Sports Law and Society

Sports Law and Society

Rules of the Game

Second Edition

Michael E. Jones

BLOOMSBURY ACADEMIC
LONDON • NEW YORK • OXFORD • NEW DELHI • SYDNEY

BLOOMSBURY ACADEMIC

Bloomsbury Publishing Inc, 1359 Broadway, New York, NY 10018, USA
Bloomsbury Publishing Plc, 50 Bedford Square, London, WC1B 3DP, UK
Bloomsbury Publishing Ireland, 29 Earlsfort Terrace, Dublin 2, D02 AY28, Ireland

BLOOMSBURY, BLOOMSBURY ACADEMIC and the Diana logo are trademarks of Bloomsbury Publishing Plc

First published in the United States of America 2026

Copyright © Bloomsbury Publishing, Inc., 2026. First edition 2016.

For legal purposes the Acknowledgments on p. xiii constitute an extension of this copyright page.

Cover design: Sally Rinehart
Cover image © iStock.com/Amir Ali

All rights reserved. No part of this publication may be: i) reproduced or transmitted in any form, electronic or mechanical, including photocopying, recording or by means of any information storage or retrieval system without prior permission in writing from the publishers; or ii) used or reproduced in any way for the training, development or operation of artificial intelligence (AI) technologies, including generative AI technologies. The rights holders expressly reserve this publication from the text and data mining exception as per Article 4(3) of the Digital Single Market Directive (EU) 2019/790.

Bloomsbury Publishing Inc does not have any control over, or responsibility for, any third-party websites referred to or in this book. All internet addresses given in this book were correct at the time of going to press. The author and publisher regret any inconvenience caused if addresses have changed or sites have ceased to exist, but can accept no responsibility for any such changes.

Library of Congress Cataloging-in-Publication Data
Names: Jones, Michael E., author.
Title: Sports law and society: rules of the game / Michael E. Jones.
Other titles: Rules of the game
Description: Second edition. | Greenbelt: Bloomsbury Publishing Inc., 2026. | Includes bibliographical references and index.
Identifiers: LCCN 2025027309 (print) | LCCN 2025027310 (ebook) | ISBN 9798881805609 (paperback) | ISBN 9798881804787 (hardback) | ISBN 9798881805616 (epub) | ISBN 9798216380702 (pdf)
Subjects: LCSH: Sports--Law and legislation--United States.
Classification: LCC KF3989 .J658 2026 (print) | LCC KF3989 (ebook) | DDC 344.73/099--dc23/eng/20250607
LC record available at https://lccn.loc.gov/2025027309
LC ebook record available at https://lccn.loc.gov/2025027310

ISBN: HB: 979-8-8818-0478-7
PB: 979-8-8818-0560-9
ePDF: 979-8-8818-0561-6
eBook: 979-8-216-38070-2

Typeset by Deanta Global Publishing Services, Chennai, India
Printed and bound in the United States of America

For product safety related questions contact productsafety@bloomsbury.com.

To find out more about our authors and books visit www.bloomsbury.com and sign up for our newsletters.

Contents

Acknowledgments xiii

Introduction 1

1 Charting the Playing Field: An Introduction to Sports Law 3

Brief History of Sports 5
    The Modern Era 6
    The Multi-Billion-Dollar Industry 9
Modern Sports and Cultural Values 10
    Social Integration and Community Building 13
The Dark Side: Winning at All Costs 14
Significance of Governing and Regulatory Bodies 16
    Communities Bidding for Sports Teams 19
Importance of Studying Legal Aspects in Sports 21
Reasons to Study Sports Law 22
    For Students 22
    For Faculty 23
    For Sports Administrators 23
    For Athletes 24
    For Leaders and the General Public 24
Key Legal Areas in Sports 25
    1. Contract Law 25
    2. Intellectual Property Rights 26
    3. Administrative Law 26
    4. Labor Relations 26
    5. Taxation and Financial Planning 27
    6. Intercollegiate Sports Governing Bodies 27
    7. Amateur vs. Professional Athlete Regulation 27

    8. Due Process, Equal Protection, and Gender Equity 28
    9. International Sports Governing Bodies 28
    10. Publicity Rights and NIL Opportunities 28
    11. Data Analytics and Artificial Intelligence 28
    12. Esports and the Metaverse 29
    13. Role of Sports Agents 29
    14. Gambling and Sports Betting 29
    15. Privacy 29
    16. Torts and Risk Management 29
    17. Social Justice, Equity, and Diversity 30
    18. Environmental Impact 30
Summary 30
Discussion Questions 32

2 The Evolution of College Sports: Tradition and Transformation 33

A Brief History of the NCAA 34
Structure and Membership 37
    Division I 37
    Division II 38
    Division III 39
    Governance 39
Regulation of Sports 43
    Legal Framework and State Action Doctrine: Due Process and Fairness 43
    Key Legal Cases Shaping NCAA Regulation 44
Criticisms and Calls for Reform 46
NCAA Constitution 47
    Article 1: Name, Purposes, and Fundamental Policy 47
    Article 2: Principles for Conduct of Intercollegiate Athletics 47
    Article 3: NCAA Membership 48
    Article 4: Organization 48
    Article 5: Legislative Authority and Process 48
    Article 6: Institutional Control and Responsibility 48
    Case Study: Penn State University and Jerry Sandusky Scandal 49

Case Study: Michigan State University and Dr. Larry
  Nassar Scandal 49
Article 7: Committees 50
Article 8: Championships and Postseason Football 50
Article 9: Enforcement 51
NCAA Bylaws 51
  Amateurism 61
  Bylaw 12 (Amateurism) 63
  Sources of NIL Money 64
  Collectives 64
  Diversity 65
  Transfer Portal 66
Division I Autonomy 66
Summary 68
Discussion Questions 70

3 Breaking Barriers: Gender Equity and Title IX in Sports 73

The History of Women's Participation in Sports 74
The Impact of Title IX on Women's Participation in
  College Sports 76
Women's Participation in the Olympic Games 76
Advancements Beyond College Sports 77
Role of Leading Women Athletes 78
Advocacy Groups 80
A Milestone for Women's Sports 80
Title IX: A Pivotal Step toward Gender Equity in Sports 81
  The OCR's 3-Prong Test for Compliance 83
  OCR Definitions 87
  Key Cases 88
  Title IX Hearing Process 90
Challenges and Inclusion of Transgender Athletes 94
  Case Studies 95
Non-Binary Athletes 99
Equal Protection Clause and Women Sports 99
Summary 103
Discussion Questions 104

4 Beyond Borders: Global Sports Governance and the Olympics and Paralympics 107

The International Olympic Committee 108
History of the Olympic Movement 108
The Olympic Charter 112
   Mission and Structure of the IOC 112
Key Olympic Rules and Regulations 117
   Promotional Limitations 120
   Athlete Safety and Welfare 122
   Anti-Doping and Performance-Enhancing Drug Restrictions 124
   The Bay Area Laboratory Co-operative (BALCO) 127
   Gender Classification 132
The Mission and Structure of the USOPC 134
   The Ted Stevens Olympic and Amateur Sports Act 135
   The Dr. Larry Nassar Scandal and SafeSport 135
   USADA 136
   Banned Substances and Techniques 137
   Categories of Banned Substances 137
   Therapeutic Use Exemptions (TUEs) 138
   Testing Protocols and Due Process 138
   The Role of CAS 138
Broadcasting and Media in the Olympics 140
Paralympics 141
   Key Points 141
Summary 143
Discussion Questions 145

5 The Business of Sports: Labor Relations and Antitrust Issues and the Role of Contracts 147

Labor and Antitrust Law in Sports 148
The Role of Contracts 149
Brief History of Professional Sport Leagues 152

Antitrust Law, Labor Law, and Collective Bargaining 156
    Unionization and Collective Bargaining in Professional Sports 157
    The National Labor Relations Act and NLRB Certification 159
Impact of the NLRB on Professional Sports 160
    Key Cases and Legislative Acts 161
The Sports Broadcasting Act of 1961 166
The Americans with Disabilities Act (ADA) 167
    Concussion Protocol 168
    Key Components of CBAs 169
Role and Power of the Commissioner in Professional Sports 173
Professional Sports Leagues 178
    Revenue Streams 180
Summary 182
Discussion Questions 184

6 Power Brokers: The Role of Agents in Sports Law 187

History, Evolution, and Influence 187
Modern Day Agents 189
Pressure Cooker Field 191
Contract Negotiations 194
Agent Certification Process and Legal Relationship 195
    Certification Procedures 196
State and Federal Regulation 199
Fiduciary Duties and Responsibilities of a Sports Agent 200
    1.   Duty of Loyalty 200
    2.   Duty of Care 200
    3.   Duty of Good Faith and Fair Dealing 201
    4.   Duty to Avoid Conflicts of Interest 201
    5.   Duty of Confidentiality 201
    6.   Duty to Act Within Scope of Authority 201
    7.   Duty to Provide Full Disclosure 201
    8.   Duty of Accountability 202
Practical Examples 202
Case Examples 203

Financial Mismanagement and Conflicts in Sports 205
   Antoine Walker 206
   Common Issues Leading to Financial Ruin 207
NIL Rights and Digital Transformation 207
Summary 210
Discussion Questions 211

7 Protecting the Game: Intellectual Property, Publicity Rights, and Privacy in the Digital Age 213

What Is Intellectual Property? 214
   Historical Genesis of Intellectual Property Law 215
Importance of IP Law in Sports Business 216
   Rights of Copyright Holders 217
   Rights of Trademark Holders 218
   Rights of Patent Holders 222
The Role of the Digital Millennium Copyright Act
     (DMCA) in Sports Broadcasting 224
The Role of International Treaties and Organizations 227
   Case Study: *Michael Jordan v. Qiaodan Sports Co., Ltd.* 230
International Recognition and Moral Rights 231
Publicity Rights and Athlete Endorsements 232
   Legal Cases Illustrating Publicity Rights 234
Publicity Rights in Digital World 236
   Esports 237
   Virtual Reality and the Metaverse 238
   Modern Developments and Challenges in AI, IP, and
     Sports 239
Summary 241
Discussion Questions 242

8 Shielding the Game: Managing Risk and Liability in Sports 245

Torts and Risk Management in Sports: An Introduction 247
   Tort Law 247
   Negligence 249
   Waivers and Releases 255

Spectator Harm and the Obligation of Facility Managers to
   Provide a Safe Environment 258
   Invitees 258
   Licensees 259
   Trespassers 259
   General Duty of Care 260
   Case Law 262
   Stadium Security and Structured Risk Management
      Process 266
   Common Defenses 267
   Intentional Torts 268
Products Liability in Sports 270
   Environmental and Sustainability Issues 272
Summary 274
Discussion Questions 276

9 Data and AI: Transforming Sports Law and Performance 279

Transforming Sports Performance with Data Analytics 282
AI Technologies in Athlete Training and Injury Prevention 287
Developing Game Strategies 289
Intellectual Property and Data: Leading Cases 291
Virtual Games and Metaverse 297
Data Privacy: A Global Challenge 299
Athlete Consent: Empowering Informed Decisions 300
Who Owns the Data Goldmine? 301
Bias, Fairness and Transparency: Ensuring a Level Playing
   Field 302
Environmental Sustainability: The Hidden Cost of Big Data 304
Summary 305
Discussion Questions 307

10 The Future of Sports: Legal, Ethical, and Environmental Dimensions 309

The Future of Sports Law: A New Era 310
Legal Challenges to Discrimination in Sports 311

Participation and Leadership 311
Intersection of Race and Gender 313
The Rooney Rule 314
Mentorship and Leadership Programs 315
Black-Owned Sports Franchises 317
Women-Owned Sports Franchises 317
Social Justice Movements on Sports 318
Impact of Activism 320
   Positive Impacts 320
   Negative Impacts 320
Modern Athlete Activism and Social Media 320
First Amendment vs. Contractual Obligations 322
LGBTQ+ Athletes and Fans 325
Reimagining Gender Classification in Sports 326
Proactive Steps for Inclusivity 329
Advocacy and Opposition 330
Disability Inclusion 331
Legal and Regulatory Frameworks for Environmental
    Protection in Sports 333
Ethical Sourcing and Supply Chain Management 336
The Future of Fan Engagement 339
Summary 344
Discussion Questions 346

Glossary 349
Bibliography 365
Index 374
About the Author 395

Acknowledgments

The creation of *Sports Law* has been a collaborative endeavor, enriched by the generous contributions of numerous individuals who have shared their expertise, insights, and unwavering support throughout this journey that began in the late 1970s. It was during this time that I had the privilege of teaching the first undergraduate course on sports law and marketing in the United States. A few years later, I authored the first book on the subject, written specifically for the general public and non-law school students.

The field of sports law, as we understand it today, owes its existence to a group of pioneers who recognized that the world of sports was not just about wins and losses, but was deeply intertwined with the complexities of contracts, torts, intellectual property, and other legal principles. Their foresight in the 1970s mirrored the observations made by Karl Llewellyn nearly a century ago in *The Bramble Bush: On Our Law and Its Study*. Llewellyn famously noted that society is "honeycombed with disputes," highlighting how conflicts pervade every aspect of life, including sports. These early scholars understood that by bringing together disparate legal subjects, they could create a cohesive field of study—sports law—that addressed the unique legal challenges faced by athletes, owners, fans, administrators, referees, and coaches.

I owe a deep debt of gratitude to these visionaries and friends, particularly Professors Bob Waters, Bob Berry, Bill Weston, and Glenn Wong, whose pioneering efforts laid the groundwork for an entire generation of legal scholars and practitioners. Their work has shaped the field of sports law into what it is today, providing a structured framework to address the evolving nature of sports, media, technology, business, and ethics.

My time at the University of Massachusetts Lowell has afforded me the privilege of guiding and instructing hundreds of students over the span of my tenure in university teaching. I extend heartfelt appreciation to the professionals, practitioners, and industry leaders who generously shared their real-world experiences and insights, infusing this book with context and practical wisdom. Your firsthand knowledge has been instrumental in bridging the gap between theory and practice in the realm of sports law.

A special acknowledgment goes to the editorial and production team at Bloomsbury, whose dedication, expertise, and meticulous attention to detail have played a pivotal role in bringing this project to fruition. Their commitment to excellence ensured the integrity and quality of the final product.

Lastly, my warmest gratitude goes to my family, particularly my spouse, Christine M. Jones, and my friends, whose love, encouragement, and understanding have been the driving force behind this endeavor. Their patience and belief in me have been pillars of support throughout this journey.

This book stands as a testament to the collective efforts of a diverse and dedicated community committed to advancing knowledge and understanding in the dynamic field of sports law.

Michael E. Jones

Introduction

Sports have long served as a unifying force, captivating audiences and inspiring individuals across the globe. Yet, beneath the excitement of intercollegiate championships, Olympic glory, and professional competition lies a complex regulatory framework that shapes the very fabric of these athletic pursuits. This book seeks to unravel that framework, offering a comprehensive introduction to the key legal and ethical issues confronting the sports industry today.

Designed for undergraduate and graduate students, sports administrators, athlete advisors, members of the media, and even passionate sports fans, this book explores the dynamic intersection of law, ethics, and sports. Whether you are preparing to advise athletes, manage a sports organization, or simply deepen your understanding of the challenges facing the sports world, this text provides the foundational knowledge you need.

The material has been developed specifically for a one-semester course and is structured to be accessible and engaging. By addressing current and controversial topics such as gender equity, name-image-likeness (NIL) rights, athlete safety, and international governance, the book reflects the rapidly evolving landscape of sports law. Case studies, real-world examples, and discussions of precedent-setting legal decisions ensure a practical and relatable approach.

For instructors teaching a course in Sports Law, the chapters are designed to offer maximum flexibility. The material can be used in any order, allowing educators to tailor the curriculum to meet the specific needs of their students or the focus of their program. While the chapters are interconnected, each stands alone as a robust examination of its respective topic.

The journey begins in **Chapter 1**, *Charting the Playing Field: An Introduction to Sports Law*, which lays the foundation by exploring the core principles and legal frameworks that underpin the field. From there, **Chapter 2**, *The Evolution of College Sports: Tradition and Transformation*, delves into the shifting dynamics of intercollegiate athletics, including NIL rights and the ongoing debates surrounding amateurism.

In **Chapter 3**, *Breaking Barriers: Gender Equity and Title IX in Sports*, we examine the pivotal role of law in advancing gender equity in sports, highlighting both successes and ongoing challenges. **Chapter 4**, *Beyond Borders: Global Sports Governance and the Olympics and Paralympics*, takes a broader perspective, addressing the legal and ethical issues within international competitions, from doping to intersex athlete regulations.

Chapter 5, *The Business of Sports: Labor Relations and Antitrust Issues and the Role of Contracts*, provides insights into collective bargaining, antitrust challenges, and the economic forces that drive professional sports. Building on this, **Chapter 6**, *Power Brokers: The Role of Agents in Sports Law*, focuses on the pivotal role agents play in negotiating contracts, endorsements, and safeguarding athletes' interests.

As we move forward, **Chapter 7**, *Protecting the Game: Intellectual Property, Publicity Rights, and Privacy in the Digital Age*, examines how athletes and organizations navigate the challenges of brand protection, digital media, and evolving privacy laws. **Chapter 8**, *Shielding the Game: Managing Risk and Liability in Sports*, shifts to safeguarding athletes, fans, and organizations, exploring risk management and the mitigation of liability.

In **Chapter 9**, *Data and AI: Transforming Sports Law and Performance*, we turn to the cutting-edge role of technology, including artificial intelligence, data analytics, and their legal and ethical implications. Finally, **Chapter 10**, *The Future of Sports: Legal, Ethical, and Environmental Dimensions*, closes the book by looking ahead at emerging trends, such as climate change's impact on sports and the need for innovative legal solutions.

It is my hope that this book not only equips readers with an understanding of legal principles but also fosters critical thinking about the ethical responsibilities that come with involvement in sports at any level. As we address the challenges of fair play, athlete welfare, and technological innovation, this resource aims to inspire informed and thoughtful dialogue.

Whether you are a student stepping into the world of sports law for the first time, a professional working to uphold integrity in athletics, or a fan curious about the mechanisms behind your favorite pastime, this book is for you. Let's investigate together the regulatory complexities and ethical debates that define the modern sports industry—and shape its future.

1

Charting the Playing Field
An Introduction to Sports Law

Chapter Outline

Brief History of Sports	5
Modern Sports and Cultural Values	10
The Dark Side: Winning at All Costs	14
Significance of Governing and Regulatory Bodies	16
Importance of Studying Legal Aspects in Sports	21
Reasons to Study Sports Law	22
Key Legal Areas in Sports	25
Summary	30
Discussion Questions	32

Sports have always held a notable place in human culture, serving as a reflection of societal values and a catalyst for social change. From ancient civilizations to modern times, sports have been a central part of social, cultural, and spiritual life. In ancient Egypt, sports were integral to royal festivals, with Pharaohs participating in physical activities to demonstrate their divine fitness to rule. The Olympic Games, founded in 776 B.C. in Greece, became a major cultural and social event, drawing thousands of spectators and continuing to influence the world today.

In the United States, sports have played a pivotal role in cultural shifts, with figures like Jackie Robinson and Muhammad Ali using their platforms to advocate for civil rights and social justice. Jackie Robinson broke Major League Baseball's color barrier in 1947, challenging the pervasive racism of the time and becoming a symbol of the civil rights movement. Muhammad Ali, renowned not only for his prowess in the boxing ring but also for his outspoken stance on racial inequality and opposition to the Vietnam War, became an iconic figure of resistance and empowerment.

Women have also been instrumental in driving social change through sports. One consequential figure is Billie Jean King, who has been a trailblazer for gender equality in sports. In 1973, she famously won the "Battle of the Sexes" tennis match against Bobby Riggs, a former world No. 1 men's player. This victory was not just about the game; it was a powerful statement against the widespread belief that women were inferior athletes. King's advocacy for equal prize money for women in tennis and her efforts to establish the Women's Tennis Association (WTA) have advanced the cause of gender equality in sports.

At the height of his Olympic success, Michael Phelps faced profound mental health struggles that he later described as some of the darkest times of his life. Despite his achievements in the pool, including becoming the most decorated Olympian in history, Phelps grappled with severe depression and thoughts of suicide. These challenges revealed the often-hidden mental toll of high-performance sports, where athletes are expected to be resilient and unbreakable.

Transgender and non-binary athletes are increasingly finding their place in United States and Olympic sports, not without controversy, marking a significant shift toward inclusivity and representation. A prime example of this progress is the inspiring journey of Nikki Hiltz, a transgender and non-binary runner who competed at the 2024 Paris Olympic Games for Team USA.

Internationally, women in Muslim communities have also harnessed the power of sports to advance social causes and break barriers. One prominent example is Fatma Samoura, who made history as the first female Secretary General of FIFA, the global governing body of soccer. Her appointment has been a significant step toward gender diversity and inclusion in international sports administration, challenging traditional gender roles and encouraging the participation of women in leadership positions within sports organizations.

Another inspiring example is Zahra Lari, an Emirati figure skater who has become a symbol of perseverance and cultural change. As the first figure skater from the United Arab Emirates to compete internationally, she has shattered stereotypes about women in sports in her region. Competing in a hijab, Lari has not only promoted the acceptance of diverse cultural practices in international sports but has also inspired young women in Muslim communities to pursue their athletic dreams regardless of societal expectations.

Together, these individuals highlight the profound impact sports can have on societal values and norms, demonstrating how athletic achievements and the public platforms they provide can be harnessed to promote equality, challenge discrimination, and inspire generations. Through their efforts, they have shown that sports are not just games but powerful tools for social change and empowerment across the globe.

Brief History of Sports

The history of sports is rich and varied, tracing back to the earliest human societies. Competitive sports emerged in ancient Mesopotamia and Egypt, evolving through the centuries into organized events like the Greek Olympics. These games were not only athletic competitions but also significant cultural and religious festivals.

In ancient Mesopotamia, sports were a part of daily life, with activities like wrestling and boxing being popular among the Sumerians. Artifacts from this period depict scenes of wrestling, indicating its importance in their culture. Similarly, in ancient Egypt, sports were integral to royal festivals and religious ceremonies. Pharaohs participated in physical activities such as running, swimming, and archery to demonstrate their divine fitness to rule. Hunting and fishing were also popular among the Egyptians, often depicted in tomb paintings as symbols of power and skill.

The Olympic Games, founded in 776 B.C. in Greece, are perhaps the most famous example of ancient sports. These games were held in Olympia every four years and included events such as running, long jump, shot put, javelin, boxing, pankration (a form of mixed martial arts), and equestrian events. The Olympics were not only a display of physical prowess but also a significant cultural and religious festival, honoring Zeus, the king of the

Greek gods. The games promoted unity among the city-states of Greece and were a testament to the importance of physical fitness and competition in Greek society.

The medieval period saw the rise of various sports across Europe. Jousting and tournaments were popular among knights, reflecting the martial culture of the time. These events were both entertainment and training for warfare, allowing knights to demonstrate their combat skills and bravery. Archery was another critical sport, with competitions held to improve and display the archery skills that were vital for both hunting and military purposes.

In addition to these martial sports, medieval Europe saw the development of ball games. Early forms of football (soccer) and rugby were played in villages and towns, often with few rules and considerable violence. These games were social events that brought communities together, though they sometimes led to conflicts and injuries.

Indigenous cultures in the Americas developed their own unique athletic traditions. The Mesoamerican ballgame, originating around 1600 B.C., was a significant sport played by the Maya, Aztec, and other Mesoamerican civilizations. The game had deep religious and cultural relevance, often associated with the myth of the Hero Twins and the gods of the underworld. Played on a large stone court, the game involved keeping a rubber ball in play using hips, forearms, or rackets, depending on the region and period. The outcome of the game could be a matter of life and death, with the losing team sometimes being sacrificed.

In North America, Native American tribes engaged in various sports, including lacrosse. Known as "baggataway" or "the Creator's Game," lacrosse was not only a physical contest but also a spiritual event, played to honor the Creator and resolve conflicts between tribes. It was a way to bring people together, fostering community and tradition.

The Modern Era

The modern era of sports began in the nineteenth century with the establishment of professional leagues and international competitions. This period marked the formalization and codification of many sports. In England, the rules of modern soccer were established in 1863 with the formation of the Football Association. Rugby split into rugby union and rugby league in the 1890s due to disagreements over professionalism.

In the United States, baseball became deeply embedded in the cultural fabric as the nation's pastime, largely due to the establishment of professional leagues such as the National League, which was founded in 1876. This league helped to standardize the game and elevate it from a casual pastime to a professional sport with widespread appeal. The sport's popularity surged through the late nineteenth and early twentieth centuries, fueled by iconic players and legendary teams that captured the American imagination.

American football, on the other hand, evolved from a blend of rugby and association football (soccer). The sport's distinctive rules began to take shape in the late nineteenth century, particularly with the introduction of key elements like the line of scrimmage and the system of downs, which were developed under the guidance of Walter Camp, often referred to as the "Father of American Football." By the turn of the century, American football had established itself as a major college sport, laying the groundwork for the professional leagues that would later dominate the American sports landscape.

Basketball was invented by Dr. James Naismith in 1891 as an innovative solution to keep athletes active during the harsh New England winters. Tasked with creating a new indoor sport at the International YMCA Training School in Springfield, Massachusetts, Naismith devised a game that combined elements of strategy and physical skill. The sport quickly gained popularity, spreading to other YMCAs and educational institutions, and by the early twentieth century, basketball had become a fixture in American sports culture. Dr. Naismith's invention is now one of the most popular sports worldwide, with a significant professional presence and a storied history of international competition.

International competitions also gained prominence during this period. The modern Olympic Games were revived in 1896 by Pierre de Coubertin, inspired by the ancient Greek tradition. These games promoted international peace and unity through sports, featuring athletes from various countries competing in a range of events.

The twentieth century saw the globalization of sports, with the establishment of numerous international competitions and governing bodies, which contributed to the spread and popularization of various sports across the globe. FIFA, founded in 1904, organized the first World Cup in 1930, making soccer a truly global sport with a massive following that continues to grow today. This century also witnessed the rise of rugby as a prominent international sport, culminating in the first Women's World Rugby Cup championship held in 1991. The expansion of professional leagues like the NBA, NHL, and MLB brought sports entertainment to millions of fans worldwide, solidifying basketball, hockey, and baseball as major global sports.

In addition to these well-known sports, the twentieth century also saw the growth of less popular but culturally valued sports. Cricket, for instance, became a central aspect of national identity in countries like India, Pakistan, and Australia, with the establishment of the ICC Cricket World Cup in 1975 providing a platform for international competition. Meanwhile, field hockey gained prominence, especially in countries like India and the Netherlands, with the men's and women's Hockey World Cups being launched in 1971 and 1974, respectively.

Sports like volleyball and handball also saw increased international participation. Volleyball, with the creation of the Fédération Internationale de Volleyball (FIVB) in 1947, and its inclusion in the 1964 Tokyo Olympics, expanded its reach, becoming one of the most widely played sports globally. Handball, on the other hand, evolved from its European roots into a globally recognized sport, with the International Handball Federation (IHF) forming in 1946 and organizing the first World Handball Championship in 1938.

Other niche sports, such as table tennis and badminton, gained traction, particularly in Asia. The International Table Tennis Federation (ITTF) was founded in 1926, and the sport's inclusion in the Olympics in 1988 further boosted its global profile. Similarly, badminton, governed by the Badminton World Federation (BWF) since 1934, saw its international appeal soar, particularly after becoming an Olympic sport in 1992.

These developments, alongside the rise of extreme sports like skateboarding and surfing, which gained global recognition and were eventually included in the Olympics, highlight the twentieth century as a period of immense growth and diversification in the world of sports. This era not only broadened the appeal of traditional sports but also brought lesser-known sports into the global spotlight, fostering a more inclusive and varied international sports landscape.

The Multi-Billion-Dollar Industry

Today, sports have evolved into a multi-billion-dollar industry encompassing a diverse array of revenue streams that extend far beyond traditional ticket sales and merchandise. The commercialization of sports has transformed how athletes, teams, and leagues generate income, leading to the development of innovative financial models that capitalize on the global appeal of sports. Ticket sales remain a significant revenue source, particularly for live events, but the digital age has expanded the market exponentially. Fans can now purchase tickets online, access exclusive content, and engage with their favorite teams through various digital platforms, enhancing the overall fan experience and creating additional revenue opportunities through premium memberships and virtual events.

Merchandise sales have also seen a substantial shift, with the integration of e-commerce platforms enabling teams to reach a global audience. Branded apparel, collectibles, and other memorabilia are now available to fans worldwide, contributing to the growing revenue streams. Additionally, the rise of digital assets like non-fungible tokens (NFTs) has revolutionized the way athletes and teams monetize their personal brands. NFTs provide a new avenue for athletes to engage with fans by offering unique digital items, such as virtual trading cards, limited-edition artwork, and exclusive experiences, all of which can be bought, sold, and traded on blockchain platforms. This digital asset boom has opened up new revenue channels and redefined the relationship between athletes and their fan bases, allowing for deeper interaction and financial gain.

Sponsorships and broadcasting rights have long been cornerstones of sports revenue, but their impact has only grown with the increasing globalization of sports. Major sports events like the Super Bowl, FIFA World Cup, and the Olympic Games attract massive global audiences, making them prime opportunities for brands to reach millions, if not billions, of viewers. These events are often supported by lucrative sponsorship deals, where companies pay significant sums to have their logos displayed on jerseys, stadiums, and broadcasts. The advertising revenue generated from broadcasting rights also plays a crucial role, with networks and streaming platforms vying for the rights to air these events to audiences worldwide. The competition for broadcasting rights has led to record-breaking deals, further inflating the financial stakes in the sports industry.

Beyond the immediate revenue generated by these events, there are extensive economic impacts on local and national economies. Hosting a major sports event can lead to job creation, both in the construction and hospitality industries, as new venues are built and tourism increases. The influx of visitors during events like the Olympic Games or the FIFA World Cup can boost local businesses, from hotels and restaurants to retail outlets. Additionally, infrastructure development, such as transportation and communication networks, often receives a boost from the need to accommodate large crowds and international media. These developments can have long-lasting benefits for the host cities and countries, contributing to economic growth long after the events have concluded.

The sports industry's expansion into digital and global markets has also led to the diversification of revenue streams, including social media and content creation. Athletes and teams now leverage their social media presence to engage directly with fans, attracting sponsorship deals and advertising revenue through platforms like Instagram, Twitter, and TikTok. This direct engagement allows for more personalized and targeted marketing, further increasing the value of sponsorship deals. In addition, content creation, such as podcasts, vlogs, and behind-the-scenes videos, has become an integral part of the sports ecosystem, providing fans with exclusive access to their favorite athletes while generating additional revenue.

Modern Sports and Cultural Values

Modern sports events serve as a mirror reflecting the cultural values and societal norms of their respective societies. In contemporary cultures, sports have shifted from sacred rituals to secular activities, emphasizing equality in competition and opportunities. This shift mirrors broader societal trends such as industrialization, urbanization, and nationalism. Sports have become a tool for addressing social issues, promoting values like liberty, equality, and fraternity, and challenging boundaries related to class, ethnicity, race, and gender. They also facilitate cultural exchange, promote health and well-being, and serve as a platform for social integration and community building.

Sports have long been seen as a means of promoting important social values. The global popularity of events like the Olympics and the World Cup provides a stage for promoting ideals of fair play, unity, and mutual respect among nations. Through these platforms, athletes can challenge societal norms and advocate for social change. For example, during the 1968 Olympics, athletes Tommie Smith and John Carlos used their medal ceremony to protest racial injustice, highlighting how sports can intersect with social activism.

Sports also play a crucial role in facilitating cultural exchange. International competitions bring together athletes and fans from diverse backgrounds, fostering a sense of global community. Events like the Olympics and world sporting championships allow countries to showcase their cultures on an international stage, promoting understanding and cooperation. The participation of diverse countries in these events encourages cross-cultural interactions and the sharing of different traditions and values.

Additionally, sports events have become powerful platforms for economic development and national branding. Countries invest heavily in hosting major sports events, not just for the immediate economic boost but also for the long-term benefits of global recognition and tourism. Hosting events like the FIFA World Cup or the Olympic Games can reshape a nation's image, attract international investment, and stimulate infrastructure development. The economic impact of sports extends to various industries, including media, fashion, and technology, illustrating the broad influence of sports on modern economies.

Moreover, the increasing commercialization of sports has raised important ethical questions. Issues such as the exploitation of athletes, the environmental impact of large-scale events, and the role of sponsorships and advertising in shaping sports culture have become central to discussions on the future of sports. These concerns highlight the need for a balanced approach that preserves the integrity of sports while embracing the opportunities for growth and innovation in the industry.

The emphasis on physical fitness and health in modern sports promotes overall well-being, benefiting individuals and society. Participation in sports, whether at the elite or recreational level, fosters a healthy lifestyle, reduces the risk of chronic diseases such as heart disease, diabetes, and obesity, and significantly improves mental health by alleviating stress, anxiety, and depression. The mental benefits of sports are particularly important, as physical activity is known to boost endorphins, improve sleep, and enhance cognitive function, all of which contribute to better mental well-being.

Governments and organizations worldwide recognize the vital role that sports play in public health, leading to meaningful investments in sports infrastructure, community programs, and public health campaigns designed to encourage physical activity among their populations. These initiatives target various demographics, ensuring that the benefits of physical activity are accessible to everyone, from young children to the elderly.

For example, the "Let's Move!" campaign in the United States, initiated by former First Lady Michelle Obama, was designed to combat childhood obesity by encouraging children to engage in at least sixty minutes of physical activity daily. The campaign also worked with schools, communities, and food providers to promote healthier eating habits and integrate physical activity into daily routines.

Similarly, in the United Kingdom, the "This Girl Can" campaign launched by Sport England aims to break down the barriers women face in sports and physical activity. The campaign's focus on inclusivity and body positivity has empowered millions of women and girls to participate in physical activities, regardless of their age, shape, or ability. This has helped reduce the gender gap in sports participation and fostered a culture where women feel confident and supported in leading active lifestyles.

At the recreational level, community sports leagues, fitness classes, and local wellness programs provide accessible opportunities for physical activity, enabling people of all ages and skill levels to engage in regular exercise. These programs often emphasize social interaction, teamwork, and fun, making physical activity an enjoyable and sustainable part of daily life.

The benefits of promoting physical activity at the recreational level extend beyond individual health. Increased participation in sports can lead to stronger community ties, reduced healthcare costs, and a more vibrant, active population. For instance, community centers that offer subsidized fitness classes or organized sports leagues can foster social cohesion, helping individuals build relationships and support networks that further enhance mental and emotional well-being.

Moreover, employers and educational institutions increasingly recognize the value of physical activity in promoting productivity and academic performance. Workplace wellness programs, which may include on-site fitness facilities, exercise breaks, and team sports, can improve employee health, reduce absenteeism, and boost morale. Schools that incorporate regular physical education and after-school sports programs report better student focus, behavior, and academic achievement.

An example of how sports can drive health initiatives on a global scale is the Livestrong Foundation, founded by cyclist Lance Armstrong in 1997. The charity aimed to support people affected by cancer and promote cancer awareness. It gained massive popularity, particularly with its iconic yellow wristbands, and at its peak, raised more than $500 million to combat cancer, making it one of the most successful charities in history in terms of fundraising. The foundation became synonymous with health, perseverance, and the fight against cancer, even forming partnerships with organizations like YMCAs to promote physical activity as a means of cancer prevention and recovery.

However, Armstrong's reputation and the charity's public perception were dramatically altered after revelations of his doping in violation of professional cycling's rules. In 2012, after Armstrong was stripped of his seven Tour de France titles and banned from competitive cycling for life, he stepped down from his leadership role at the Livestrong Foundation and resigned from its board. The scandal led to a significant shift in how the charity was viewed, and many of its partnerships, including those with health and fitness organizations like YMCAs, were severed as a result. Despite this, the Livestrong Foundation has continued its work, albeit with a diminished public profile, focusing on its mission to support those affected by cancer.

Social Integration and Community Building

Sports serve as a powerful tool for social integration and community building. Local sports events and community leagues provide opportunities for individuals from different backgrounds to come together, fostering social cohesion. The following program uses sports to address social issues, combat isolation, and promote community involvement.

Examples of Sports Promoting Social Integration and Community Building

1. **Skateboarding in Public Spaces:** Skateboarding has been used as a tool for social integration by creating inclusive public spaces where people from diverse backgrounds can interact and build social trust.
2. **Women's Sports Initiatives:** Programs targeting underrepresented groups, such as women from ethnic communities, help promote nondiscrimination and empower participants by providing a sense of ownership and equality.
3. **London Together Projects:** Initiatives like the London Together projects use sports to address isolation and drive social integration by fostering social connections and a sense of community belonging among participants.
4. **NBA Cares Program:** The NBA Cares program leverages the popularity of basketball to create positive social impacts through education, youth and family support, and health and wellness initiatives.
5. **Sport for Development (S4D):** The S4D approach promotes tolerance, inclusion, and reconciliation in conflict-affected regions, fostering social cohesion and empowering youth through sports.

The Dark Side: Winning at All Costs

However, the pursuit of victory in sports can also lead to negative consequences. The pressure to win has sometimes led to unethical practices, such as systematic doping and cheating, undermining the values of fair play and integrity.

One of the most prominent examples of this dark side is the state-sponsored doping programs in countries like Russia and China. These programs have been designed to enhance athletic performance through illegal means, compromising the integrity of sports.

- **Russia:** The Russian doping scandal, exposed in 2014, continues to cast a long shadow over international sports. While the initial revelations of a state-sponsored doping program orchestrated by the Russian government and sports officials were shocking, the full picture is still emerging. Ongoing investigations raise the possibility of new evidence or whistleblowers coming forward, potentially leading to further sanctions. Further complicating the issue is Russia's lack of full acceptance of responsibility, hindering efforts to rebuild trust with international anti-doping agencies like WADA (World Anti-Doping Agency) and the IOC (International Olympic Committee). Even after the initial scandal and the suspension of the Russian Anti-Doping Agency (RUSADA), new doping cases involving Russian athletes continue to surface across various sports, raising concerns about the effectiveness of anti-doping measures within Russia. The case of fifteen-year-old figure skater Kamila Valieva at the 2022 Beijing Olympics perfectly exemplifies the complexities of the issue. Valieva's positive test for a banned substance, coupled with questions about her age and potential manipulation by her entourage, sparked controversy and debate about how to handle such sensitive cases. These ongoing factors demonstrate that concerns over doping by Russian athletes remain an important and unresolved issue in international sports.

- **China:** Similarly, China has faced allegations of systematic doping, particularly during the 1990s and then again at the Tokyo and Paris Summer Olympic Games. Reports surfaced about Chinese athletes in sports like swimming and track and field using performance-enhancing drugs to gain an unfair advantage. Although China claims to have made efforts to clean up its sports programs, the legacy of these allegations continues to affect perceptions of Chinese athletes.

These doping scandals highlight the other side of the winning-at-all-costs mentality, which stands in stark contrast to the Olympic motto of "Citius, Altius, Fortius" (Faster, Higher, Stronger). The essence of the Olympics is to promote peace, unity, and fair competition among nations. When countries engage in systematic cheating, it tarnishes the spirit of the Games and undermines the credibility of the sporting community.

To combat doping and preserve the integrity of sports, independent bodies like the World Anti-Doping Agency (WADA), newly formed International Testing Agency (ITA), and national anti-doping bodies like the United States Anti-Doping Agency (USADA) play a pivotal role. These organizations conduct rigorous testing and investigations to ensure that athletes compete on a level playing field. The development of the biological passport, which tracks athletes' biological markers over time to detect abnormalities, has been a hopeful advancement in anti-doping efforts.

Significance of Governing and Regulatory Bodies

The organization and regulation of sports have become increasingly important as the industry has grown. Governing bodies such as the International Olympic Committee (IOC), Fédération Internationale de Football Association (FIFA), and the NCAA play crucial roles in setting rules, ensuring fair play, and maintaining the integrity of sports. These organizations also address issues like doping, match-fixing, and athlete welfare, providing a structured framework that supports the global sports ecosystem. They ensure that sports events reflect and uphold societal values, promoting sports as a means of social and cultural development.

Soccer, or football as it is known outside North America, is the world's most popular sport and a dynamic economic powerhouse. FIFA, the global governing body for soccer, generates vast sums of money through the World Cup, sponsorship deals, and broadcasting rights. The 2022 World Cup in Qatar shattered financial records, reaching an estimated $7.5 billion in revenue. Broadcaster rights remained a major source of income, and sponsorships from major brands like Coca-Cola, Adidas, and Visa continued to play a key role. The 2026 World Cup co-hosted by Canada, Mexico, and the United States is poised to be the biggest yet, with FIFA targeting a record-breaking $11 billion in revenue and expecting an attendance of 5.8 million fans. Additionally, the transfer market for players sees clubs spending hundreds of millions of dollars on top talent, further highlighting soccer's economic impact.

Saudi Arabia's involvement in professional golf has markedly disrupted the traditional landscape of the sport. The Saudi-backed LIV Golf series has attracted some of the biggest names in golf with lucrative contracts and prize money, challenging the dominance of the PGA Tour. This influx of money has led to a shift in the sport's dynamics, with increased prize funds and competition for top talent. The Saudi investment is part of a broader strategy to diversify the country's economy beyond oil production and enhance its global sporting profile, demonstrating the profound financial impact such investments can have on a sport.

In the United States, major team sports like the NFL, NBA, MLB, and NHL continue to be economic powerhouses, generating billions of dollars annually. The NFL remains the most profitable, exceeding $15 billion in annual revenues. This financial strength is fueled by a recently negotiated broadcast rights deal expected to pay the league a staggering $11 billion per year over the 2023–33 seasons.

The NBA is also thriving, with its global popularity and star power driving appreciable income. In 2024, the NBA secured a record-breaking media rights deal valued at $77 billion over eleven years (2025–36). This translates to an estimated $6.9 billion distributed annually to the league and its teams, solidifying the NBA's position as the second-highest revenue-generating sports league in the United States. These lucrative deals not only benefit the leagues and teams, including players like Jason Tatum who is paid more than $60 million per year, but also contribute significantly to local economies through game-day spending, tourism, and job creation.

The Olympic Games are a financial juggernaut, generating billions through a complex web of revenue streams. The International Olympic Committee (IOC) sits at the heart of this system, securing multi-billion dollar deals with broadcasters worldwide. These deals, estimated to be worth over $4 billion per Olympic cycle (Summer and Winter Games combined), ensure extensive global coverage and a major portion of the IOC's revenue.

Sponsorships are another major source of income, with large corporations vying for coveted Olympic partnerships. The TOP (The Olympic Partners) program alone brings in billions, with companies like Coca-Cola, Visa, and Alibaba securing exclusive marketing rights across all Olympic Games. Ticket sales also contribute, though the impact can vary depending on the host city, event popularity, and overall economic climate.

However, hosting the Games is a double-edged sword. Host cities often invest heavily in infrastructure development, new venues, and security measures. These costs can easily balloon into the tens of billions, raising questions about the long-term return on investment. While some cities experience a tourism boom and increased international exposure, others struggle with post-Olympic debt and underutilized facilities.

The economic impact remains a subject of debate, with studies showing mixed results. Some argue that the Games act as a catalyst for urban renewal and infrastructure upgrades, while others highlight the risk of cost overruns and white elephant venues. Ultimately, the financial success of the Olympics hinges on careful planning, realistic budgeting, and a focus on long-term economic benefits that extend beyond the closing ceremony.

Prize money in professional sports has skyrocketed in recent years, reflecting the booming commercialization and ever-increasing financial stakes involved. This growth is particularly evident in major tournaments and established leagues.

Tennis: Grand Slam tournaments like Wimbledon and the US Open offer the pinnacle of prize money. Wimbledon boasts a total prize pool exceeding £40 million (over $50 million), with the champions taking home a cool £2 million ($2.5 million) each. Even earlier rounds offer substantial payouts, ensuring financial security for a wider range of players.

Golf: Similar to tennis, major golf tournaments like the Masters and PGA Championship offer hefty prize purses. Winners at the Masters can walk away with a life-changing sum exceeding $12 million, while the PGA Championship champion pockets over $3 million.

Beyond the Big Leagues: While tennis and golf are prime examples, prize money growth extends to other sports. Esports, a relatively young competitive gaming scene, boasts lucrative tournaments like The International (Dota 2) with a prize pool exceeding $40 million distributed among winning teams. The virtual sports economy also includes digital sports betting, fantasy sports, and the sale of virtual goods and skins, contributing to the overall financial impact of this sector. Formula One racing offers significant prize money as well, with constructors' championships awarding tens of millions to the winning teams.

However, the financial landscape of professional sports remains uneven. While star athletes and participants in major events can command amazing prize money, many professional athletes, particularly those in less-established sports like the triathlon or curling, struggle to make ends meet solely on prize money. Here's where sponsorship deals come into play.

Brands across industries understand the immense value that top athletes bring. Their popularity, influence, and dedication translate into valuable marketing opportunities. Sponsorship deals can be lucrative, with major brands like Nike, Adidas, and Gatorade investing millions in partnerships with top athletes to leverage their reach and enhance their brand image. The mixed martial arts organization UFC partnered with Crypto.com to pay bonuses to fighters in bitcoins as a marketing strategy.

The interplay between prize money and sponsorships creates a complex financial ecosystem in professional sports. While the top earners enjoy significant financial rewards, the disparity between established sports and lesser-known ones remains a challenge.

Communities Bidding for Sports Teams

Cities across the globe fiercely compete to attract or retain professional sports teams. This drive stems from the economic impact these teams can have on local communities. The overall financial impact of sports teams remains a subject of debate among leading sports economists. Some argue that the costs outweigh the benefits, particularly when considering the long-term debt burden of publicly financed stadiums and the displacement of residents due to development projects. Others highlight the positive long-term effects like increased tourism, job creation, and a revitalized downtown area.

Positive Impacts

- **Tourism Boost:** Major sporting events like the Super Bowl and the FIFA World Cup act as powerful tourism magnets. By way of example, the Super Bowl can generate an economic impact in excess of $1 billion reflecting the significant influx of visitors, increased spending at local hotels, restaurants, and entertainment venues, and the overall boost to the local economy.
- **Job Creation Engine:** Sports teams and events create jobs across various sectors. From direct stadium staff like security and concessions to ancillary industries like hospitality, retail, and transportation, the sports ecosystem supports a significant number of jobs. A recent study by the AFL-CIO found that the NFL alone supports over 800,000 jobs across the United States.

- **Community Revitalization:** Successful sports franchises can act as catalysts for urban renewal. Take, for example, the recent development surrounding the new UBS Arena, home to the New York Islanders. The project has spurred a wave of investment in Belmont Park, Long Island, with new restaurants, bars, and entertainment venues popping up, creating a vibrant and revitalized atmosphere.
- **Increased Local Spending:** Whether it's attending games, purchasing merchandise, or subscribing to streaming services, sports fans contribute significantly to local economies. The rise of legalized sports betting in the United States has also created a new revenue stream for some cities and states.

Recent Examples of Positive Impact

- **The LIV Golf Series:** Despite controversy surrounding its funding source, the Saudi-backed LIV Golf Series has injected significant capital into the professional golf landscape. The series offers players record-breaking prize purses, attracting top talent and sparking a potential shakeup in the sport's traditional structure.
- **Esports Boom:** The burgeoning esports industry is a testament to the growing economic power of competitive gaming. The global esports market is expected to reach a staggering $1.6 billion soon, with sponsorships, advertising, and media rights driving dramatic revenue growth. This creates new opportunities for players, teams, and content creators within the esports ecosystem.

Negative Impacts

- **Strained Public Finances:** Cities often face pressure to secure major sporting events or franchises, leading to hefty financial commitments. Building new stadiums and upgrading infrastructure can be costly, sometimes burdening taxpayers with long-term debt. For instance, the construction of Mercedes-Benz Stadium in Atlanta for the Super Bowl in 2017 raised concerns about public financing and its impact on other essential city services.
- **Displacement of Communities:** Large-scale stadium projects can sometimes lead to the displacement of residents and businesses in

surrounding neighborhoods. Concerns regarding gentrification and rising property costs often accompany major sporting developments.
- **Environmental Impact:** The construction and operation of sports stadiums can have environmental consequences. Resource consumption, energy use, and waste generation are all factors to consider. Additionally, large-scale events may increase carbon emissions due to travel and infrastructure demands.
- **Ethical Concerns:** Issues like doping, performance-enhancing drugs, and gambling addiction remain challenges within the sports industry. Additionally, the working conditions of athletes and stadium staff, particularly in developing countries, raise ethical concerns that need to be addressed.

The economic impact of sports is undeniable. While the industry undoubtedly generates revenue, creates jobs, and fosters community pride, it's crucial to acknowledge and address the potential downsides. Careful planning, responsible financial management, and a focus on ethical considerations are essential for ensuring that the positive aspects of sports continue to thrive and contribute meaningfully to economies and societies worldwide.

Importance of Studying Legal Aspects in Sports

The world of sports is a complex ecosystem fueled by passion, competition, and big business. Beneath the roar of the crowd and the thrill of victory lies an intricate web of legal frameworks that strive to ensure fairness, protect rights, and maneuver through the ever-evolving sports panorama. Studying sports law is essential for several reasons, including the protection of stakeholders' rights, the integrity of competitions, and the traversing of complex legal and ethical challenges in an increasingly technology-driven industry.

However, it wasn't until the mid to late 1970s that the legal aspects of sports were seriously considered as a distinct field of study. This shift was pioneered by law school professors such as John Weistart at Duke University, Cym Lowell at Indiana University, Bob Barry at Boston

College, and Robert Waters at the University of Miami. Their groundbreaking work laid the foundation for sports law as an academic discipline. Following in their footsteps, Glenn Wong, a student of Professor Barry, and your author Michael Jones, a student of Professor Waters, markedly expanded the field through their teaching, research, scholarship, media presence, and real-world contributions at both the professional sports and Olympic levels. Their efforts demonstrated that integrating contract law, property rights, torts, labor laws, marketing, management, and agency issues in a comprehensive manner could create a holistic field of sports law. This new perspective helped the world appreciate the complexities of legal frameworks in the sports industry.

By studying and learning about the legal and business complexities of sports in an increasingly tech-driven industry, students are not only gaining knowledge but are also being prepared to become the next generation of leaders in this evolving field. Understanding the legal intricacies involved is essential for ensuring fair play, protecting the rights of all stakeholders, and effectively managing the multifaceted challenges that arise in modern sports. This underscores the importance of studying sports law, making it a rewarding and impactful pursuit for those passionate about the intersection of law, technology, and sports. Through this education, future professionals will be equipped to maneuver through the dynamic landscape of sports, shaping their future while upholding the principles of justice and ethical conduct.

Reasons to Study Sports Law

For Students

1. **Career Opportunities:** Sports law offers diverse career paths, including roles as sports agents, team counsels, arbitrators, and intellectual property lawyers. These positions allow students to combine their passion for sports with legal expertise, opening doors to exciting and dynamic careers.
2. **Interdisciplinary Knowledge:** Studying sports law provides students with a comprehensive understanding of various legal fields such as contract law, labor law, intellectual property, and

dispute resolution. This interdisciplinary approach equips them with versatile skills applicable in numerous legal contexts.
3. **Real-World Applications:** Through internships, clinics, and simulation courses, students can gain practical experience in handling sports-related legal issues, preparing them for the complexities of the professional world.

For Faculty

1. **Research and Scholarship:** Faculty members can contribute to the development of sports law through research and scholarship, exploring emerging legal challenges and proposing innovative solutions. Their work can influence policy and shape the future of the sports industry.
2. **Teaching and Mentorship:** Educators have the opportunity to inspire and mentor the next generation of sports lawyers, sharing their expertise and guiding students through the intricacies of sports law.
3. **Industry Engagement:** Faculty can collaborate with sports organizations, governing bodies, and legal practitioners, bridging the gap between academia and industry and ensuring that their research has practical relevance.

For Sports Administrators

1. **Compliance and Governance:** Understanding sports law is essential for administrators to ensure compliance with regulations, manage legal risks, and uphold the integrity of their organizations.
2. **Contract Negotiations:** Administrators often handle complex contract negotiations with athletes, sponsors, and media partners. Knowledge of sports law enables them to draft and negotiate agreements that protect their organization's interests.
3. **Crisis Management:** In the event of legal disputes or scandals, administrators with a background in sports law are better equipped to manage crises, mitigate damage, and navigate the legal landscape effectively.

For Athletes

1. **Rights and Protections:** Athletes benefit from understanding their legal rights and protections, including issues related to contracts, endorsements, and intellectual property. This knowledge empowers them to make informed decisions about their careers.
2. **Dispute Resolution:** Familiarity with sports law helps athletes navigate disputes with teams, sponsors, or governing bodies, ensuring that their interests are represented and protected.
3. **Career Management:** Athletes can leverage legal knowledge to manage their careers strategically, from negotiating contracts to protecting their brand and image.

For Leaders and the General Public

1. **Informed Leadership:** Leaders in sports organizations, including team owners and executives, benefit from a deep understanding of sports law to make informed decisions that align with legal and ethical standards.
2. **Public Awareness:** The general public gains a better appreciation of the complexities and challenges within the sports industry, fostering a more informed and engaged fan base.
3. **Advocacy and Social Change:** Knowledge of sports law enables individuals to advocate for fair play, integrity, and social justice within the sports community, driving positive change and promoting equity.

Sports law goes beyond just the athletes on the field. It encompasses a diverse group of affected and interested parties, each with their own legal needs and considerations. Athletes benefit from understanding their contractual rights, endorsement deals, and image usage protections. Teams require expertise in areas like labor relations, intellectual property (logos, trademarks), and media rights. Sponsors need legal guidance on sponsorship agreements and marketing strategies. Sports administrators are entrusted to make sure their venues are not merely comfortable, but safe and conflict-free. Even fans have rights regarding ticket sales, data privacy, and fair competition within the sport they love. Studying sports law equips individuals to advocate for the fair treatment of all parties involved in the sports industry.

The world of sports is not static. As technology advances and the industry grows, new legal challenges arise. Data analytics and artificial intelligence are revolutionizing player performance analysis and scouting, raising questions about data ownership, privacy, and potential algorithmic biases. Students of sports law need to be at the forefront of these developments, ensuring responsible use of technology and upholding the integrity of competition.

The burgeoning world of esports presents a unique legal frontier. Issues surrounding intellectual property rights for video games, player contracts, and athlete representation in the digital realm, and broadcast rights require specialized knowledge and legal frameworks still under development. Similarly, the metaverse, a virtual world with potential applications in sports viewership and training, throws up new challenges regarding data security, virtual ownership of assets, and the legal implications of virtual sporting events. Those who understand these emerging areas will be highly sought after to understand and lead in this uncharted territory.

Sports law plays a vital role in maintaining the integrity and ethical standards of competition. Anti-doping regulations, player safety protocols, and fair play rules all fall under the purview of sports law. Understanding these frameworks empowers individuals to advocate for a level playing field and combat practices that compromise the spirit of sportsmanship.

Key Legal Areas in Sports

1. Contract Law

Sports lawyers assist in drafting, reviewing, and negotiating contracts. These contracts may involve publicity rights, mergers, acquisitions, or the formation of sports organizations. Player agents represent professional athletes in contract negotiations with their teams. A notable example is the contract negotiation of LeBron James with the Los Angeles Lakers. His agent ensured that the contract included specific provisions related to sponsorships and endorsements, which are crucial for an athlete of his stature. Another example is the landmark case of *Adrian Peterson v. NFLPA*, where the court examined the terms of Peterson's contract and the arbitration process within the NFL.

2. Intellectual Property Rights

Protecting intellectual property rights is vital in the sports industry. This includes handling matters related to trademark and copyright infringement, licensing agreements, and the use of athletes' NIL. The proliferation of NIL rules and regulations has made this a growth area in sports law. For instance, the case of *O'Bannon v. NCAA* significantly impacted how student-athletes can profit from their image or publicity rights. This case established that the NCAA's previous restrictions violated antitrust laws, thus allowing athletes to receive compensation for their NIL.

3. Administrative Law

This area involves traversing the regulation and governance of sports organizations and leagues, including compliance with rules and regulations set by governing bodies such as the NCAA. It also extends to licensing and permitting processes for sports venues and issues related to sports betting. The case of *Jerry Sandusky and Penn State University* serves as an example of administrative law in sports, where the university faced severe sanctions for failing to comply with NCAA regulations. Another example is the *Murphy v. NCAA* case, where the Supreme Court struck down the *Professional and Amateur Sports Protection Act* (PASPA), allowing states to legalize sports betting.

4. Labor Relations

The ongoing debate around whether college athletes should be paid has been a significant labor relations issue. The case of *Northwestern University and College Athletes Players Association* (CAPA) highlighted this, where the National Labor Relations Board (NLRB) examined whether college football players could unionize and be considered employees. Additionally, federal antitrust laws have been enacted to prevent monopoly practices, unfair competition, and illegal tying arrangements. The case of *American Needle, Inc. v. National Football League* is a key example, where the Supreme Court ruled that NFL teams are separate entities and thus subject to antitrust laws.

5. Taxation and Financial Planning

This includes tax and estate planning and counseling for individuals with backgrounds in sports, such as athletes, members of ownership groups, and team executives. It also involves reviewing legal documents associated with investment opportunities. The case of *US v. Tim Duncan* involved the NBA star's lawsuit against his former financial advisor for mismanagement of his finances and poor investment advice, showcasing the importance of proper financial and tax planning in sports.

6. Intercollegiate Sports Governing Bodies

Addressing the complex landscape of intercollegiate sports requires understanding the roles of various governing bodies such as the NCAA. These bodies enforce regulations that differ significantly from those governing professional sports. The *Alston v. NCAA* case, where the Supreme Court ruled that the NCAA's restrictions on education-related benefits for athletes violated antitrust laws, illustrates the ongoing legal challenges in this area.

7. Amateur vs. Professional Athlete Regulation

The distinction between regulating amateur and professional athletes is significant in sports law. Amateur athletes, often governed by organizations like the NCAA, face different rules and regulations compared to professional athletes who are represented by unions and agents. Yet, the growth of sponsorship money via NIL deals erases some of the boundary lines between college and professional athletes.

8. Due Process, Equal Protection, and Gender Equity

Legal issues surrounding constitutional rights and protections like due process, equal protection, and gender equity are at the heart of fairness in sports. The Title IX legislation, which prohibits gender discrimination in federally funded education programs, has had a profound impact on women's sports. Cases involving transgender athletes, such as the debate over their participation in women's sports, continue to challenge existing legal frameworks.

9. International Sports Governing Bodies

International sports governing bodies like the IOC, international sports federations, and FIFA play formative roles in regulating sports globally. They interact with national governing bodies to ensure the uniform application of rules and standards. The role of independent bodies like WADA and USADA in addressing doping and ensuring a level playing field is also vital.

10. Publicity Rights and NIL Opportunities

Publicity rights, including NIL opportunities for college athletes, are a rapidly evolving area of sports law. Copyrights protect media content, while trademarks are essential for brand sponsorships, athlete endorsements, and the names of teams. Social media's role in defamation cases and the protection of athletes' reputations is increasingly important.

11. Data Analytics and Artificial Intelligence

The growth and use of data analytics to improve performance and the application of artificial intelligence to evaluate teams and strategies have transformed sports. These technologies enhance game strategy and provide new insights into athlete performance.

12. Esports and the Metaverse

Esports and the metaverse represent a new frontier in sports. The rapid growth of video games and virtual reality sports presents unique legal challenges and opportunities. Legal issues in this area include intellectual property rights, player contracts, and the regulation of virtual sports competitions.

13. Role of Sports Agents

Sports agents play a critical role in negotiating contracts, licensing agreements, and managing the careers of athletes. They have fiduciary duties to their clients, and cases where these duties have been breached, such as in the civil lawsuit against powerful sports agent Leigh Steinberg, highlight the importance of ethical practices in sports management.

14. Gambling and Sports Betting

Recent legislation and Supreme Court cases have opened up gambling on sports games, leading to significant revenue growth for states. However, concerns over the integrity of games and the regulation of betting activities are ongoing issues. The use of AI and technology to detect suspicious betting patterns is becoming increasingly important.

15. Privacy

Privacy concerns in sports include data privacy, social media exploitation, and the use of biometric data and facial recognition at events. Issues of free speech and defamation, as well as the risk of hacking, are critical areas of focus.

16. Torts and Risk Management

Torts in sports law involve risk management, product liability, and the standard of care required from coaches, medical personnel, and equipment manufacturers. Crisis management and the handling of injuries and accidents are also crucial aspects of sports law.

17. Social Justice, Equity, and Diversity

Social justice and equity issues, including the Black Lives Matter movement and athletes as advocates, are prominent in sports. The inclusion of LGBTQ+ athletes and the promotion of diversity in sports organizations are critical areas of study and examination.

18. Environmental Impact

The environmental impact of sports includes green initiatives and the organization of eco-friendly events. The future of sports will likely involve increased emphasis on sustainability and reducing the ecological footprint of sporting events.

By looking into these key legal areas, this chapter provides a comprehensive understanding of how various legal disciplines intersect with the world of sports. Through case examples, the dynamic and multifaceted nature of sports law is illustrated, highlighting its critical role in the sports industry.

Summary

Studying sports law is essential for ensuring the fair and ethical operation of the sports industry. It provides students, faculty, administrators, athletes, leaders, and the general public with the tools to appreciate the legal complexities of sports, protect stakeholders' rights, and uphold the integrity of competitions. As the sports industry continues to develop, the importance of sports law will only grow, making it an indispensable field of study for those passionate about the intersection of law and sports.

Through exploring these multifaceted issues, readers will gain a deeper understanding of the essential role that legal frameworks play in shaping the sports industry. This book emphasizes the need for continuous adaptation and innovation in legal practices to keep pace with technological advancements and emerging trends. The dynamic nature of sports law necessitates a proactive approach to addressing issues such as data analytics, artificial intelligence, esports, and the metaverse, all of which are transforming the way sports are played, managed, and consumed.

By providing a comprehensive analysis of both traditional and contemporary legal challenges, this book aims to ensure the orderly and equitable progression of the sports industry in an ever-evolving landscape. It examines the historical development of sports law, highlighting key milestones and pivotal cases that have shaped the field. This historical context provides a foundation for understanding current legal principles and their application in today's sports environment.

Furthermore, the book explores the intricate relationship between sports law and various legal disciplines, such as contract law, intellectual property rights, labor law, and torts. This interdisciplinary approach equips readers with a holistic view of the legal environment, enabling them to appreciate the interconnectedness of different legal areas and their collective impact on the sports industry.

In addition to theoretical knowledge, practical insights are provided through real-world case studies and examples. These practical applications illustrate how legal principles are implemented in actual sports scenarios, offering readers a tangible understanding of how sports law operates in practice. This pragmatic approach ensures that readers are well prepared to tackle real-world legal issues in the sports industry.

Moreover, the book underscores the importance of ethical considerations and social responsibility in sports law. It emphasizes the role of sports leaders in advocating for fair play, equality, and social justice within the sports community. By promoting these values, sports law contributes to the overall positive impact of sports on society, fostering a more inclusive and equitable environment for all stakeholders.

For students, studying sports law opens up diverse career opportunities, allowing them to combine their passion for sports with legal expertise. For faculty, it offers a platform to contribute to the development of the field through research and scholarship. For sports administrators, it provides the knowledge needed to manage legal risks and ensure compliance. For athletes, it empowers them to make informed decisions about their careers and protect their rights. For leaders and the general public, it fosters informed decision-making and advocacy for integrity and fairness in sports.

In conclusion, this book aims to serve as an extensive guide for anyone interested in the field of sports law. By surveying both the theoretical and practical aspects of sports law, it provides a solid foundation for understanding the complex legal landscape of the sports industry. It encourages continuous learning and adaptation to keep pace with the evolving nature of sports and ensures that the legal frameworks governing sports remain robust, fair, and effective. Through this exploration, readers will be equipped to contribute to the sustainable and equitable growth of the sports industry, making a meaningful impact in a field that continues to captivate and inspire people around the world.

Discussion Questions

1. How did sports law emerge as a distinct field of study in the mid to late 1970s, and why was this development significant?
2. What role does sports law play in promoting ethical behavior in the sports industry?
3. How does sports law protect the rights and interests of different stakeholders in the sports industry?
4. What are some of the career paths available in sports law, and what makes these roles unique?
5. Why are regulatory frameworks and compliance important in the context of sports law?
6. In what ways does sports law contribute to social justice and equity in sports?
7. How can knowledge of sports law help in managing crises within sports organizations?
8. What are some emerging trends in sports law, and why is it important for legal professionals to stay updated?
9. What are some of the contemporary legal challenges faced by the sports industry?
10. Why is it important for educational institutions to offer courses and programs in sports law?

2

The Evolution of College Sports

Tradition and Transformation

Chapter Outline

A Brief History of the NCAA	34
Structure and Membership	37
Regulation of Sports	43
Criticisms and Calls for Reform	46
NCAA Constitution	47
NCAA Bylaws	51
Division I Autonomy	66
Summary	68
Discussion Questions	70

College sports in the United States represent a unique and vibrant segment of the sports industry, blending in theory the pursuit of academic excellence with athletic achievement. College athletics provide students with opportunities to excel in their chosen sports while receiving what one hopes is a quality education. These programs foster school spirit, build community, and often serve as a stepping-stone to professional sports careers.

At the heart of this intricate ecosystem is the National Collegiate Athletic Association (NCAA), the major governing body responsible for regulating the activities of student-athletes across hundreds of institutions. The NCAA plays a crucial role in maintaining the integrity of college sports through the enforcement of rules and regulations that govern all aspects of athletic competition and student-athlete conduct.

The NCAA's bylaws and constitution are foundational to maintaining fairness, health, and safety in collegiate sports, ensuring that the rights and well-being of student-athletes are protected. The organization's regulatory framework addresses a wide range of issues, including academic eligibility, recruitment practices, financial aid, and the conduct of coaches and athletes. This comprehensive governance system aims to promote a level playing field, preventing any institution from gaining an unfair advantage.

In addition to regulating competition, the NCAA also hosts national championships in multiple sports, providing student-athletes with the opportunity to compete at the highest levels and gain national recognition. These events not only showcase the talents and hard work of the athletes but also generate significant revenue and exposure for the participating institutions, especially in the revenue-generating sports of football and men's and women basketball.

The ever-changing landscape of college sports, including recent debates over student-athlete compensation, unionization, transfer portal, and the use of their names, images, and likenesses (NIL), highlights the dynamic nature of the NCAA's role. As it addresses these and other challenges, the NCAA seeks to adapt its policies and practices to uphold the evolving principles of amateurism while addressing the rights and needs of modern student-athletes and still remain relevant as a power broker in the world of college sports.

A Brief History of the NCAA

The history of college sports in the United States dates back to the nineteenth century, reflecting the nation's shifting relationship with athletics and education. The first recorded intercollegiate competition took place on August 3, 1852, when Harvard and Yale faced off in a rowing race on Lake Winnipesaukee in New Hampshire. This event marked the beginning of a long tradition of intercollegiate athletics. In the following decades, college sports grew rapidly in popularity. Football, in particular, became a major sport on college campuses. The first intercollegiate football game was played on November 6, 1869, between Rutgers and Princeton, setting the stage for what would become one of the most popular sports in American colleges. Other sports such as baseball, track and field, and basketball soon followed, each establishing their own traditions and rivalries. By the early twentieth century, the need for standardized rules and regulations became apparent. Issues such as player eligibility, safety, and fairness were often disputed, leading to the formation of various regional athletic associations. These early organizations laid the groundwork for the establishment of a national governing body to oversee college sports.

The NCAA, originally known as the Intercollegiate Athletic Association of the United States (IAAUS), was founded on March 31, 1906, in response to the alarming brutality and fatalities that plagued college football at the turn of the twentieth century. The formation of the IAAUS was largely driven by the decisive intervention of President Theodore Roosevelt, whose role was instrumental in the organization's creation. College football at the time was notoriously violent, with the 1904 season alone resulting in eighteen deaths and 159 serious injuries on the field. This level of danger prompted widespread public outcry and concern for the safety of student-athletes.

As both a football fan and a staunch advocate for reform, President Roosevelt was deeply disturbed by the sport's increasingly dangerous nature. He feared that without significant changes, the sport could face a complete ban, which would undermine the development of character and physical fitness that Roosevelt believed football fostered in young men. In October 1905, Roosevelt took a bold step by convening a meeting at the White House with representatives from Harvard, Princeton, and Yale, three of the most influential football programs of the time. The purpose of this meeting was to discuss and devise potential reforms to make the sport safer while preserving its competitive spirit.

Roosevelt's push for reform was not merely a symbolic gesture; he exerted considerable pressure on these institutions to take concrete actions. His involvement helped galvanize support for change, and his influence extended beyond this initial meeting. Concurrently, New York University Chancellor Henry M. MacCracken also advocated for the reform of college athletics, organizing a conference of thirteen schools that further highlighted the need for a regulatory body to oversee college sports.

These efforts culminated in the establishment of the IAAUS, which was constituted as a rules-making body on March 31, 1906. The organization's primary mission was to create and enforce standardized rules for college sports to reduce violence and ensure the safety of athletes. In 1910, the organization was renamed the National Collegiate Athletic Association (NCAA). Over the next several decades, the NCAA expanded its role and influence, introducing regulations on player eligibility, academic standards, and amateurism. The NCAA's efforts were aimed at ensuring a balance between athletics and academics, promoting fair competition, and safeguarding the health and safety of student-athletes. The mid-twentieth century saw dramatic changes and challenges for the NCAA. Television began to play a major role in college sports, bringing both increased revenue and new issues related to broadcasting rights and commercialization. The NCAA adapted by negotiating television contracts and sharing revenues among member institutions after numerous court disputes.

In recent years, the NCAA has faced ongoing debates and legal challenges related to student-athlete compensation, particularly around the use of athletes' names, images, and likenesses (NIL). In response to these pressures, the NCAA has implemented reforms allowing student-athletes to earn money from endorsements and other commercial activities, reflecting the shifting terrain of college sports.

However, NIL is not the only issue the NCAA is contending with. The growth and use of the transfer portal have introduced new challenges and opportunities. The transfer portal allows student-athletes to enter their names into a database indicating their desire to transfer to another school, facilitating movement between institutions. While this system promotes greater autonomy for athletes, it has raised concerns about competitive balance, recruiting practices, and the potential for individual schools and conferences to use the portal to build "super teams."

Additionally, gender equity remains a critical concern. Title IX, a federal civil rights law passed in 1972, mandates that no person in the United States shall be discriminated against on the basis of sex under any education program or activity receiving federal financial assistance.

Despite this, achieving true gender equity in college sports has fallen short of its mark. Issues persist regarding equal funding, facilities, scholarships, and media coverage for male and female sports programs.

The current binary system of gender classification also faces scrutiny as the number of non-binary athletes grows. Traditional male or female classifications do not adequately address the needs and identities of non-binary athletes. This gap in policy raises complex questions about how to classify and accommodate these athletes within the existing framework of college sports.

Transgender athletes present another layer of complexity in the quest for a level playing field. The inclusion of transgender athletes has sparked debates over fairness, particularly regarding the potential advantages transgender women might have in female sports. Balancing the rights of transgender athletes with concerns over competitive equity and safety remains a contentious issue. Policies must consider scientific, ethical, and social perspectives to ensure inclusivity while maintaining fairness in competition.

Due process and inclusion are integral components of these discussions. The NCAA must confront these sensitive issues carefully, ensuring that all athletes' rights are respected and protected. This involves creating transparent, fair processes for addressing grievances and disputes while fostering an inclusive environment that supports diversity in all its forms.

Structure and Membership

The NCAA is a member-led organization comprising over 1,100 member institutions, including four-year colleges and universities across the United States and Canada. These institutions are divided into three divisions (I, II, and III), each with its own legislative powers, governance structures, and championships. The divisions are based on the size of the institution, the level of competition, and the scope of athletic scholarships offered.

Division I

Division I is the most competitive and includes the largest schools with the most extensive athletic programs. Institutions in this division are typically characterized by significant financial resources, extensive athletic facilities, and substantial fan bases. Division I schools are divided into two subdivisions for football: the Football Bowl Subdivision (FBS) and the Football Championship Subdivision (FCS).

- **Football Bowl Subdivision (FBS):** The FBS includes schools with large football programs like the University of Alabama, Texas A&M, Stanford University, and The Ohio State University that participate in bowl games rather than a traditional playoff system. These institutions must meet minimum attendance requirements and sponsor a certain number of sports.
- **Football Championship Subdivision (FCS):** The FCS includes schools like South Dakota State, Dartmouth College, William and Mary, and Southern University that participate in a playoff system to determine the national champion. These schools have fewer athletic scholarships and lower attendance requirements compared to FBS schools.

Division I schools must meet basic academic and financial standards and are subject to extensive regulations to ensure competitive equity and athlete welfare. They offer a wide range of athletic scholarships to attract top-tier athletes.

Division II

Division II institutions are smaller than those in Division I but still emphasize a high level of competition. These schools often provide a balance between athletics, academics, and extracurricular activities. Division II schools like Bentley University, Central State University, Franklin Pierce University, and Slippery Rock University offer partial athletic scholarships, allowing athletes to receive a mix of athletic and academic aid.

Division II emphasizes the "Life in the Balance" approach, encouraging student-athletes to participate in a variety of campus and community activities. The division sponsors championships in various sports and aims to provide a comprehensive collegiate experience.

Division III

Division III schools like Denison University, University of Chicago, NYU, and Emory University focus on the overall college experience, prioritizing academics and extracurricular activities over athletics. Institutions in this division do not offer athletic scholarships, although they may provide other forms of financial aid based on need or merit.

Division III is the largest division in terms of the number of member institutions, emphasizing participation, sportsmanship, and community engagement. Student-athletes in Division III are encouraged to integrate their athletic commitments with their academic and personal lives, fostering a well-rounded college experience rather than looking to compete later in life as a professional athlete.

Governance

The governance structure of the NCAA is designed to ensure that member institutions have a voice in the decision-making process. Each division operates with its own set of rules and governing bodies:

- **Board of Governors:** The Board of Governors is the highest governing body in the NCAA, providing overall strategic direction and oversight. It includes representatives from all three divisions and ensures that the organization adheres to its core values and mission.
- **Division Councils:** Each division has its own council responsible for overseeing legislative processes, enforcing rules, and addressing issues specific to their member institutions. These councils include representatives from member schools, conferences, and student-athletes.
- **Committees:** Various committees within each division address specific areas such as championships, student-athlete welfare, academic standards, and compliance. These committees play a crucial role in shaping policies and regulations.

The NCAA's structure and governance model are designed to ensure that it can effectively manage a diverse membership while maintaining a focus on fairness, safety, and the physical and mental development of student-athletes. Its regulations and policies aim to integrate sports as an essential part of the educational experience, promoting both athletic excellence and academic achievement.

Despite its efforts, the NCAA has faced mounting criticism and disapproval over the years. One of the primary criticisms is that the organization exploits student-athletes by generating substantial revenue from their performances while historically restricting their ability to profit from their own likenesses. This has been a point of contention, particularly as college sports have grown into a multi-billion-dollar industry, with television deals, merchandise sales, and other revenue streams heavily reliant on the athletes themselves, who until recently, saw little to none of this financial benefit.

Another major criticism centers around the fairness and consistency of NCAA regulations and enforcement practices. The organization has been accused of inconsistent disciplinary actions, where similar infractions receive disparate penalties depending on the institution or sport involved. For example, schools from powerful football and basketball conferences such as the ACC, SEC, Big Ten, and Big Twelve have often been perceived as receiving preferential treatment.

One notable instance of inconsistent treatment involves the sanctions imposed on the University of Southern California (USC) compared to those on other institutions. USC received severe penalties, including a two-year postseason ban, scholarship reductions, and the vacating of wins, due to improper benefits received by star football player Reggie Bush. The NCAA determined that Bush and his family had accepted substantial gifts and financial assistance from sports marketers, which constituted major violations of NCAA rules.

In contrast, similar violations at other high-profile programs, such as Ohio State and Auburn, resulted in comparatively lenient punishments. At Ohio State, several football players were found to have received improper benefits, including selling memorabilia and receiving discounted or free tattoos from a local tattoo parlor, in violation of NCAA rules. Despite the clear violations, the penalties were notably lighter than those imposed on USC; to wit, Ohio State received a one-year postseason ban, scholarship reductions, and the vacating of wins

Similarly, Auburn faced scrutiny during the season when reports surfaced that star quarterback Cam Newton's father had solicited money from other schools during the recruiting process. Although Auburn was ultimately cleared of wrongdoing, the controversy raised questions about the consistency of NCAA enforcement. Critics pointed out that Auburn faced no significant penalties despite the serious nature of the allegations, particularly when compared to the harsh sanctions imposed on USC.

These disparities in enforcement not only undermine the NCAA's credibility but also create an uneven playing field, where the severity of consequences appears to be influenced by the prominence and influence of the schools involved. The perceived favoritism and lack of uniformity in the NCAA's disciplinary actions continue to fuel debates about the fairness and integrity of college sports governance.

Concerns about athlete welfare remain an unresolved issue within the NCAA, despite some improvements over the years. One of the primary concerns is the adequacy of medical care provided to student-athletes. While the NCAA has implemented protocols to address injuries, particularly concussions, critics argue that these measures are not uniformly enforced across all member institutions. For example, high-profile incidents such as the death of Maryland football player Jordan McNair, who suffered a fatal heatstroke during a team practice, have highlighted the shortcomings in athlete safety protocols. The University of Maryland faced severe backlash for failing to provide timely and appropriate medical care, leading to calls for more stringent oversight and standardized care across all schools.

In addition to physical health, the lack of mental health resources for student-athletes has become a growing concern. The pressures of maintaining athletic performance, academic responsibilities, and dealing with the public scrutiny that comes with being a high-profile athlete can lead to significant mental health challenges, including anxiety, depression, and burnout. Recent years have seen a troubling rise in reports of mental health crises among college athletes, with some tragically leading to suicides.

One example is the case of Washington State quarterback Tyler Hilinski, who took his own life in 2018. His death sparked a national conversation about the mental health of student-athletes and the perceived lack of support from institutions. Observers argue that the NCAA has not done enough to address these issues, with many schools lacking adequate mental health resources and professionals trained to deal with the unique challenges faced by student-athletes.

The physical demands placed on student-athletes also continue to be a not fully addressed concern. The rigorous training schedules, coupled with the expectation to perform at a high level both athletically and academically, can take a toll on their physical and mental well-being. This issue is compounded by the fact that many athletes, particularly in revenue-generating sports like football and basketball, face pressure to play through injuries, sometimes risking long-term health consequences. The demands of these sports seasons, which often extend year-round, leave little time for recovery, further exacerbating the risks to athletes' health.

In response to these concerns, the NCAA and its member schools have taken some steps to improve athlete welfare. The NCAA has introduced policies aimed at reducing the risk of concussions, such as limiting contact practices and implementing return-to-play protocols. Additionally, the NCAA has begun to place more emphasis on mental health, encouraging schools to provide resources and support for athletes struggling with mental health issues. Some schools have responded by hiring full-time sports psychologists and creating dedicated mental health programs for their athletes.

However, these efforts are often seen as insufficient, with critics arguing that the NCAA's actions are reactive rather than proactive. There is a growing call for the NCAA to take a more active role in enforcing uniform standards for both physical and mental health care across all its member institutions. Advocates suggest that the NCAA should mandate mental health screenings, provide funding for mental health resources, and implement stricter oversight of medical care practices to ensure the safety and well-being of student-athletes.

The debate over athlete welfare is ongoing, with the NCAA facing increasing pressure to evolve its policies to better protect the physical and mental health of those who compete under its banner. As the demands on student-athletes continue to grow, the NCAA's ability to address these concerns effectively will be decisive in shaping the future of collegiate sports. Should the NCAA fail to take meaningful action, it is likely that schools and the NCAA itself will face civil lawsuits from athletes and their families, seeking accountability and reform through judicial action. Such legal challenges could force improvements that the NCAA has been slow to implement, compelling the organization to adopt more rigorous standards and protections for athlete welfare. The stakes are high, and the consequences of inaction could lead to exponential legal and financial repercussions, as well as a potential erosion of public trust in collegiate athletics.

Regulation of Sports

The NCAA is a voluntary, non-state, membership organization, meaning colleges and universities can choose to join or remain independent from its governance practices. The NCAA's governance model is designed to manage a membership of small and large institutions with different focuses on the roles of sports participation within the mission of each school while concentrating on the holistic development of student-athletes.

Over the years, since the founding of the NCAA more than a century ago, it has evolved into a comprehensive regulatory body that oversees various aspects of collegiate athletics through its bylaws, including player eligibility, academic standards, recruitment, health and safety, compliance, and amateurism. The organization's rules and regulations are designed to ensure a level playing field, promote athlete welfare, and integrate athletics into the broader educational mission of institutions.

Legal Framework and State Action Doctrine: Due Process and Fairness

However, as a private, voluntary membership organization receiving no state or federal funds, the distinction between the NCAA and state actors is precarious from a due process and fairness perspective. State actors are subject to constitutional constraints, including due process and equal protection under the law, ensuring that individuals have legal recourse if their rights are violated. In contrast, as a private organization, the NCAA is not bound by these constitutional requirements, giving it more flexibility in setting and enforcing its rules against coaches, student-athletes, administrators, and member institutions. However, this also means that athletes and member institutions must rely on the NCAA's internal processes for dispute resolution, which may not always align with constitutional standards of fairness and transparency.

The state action doctrine is a legal principle that determines whether an entity's actions can be attributed to the state, thereby subjecting it to constitutional scrutiny. According to the US Supreme Court, private entities can be considered state actors in certain circumstances, such as when they perform functions traditionally reserved for the state, when the government compels the private entity to act, or when the government and the private entity act jointly. However, the NCAA has been consistently ruled as a private entity, not a state actor, which exempts it from traditional constitutional due process requirements.

Key Legal Cases Shaping NCAA Regulation

NCAA v. Tarkanian (1988)

A landmark case illustrating the distinction between state actors and private entities.

Facts: Jerry Tarkanian, the head basketball coach at the University of Nevada, Las Vegas (UNLV), was disciplined by the NCAA for alleged recruiting violations and associations with known gamblers. Tarkanian contended that the NCAA's disciplinary actions violated his due process rights, arguing that the NCAA should be considered a state actor because it was working closely with the state university.

Legal Issues: The central issue was whether the NCAA's actions could be attributed to the state, making it a state actor and subjecting it to constitutional scrutiny.

Outcome: The US Supreme Court ruled that the NCAA was not a state actor. The Court found that the NCAA was a private organization and that its actions, even though they affected a state university employee, did not convert the NCAA into a state actor.

Impact: This decision underscored the NCAA's status as a private entity, affirming that its regulations and enforcement actions are not subject to the constitutional requirements of due process that apply to state actors.

It is important to note that there is no constitutional right to play sports. This distinction, like that between "state" actors and private voluntary organizations, is vital because it means that the regulatory powers of high school sports associations and the NCAA are not inherently limited by constitutional protections. Instead, these organizations can set and enforce rules that they deem necessary to maintain the integrity and fairness of athletic competition. However, they must still ensure that their regulations and enforcement practices are fair and transparent to avoid legal challenges.

The regulation of college and even high school sports also intersects with **First Amendment** issues, particularly concerning freedom of speech and expression. Student-athletes, like all students, have the right to express their views, but this right can be limited by the NCAA's rules and the policies of individual institutions. Restrictions on social media use or public statements by athletes can raise First Amendment concerns, especially if such restrictions are seen as overly broad or punitive.

Cohen v. San Bernardino Valley College (1996)

Facts: A student-athlete was disciplined for making critical comments about the college's athletic program on social media.

Legal Issues: The case centered on whether the college's actions violated the student's First Amendment rights.

Outcome: The court ruled in favor of the student-athlete, finding that the college's actions were overly broad and punitive, thus violating the student's free speech rights.

Impact: This case highlighted the need for colleges and the NCAA to carefully consider the scope and enforcement of their social media policies to avoid infringing on student-athletes' First Amendment rights.

Tinker v. Des Moines Independent Community School District (1969)

Facts: Although not directly related to sports, this landmark case involved students wearing black armbands to protest the Vietnam War.

Legal Issues: The central issue was whether the school's actions in disciplining the students violated their First Amendment rights.

Outcome: The US Supreme Court ruled that students do not "shed their constitutional rights to freedom of speech or expression at the schoolhouse gate."

Impact: This case set a precedent for student free speech rights, which extends to student-athletes and their expression on social media and other platforms.

Despite not being bound by constitutional due process requirements, the NCAA has established its own internal processes in an attempt to ensure some minimum level of fairness in its regulatory practices. These processes include various levels of investigation and resolution methods, such as negotiated resolution, summary disposition, written record hearings, and full hearings. The NCAA's enforcement staff is responsible for investigating potential violations and working collaboratively with institutions to ensure compliance with NCAA rules.

Criticisms and Calls for Reform

Over the years the NCAA's internal processes have faced significant criticism for lacking transparency and fairness. Observers argue that the NCAA's procedures are often inconsistent and biased, leading to perceptions of selective prosecution and unchecked power. To address these concerns, there have been calls for reforms to enhance due process protections within the NCAA's regulatory framework.

For instance, were the NCAA to fully integrate traditional standards of due process as provided by the Fourth and Fourteenth Amendments to the US Constitution, then the following protections would apply not only to the NCAA but also to its member institutions.

In athletic administration, due process involves several critical elements to ensure fairness. First, individuals must be given notice of specific charges or accusations against them, with timely notification before any disciplinary action is taken. Second, a fair and impartial hearing must be conducted where the individual can present their case, including evidence, witnesses, and a defense. Third, individuals have the right to be represented by counsel or an advisor during hearings or disciplinary proceedings. Fourth, decisions should be based on substantial evidence presented during the hearing, with opportunities to cross-examine witnesses and challenge the evidence. Finally, individuals should have the right to appeal decisions to a higher authority or an independent body, with the appeals process being fair and accessible.

The issue of due process for students accused of sexual harassment or abuse on college campuses has been a topic of enormous debate and concern. Under Title IX, a federal law prohibiting sex discrimination in educational institutions that receive federal funding, schools are required to address and remedy instances of sexual harassment and violence. However, the procedures for handling such accusations have raised concerns about fairness and due process for the accused, as will be discussed further later.

NCAA Constitution

The NCAA Constitution outlines the core principles and operational framework governing college athletics. Here are the main articles of the NCAA Constitution and how they work in practice, along with examples of major breaches and their consequences.

Article 1: Name, Purposes, and Fundamental Policy

Purpose: This article establishes the name and fundamental policy of the NCAA, emphasizing the promotion of student-athlete well-being, educational values, and competitive fairness.

Practice: In practice, this article ensures that all NCAA activities and regulations are aimed at balancing athletic competition with educational priorities and student-athlete welfare. It underpins every decision and policy the NCAA implements.

Article 2: Principles for Conduct of Intercollegiate Athletics

Purpose: This article outlines key principles such as amateurism, fair competition, and the overall educational experience of student-athletes. It includes policies on nondiscrimination, sportsmanship, and ethical conduct.

Practice: Schools must adhere to these principles by ensuring their athletic programs align with the educational mission of the institution and uphold high ethical standards. Violations can lead to sanctions and loss of eligibility for student-athletes.

Article 3: NCAA Membership

Purpose: Article 3 defines the criteria and process for becoming and maintaining membership in the NCAA.

Practice: Institutions must meet certain academic and operational standards to join the NCAA. Membership is reviewed periodically, and schools that fail to meet these standards may face probation or expulsion.

Article 4: Organization

Purpose: This article details the organizational structure of the NCAA, including the roles and responsibilities of the Board of Governors, councils, and committees.

Practice: The Board of Governors oversees major decisions and policies, while various councils and committees handle specific aspects of NCAA governance, such as rules enforcement and championships.

Article 5: Legislative Authority and Process

Purpose: Article 5 describes the legislative process within the NCAA, including how rules and regulations are proposed, reviewed, and implemented.

Practice: Members can propose changes to NCAA rules, which are then reviewed by committees and voted on by member institutions. This ensures a democratic process where all members have a voice.

Article 6: Institutional Control and Responsibility

Purpose: This article emphasizes the importance of institutional control over athletic programs and holds institutions accountable for the actions of their representatives.

Practice: Institutions must maintain control over their athletic programs, ensuring compliance with NCAA rules. Failure to do so can result in severe penalties, as seen in the Penn State and Michigan State cases.

Case Study: Penn State University and Jerry Sandusky Scandal

Violation: Lack of institutional control and failure to protect student-athletes from sexual abuse. **Breached Articles**: Articles 2 and 6.

Facts and Participants: Jerry Sandusky, a former assistant coach for Penn State's football team, was found guilty of sexually abusing multiple young boys over a period of at least fifteen years. The abuse often occurred on Penn State's campus and involved boys Sandusky met through his charity, The Second Mile. Key figures involved included head coach Joe Paterno, Athletic Director Tim Curley, Vice President Gary Schultz, and President Graham Spanier, who were accused of failing to report Sandusky's actions to law enforcement and adequately protect the victims.

Harm Caused: The scandal caused immense harm to the victims, who suffered long-term psychological and emotional trauma. It also severely damaged Penn State's reputation and led to draconian financial costs, including over $100 million in settlements to victims.

Outcome: The NCAA imposed a $60 million fine, a four-year postseason ban, scholarship reductions, and vacated 112 wins from the football program's record. These penalties aimed to address the systemic failures in oversight and ensure future compliance. Additionally, Curley, Schultz, and Spanier were found guilty of misdemeanor charges of child endangerment and received jail sentences.

Governance Changes: The scandal led to increased scrutiny of institutional control and prompted the NCAA to implement stricter oversight and compliance measures. Penn State also made significant changes to its policies and procedures to prevent future abuses and improve reporting mechanisms.

Case Study: Michigan State University and Dr. Larry Nassar Scandal

Violation: Failure to address and prevent sexual abuse by a university-employed doctor. **Breached Articles**: Articles 2 and 6.

Facts and Participants: Larry Nassar, a former team doctor for Michigan State University and USA Gymnastics, was convicted of sexually abusing hundreds of female athletes under the guise of medical treatment.

Key figures involved included university administrators and athletic staff who failed to act on numerous complaints and reports of Nassar's abuse over two decades.

Harm Caused: The abuse caused severe physical and emotional trauma to the victims, many of whom were minors at the time. The scandal also led to a significant loss of trust in Michigan State's ability to protect its students and athletes.

Outcome: The NCAA fined Michigan State $4.5 million and imposed corrective measures to enhance institutional control and safeguard athlete welfare. Nassar was sentenced to 40 to 175 years in prison. The university also reached a $500 million settlement with over 300 victims and faced ongoing legal and financial repercussions.

Governance Changes: The scandal prompted Michigan State to overhaul its Title IX office and procedures for handling sexual misconduct cases. The university implemented new policies to ensure better reporting, transparency, and accountability. The US Department of Education also placed the university under a five-year period of special compliance monitoring.

Article 7: Committees

Purpose: This article establishes various committees responsible for different aspects of NCAA governance, including infractions, eligibility, and championships.

Practice: These committees ensure specialized and focused oversight in their respective areas, enabling effective regulation and enforcement of NCAA rules.

Article 8: Championships and Postseason Football

Purpose: Article 8 outlines the organization and administration of NCAA championships and postseason football.

Practice: The NCAA ensures that these events are conducted fairly and in alignment with the organization's principles, providing student-athletes with opportunities to compete at the highest levels.

Article 9: Enforcement

Purpose: This article describes the enforcement procedures for investigating and addressing violations of NCAA rules.

Practice: The NCAA's enforcement division investigates alleged violations, conducts hearings, and imposes penalties on institutions and individuals found guilty of breaking NCAA rules. This process ensures accountability and compliance within college sports

The NCAA Constitution provides a comprehensive framework for regulating college athletics, emphasizing principles like fairness, safety, and institutional control. The examples of Penn State and Michigan State illustrate the severe consequences of failing to adhere to these principles, highlighting the importance of rigorous oversight and compliance in maintaining the integrity of collegiate sports. These cases have led to changes in governance and procedures, aiming to prevent future abuses and ensure a safer environment for student-athletes.

NCAA Bylaws

The NCAA member institutions enact legislation annually to update their operating bylaws, which govern various aspects of college athletics. This process involves proposing, reviewing, and voting on changes to ensure that the rules remain relevant and effective in promoting fairness, safety, and integrity in collegiate sports. The key bylaws cover areas such as recruitment, academic standards, health and safety, fairness, integrity, compliance, and amateurism.

Recruitment (Bylaw 13) governs the recruitment of student-athletes, including contact with prospective students, official and unofficial visits, and offers of financial aid. Recent updates have included specific rules regarding social media and digital communication. Coaches are allowed to send direct messages to prospective student-athletes on social media platforms, regulated by specific timing rules. They can "like," "favorite," or publicly comment on recruits' posts, but these actions are subject to overall recruitment period restrictions. Recruitment periods include contact periods, when coaches can communicate with recruits in person, via phone, or through electronic communication such as social media direct messages; evaluation periods, when coaches can watch recruits play but cannot engage in off-campus contact, with digital communication also restricted; quiet periods, when coaches can communicate with recruits only on the college campus, with digital communication allowed but no in-person off-campus interactions; and dead periods, when no in-person recruiting contacts or evaluations can occur, though certain types of digital communication, such as direct messaging, may still be allowed.

Specific rules for social media contact include timing and frequency guidelines, where coaches can initiate social media contact with prospective student-athletes starting September 1 of their junior year in high school, with no limits on the number of permissible electronic communications once initial contact is allowed. Digital communications must adhere to the same content guidelines as other forms of recruitment communication, meaning no offers or inducements that would violate NCAA rules. Public interactions (likes, retweets, comments) are allowed but should be appropriate and not suggest any form of impermissible inducement. Coaches are not allowed to publicize a recruit's visit to the campus via social media until after the recruit has signed a National Letter of Intent or a written offer of admission and/or financial aid, and recruits are discouraged from announcing unofficial visits on social media to prevent undue pressure or influence.

An example of social media abuse involved a Division I basketball coach contacting recruits through direct messages during a dead period, violating NCAA contact rules. Penalties included restrictions on recruiting activities, a fine, and the coach's suspension, with additional compliance training required. The NCAA has enhanced its monitoring and compliance efforts to seek to ensure adherence to these updated rules, requiring institutions to educate coaches, staff, and student-athletes on the appropriate use of social media in recruitment and using various tools to monitor social media interactions to ensure compliance.

The **National Letter of Intent (NLI)** is a binding agreement between a prospective student-athlete and an NCAA Division I or II institution. By signing an NLI, the student-athlete commits to attending the institution for one academic year, and the institution, in return, agrees to provide athletic financial aid for that year. Division III institutions are not subject to NLI rules. Once an NLI is signed, other institutions are prohibited from recruiting the student-athlete.

Recently, the NCAA made changes to the NLI rules to provide greater flexibility for student-athletes. Now, if a student-athlete fails to honor the NLI, they may still retain eligibility to compete at a new institution without the penalty of sitting out a full academic year, depending on the circumstances. However, the NLI must still be accompanied by an offer of athletic financial aid for the entire academic year and can only be signed during designated signing periods specific to each sport. Signing an NLI is not mandatory, but it offers security, assures athletic aid, and concludes the recruiting process.

The **NCAA Eligibility Center**, formerly known as the NCAA Clearinghouse, is responsible for determining the academic and amateurism eligibility of prospective student-athletes who wish to compete in NCAA Division I or II sports. The Eligibility Center reviews high school transcripts, SAT/ACT scores, and core course completions to ensure the student-athlete meets the academic requirements. It also verifies that the student-athlete adheres to NCAA amateurism rules, which include restrictions on receiving payments or benefits related to their sport. Prospective student-athletes must register with the NCAA Eligibility Center, typically during their junior year of high school, to begin the certification process. Before a student-athlete can compete, their academic and amateurism status must be certified by the NCAA Eligibility Center, ensuring that all participants meet the NCAA's standards for academic performance and amateur status.

Historically, the NCAA has been scrutinized for failing to impose higher academic standards among its member institutions, particularly Division I schools. Commentators argue that the NCAA often looks the other way when institutions create one educational experience for their student-athletes and another, more challenging academic experience for the remainder of the student body. This discrepancy undermines the core values of higher education and the integrity of collegiate sports. In response, the governing bodies of the NCAA are beginning to take a renewed view of intercollegiate athletics as an integral component of the educational enterprise. Moving forward, schools must complement and align athletics with the values of higher education. The NCAA now emphasizes the need for intercollegiate athletics to remain a positive contributing factor within the higher education model. This includes ensuring that athletic programs support the overall mission of educational institutions and contribute to the holistic development of student-athletes.

Intercollegiate athletics schools must establish a level of academic rigor and commitment for all student-athletes that is commensurate with that of the general student body. This involves creating academic environments that enable student-athletes to be educated, graduate, and succeed in their chosen careers. Key initiatives and policies include establishing and enforcing academic standards that are consistent across all member institutions to ensure that student-athletes receive a quality education, requiring student-athletes to make consistent progress toward their degrees, maintaining a course load and GPA similar to non-athlete students, providing comprehensive academic support services, including tutoring, study halls, and academic advising tailored to the unique needs of student-athletes, and implementing rigorous monitoring and accountability measures to ensure that institutions adhere to academic standards and provide a challenging educational experience for all students.

The **Academic Performance Program (APP)** includes the Academic Progress Rate (APR) and Graduation Success Rate (GSR) metrics, which hold institutions accountable for the academic performance of their student-athletes. Schools that fail to meet these benchmarks can face penalties, including scholarship reductions and postseason bans. The NCAA has raised initial and continuing eligibility standards to ensure that student-athletes are better prepared for the rigors of college academics. Partnering with educational organizations and institutions, the NCAA develops programs that promote academic excellence and career readiness for student-athletes. The renewed focus on aligning intercollegiate athletics with the broader values of higher education aims to create an academic experience that prepares student-athletes not only for success on the field but also for meaningful careers and lifelong achievements beyond participation as professional athletes.

Bylaw 14 sets the academic eligibility standards for student-athletes, including initial eligibility, continuing eligibility, and progress-toward-degree requirements. Student-athletes must maintain specific GPAs in core courses, which are fundamental subjects like math, science, and English. Division I requires a minimum 2.3 GPA in core courses, while Division II requires a minimum 2.2 GPA. Minimum ACT or SAT scores are required to receive aid and participate in sports. By the end of the first year, student-athletes must complete at least twenty-four semester hours or thirty-six quarter hours. By the end of the second year, they must declare a major and complete at least 40 percent of the coursework required for their degree. By the end of the third year, they must complete at least 60 percent of the coursework required for their degree. By the end of the fourth year, they must complete at least 80 percent of the coursework required for their degree. In addition, institutions are required to provide vigorous academic support services, including tutoring, study halls, and dedicated academic advisors for student-athletes. Institutions must report academic performance data to the NCAA, ensuring transparency and enabling the NCAA to monitor compliance with academic standards.

An example of abuse occurred at the University of North Carolina at Chapel Hill, where student-athletes were enrolled in fraudulent courses to maintain their eligibility. Although the NCAA did not impose sanctions due to the courses being available to all students, the case led to increased scrutiny and reforms in academic oversight. Another example, the Jan Kemp saga, involved a former academic counselor at the University of Georgia who exposed the practice of keeping athletes eligible through academic fraud by forcing faculty to change grades to keep their athletes eligible to compete in a football bowl game. This led to heightened awareness and stricter academic standards across the NCAA, including requiring all student-athletes to declare a major by their junior year and maintain satisfactory academic progress each semester.

Health and Safety (Bylaw 17) originally focused on regulating playing and practice seasons to ensure student-athletes had adequate time for rest and recovery. Recent changes by the NCAA in health and safety protocols, particularly regarding concussion protocols, social media exposure, mental health, and suicide prevention, reflect a growing commitment to ensuring the well-being of student-athletes.

Concussion protocols have been enhanced significantly. The NCAA now requires member schools to have a concussion management plan that includes baseline testing, proper medical evaluation, and a step-by-step return-to-play protocol. Schools must provide independent medical care for student-athletes to ensure unbiased decision-making in concussion management. Additionally, regular education for coaches, staff, and student-athletes about concussion signs, symptoms, and the importance of reporting them is mandated. Updated guidelines emphasize return-to-learn protocols, ensuring that student-athletes receive academic accommodations during recovery, and standardized concussion care protocols across divisions to ensure consistent treatment and management.

Social Media Exposure is another area of focus, with the NCAA implementing educational programs to help student-athletes navigate the pressures and risks associated with social media. This includes understanding the impact of their digital footprint and promoting positive online behavior. Schools are encouraged to monitor social media activity and provide support when student-athletes face online harassment or cyberbullying.

Mental Health and Suicide Prevention efforts have been bolstered with comprehensive mental health support. The NCAA has developed a set of best practices for mental health care, which includes recommendations for mental health screening, management, and referral processes. Member schools are required to provide access to licensed mental health professionals for student-athletes, including on-campus counseling centers and referrals to external mental health services if necessary. Suicide prevention initiatives include crisis intervention training for coaches, athletic trainers, and staff to recognize and respond to signs of mental distress and potential suicide risk among student-athletes. The NCAA supports peer mentoring and support programs where student-athletes can provide support to their peers who may be struggling with mental health issues. In the unfortunate event of a student-athlete suicide, the NCAA has guidelines for postvention programs to support the affected community and prevent additional trauma.

Case studies highlight the effectiveness of these protocols. The University of Michigan's updated concussion protocol includes mandatory baseline testing, immediate removal from play after a suspected concussion, and a structured return-to-play protocol supervised by medical professionals, reducing the risk of long-term brain injuries and ensuring proper care and recovery time. The University of Florida's social media education program includes workshops on digital literacy, privacy settings, and managing public perception, helping student-athletes maintain a positive online presence and avoid potential pitfalls. Following the tragic suicide of Washington State University quarterback Tyler Hilinski, the university implemented comprehensive mental health programs, including mandatory mental health check-ins, increased counseling services, and a partnership with the Hilinski's Hope Foundation to raise mental health awareness, increasing support availability and reducing the stigma associated with seeking help.

Bylaw 17 has also been updated to address the use of doping and performance-enhancing drugs as well as the prevention of sexual harassment. The NCAA's commitment to maintaining the integrity and safety of collegiate sports is reflected in these changes. Anti-doping regulations include a comprehensive list of banned substances, such as anabolic steroids, stimulants, hormones, and other performance-enhancing drugs, aligning with World Anti-Doping Agency (WADA) standards. Regular and random drug testing of student-athletes is mandated to detect and deter the use of banned substances, both in and out of competition. Penalties for violations include a minimum suspension of one calendar year and the loss of a season of eligibility for the first offense, with progressively harsher penalties for additional violations, including potential permanent ineligibility. Annual educational sessions on the dangers of doping and the importance of competing clean are mandatory for all student-athletes, coaches, and athletic staff, with resources provided to educate athletes about nutrition, proper training techniques, and the health risks associated with performance-enhancing drugs.

Sexual Harassment Prevention policies and procedures have been strengthened, with a zero-tolerance policy for sexual harassment and assault within NCAA member institutions. This includes harassment by coaches, staff, teammates, or any other individuals involved in athletics. Institutions must have clear and accessible reporting mechanisms for student-athletes to report incidents of sexual harassment, ensuring confidentiality and protection from retaliation. Immediate and appropriate action is required upon receiving a report of sexual harassment, including conducting thorough investigations and providing support to affected individuals. Sanctions for individuals found guilty of sexual harassment range from suspension to permanent removal from the program, depending on the severity of the offense. Annual training on sexual harassment prevention, including recognizing, reporting, and responding to such incidents, is mandatory for all student-athletes, coaches, and athletic staff. Ongoing awareness programs are implemented to educate the athletic community about the impact of sexual harassment and the importance of creating a safe and respectful environment. Schools must provide access to counseling services and advocacy support for victims of sexual harassment, including mental health services and guidance on navigating the reporting process, with coordination with Title IX offices to ensure compliance with federal regulations and provide comprehensive support to affected student-athletes.

NCAA Bylaw 10, which governs ethical conduct and compliance, reflects the NCAA's ongoing efforts to enhance integrity and ethical behavior in college sports. Recent governance updates address various areas, including honesty, sportsmanship, gambling, and other ethical standards. Under this bylaw, student-athletes, coaches, and athletic staff must conduct themselves with honesty and sportsmanship at all times, avoiding dishonest or fraudulent behavior in their academic and athletic pursuits. Compliance with NCAA, conference, and institutional rules is mandatory for all individuals associated with NCAA athletics, with significant penalties for violations.

Gambling and Sports Wagering have enhanced restrictions under **Bylaw 10**. The bylaw reinforces the prohibition on gambling by student-athletes, coaches, and athletic staff on any sporting event, amateur or professional, in which the NCAA conducts championships. This includes betting on their sports, other NCAA sports, and professional sports. It explicitly forbids using inside information for gambling purposes and sharing confidential information that could affect a game's outcome for gambling purposes. Institutions must provide annual education sessions on the risks and consequences of gambling and sports wagering to raise awareness and prevent gambling-related issues among student-athletes and staff. The NCAA has enhanced its monitoring capabilities to detect and prevent gambling activities through partnerships with gambling monitoring organizations. Institutions must have clear procedures for reporting suspected gambling violations, which must be investigated promptly, with appropriate actions taken.

Ethical Conduct and Integrity measures have been strengthened. All individuals associated with NCAA athletics are required to participate in regular ethics training sessions covering topics such as honesty, integrity, sportsmanship, and compliance with NCAA rules. Institutions may require student-athletes and staff to sign integrity pledges, affirming their commitment to ethical behavior and compliance with NCAA rules. The NCAA has strengthened its investigative powers to ensure thorough and timely investigations of ethical conduct violations, including the ability to gather evidence, conduct interviews, and collaborate with external agencies when necessary. Ensuring due process protections for individuals accused of violations remains a priority, including the right to a fair hearing, the right to present evidence, and the right to appeal decisions.

Social Media and Public Statements are also regulated under **Bylaw 10.** The bylaw includes guidelines for appropriate conduct on social media. Student-athletes, coaches, and staff are expected to use social media responsibly and refrain from posting content that could harm the reputation of their institution or the NCAA. Any form of harassment, bullying, or inappropriate conduct on social media is strictly prohibited and subject to disciplinary action.

A recent example of a violation occurred when a student-athlete made inappropriate and offensive comments on social media, violating the NCAA's ethical conduct standards. The student-athlete was suspended for part of the season, required to issue a public apology, and mandated to attend social media conduct training. The institution implemented additional social media monitoring policies.

Bylaw 19 establishes the framework for the NCAA's infractions program, which aims to uphold integrity and fair play among member schools. Violations are categorized into different levels based on their severity. Level I violations are severe breaches of conduct that seriously undermine or threaten the integrity of the NCAA collegiate model. Level II violations are significant breaches of conduct that provide more than a minimal but less than a substantial or extensive recruiting, competitive, or other advantage. Level III violations are breaches of conduct that are isolated or limited in nature and provide no more than a minimal recruiting, competitive, or other advantage. Level IV violations are incidental infractions that are technical and do not constitute a breach of conduct.

Institutions, staff members, student-athletes, and other associated individuals have an enhanced responsibility to cooperate with NCAA investigations. This includes preserving documentation related to potential violations, disclosing and providing access to relevant electronic devices and accounts, encouraging cooperation from spouses, family members, boosters, and other associates, and participating in interviews and providing requested materials. The enforcement process involves several key steps: investigation by NCAA enforcement staff, importation of facts from other legal or administrative proceedings, and inferences of violations if there is a failure to cooperate. The Committee on Infractions has the authority to impose various sanctions on institutions and individuals found to have committed violations, including loss of revenue sharing during a postseason ban, postseason bans, suspension of individuals, reductions in recruiting visits, and other penalties deemed appropriate based on the severity of the violation.

The infractions process includes multiple resolution methods. Full hearings are reserved for cases with significant disagreement on facts or violations. Written record hearings are used for cases with limited disagreement on facts or violations. Summary disposition is an agreement on facts and violations but not on classification or penalties. Negotiated resolution involves agreement on all aspects, including facts, violations, classification, and penalties. The NCAA has created a public dashboard to provide a procedural timeline of Level I and II infractions cases, enhancing transparency in the enforcement process.

Recent additions to the investigative process now incorporated into **Bylaw 19** include strengthened investigative powers, streamlined processes, advanced technology and data analysis, increased transparency, and support for whistleblowers. The NCAA can now employ independent external investigators to ensure thorough and unbiased investigations, improving credibility and impartiality. Additionally, there is an increased emphasis on collaboration with law enforcement agencies when investigating potential criminal activities associated with NCAA violations.

To streamline processes, the NCAA has introduced expedited hearing procedures for certain cases to resolve issues more quickly while maintaining fairness and due process. A preliminary review process has also been instituted to assess whether allegations warrant a comprehensive investigation, helping prioritize cases and allocate resources efficiently.

In terms of technology and data analysis, the NCAA now employs advanced data analytics and forensic tools to identify patterns of behavior indicative of rule violations, including monitoring financial transactions, communication patterns, and social media activity. Upgraded protocols for collecting and preserving digital evidence, such as emails, text messages, and social media interactions, have been implemented to ensure more thorough investigations.

The NCAA has committed to greater transparency in its investigative processes, including public disclosure of investigation timelines, findings, and sanctions to ensure accountability. Institutions under investigation now receive regular updates on the status of their cases.

Support for whistleblowers has also been strengthened, as the lack of support had been a long-time criticism of the NCAA. The NCAA has guaranteed confidentiality and protection from retaliation for those who report violations, and improved anonymous reporting mechanisms have been put in place to encourage individuals to report potential violations without fear of repercussions.

For example, the University of Kansas men's basketball program faced allegations of recruiting violations and improper benefits. The investigation employed independent external investigators and advanced data analytics to gather evidence. Due to overlapping criminal investigations, the case involved collaboration with federal law enforcement agencies. Preliminary reviews were conducted to streamline the process, and regular updates were provided to the institution. The investigation led to major sanctions, including postseason bans, scholarship reductions, and show-cause penalties for implicated individuals.

Another case involved the University of Louisville's men's basketball program, which provided improper benefits, including escorts to recruits. As a result, Louisville received a postseason ban, scholarship reductions, and vacated wins, including their national championship.

The harshest sanction for lack of institutional control, known as the Death Penalty, was used only once against Southern Methodist University (SMU) in 1987 for repeated and severe bylaw violations. The sanctions included the cancellation of one football season, the suspension of another, coupled with the loss of scholarships and recruiting restrictions, and limitations on coaching staff, which had a profound and long-lasting impact.

Amateurism

The concept of amateurism in college sports has its roots in nineteenth-century England, where it was defined by the London Amateur Athletic Club in 1866. An amateur was someone who had never competed for money, admission fees, or with professionals, and who did not earn a living through manual labor. This definition was inherently classist, favoring the wealthy who could afford to compete without financial compensation. When the NCAA was formed in 1906, it adopted amateurism as a core value, influenced by these British ideals. The NCAA's version of amateurism aimed to maintain the educational integrity of college sports by ensuring that athletes were students first and foremost, not professionals. Initially, the NCAA prohibited any form of compensation for athletes, including scholarships. It wasn't until 1956 that the NCAA allowed schools to offer "grants-in-aid" covering educational expenses, but strictly for tuition, room, board, and books.

Despite these strict rules, abuse was rampant. Schools often found ways to circumvent the regulations, leading to various scandals. Initially, each school was responsible for policing its own adherence to amateurism rules, which led to inconsistent enforcement and widespread violations. The NCAA eventually established a system to investigate violations and enforce penalties, but issues persisted. Walter Byers, the NCAA's first executive director, played a significant role in shaping the organization's policies. Byers later criticized the system he helped build in his book *Unsportsmanlike Conduct: Exploiting the Student-Athlete* (1995). He argued that college sports had become a high-dollar commercial enterprise, with schools and athletic directors making millions while student-athletes received little in return. Byers highlighted the hypocrisy of the NCAA's amateurism rules, which he believed exploited athletes under the guise of maintaining educational integrity.

The myth of amateurism began to unravel through various legal challenges. Notable cases include:

***O'Bannon v. NCAA* (2015)**: This case challenged the NCAA's prohibition on compensating athletes for the use of their names, images, and likenesses (NILs). The court ruled that the NCAA's rules were an unlawful restraint of trade under the Sherman Antitrust Act, leading to a partial victory for the plaintiffs. The ruling allowed schools to provide scholarships up to the full cost of attendance and permitted deferred compensation for athletes.

***NCAA v. Alston* (2021)**: This Supreme Court case further eroded the NCAA's amateurism rules. The court ruled that the NCAA could not restrict education-related benefits for student-athletes, such as scholarships for graduate school or paid internships. The decision emphasized that while the NCAA could limit cash payments unrelated to education, it could not cap benefits that were clearly educational.

Several other important cases have shaped the concept of NCAA amateurism:

NCAA v. Board of Regents (1984): This case dealt with television rights and the NCAA's control over broadcasting. The Supreme Court ruled that the NCAA's television plan violated antitrust laws, which significantly reduced the NCAA's control over college sports broadcasting.

White v. NCAA (2008): This case challenged the NCAA's restrictions on the value of athletic scholarships. The settlement allowed schools to purchase health insurance for athletes and set up a fund for additional educational benefits.

These legal battles have progressively dismantled the NCAA's strict amateurism rules, highlighting the tension between maintaining amateur status and addressing the financial realities of modern college sports, leading to changes in the NCAA rules regarding amateurism as found in **Bylaw 12**.

Bylaw 12: This bylaw ensures that student-athletes maintain amateur status, prohibiting them from receiving compensation related to their athletic abilities with a multitude of exceptions and waiver possibilities to the general rule including the newly enacted Name, Image and Likeness (NIL) Rights.

Bylaw 12 (Amateurism)

- **NIL Compensation:** Significant changes have been made to allow student-athletes to profit from their name, image, and likeness. This includes the ability to sign endorsement deals, participate in commercial activities, and receive compensation for social media activities.
- **Institutional Involvement:** Institutions are prohibited from directly compensating student-athletes for NIL activities, but they can provide education and resources to help athletes navigate these opportunities.
- **Disclosure Requirements:** Student-athletes must disclose NIL agreements to their institutions to ensure compliance with NCAA regulations.

NIL (Name, Image, and Likeness) money for college athletes comes from a variety of sources, including brand endorsements, social media promotions, personal appearances, and more. For instance, EA Sports will pay thousands of college athletes through a name, image, and likeness deal. Players who opt in to have their name, image, and likeness used in their video games will receive $600 and a copy of the game. A major portion of NIL deals is facilitated through collectives, which are groups or organizations that pool resources to support athletes in monetizing their NIL rights. Here's a detailed look at how NIL money is sourced and examples of both women and men athletes profiting from these opportunities:

Sources of NIL Money

1. **Brand Endorsements:** Companies sponsor athletes to promote their products or services. This can include apparel, equipment, food and beverages, and more.
2. **Social Media Promotions:** Athletes with large social media followings can earn money by posting sponsored content on platforms like Instagram, TikTok, and Twitter.
3. **Personal Appearances:** Athletes are paid to make appearances at events, including autograph signings, meet-and-greets, and promotional events.
4. **Merchandising:** Athletes can create and sell their own branded merchandise, such as clothing, accessories, and other products.
5. **Training Camps and Clinics:** Athletes can host or participate in sports camps and clinics, earning money through participation fees and sponsorships.
6. **Media and Content Creation:** Some athletes monetize their YouTube channels, podcasts, and other content platforms by leveraging their fame and expertise.

Collectives

Collectives are groups, often formed by alumni, boosters, and fans, that pool financial resources to help athletes capitalize on their NIL opportunities. These collectives can provide direct financial support, facilitate deals, and offer guidance on how to manage and maximize NIL earnings. Collectives aim to ensure that athletes can benefit financially while maintaining compliance with NCAA regulations.

Florida State University faced penalties for an NIL-related recruiting violation. An assistant football coach facilitated an impermissible recruiting contact between a transfer prospect and a booster, who offered the prospect an NIL deal as a recruiting inducement. Florida State received a two-year probation, a three-year disassociation from the booster, a one-year disassociation from the NIL collective, a $5,000 fine plus 1 percent of the football budget, a reduction of five football scholarships over the probationary period, and restrictions on recruiting communications and in-person recruiting days.

Modern college athletes who sign endorsements and sponsorship deals are significantly altering the business aspect of college sports. There are numerous examples of star high school athletes receiving NIL deals in excess of a million dollars before even starting a college game.

Diversity

The NCAA has incorporated diversity and inclusion into its operating bylaws through **Bylaw 20**, reflecting the association's commitment to promoting these values at all levels of college athletics. This bylaw mandates that member institutions and conferences develop and implement policies and procedures to support diversity and inclusion initiatives. Among these initiatives, the NCAA conducts annual social media campaigns to raise awareness about the importance of diversity and inclusion in sports. These campaigns engage student-athletes, coaches, and fans in conversations about inclusivity. Additionally, the NCAA hosts an annual Equity and Inclusion Forum, bringing together administrators, coaches, and student-athletes to discuss best practices and strategies for fostering inclusive environments. The NCAA also provides resources and support for LGBTQ student-athletes and staff, promoting a safe and inclusive environment for all individuals regardless of sexual orientation or gender identity.

The NCAA encourages diversity in leadership positions within its member institutions and governance structures, including efforts to increase the representation of women and ethnic minorities in coaching, administrative roles, and committees. Programs such as the NCAA Leadership Development Program focus on preparing student-athletes from diverse backgrounds for leadership roles both within and outside of sports, aiming to equip participants with the skills and knowledge necessary to succeed in their future careers. The NCAA sets goals for diverse representation in various roles, including coaches, athletic directors, and committee members, with progress regularly reviewed to ensure accountability. Regular training sessions on diversity, equity, and inclusion are conducted for student-athletes, coaches, and administrators. Enhanced support services are also provided for student-athletes from underrepresented groups, including academic support, mental health services, and career counseling.

Transfer Portal

Under **Bylaw 14**, the NCAA Transfer Portal allows student-athletes to transfer between schools more easily, leading to increased mobility among athletes, with thousands across all NCAA-sponsored sports entering the portal each year. The introduction of the transfer portal has streamlined the transfer process, allowing student-athletes to publicly declare their intention to transfer and communicate with other institutions. This system provides more flexibility and autonomy in their athletic careers, as student-athletes in many sports can now transfer once without having to sit out a year. For second-time transfers, waivers can be granted based on specific circumstances such as health, family issues, or other personal reasons. In the most recent year reported, over 1,600 football players entered the transfer portal, reflecting the growing trend of athletes seeking new opportunities.

The impact of the transfer portal has been particularly significant in men's and women's basketball and football, where the increased player movement has affected team dynamics, competitive balance, and championship outcomes. Coaches and athletic programs have had to adapt to the new landscape by focusing on recruiting both high school athletes and transfer students. This shift has led to concerns about team stability and the academic impact on transferring athletes, as frequent transfers can disrupt a player's educational progress.

Division I Autonomy

Division I institutions, particularly the Power Five (now Power 4 with the demise of the Pac 10) conferences, have legislative autonomy to address specific needs such as athlete welfare, scholarships, and financial aid. This autonomy allows them to implement policies tailored to their unique challenges and resources. In a groundbreaking development, the NCAA and its five (or four now) major conferences have reached an agreement to permit colleges to directly compensate athletes for the first time in over a century of college sports. This settlement will pay over $2.7 billion in damages over ten years to past and present athletes.

Each school can set aside up to $21 million in revenue to share with athletes per year, with athletes in all sports eligible for payments. Schools have the freedom to decide how the money is distributed among sports programs, and scholarship limits by sport will be replaced by roster restrictions. This new model allows athletes to receive direct payments, significantly altering the landscape of college sports.

Despite these advancements, the settlement's impact on Title IX gender equity law and schools' ability to bring NIL activities in-house remains uncertain, potentially leading to more lawsuits. Additionally, the increased focus on NIL deals and direct payments may exacerbate inequities between revenue and non-revenue sports.

The NCAA Constitution and its Bylaws provide a comprehensive framework for regulating college athletics, emphasizing principles like fairness, safety, and institutional control. The examples of Michigan, North Carolina, Maryland, Florida State, and Louisville illustrate the consequences of failing to adhere to these principles, highlighting the importance of rigorous oversight and compliance in maintaining the integrity of collegiate sports. These cases have led to changes in governance and procedures, aiming to prevent future abuses and ensure a safer environment for student-athletes.

The distinction between Division I autonomy and the Governance Council ensures that the specific needs of Division I institutions, particularly the Power Five (now Four) conferences, are met while maintaining overall coherence and integrity within NCAA governance. Division I autonomy allows these institutions to deal with their unique challenges by implementing policies tailored to their resources and needs, such as athlete welfare and financial aid. Meanwhile, the Governance Council oversees broader NCAA policies and ensures that all member institutions adhere to the overarching principles of fairness, safety, and institutional control. This dual structure helps balance the flexibility needed by larger, resource-rich institutions with the consistent regulation required to maintain the integrity of college athletics as a whole.

This rebalancing also occurred in response to fears that the major football and basketball conferences might seek to break away from the NCAA and form their own governing body. These conferences have substantial financial resources and generate significant revenue from television rights, sponsorships, and ticket sales. By forming their own governing body, these conferences would not have to share revenue with smaller schools and could create rules and policies that better reflect the commercial realities of their sports programs. This potential move could lead to a more efficient distribution of resources and increased control over their operations, ensuring that their financial and competitive interests are prioritized.

The autonomy granted to Division I institutions under the current NCAA structure aims to address these concerns by allowing the Power Four conferences more flexibility in managing their affairs. This approach seeks to retain these influential conferences within the NCAA framework while providing them with the ability to negotiate their unique challenges. However, the balance remains delicate, as the pressures and incentives for these conferences to consider independence persist, driven by the desire for greater financial control and tailored governance that better aligns with their substantial economic impact on college athletics.

Summary

This chapter provides a brief history of college athletics and an in-depth look at the NCAA's role in governing collegiate sports, emphasizing its dedication to integrity, fairness, and safety. College athletics have evolved significantly, with the NCAA emerging as a central governing body. The NCAA operates through a democratic legislative process as outlined in its Constitution, allowing member institutions to propose, review, and vote on rule changes. This process ensures that all stakeholders, including student-athletes to a limited degree, have a voice in shaping regulations.

The key bylaws and recent changes in NCAA governance address several critical areas to ensure fairness, safety, and integrity in collegiate sports. Recruitment governs the recruitment of student-athletes, covering contact periods, official visits, and financial aid offers. Recent updates address digital communication and social media interactions, reflecting modern recruitment practices. Academic standards set academic eligibility requirements, including minimum GPAs, standardized test scores, and progress-toward-degree criteria. Emphasis is placed on support and monitoring to ensure student-athletes maintain academic rigor.

Health and safety regulate playing and practice seasons, focusing on concussion protocols, mental health resources, and sexual harassment prevention. The bylaws mandate independent medical care, mental health support, and comprehensive education programs to safeguard student-athletes' well-being. Fairness, integrity, and compliance address ethical conduct, including honesty, sportsmanship, and compliance with NCAA rules. Recent enhancements include stricter anti-gambling measures, advanced data analytics for investigations, and robust whistleblower protections.

Amateurism and NIL rights ensure student-athletes maintain amateur status while allowing them to profit from their name, image, and likeness (NIL). This has significantly altered the landscape, enabling athletes to secure endorsements and sponsorships. The transfer portal streamlines the transfer process, allowing student-athletes to declare their intention to transfer and communicate with other institutions. Changes include immediate eligibility for first-time transfers and specific waiver criteria for second-time transfers.

The NCAA's improved investigative procedures include independent external investigations, collaboration with law enforcement, and the use of advanced technology for evidence collection. These measures try to ensure thorough, fair, and transparent investigations of rule violations. Power Five (Four) conferences under Division I have legislative autonomy to address specific needs related to athlete welfare and financial aid. The Governance Council oversees broader NCAA regulations to maintain consistency and integrity across all divisions.

The NCAA emphasizes diversity and inclusion, mandating regular training, inclusive policies, and equitable resource distribution. This establishes a policy that collegiate sports environments are supportive and representative of all student-athletes. The NCAA has placed a renewed focus on aligning intercollegiate athletics with the broader values of higher education. Key initiatives include establishing consistent academic standards across all member institutions, requiring consistent academic progress, providing robust academic support, and implementing more rigorous monitoring and accountability measures.

This chapter underscores the NCAA's changing role in regulating college sports, adapting to modern challenges while upholding core values of fairness, integrity, and safety. Through continuous updates to its bylaws and a commitment to comprehensive governance, the NCAA strives to create an equitable and supportive environment for all student-athletes, preparing them for success both on and off the field. This includes a renewed emphasis on academic integrity, ensuring that athletic participation complements and enhances the overall educational experience.

Discussion Questions

1. What are the main functions of the NCAA's legislative process, and how does it attempt to guarantee that all stakeholders have a voice in shaping the regulations that govern college athletics?
2. How have recent changes impacted the recruitment of student-athletes, particularly regarding digital communication and social media interactions?
3. In what ways do academic standards attempt to require that student-athletes maintain academic rigor comparable to their non-athlete peers, and do you think it meets this objective?
4. What are the key components of concussion protocols and mental health resources, and how do they contribute to the overall well-being of student-athletes?
5. How do anti-gambling measures and advanced data analytics enhance the NCAA's ability to uphold ethical conduct and integrity in collegiate sports?
6. What are the potential benefits and challenges associated with allowing student-athletes to profit from their name, image, and likeness (NIL)?
7. What are the pros and cons of the transfer portal for student-athletes and institutions?
8. What roles do diversity, equity, and inclusion initiatives play in NCAA governance, and how do they contribute to creating

a supportive and representative environment for all student-athletes?
9. In what ways has the NCAA improved its investigative processes to verify thorough, fair, and transparent investigations of rule violations?
10. How does NCAA governance aim to align intercollegiate athletics with the broader values of higher education, and what measures have been implemented to improve the academic experience for college athletes?

3

Breaking Barriers
Gender Equity and Title IX in Sports

Chapter Outline

The History of Women's Participation in Sports	74
The Impact of Title IX on Women's Participation in College Sports	76
Women's Participation in the Olympic Games	76
Advancements Beyond College Sports	77
Role of Leading Women Athletes	78
Advocacy Groups	80
A Milestone for Women's Sports	80
Title IX: A Pivotal Step toward Gender Equity in Sports	81
Challenges and Inclusion of Transgender Athletes	94
Non-Binary Athletes	99
Equal Protection Clause and Women Sports	99
Summary	103
Discussion Questions	104

> Inherent differences between men and women, we have come to appreciate, remain cause for celebration, but not for denigration of the members of either sex or for artificial constraints on an individual's opportunity.
> —Justice Ruth Bader Ginsburg (from the Supreme Court decision in *United States v. Virginia*, 518 U.S. 515 (1996))

The History of Women's Participation in Sports

In the early days of organized sports, women faced formidable barriers to participation. Societal norms and beliefs about women's physical capabilities often excluded them from competitive sports. Physical education for women was limited and focused more on activities deemed appropriate for their perceived delicate constitutions, such as calisthenics, dance, and light exercise. This exclusion was rooted in deeply ingrained gender roles and the belief that strenuous physical activity was unsuitable and potentially harmful to women.

Women's participation in sports has a resilient history, marked by noteworthy milestones and persistent challenges. The first modern Olympics in 1896 did not include any events for women. It wasn't until the 1900 Paris Olympics that women were allowed to compete, and even then, they could only participate in five sports: tennis, golf, sailing, croquet, and equestrianism. The number of female athletes was small, with only 22 women out of 997 total participants.

Over the years, the inclusion of women in the Olympics gradually expanded. By 1912, women were competing in swimming and diving. The 1928 Amsterdam Olympics marked a jump with the introduction of women's athletics in track and field, including events like the 100-meter dash and high jump. Despite these advancements, women still faced considerable resistance. Pierre de Coubertin, the founder of the International Olympic Committee (IOC), famously opposed women's participation, believing their role should be limited to crowning male victors.

While controversies and resistance to gender equality in sports persisted, one notable protest against gender discrimination was the establishment of the Women's World Games by Alice Milliat. Frustrated by the IOC's refusal to include more women's events in the Olympics, Milliat organized the Women's World Games, held from 1922 to 1934. These games provided a platform for women to demonstrate their athletic abilities and challenged the male-dominated sports establishment. The success and visibility of the Women's World Games eventually pressured the IOC to expand the number of women's events and participants in the Olympics, marking a major victory in the fight for gender equality in sports.

Despite these barriers, several pioneering women athletes emerged, challenging societal norms and paving the way for future generations. Babe Didrikson Zaharias stands out as one of the most versatile and talented athletes of any generation. Excelling in multiple sports, including track and field, golf, and basketball, Zaharias broke barriers and set numerous records. In the 1932 Olympics, she won two gold medals and one silver in track and field events. Her prowess in golf later earned her ten LPGA major championships, demonstrating her exceptional versatility and challenging the stereotype that women could not compete at the highest levels across multiple sports.

Wilma Rudolph, another trailblazing athlete, overcame numerous obstacles to achieve greatness. Stricken with polio as a child, Rudolph defied the odds to become a three-time Olympic gold medalist in track and field during the 1960 Rome Olympics. Her achievements not only showcased her incredible talent but also served as a powerful symbol of perseverance and the potential of women in competitive sports. Rudolph's success inspired countless young women to pursue their athletic dreams, breaking down racial and gender barriers and like Zaharias helped set the stage for expanding athletic opportunities for future generations.

The enactment of Title IX of the Education Amendments of 1972 marked a pivotal moment in the struggle for gender equity in sports. This landmark civil rights law prohibited sex or gender discrimination in any educational institution receiving federal funding, leading to a dramatic increase in the participation of women in sports. Prior to Title IX, opportunities for women in collegiate athletics were severely limited, with minimal funding and little administrative support. The law's implementation mandated equal treatment and resources for male and female athletes, subject to controversial administrative law and judicial exceptions, seeking to come closer to leveling the playing field.

The Impact of Title IX on Women's Participation in College Sports

The impact of Title IX has been profound, remarkably increasing the participation of women in collegiate sports. Before Title IX, women's opportunities in college sports were extremely limited. In the 1971–2 academic year, only 29,972 women participated in college athletics. By the 2007–8 academic year, this number had surged to 166,728, representing a 456 percent increase. Today, women make up nearly 50 percent of all student-athletes in NCAA Division I sports. This transformation has not only increased the number of female athletes but also improved the quality of women's sports programs, leading to better facilities, coaching, and competitive opportunities. Title IX has also had an immense impact on high school sports, where female participation increased from 294,015 in 1971–2 to over 3 million today according to the Women's Sports Foundation. It is fascinating to note that around 60 percent of all high school girls participate in some sport, whereas 75 percent of all boys join a high school sports team. Nevertheless, the participation growth for girls at the high school level has created a pipeline of talent that feeds into college sports, further enhancing the competitive playing field for women. Even with these gains, challenges remain. Women still hold only 25 percent of all NCAA head coaching and athletic director positions, and the spending on men's sports programs continues to outpace that of women's programs, particularly in Division I. These disparities highlight the ongoing need for policy improvements and better compliance structures to ensure equitable treatment and opportunities for female athletes, coaches, and administrators.

Women's Participation in the Olympic Games

The transformation in women's sports is also evident in the Olympic Games, where the number of female athletes has continued to rise. Over the years, the inclusion of women in the Olympics has steadily increased from a mere 2.2 percent of participants at the Paris Olympics in 1900 to the 1996 Atlanta Olympics, where women made up 34 percent of the total athletes, and this number rose to 50 percent at the Paris 2024 Olympics. The Paris Olympic Summer Games also introduced new opportunities for women, including twenty mixed-gender events and less traditional sports such as breaking (breakdancing), skateboarding, sport climbing, surfing, and 3x3 basketball. Baseball/softball, cricket, flag football, lacrosse, and squash are five new sports for the Los Angeles Summer Olympic Games. The IOC has played a crucial, if not late, role in promoting gender equality, implementing policies to increase female participation and visibility. For example, for the first time, the IOC allowed male and female athletes to jointly carry their nation's flag during the Opening Ceremony in the Tokyo 2020 Olympics, increasing the appearance of female athletes before television viewers and sponsors. In addition to introducing new mixed-gender events in sports like triathlon, swimming, and track and field, the IOC has sought to balance the competition schedule to ensure fairer coverage of women's sports on prime-time media.

Advancements Beyond College Sports

The cultural acceptance of women in sports has changed considerably, leading to advancements beyond college athletics. In professional sports, women have made substantial gains in tennis, golf, track and field, skiing, swimming, mixed martial arts, and soccer. The Women's Tennis Association (WTA), founded in 1973, has been instrumental in advocating for equal prize money, with Wimbledon and the French Open offering equal prize money to male and female champions since 2007. Similarly, the Ladies Professional Golf Association (LPGA), established in 1950, has provided a platform for women golfers to compete at the highest level. In 2013, twenty years after the beginning of the UFC (Ultimate Fighting Championship), women were permitted to compete in the octagon and receive promotional fees. Professional women's sports leagues have also seen significant growth. The Women's National Basketball Association (WNBA), founded in 1996, and the National Women's Soccer League

(NWSL), established in 2013, are prominent examples of successful women's professional leagues. These leagues have provided a platform for female athletes to showcase their talents and have garnered substantial fan support.

Role of Leading Women Athletes

Leading women athletes and advocates have played a crucial role in advancing gender equity in sports. Billie Jean King, a tennis legend, has been a tireless advocate for women's rights in sports. She founded the Women's Sports Foundation in 1974 to promote and protect the sports side of Title IX and has been instrumental in fighting for equal prize money in tennis. King's efforts culminated in the US Open becoming the first major tournament to offer equal prize money to both sexes. Her advocacy extended beyond tennis, influencing broader societal attitudes toward women's sports. Nancy Lieberman, known as "Lady Magic," has also made enormous contributions to women's basketball. As a player, coach, and broadcaster, Lieberman has been a trailblazer in the sport. She was the first woman to play in a men's professional basketball league and later became the first female head coach in the NBA's Development League. Lieberman has also served as president of the Women's Sports Foundation, furthering her impact on gender equity in sports. Martina Navratilova, one of the greatest tennis players of all time, has been a vocal advocate for fair competition and equal rights for female athletes. She has been involved in the Women's Sports Policy Working Group and has spoken out on issues related to transgender athletes in women's sports. Navratilova's advocacy has helped raise awareness about the importance of maintaining fair competition while respecting the rights of all athletes. Marta Vieira da Silva, widely known as Marta, is one of the world's most celebrated soccer players, recognized for being the top scorer in Women's World Cup history and winning FIFA World Player of the Year for five consecutive years. Her contributions to women's soccer have made her a global icon and an inspiration, particularly for aspiring Hispanic female athletes.

While there are many examples of successful women professional athletes, Janet Guthrie's achievements in 1977 are particularly noteworthy.

Guthrie made history as the first woman to qualify and compete in the Indianapolis 500, breaking gender barriers in the male-dominated world of motorsports. In a sidebar, your author trained Guthrie for the ABC network special known as the "Superstars" featuring ten top athletes from ten different sports competing in events that were not their own.

Guthrie's pioneering success paved the way for future female drivers like Danica Patrick. Patrick stands out as the only woman to win an IndyCar Series race, securing victory at the 2008 Indy Japan 300. Transitioning to NASCAR, Patrick continued to hurdle obstacles by becoming the first woman to win a NASCAR Sprint Cup Series pole position at the Daytona 500. Over her seven-year NASCAR career, Patrick's annual earnings from salary and endorsements peaked at over $10 million. Patrick's net worth is estimated to be around $80 million, reflecting her marketing and sponsorship success on and off the track.

Another groundbreaking athlete is Serena Williams, whose career has had a remarkable impact on both gender and racial equality in sports. Serena Williams is widely regarded as one of the greatest tennis players of all time, having won twenty-three Grand Slam singles titles, the most by any player in the Open Era. Her dominance on the court has not only set new records but also paved the way for greater visibility and participation of women, particularly women of color, in tennis.

Williams has faced and overcome substantial challenges throughout her career, including issues related to racial and gender discrimination and body shaming. Her tenacity, inner strength and achievements have made her an inspirational figure worldwide. Financially, Serena Williams has also broken new ground. Her career prize money exceeds $94 million, making her the highest-earning female tennis player in history. Beyond her earnings from tennis, Williams has garnered substantial income through endorsements and business ventures, including partnerships with Nike, Gatorade, and Wilson, among others. Her estimated net worth is approximately $225 million.

These pioneering women—Janet Guthrie, Danica Patrick, and Serena Williams and many others—demonstrate the profound impact that female athletes can have in their respective sports. They have not only broken barriers but also inspired future generations to pursue their athletic dreams, contributing to a more inclusive and equitable sporting world.

Advocacy Groups

Several advocacy groups have been instrumental in nurturing gender equity in sports. The Women's Sports Foundation, founded by Billie Jean King, has been at the forefront of this movement. The foundation works to ensure that all girls and women have equitable access to physical activity and sports, advocating for policy changes and providing resources to support female athletes.

Champion Women, founded by Nancy Hogshead-Makar, another prominent advocate and former Olympic swimmer, focuses on promoting, protecting, and supporting girls and women in sports. The organization addresses issues such as sexual harassment, discrimination, and the enforcement of Title IX, working to create a fair and inclusive environment for female athletes.

The Institute for Diversity and Ethics in Sport (TIDES) is another vital advocacy group that seeks to counter negative stereotypes that may discourage girls and women of color from pursuing sports. In particular, they conduct research, provide educational resources, and offer consulting services to organizations on creating more inclusive sports environments.

A Milestone for Women's Sports

For the first time in history, a stadium built exclusively for a women's professional sports team opened in Kansas City, Missouri. Named CPKC Stadium, this groundbreaking facility is the new home of the Kansas City Current, an expansion soccer team in the NWSL. The stadium, which opened its doors in 2024, boasts a seating capacity of 11,500 with design features that allow for future expansion to accommodate up to 20,000 spectators. The team itself is co-owned by two women. The creation of this stadium is a testament to the explosive growth and investment in women's soccer, while providing the team and league with greater autonomy over scheduling and revenue streams.

Notwithstanding these advancements, disparities in compensation, media coverage, professional teams, and sponsorships persist. Women athletes often receive less prize money and sponsorship compared to their male counterparts. However, the increasing popularity of women's sports and the growing recognition of their commercial potential are driving positive changes. This year women's elite sports are projected to generate over $1 billion in revenue, a substantial increase from previous years. The history of women's participation in sports is a testament to the resilience and determination of female athletes who have overcome numerous obstacles to achieve recognition and equality. From the early days of limited Olympic participation to the transformative impact of Title IX and the ongoing growth of professional women's sports, the journey toward gender equity in sports continues. While challenges remain, the progress made thus far provides a strong foundation for future advancements, ensuring that women athletes receive the opportunities and support they deserve.

Title IX: A Pivotal Step toward Gender Equity in Sports

The fight for gender equity in sports took a monumental leap forward with the passage of Title IX. This landmark legislation, signed into law by President Richard Nixon on June 23, 1972, prohibited sex-based discrimination in any federally funded education program or activity. While Title IX's reach extends far beyond athletics, its impact on creating a more level playing field for female athletes has been nothing short of transformative.

The journey toward Title IX began long before its official enactment. Pioneering women like Alice Paul, who tirelessly advocated for the 19th Amendment granting women the right to vote, and Bernice Sandler, often called the "Godmother of Title IX," dedicated their careers to dismantling gender discrimination in education. Throughout the twentieth century, female athletes faced significant obstacles. For example, in 1972, women received only 2 percent of college athletic budgets, while scholarships for female athletes were virtually nonexistent. Girls and women had far fewer opportunities to participate in organized sports compared to boys and men. Many schools offered only a handful of women's sports, with limited resources and coaching support. Female athletes often had to practice and compete in outdated or inadequate facilities or odd practice times compared to their male counterparts. Women's sports received minimal media attention, discouraging participation and sponsorship opportunities.

The push for Title IX was part of a broader civil rights movement that sought to address systemic inequalities faced by women across various sectors of society. Title IX emerged from a broader wave of civil rights legislation enacted during the 1960s and 1970s. It was originally part of the Education Amendments of 1972, and its passage owed much to the efforts of key figures like Representative Patsy Mink, the first woman of color elected to the US House of Representatives, who championed Title IX as a critical step toward educational equity for women, and Senator Birch Bayh, a leading advocate for gender equality, who played a crucial role in garnering bipartisan support for Title IX's passage.

The core principle of Title IX is enshrined in Section 901:

> No person in the United States shall, on the basis of sex, be excluded from participation in, be denied the benefits of, or be subjected to discrimination under any education program or activity receiving Federal financial assistance.

This simple yet powerful statement requires schools receiving federal funding to provide equal opportunities for both men and women in all aspects of their athletics programs, including:

- **Scholarships**: Schools must offer athletic scholarships to women in proportion to their participation in athletics. In 1972, there were only 156 athletic scholarships available to women nationwide. Today that number has grown to over 180,000.
- **Facilities and Equipment**: Schools must provide facilities and equipment for female sports that are comparable to those provided for men's sports. Prior to Title IX, many female athletes had to change in cramped locker rooms or makeshift spaces or travel in personal vehicles to attend games, while male teams had access to well-equipped facilities and traveled at schools' expense on buses or planes.
- **Coaching and Staffing**: Opportunities for coaching and other athletic staff positions must be made available to qualified women. Title IX eventually led to an increase in the number of paid full-time

female coaches in women's sports, creating role models and mentors for the next generation.
- **Participation Opportunities**: Schools must provide women with opportunities to participate in a variety of sports, ensuring these opportunities are proportional to the number of women interested in competing or reflective of their percentage within the undergraduate student body. The ratio of male to female athletes should closely align with their respective enrollments at the institution. Title IX led to the expansion of women's sports offered at the high school and college levels, including sports like softball, volleyball, field hockey, lacrosse, and rowing.

The scope and enforcement of Title IX faced significant challenges, notably with the 1984 Supreme Court decision in *Grove City College v. Bell*. The Court ruled that Title IX applied only to those specific programs within an institution that directly received federal funds, rather than the institution as a whole. This decision significantly limited the application of Title IX, reducing its impact on ensuring gender equity across entire educational institutions.

In response, Congress passed the *Civil Rights Restoration Act* of 1987, which reversed the Grove City decision by stipulating that if any part of an institution receives federal funding, then all programs within that institution must comply with Title IX. This legislative fix reaffirmed the broad scope of Title IX, ensuring that the law could be effectively used to combat gender discrimination across all educational programs and activities.

The Department of Education, through its Office for Civil Rights (OCR), plays a crucial role in enforcing Title IX. The OCR is responsible for ensuring that educational institutions comply with Title IX by investigating complaints of discrimination, providing guidance on the implementation of the law, and enforcing compliance when violations occur.

The OCR's 3-Prong Test for Compliance

To ensure compliance with Title IX, schools must pass the OCR's 3-prong test, which evaluates whether an institution effectively accommodates the interests and abilities of both male and female students.

Prong 1: Proportionality

This prong focuses on the ratio of athletic participation opportunities for women compared to men relative to the overall student enrollment. The goal is to ensure a proportional representation of female athletes to their enrollment.

Landmark Case: *Cohen v. Brown University* (1992) In this case, Brown University cut women's gymnastics and volleyball from varsity status. The court ruled this violated Title IX because the remaining women's sports opportunities were not proportionate to the female student body compared to men's sports participation. This case established the "substantial proportionality test," emphasizing that universities must demonstrate a proportional number of female athletes to their enrollment, considering factors like scholarship distribution and the range of sports offered for each gender.

Prong 2: Expansion

This prong assesses a school's history and ongoing efforts to expand athletic opportunities for women. It acknowledges that pre-Title IX realities may necessitate an ongoing effort to achieve proportionality.

Landmark Case: *Mercer v. Duke University* (1997) This case introduced the concept of the "safe harbor rule." Mercer, a female kicker, was allowed to try out for the football team but faced discrimination and was cut from the team. The court ruled that once a woman is allowed to try out for a men's team, she cannot be treated differently based on her gender. Schools can demonstrate Title IX compliance by showing a documented history of expanding their women's sports programs in response to increased female interest. Universities present evidence of adding new women's sports, increasing coaching staff for female athletes, and actively promoting sports participation opportunities for girls.

Prong 3: Accommodation of Interests and Abilities

This prong focuses on a school's efforts to meet the interests and abilities of female students in athletics, even if full proportionality isn't immediately achieved.

Case Example: The OCR considers factors like student surveys gauging interest in specific sports for women, offering introductory clinics and intramural opportunities, and providing adequate facilities and equipment for emerging female sports programs. Schools can demonstrate proactive measures to identify and nurture female athletic interests, even in sports with lower participation initially.

Schools must consider several factors to ensure compliance with Title IX, including:

- **Athletic Scholarships**: Providing equitable athletic financial assistance to male and female athletes.
- **Accommodation of Interests and Abilities**: Offering a range of sports that meet the interests and abilities of both male and female students.
- **Equipment and Supplies**: Ensuring that both male and female sports teams have access to comparable quality and quantity of equipment and supplies.
- **Scheduling of Games and Practice Times**: Providing equal opportunities for male and female teams to practice and compete.
- **Travel and Per Diem Allowances**: Equitably distributing travel and per diem allowances for male and female teams.
- **Coaching and Tutoring**: Ensuring equitable quality and availability of coaching staff and academic tutoring for male and female teams.
- **Locker Rooms, Practice, and Competitive Facilities**: Providing comparable facilities for male and female teams.
- **Medical and Training Facilities and Services**: Ensuring equal access to medical and training facilities and services for all athletes.
- **Publicity**: Offering equal opportunities for promotion and media coverage for male and female sports.

Court rulings in different federal courts of appeals circuits can lead to slightly different interpretations of Title IX's three-prong test. As a result, a school might be compliant in one region but not in another. For instance, the First Circuit Court of Appeals, which covers the New England states, decided in *Cohen v. Brown University* that educational institutions cannot justify non-compliance with Title IX based on the revenue-generating potential of certain sports like football. While this decision theoretically applies to schools only within this circuit, it has influenced practices nationwide, though not without pushback and controversy.

As stated earlier, Title IX requires that educational institutions receiving federal funding provide equal opportunities for men and women in athletics. Despite the enormous revenue generated by football programs like the University of Alabama generating well in excess of $130 million a year, Title IX compliance does not permit institutions to justify unequal treatment based on the financial success of a particular sport. The law mandates that resources and opportunities be distributed fairly across all sports, ensuring that female athletes receive the same level of support and investment as their male counterparts, proportional to their respective campus-wide undergraduate population. Striking a balance between proportionality and preserving these programs remains a complex issue, particularly for Power 4 conference schools with enormous football rosters compared to any other male or female sport. To achieve proportional equity, many schools have resorted to cutting men's sports programs, such as wrestling, swimming, and gymnastics, rather than adding women's sports opportunities—a practice known as "addition by subtraction."

In terms of compliance, some schools have faced challenges from women students who have filed Title IX complaints against their schools. For instance, the University of California, Berkeley, faced scrutiny and was required to increase opportunities for female athletes by adding golf, water polo, lacrosse, and later beach volleyball to comply with Title IX. Similarly, Quinnipiac University was found non-compliant for attempting to classify competitive cheerleading as a varsity sport to appear in compliance with Title IX requirements when cheerleading was not recognized by the NCAA as a competitive sport. The University of South Florida added women's lacrosse and beach volleyball to its athletics program to meet Title IX requirements. Clemson University added women's lacrosse and gymnastics to bolster their compliance efforts. The University of Maryland added women's beach volleyball to its roster, reflecting a growing trend among universities to provide more athletic opportunities for female students. These efforts illustrate how institutions can work toward gender equity in athletics by expanding opportunities for female athletes rather than reducing men's programs.

Schools can achieve Title IX compliance by meeting any one of the three prongs, depending on the judicial jurisdiction of the educational institution. For example, schools within the jurisdiction of the 1st Circuit Court of Appeals must adhere to the proportionality standard due to the precedent set by the *Cohen v. Brown* decision. In contrast, many Power 4 colleges and universities located in the South with large football and basketball programs may choose the easiest path to Title IX compliance, often opting to conduct surveys to gauge student interest in adding new sports for women athletes. Furthermore, under the *Equity in Athletics Disclosure Act* (EADA), schools are required to publicly submit detailed reports on revenue and expenses for all sports, including coaches' salaries, recruiting costs, and administrative expenses, making this information available for public scrutiny.

Title IX not only requires schools to comply with factors related to recruiting, financial aid, scheduling, and other areas, but it also includes protection against sexual harassment, sexual abuse, and hostile work environments as interpreted by the Department of Education and their administrative regulations, along with the Office for Civil Rights (OCR). The law's scope ensures a broader protection framework encompassing the safety and equitable treatment of all students.

OCR Definitions

- **Sexual Harassment:** Conduct on the basis of sex that satisfies one or more of the following:
  1. Quid pro quo harassment, where an employee conditions the provision of aid, benefit, or service on an individual's participation in unwelcome sexual conduct.
  2. Unwelcome conduct that a reasonable person would find so severe, pervasive, and objectively offensive that it effectively denies a person equal access to the education program or activity.
  3. Sexual assault, as defined by the Clery Act regulations, including dating violence, domestic violence, or stalking as defined in the Violence Against Women Act (VAWA).

- **Sexual Assault:** An offense that meets the definition of rape, fondling, incest, or statutory rape as used in the FBI's Uniform Crime Reporting system.
- **Hostile Work Environment:** Unwelcome conduct based on sex that is so severe, pervasive, and objectively offensive that it effectively denies a person equal access to the education program or activity.

Key Cases

In the matter of *Simpson v. University of Colorado Boulder*, two female students sued the University of Colorado, alleging the university's failure to properly supervise football recruits and players led to their sexual assault during a recruiting party. The court ruled that the university could be held liable under Title IX if it showed deliberate indifference to sexual harassment or assault risks. The university settled the case by agreeing to pay the harmed women and implement measures to improve campus safety. This case led to increased scrutiny of university athletic programs across the country and their compliance with Title IX, prompting stricter recruitment policies and better support systems for assault survivors.

A few years after the *Colorado* decision, an investigation by the OCR and the Department of Justice into the University of Montana's handling of sexual harassment and assault complaints found the university's policies and responses to be inadequate. As a result, the University of Montana entered into a Resolution Agreement, committing to revise its policies and procedures, provide mandatory training on Title IX obligations, and implement measures to monitor the effectiveness of its revised policies. This case became a model for other institutions, emphasizing the need for comprehensive and effective policies to address sexual harassment and assault.

One of the leading early sexual harassment cases that is still good law occurred in *Davis v. Monroe County Board of Education*. LaShonda Davis, a fifth-grade student, experienced severe sexual harassment from a male classmate, G.F. Despite multiple reports to teachers and administrators, the school took no meaningful action. The Supreme Court addressed whether a school can be held liable under Title IX for student-on-student harassment if it shows deliberate indifference to known acts of harassment, and the harassment is so severe, pervasive, and objectively offensive that it deprives victims of access to educational opportunities. The Court held that a school board can be liable under Title IX for student-on-student harassment under these conditions, finding deliberate indifference by the school, with the harassment being severe, pervasive, and objectively offensive, effectively denying LaShonda equal access to her education. This decision established that schools must address student-on-student harassment under Title IX, leading to more stringent anti-harassment policies and grievance procedures.

The primary significance of the *Davis* decision is that it provided a clear definition of a hostile environment under Title IX, emphasizing the need to consider both the subjective impact on the complainant and the objective severity of the conduct. Schools are required to designate a Title IX Coordinator to oversee compliance and handle complaints, ensuring that policies and procedures are accessible and widely disseminated to students, staff, and faculty. These updates aim to balance the rights of complainants and respondents, maintaining protections against sex-based discrimination and harassment.

In another monumental Title IX Supreme Court case that began with an intriguing fact pattern, Roderick Jackson, a male teacher and the girls' basketball coach at Ensley High School in Birmingham, Alabama, noticed significant disparities between the resources provided to the boys' and girls' basketball teams. (See: *Jackson v. Birmingham Board of Education* (2005))

The girls' team had inferior practice facilities, such as a court with a broken hoop, limited access to quality equipment, fewer opportunities for travel and competition (relying on parents for transportation while the boys' team had a school-provided bus), and inadequate funding and support from the school's athletic department.

The central legal issue was whether Jackson had a valid claim under Title IX after being fired for complaining about the unequal resources for the girls' basketball team. Specifically, the question was whether Title IX's protection against sex discrimination included retaliation against someone who reports such discrimination.

Although Jackson himself was not directly discriminated against based on his sex, he argued that his firing was retaliation for reporting sex discrimination against the girls' basketball team. In a 5–4 decision, the Supreme Court ruled in favor of Jackson. The Court reasoned that retaliation for reporting sex discrimination is itself a form of "discrimination based on sex." By retaliating against Jackson, the school board was essentially discriminating against him due to his association with the female athletes and his advocacy for their equal treatment. The Court found that Title IX's broad language prohibiting discrimination "on the basis of sex" encompasses retaliation for reporting such discrimination. They emphasized the importance of protecting individuals who advocate for gender equality, noting that effective enforcement of Title IX relies on the ability of individuals to report discrimination without fear of retaliation.

Furthermore, the administrative regulations under Title IX stipulate that schools must take immediate and appropriate action to investigate and resolve complaints of sexual harassment and violence. Specifically, the Department of Education's Office for Civil Rights (OCR) mandates that educational institutions adopt and publish grievance procedures that provide for prompt and equitable resolution of student and employee complaints alleging any action prohibited by Title IX, including sexual harassment and assault (34 C.F.R. § 106.8(b)).

Title IX Hearing Process

The US Department of Education has recently updated Title IX regulations that took effect on August 1, 2024. These politically charged changes are significant and cover various aspects such as the rights of victims and the accused, the hearing process, and the standard of proof. Below are the key updates:

Rights of Victims and the Accused:

Victims:
- **Broadened Definition of Harassment:** The new regulations define sex-based harassment to include harassment based on sex stereotypes, sex characteristics, parental, family, or marital status, pregnancy, lactation, sexual orientation, and gender identity.
- **Prompt and Effective Response:** Schools are required to respond promptly and effectively to complaints of sex discrimination, taking steps to prevent recurrence and remedy its effects.
- **Supportive Measures:** Schools must offer and coordinate supportive measures for complainants, ensuring their safety and well-being throughout the process.

Accused:
- **Equitable Treatment:** The regulations mandate that both complainants and respondents be treated equitably, with a fair and transparent process.
- **Presumption of Non-Responsibility:** The accused are presumed not responsible until a determination is made at the conclusion of the grievance process.

Hearing Process:
- **Single-Investigator Model:** Schools now have the option to adopt a single-investigator model, where the Title IX coordinator or investigator can also serve as the decision-maker.
- **Live Hearings:** The requirement for live hearings and cross-examinations has been removed. Schools can now decide whether to include these elements based on their specific needs and contexts.

Standard of Proof:
- **Preponderance of the Evidence:** The default standard of proof for adjudicating cases of sex-based harassment is now the preponderance of the evidence, which means that it is more likely than not that the harassment occurred. This is a lower standard compared to the "clear and convincing evidence" standard, which some institutions may still use if applied consistently across all comparable proceedings.

Additional Provisions:
- **Off-Campus Conduct:** The regulations cover conduct that occurs off-campus, including online behavior, as long as the institution has disciplinary authority over the respondent's conduct in the context in which it occurred.
- **Retaliation Protections:** The regulations provide clear protections against retaliation for individuals who report sex discrimination or participate in the Title IX process.

Legal and Political Challenges:
1. **Due Process Concerns:** Several states and advocacy groups have filed lawsuits against the new regulations, arguing that they discard essential due process protections. The Alabama-led lawsuit specifically criticizes the single-investigator model and the removal of mandatory live hearings. The American Civil Liberties Union (ACLU) has also expressed concerns about the single-investigator model, although it supports other aspects of the regulations.
2. **Free Speech Issues:** The new definition of harassment as "unwelcome sex-based conduct" that is "subjectively and objectively offensive" has raised free speech concerns. Critics argue

that this could lead to censorship of speech, including opinions on controversial topics or refusal to use preferred pronouns.
3. **LGBTQ+ Protections:** The regulations expand protections to include discrimination based on sexual orientation and gender identity. This has led to legal challenges from states arguing that such protections are not within the original scope of Title IX. A federal judge in Kansas has blocked the enforcement of these protections in several states, adding to the legal complexity.

Support and Opposition:
- **Supporters:** Advocates for the new regulations argue that they provide necessary protections for victims of sexual harassment and assault, making it easier for them to report incidents and receive support. The regulations are seen as a step forward in protecting LGBTQ+ students and ensuring a safe and inclusive educational environment.
- **Opponents:** Critics, including some conservative groups and state governments, argue that the regulations undermine due process rights and impose unconstitutional speech restrictions. There is also concern that the changes could lead to inconsistent application of Title IX protections across different states and institutions.

The 2024 Title IX regulations have introduced significant changes to the hearing process for sexual misconduct cases, leading to a polarized debate. While the regulations aim to enhance protections for victims and expand coverage to LGBTQ+ students, they face substantial legal challenges and criticism over due process and free speech concerns. The outcome of ongoing lawsuits and potential further modifications depending on which political party is in power will shape the future implementation and impact of these regulations.

Real-life examples illustrate these controversies even before these new administrative law interpretations of Title IX. The case of Keith Mumphery, a former Michigan State University (MSU) student and football player, is a relevant example of Title IX controversies that have garnered national attention. Mumphery was accused of sexual assault by another student, leading to multiple investigations. Initially, the police investigated the allegations, but due to the accuser's lack of cooperation, no criminal charges were filed. MSU's Title IX office conducted its own investigation and cleared Mumphery of the charges. However, after the accuser appealed the decision,

MSU reopened the case without informing Mumphery. This time, the university found him responsible for relationship violence and sexual misconduct, resulting in his expulsion and barring him from campus.

Mumphery challenged the expulsion, arguing that the investigation violated his due process rights. Key concerns included the lack of proper notification, as Mumphery was not informed about the appeal and subsequent reinvestigation. Additionally, he was not given a fair chance to present his case or question his accuser, and the investigation was criticized for being biased and not adhering to fair procedures.

The case drew media attention, highlighting broader issues with Title IX procedures. It underscored concerns about the fairness and impartiality of university-led investigations, sparked debates about the potential for bias against accused students, and emphasized the need for due process protections. The controversy also highlighted the challenge of balancing the protection of sexual assault victims with ensuring the rights of the accused.

Ultimately, the case was settled, with MSU agreeing to pay Mumphery $725,000 to drop his lawsuit and $475,000 to the accuser to settle her claims. As part of the settlement, Mumphery's record was cleared, potentially allowing him to resume his professional football career.

Another controversial Title IX case involving Emma Sulkowicz and Paul Nungesser at Columbia University illustrates the complexities surrounding Title IX investigations on college campuses. Emma Sulkowicz accused fellow student Paul Nungesser of raping her in her dorm room. Despite multiple complaints, Columbia University found Nungesser not responsible for the allegations. In response, Sulkowicz protested the university's handling of her complaint by carrying a mattress around campus as part of her senior thesis, titled Mattress Performance (Carry That Weight) until her graduation.

The legal issues in this case centered on due process and sex bias. Nungesser argued that the university's actions constituted gender-based harassment and violated his rights under Title IX. He claimed that Columbia's support of Sulkowicz's project and the ensuing harassment he faced were discriminatory based on his gender. Nungesser filed a Title IX lawsuit against Columbia University, its president, and Sulkowicz's thesis advisor, alleging that the university facilitated a hostile environment by allowing Sulkowicz's project to proceed.

The case was initially dismissed but later refiled. Eventually, Columbia University and Nungesser reached a confidential settlement. The university acknowledged the difficulties Nungesser faced and pledged to review and update its gender-based misconduct policies. Despite the ongoing controversy and his subsequent lawsuit against the institution, Paul Nungesser graduated from Columbia University. The settlement with Columbia marked the conclusion of the legal battle, with the university agreeing to undisclosed terms and committing to policy reforms.

The controversy surrounding schools handling complaints of sexual harassment and assault primarily stems from concerns about the adequacy of traditional due process protections within the academic setting. Critics argue that universities and colleges, when dealing with such sensitive and serious allegations, often lack the necessary experience and framework to ensure fairness and justice for all parties involved. Unlike the criminal justice system, school-based investigations and disciplinary proceedings may not uphold the right to presumption of innocence, the right to legal counsel, the opportunity to cross-examine witnesses including the victim, and the thorough examination of exculpatory evidence.

Furthermore, the informal nature of campus tribunals can result in procedural flaws and biases, undermining the accused's ability to mount an effective defense. This has led to calls for these matters to be addressed primarily by external criminal justice departments, which are equipped with the expertise and legal mechanisms to handle such cases impartially.

There is nothing preventing law enforcement agencies from conducting their own investigations and bringing criminal charges against the accused. By involving law enforcement, allegations of sexual harassment and assault can be addressed with the gravity they deserve, ensuring both the protection of victims and the preservation of the accused's legal rights. This approach advocates for a dual-track system where educational institutions provide support and accommodations to survivors while deferring to the criminal justice system for investigation and adjudication, thereby safeguarding the principles of due process and fairness.

Challenges and Inclusion of Transgender Athletes

The inclusion of transgender athletes in sports, particularly post-puberty male-to-female (MtF) athletes, has become a highly contentious issue.

This debate centers around balancing fairness, competitive integrity, and the rights of transgender individuals to participate in sports consistent with their gender identity. High-profile cases such as Lia Thomas and Caster Semenya have brought significant attention to this issue.

The NCAA updated its transgender participation policy in 2022 to align with the Olympic Movement, adopting a sport-by-sport approach. This policy requires transgender athletes to follow the guidelines set by the national governing body (NGB) of their sport. If no NGB policy exists, the international federation's policy applies, and if neither exists, the International Olympic Committee (IOC) policy is used. Transgender athletes must document sport-specific testosterone levels before and during the competitive season.

Research indicates that while gender-affirming hormone therapy (GAHT) reduces some of the physiological advantages retained from male puberty, it may not entirely eliminate them. Studies have shown that transgender women retain some advantages in muscle mass, strength, and aerobic capacity even after a year of hormone therapy. This has led to calls for longer periods of hormone suppression before allowing transgender women to compete in women's sports.

Case Studies

Lia Thomas

Lia Thomas, a transgender swimmer from the University of Pennsylvania, made history as the first openly transgender woman to win an NCAA Division I championship. Her participation ignited a widespread and heated debate surrounding fairness, inclusion, and the evolving landscape of sports. Critics of Thomas's participation argue that she retained physiological advantages from male puberty, raising concerns about the level playing field in women's sports. On the other hand, supporters of Thomas emphasize the importance of allowing transgender athletes to compete in alignment with their gender identity, underscoring her right to compete as her true self.

Amid the controversy, it is important to note that Thomas fully adhered to the transgender policies in effect under the existing NCAA rules and regulations, which at the time allowed her to compete in women's events. However, the debate has not been limited to NCAA policies. Thomas has also taken legal action against World Aquatics (formerly FINA), challenging their policy that restricts transgender women from competing in women's events unless they transitioned before the age of twelve. This policy has sparked further debate over the inclusion of transgender athletes and the balance between fairness in competition and the rights of individuals to participate in sports according to their gender identity.

The case of Lia Thomas represents a complex intersection of sports, law, ethics, and human rights, highlighting the ongoing challenges in creating inclusive and equitable policies for transgender athletes in competitive sports.

Caster Semenya

Caster Semenya, a South African middle-distance runner, has been at the center of intense scrutiny and legal battles due to her naturally high testosterone levels, a result of Differences of Sex Development (DSD). Semenya's condition, while naturally occurring, has placed her in a controversial position within the world of athletics, where the regulation of testosterone levels has become a focal point in determining eligibility for women's competitions. Despite her undeniable talent and numerous victories, including Olympic and World Championship titles, Semenya has faced significant challenges and discrimination based on her biology.

In a significant legal victory, Semenya won her case in the European Court of Human Rights, which ruled that her rights had been violated by previous restrictions imposed on her participation. However, despite this victory, Semenya remains barred from competing in her preferred events, such as the 800 meters, unless she undergoes medical interventions to lower her testosterone levels. These interventions, which include hormone therapy or surgery, have sparked widespread debate over their ethical implications, the potential health risks to athletes, and the fairness of requiring such measures as a condition for competition.

Semenya's case highlights the broader and deeply contentious issue of using testosterone levels as a criterion for eligibility in women's sports. Critics argue that such policies are discriminatory and based on flawed science, failing to account for the natural variations in human biology. They also raise concerns about the potential physical and psychological harm caused by forcing athletes to alter their bodies in order to compete. On the other hand, proponents of testosterone regulation in women's sports contend that it is necessary to ensure a level playing field and maintain the integrity of female competitions.

The ongoing legal and medical challenges faced by Caster Semenya underscore the complexities of gender, biology, and fairness in sports. Her case, much like those of other athletes with DSD, continues to shape the global conversation around the rights of athletes, the role of medical interventions in sports, and the evolving definitions of gender and fairness in competitive athletics. Similarly, the controversy surrounding the two female boxers who competed in the Paris Olympic Games highlights the ongoing tension between traditional gender classifications and the realities of biological diversity. These boxers, whose birth certificates and passports indicated that they were girls but who apparently fall within the intersex category, had previously been banned from boxing competitions due to high testosterone levels by the now-defunct international federation governing boxing. Their participation in the Olympics was questioned by some yet supported by the International Olympic Committee (IOC), reflecting the broader debate about inclusivity versus competitive fairness. As the debate continues, the outcomes of such cases will likely have far-reaching implications for the future of women's sports and the inclusion of athletes with diverse biological characteristics.

Advocates for the inclusion of transgender athletes emphasize the importance of respecting the gender identity of all athletes and ensuring their right to participate in sports. They argue that excluding transgender women from women's sports is a violation of their human rights, including the right to equality, non discrimination, and participation in sports. These advocates highlight that transgender athletes are following the rules in place and should be allowed to compete based on their gender identity. They also stress the mental and physical health benefits of sports participation for transgender individuals.

Some scientific studies suggest that transgender women who undergo hormone therapy experience significant reductions in muscle mass, strength, and aerobic capacity, which could mitigate some of the advantages retained from male puberty. However, the extent of these changes and their impact on competitive fairness vary across different sports. For example, sports that rely heavily on strength and speed may see more pronounced differences than those that emphasize skill and technique. This has led to calls for sport-specific guidelines and ongoing research to better understand the impact of hormone therapy on athletic performance.

The inclusion of transgender athletes, particularly post-puberty male-to-female (MtF) athletes, in women's sports raises multiple Title IX concerns that remain unresolved. Title IX, as described extensively above, is a federal civil rights law passed as part of the Education Amendments of 1972, prohibiting sex-based discrimination in any school or education program that receives federal funding. While Title IX aims to ensure equal opportunities for all genders, its application to transgender athletes remains a contentious issue.

Denying post-puberty male-to-female athletes the right to compete in women's sports might be viewed as a violation of Title IX, as it could be interpreted as sex-based discrimination. Advocates argue that transgender women should have the right to participate in sports consistent with their gender identity, in line with Title IX's broader goal of promoting equality. However, opponents contend that this inclusion could compromise the competitive integrity of women's sports, given the potential physiological advantages retained from male puberty.

The use of locker rooms by transgender athletes has also become a significant issue under Title IX. For example, at the University of Pennsylvania, Lia Thomas's participation in the women's swim team raised concerns among some swimmers and their families about privacy and safety in locker rooms. Title IX requires schools to provide equal access to facilities for all students, but it also mandates that schools ensure a safe and non-discriminatory environment. This has led to heated debates about how best to accommodate the needs of transgender athletes while respecting the privacy and comfort of all students.

At the high school level, differences in strength and size between post-puberty transgender women and cisgender female athletes can impact the fairness and safety of the competitive playing field. For example, in Connecticut, the success of transgender sprinters in girls' track events has sparked controversy, with critics arguing that their participation creates an uneven playing field and jeopardizes the competitive opportunities for cisgender female athletes. Title IX requires that sports programs provide equal opportunities and safe environments for all participants, which complicates the inclusion of transgender athletes in certain contexts.

Organizations like Champion Women, a women's sports advocacy group, express concerns that the inclusion of post-puberty transgender women in women's sports could undermine opportunities for cisgender female athletes. They argue that allowing transgender women to compete may lead to a loss of scholarships and participation opportunities for biologically born women, from high school to college levels. These groups advocate for policies that ensure fair competition while protecting the integrity of women's sports and the opportunities for female athletes.

Non-Binary Athletes

The rise of non-binary athletes presents additional challenges to the traditional binary model of sports competition under Title IX legal analysis. Non-binary athletes, who do not identify strictly as male or female, often face difficulties in finding categories that align with their gender identity. This has led to the introduction of non-binary competition classifications in some sports, such as triathlon and marathon running, allowing more athletes to participate authentically.

The inclusion of transgender athletes in women's sports remains a complex and evolving issue. Balancing fairness, inclusion, and competitive integrity requires nuanced policies informed by scientific research and ethical considerations. As the debate continues, it is crucial to ensure that all athletes are treated with respect and dignity while maintaining the integrity of competitive sports. Advocates for transgender athletes, particularly those who have transitioned post-puberty, emphasize that they are following the rules in place and should be allowed to participate. They highlight the human rights concerns associated with excluding individuals based on their gender identity. The participation of transgender athletes in events like the Olympics will continue to shape the discourse around this issue, reflecting the broader societal debates about gender, fairness, and equality in sports.

Equal Protection Clause and Women Sports

The 14th Amendment's Equal Protection Clause, ratified in 1868, mandates that no state shall "deny to any person within its jurisdiction the equal protection of the laws." Originally intended to protect the rights of newly freed slaves, the broad wording of the clause has allowed it to be applied to various forms of discrimination, including gender discrimination. Over time, the Supreme Court has interpreted the Equal Protection Clause to prohibit not only racial discrimination but also discrimination based on gender, national origin, religion, alienage, and even immigration status, and legitimacy at birth. This broad interpretation has had significant implications for women's sports, ensuring that female athletes receive equal opportunities and treatment under the law.

Professional sports leagues and teams are often private entities. The 14th Amendment does not apply to purely private conduct. However, if there is significant government involvement, such as funding the sports arena where professional teams play, then the amendment could be invoked.

The Equal Protection Clause has been instrumental in helping women college and high school athletes achieve gender equity. By mandating that states provide equal protection under the law, the clause has been used to challenge and dismantle discriminatory practices in educational institutions, particularly in high school and college athletics. Notable cases highlight this impact. For example, in *Communities for Equity v. Michigan High School Athletic Association (2001)*, high school girls in Michigan argued that the MHSAA violated Title IX and the Equal Protection Clause by scheduling girls' sports in nontraditional and disadvantageous seasons, providing inferior facilities, and refusing to sanction additional sports for girls. The court ruled in favor of the plaintiffs, holding that MHSAA's practices discriminated against female athletes and violated both Title IX and the Equal Protection Clause, underscoring the importance of equitable treatment in high school athletics and setting a precedent for future gender equity suits.

Another landmark case is *United States v. Virginia (1996)*, where the Supreme Court addressed the constitutionality of the Virginia Military Institute's (VMI) male-only admissions policy. VMI, a state-supported military college, had a long-standing tradition of excluding women. The United States challenged this policy, arguing that it violated the Equal Protection Clause. The Supreme Court, applying heightened scrutiny, ruled that VMI's exclusion of women was unconstitutional. Justice Ruth Bader Ginsburg, writing for the majority, stated that any gender-based classification must serve an important governmental objective and must be substantially related to achieving that objective. The decision emphasized that equal protection under the law means providing genuinely equal opportunities, not merely separate but purportedly equal programs. The VMI decision significantly impacted women's participation and opportunities in college sports by strengthening the legal standards for challenging discriminatory practices in educational institutions.

In *O'Connor v. Board of Education of School District No. 23*, the court addressed the issue of gender-based classifications in school sports. The defendants' policy of providing separate teams for boys and girls was based on generalizations about the relative basketball skills of boys and girls. The court held that while gender-based classifications are not inherently suspect, they must still meet the heightened scrutiny standard, meaning they must serve an important governmental objective and be substantially related to achieving that objective.

The issue of transgender and non-binary athletes competing in sports intersects with the Equal Protection Clause, which has been interpreted to prohibit states from discriminating against individuals or groups without sufficient justification. Courts consider whether a law or policy discriminates based on a suspect classification. Gender identity, including transgender and non-binary status, can be argued as such a classification. Relevant cases in this context include *Grimm v. Gloucester County School Board (2020)*, where the Fourth Circuit Court of Appeals ruled that the school board's policy violated the Equal Protection Clause and Title IX by discriminating against a transgender student's right to use the bathroom corresponding to his gender identity. In *Hecox v. Little (2020)*, a federal district court in Idaho issued a preliminary injunction against Idaho's "Fairness in Women's Sports Act," which barred transgender women from participating in women's sports. The court found that the plaintiffs were likely to succeed on their Equal Protection Clause claim because the law discriminated against transgender individuals without adequate justification. Additionally, in *Bostock v. Clayton County (2020)*, a Title VII employment discrimination case, the Supreme Court decided that discrimination based on transgender status is sex discrimination, which could influence how courts interpret similar claims under the Equal Protection Clause.

The Equal Protection Clause applies different standards of scrutiny depending on the classification involved. *Strict Scrutiny* is applied to classifications based on race, national origin, or alienage and requires a compelling governmental interest and narrowly tailored means to achieve that interest. *Heightened Scrutiny* is applied to gender-based classifications and requires that the classification must serve an important governmental objective and must be substantially related to achieving that objective. *Rational Basis Review* is applied to other classifications, where the state only needs to show a legitimate interest, and the law or policy is rationally related to that interest. Notable cases involving these standards include *Brown v. Board of Education (1954)*, where the Supreme Court applied strict scrutiny to racial segregation in public schools, ruling that "separate but equal" facilities are inherently unequal, and *Sherbert v. Verner (1963)*, where the Court ruled that denying unemployment benefits to a person because their religion prohibited them from working on Saturdays violated the Free Exercise Clause of the First Amendment.

Significant equal protection cases involving religion include issues faced by Muslim women athletes who wear hijabs, leading to FIFA lifting its ban on hijabs in official competitions in 2011 after advocacy and pressure from various groups. Jewish athletes have also faced challenges when sporting events are scheduled on religious holidays such as the Sabbath. While there are no widely known Supreme Court cases specifically involving Jewish women and sports, broader legal discussions and cases concerning religious accommodations in education and public life generally uphold the principle that reasonable accommodations should be made for religious observance.

The issue of transgender and non-binary athletes in sports engages fundamental questions of equality and fairness under the Equal Protection Clause. Courts examining these issues will balance state interests in maintaining fair competition and safety against the constitutional mandate to prevent discrimination and ensure equal protection for all individuals, including those whose gender identity does not align with traditional binary classifications. The principles established in cases involving gender discrimination in women's sports provide a legal framework for addressing these complex and evolving issues. The different standards of scrutiny applied to various classifications ensure that the Equal Protection Clause continues to protect individuals from discrimination based on race, gender, and religion, promoting fairness and inclusivity in all aspects of public life, including sports.

Summary

The evolution of women's sports has been marked by numerous milestones and persistent challenges. Historically, women faced considerable barriers to participation in sports, including societal norms that deemed athletic pursuits inappropriate for females. However, over the decades, women have gradually broken through these barriers, achieving recognition and success in various sports. The growth of women's sports has been bolstered by landmark legislation, increased visibility, and the tireless efforts of female athletes advocating for equality.

Title IX of the Education Amendments of 1972 has played a pivotal role in promoting gender equity in sports. This federal law prohibits sex-based discrimination in any education program or activity receiving federal financial assistance. Title IX has been instrumental in increasing opportunities for female athletes at both the high school and college levels, leading to a dramatic rise in female sports participation. Compliance with Title IX requires institutions to provide equitable resources, facilities, and opportunities for female athletes, ensuring that sports programs are not skewed in favor of male athletes.

The Office for Civil Rights (OCR) is responsible for enforcing Title IX and ensuring that educational institutions comply with its requirements. The OCR investigates complaints of gender discrimination and provides guidelines to help institutions foster gender equity in sports. This includes addressing disparities in athletic scholarships, equipment, facilities, coaching, and competition opportunities.

Title IX also mandates that schools take steps to prevent and address sexual harassment, assault, and hostile work environments. Educational institutions must implement policies and procedures to protect students and athletes from these issues, ensuring a safe and supportive environment. This includes providing training, establishing clear reporting mechanisms, and taking prompt and effective action when incidents occur.

The processes used by schools to handle complaints of sexual harassment and assault have been the subject of significant controversy. Critics argue that university-led investigations often lack the traditional due process protections found in the criminal justice system, such as the presumption of innocence, the right to legal counsel, and the opportunity to cross-examine witnesses. This has led to calls for reforms to ensure that both accusers and the accused receive fair and impartial treatment.

The inclusion of transgender athletes, particularly post-puberty male-to-female (MtF) athletes, in women's sports has become a highly contentious issue raising both Title IX and Equal Protection under the law arguments. Advocates for transgender athletes emphasize their right to compete in accordance with their gender identity, highlighting human rights concerns. However, critics argue that physiological advantages retained from male puberty can compromise competitive fairness. The law's application to transgender athletes continues to evolve, with ongoing debates about how to balance inclusion with the integrity of women's sports while recognizing the need for more scientific studies.

The landscape of women's sports has undergone significant transformation, driven by legislative advancements, advocacy, and increasing societal acceptance. Title IX and the Equal Protection Clause have been cornerstones in promoting gender equity, ensuring that female athletes receive equal opportunities. However, challenges remain, including addressing sexual harassment and assault, ensuring fair hearing processes, and navigating the complexities of transgender athlete participation. As the field of sports law continues to unfold, it remains crucial to uphold the principles of fairness, inclusion, and respect for all athletes.

Discussion Questions

1. What were some of the major historical barriers that women faced in gaining access to sports, and how have these barriers been overcome over time?
2. How has Title IX transformed women's sports in the United States, and what are some of the most major changes it has brought about in terms of participation and resources?
3. What measures must educational institutions take to comply with Title IX, and what are the consequences of noncompliance?
4. How does the Office for Civil Rights enforce Title IX in educational institutions, and what is its impact on promoting gender equity in sports?

5. What are the key components of effective policies to prevent and address sexual harassment and assault in sports programs, and how can institutions ensure these policies are properly implemented?
6. What are the main criticisms of the hearing processes used in Title IX cases involving sexual harassment and assault, and what reforms have been proposed to address these concerns?
7. How does Title IX apply to transgender athletes, and what are the main arguments for and against the inclusion of post-puberty male-to-female athletes in women's sports?
8. How can institutions balance the goals of fairness, competitive integrity, and inclusion when developing policies for transgender athletes?
9. What challenges do women face in obtaining coaching and administrative positions in sports, and what strategies can be implemented to promote gender equity in these areas?
10. What are the emerging issues in gender equity in sports, and how can policymakers, institutions, and athletes work together to address these challenges and continue to advance the cause of gender equity?

4

Beyond Borders

Global Sports Governance and the Olympics and Paralympics

Chapter Outline

The International Olympic Committee	108
History of the Olympic Movement	108
The Olympic Charter	112
Key Olympic Rules and Regulations	117
The Mission and Structure of the USOPC	134
Broadcasting and Media in the Olympics	140
Paralympics	141
Summary	143
Discussion Questions	145

Global sports are powered by a dynamic network of organizations, each playing a crucial role in keeping competitions fair and exciting on the world stage. Leading the charge is the International Olympic Committee (IOC), which not only manages the Olympic Games but also works hand in hand with international federations like FIFA for soccer and World Aquatics for swimming to orchestrate world championships and other marquee events. On the national level, organizations like the United States Olympic & Paralympic Committee (USOPC) dedicate themselves to nurturing athletes, enforcing rules, and boosting sports at every level. These organizations are united in their mission to foster an environment where athletes' rights are respected and fair play is the standard in all competitions.

In this chapter, we dive into the structure, goals, and challenges that these major sports governing bodies face. We'll explore the intricate process of choosing host cities for events like the Olympics, uncovering the logistical and political hurdles along the way. The chapter also tackles the tough questions around competition rules, athlete eligibility, and the governance disputes that these organizations must address. We'll shine a light on pressing issues such as doping, match-fixing, and corruption, with a focus on the pivotal role of the Court of Arbitration for Sport (CAS) in settling these disputes. Through their oversight and conflict resolution mechanisms, these organizations play a vital role in keeping global sports events credible and exciting within the confines of a political environment.

The International Olympic Committee

The International Olympic Committee (IOC) is a nongovernmental organization responsible for organizing the modern Olympic Games and promoting the principles of Olympism worldwide with its headquarters located in Lausanne, Switzerland. Established in 1894, the IOC aims to foster a spirit of friendship, solidarity, and fair play across nations through sports. Central to its mission is the Olympic Charter, a comprehensive set of rules and guidelines that govern the organization of the Olympic Games and the broader Olympic Movement.

History of the Olympic Movement

The Olympic Games trace their origins to ancient Greece, where they were first held in Olympia starting in 776 B.C. These ancient Games were much more than a series of athletic competitions; they were part of a grand festival that also celebrated the arts, including music, poetry, and dance. This blend of athleticism and cultural events made the Olympics a comprehensive celebration of Greek culture and religious devotion to Zeus, the king of the Greek gods.

Initially, the Games featured sports such as running, wrestling, boxing, and chariot racing, but they expanded over time to include events like the pentathlon, which combined running, jumping, discus throw, javelin throw, and wrestling. The festival also featured artistic competitions where poets, musicians, and dancers showcased their talents, adding a rich cultural dimension to the event.

The ancient Olympic Games lasted for five days, although the entire festival period was longer, including time for arrival, religious ceremonies, and departures. Major city-states like Athens, Sparta, Corinth, and Thebes were regular competitors, and their athletes were chosen based on their physical prowess and local reputations. Participation in the Games was an honor, reflecting the athletes' status and their city's prestige.

The Games held immense value in ancient Greek society, promoting unity among the often-warring city-states and offering a venue for displaying the physical and artistic talents of the Greek people. They were a time for establishing truces, fostering diplomacy, and celebrating shared cultural and religious values. The Olympic Games continued for nearly twelve centuries until they were abolished in 393 A.D. by the Roman Emperor Theodosius I, who sought to suppress pagan festivals in favor of Christianity.

The modern Olympic Games, revived in the late nineteenth century by Baron Pierre de Coubertin, sought to resurrect the spirit of the ancient Games while promoting physical education and international peace through sport. Coubertin's vision materialized at the International Congress of Paris in 1894, leading to the first modern Olympics held in Athens in 1896. These Games featured 241 athletes from fourteen nations competing in forty-three events, marking the beginning of a global sporting tradition.

Over the years, the Olympic Games have witnessed dramatic growth and numerous milestones. Women first participated in the 1900 Paris Games, where twenty-two female athletes competed in five sports: tennis, sailing, croquet, equestrianism, and golf. This marked the beginning of a gradual increase in women's involvement, culminating in the 2012 London

Games where women competed in all Olympic sports. The inclusion of new sports has also been a hallmark of the Games' evolution, with disciplines such as snowboarding, skateboarding, surfing, and BMX racing adding modern flair to the traditional lineup.

The Olympic Games have not been without controversy. The 1936 Berlin Games, held under Nazi Germany, were intended by Adolf Hitler to showcase Aryan supremacy. However, Black athlete Jesse Owens famously defied this agenda by winning four gold medals, undermining the Nazi ideology of racial superiority. This highlighted the inherent political nature of the Games, despite efforts to maintain political neutrality. Further complicating the notion of neutrality, the United States boycotted the 1980 Summer Olympics hosted in Moscow as a protest against the Soviet invasion of Afghanistan. In response, the Soviet Union led a boycott of the 1984 Los Angeles Games, citing security concerns and alleged commercialization of the event. More recently, in 2024, the IOC banned Russia from participating in the Paris Olympic Games due to its ongoing invasion of Ukraine, demonstrating how geopolitical tensions continue to impact the global sporting event.

In 1960, the first official Paralympic Games were held in Rome, providing a platform for athletes with disabilities to compete at an international level. The Paralympics have since grown in prominence, yet they continue to face challenges such as securing adequate funding, ensuring accessibility, and achieving media coverage comparable to the Olympics.

Since 1960, the event has seen significant growth in both the number of athletes participating and the variety of sports included. The first Paralympics featured 400 athletes from twenty-three countries, primarily competing in wheelchair events. In the most recent summer Paralympics, the number of athletes had grown to over 4400 from 162 nations, competing in more than 20 sports.

The Paralympics have expanded to include athletes with various disabilities, including physical impairments, visual impairments, and intellectual disabilities. This growth has not only increased the visibility of Paralympic sports but also fostered greater inclusion and recognition of athletes with disabilities.

The selection of host cities for both the Summer and Winter Olympics has become a complex process, requiring a balance of logistical capabilities, political considerations, and legacy impacts. Cities like Tokyo, London,

Paris, Rio de Janeiro, and Los Angeles have faced immense challenges in hosting the Games, including construction delays, economic burdens, environmental concerns, social disruptions, and even allegations of foreign hacking targeting infrastructure. The selection process has not been without controversy. Past charges have surfaced alleging rigged selection processes, with instances of bribes and even threats from the IOC. A notable case involved the selection of Salt Lake City for the Winter Olympic Games, where the IOC allegedly threatened to pull the Games unless US Olympic officials, specifically the U.S. Anti-Doping Agency (USADA), ceased their criticism of the IOC's failure to enforce global anti-doping rules fairly. These tensions were exacerbated by accusations that China had repeatedly hidden positive drug tests of its swimmers, and the World Anti-Doping Agency (WADA) failed to ban these athletes, further fueling suspicions of bias and inadequate oversight. Such incidents highlight the complex interplay between global sports governance, national interests, and the ethical challenges of maintaining fair competition on the world stage.

The Olympics have continually evolved, expanding to include new sports and integrating cutting-edge technology to enhance both competition and the spectator experience. The Games now feature a diverse array of events, ranging from traditional disciplines like track and field and gymnastics to more recent additions such as karate, rugby sevens, and sport climbing. This evolution reflects the Olympic commitment to staying relevant and engaging for a global audience. Each edition of the Games strives to foster international unity and celebrate human achievement, echoing the ancient ideals of excellence, harmony, and cultural exchange. Through these efforts, the Olympics continue to stand as a powerful symbol of global cooperation and the pursuit of greatness.

The history of the Olympic Games reflects a deep commitment to inclusivity, competitive fairness, and the celebration of human potential. Despite facing numerous challenges and controversies, the Games continue to be a powerful symbol of global unity and an enduring testament to the ancient Olympic spirit. Over time, the Olympics have expanded to include a diverse range of sports and athletes from around the world, striving to uphold the ideals of excellence and sportsmanship. This ongoing journey demonstrates the resilience and adaptability of the Olympic movement, highlighting its role in promoting peace, understanding, and shared human achievement across cultures and nations.

The Olympic Charter

The Olympic Charter is the codification of the fundamental principles of Olympism, the rules, and the by-laws adopted by the International Olympic Committee. It serves as a foundational document that governs the organization, action, and operation of the Olympic Movement, setting forth the conditions for the celebration of the Olympic Games. The Charter is designed to ensure that the values of Olympism—excellence, friendship, and respect—are upheld throughout the global sporting community. It outlines the responsibilities of the IOC, National Olympic Committees (NOCs), International Federations (IFs), and other stakeholders within the Olympic Movement.

The Charter consists of several key components:

- **Fundamental Principles of Olympism:** These principles emphasize the philosophy of life that combines sport with culture and education, aiming to promote a harmonious development of humankind with a view to creating a peaceful society concerned with the preservation of human dignity.
- **Rules and By-laws:** These provide detailed guidelines on the organization of the Olympic Games, the roles and responsibilities of various entities within the Olympic Movement, and the protocols for ensuring fair competition and ethical behavior.
- **Rights and Responsibilities:** The Charter delineates the rights of athletes, officials, and other participants, as well as their obligations to adhere to the rules and uphold the spirit of fair play.

Mission and Structure of the IOC

Mission

The mission of the IOC is to promote Olympism throughout the world and lead the Olympic Movement. Its roles include:

- **Encouraging and Supporting the Promotion of Ethics and Good Governance in Sport:** The IOC works to uphold high standards of ethical behavior and governance within the sporting community. This includes implementing measures to combat corruption, ensuring transparency, and promoting accountability among sports organizations.
- **Ensuring the Regular Celebration of the Olympic Games:** The IOC is responsible for organizing the Summer and Winter Olympic Games every four years. This involves selecting host cities, overseeing the preparation and execution of the Games, and ensuring they adhere to the standards and principles set forth in the Olympic Charter.
- **Promoting Peace Through Sport:** The IOC advocates for the use of sport as a tool for fostering peace and understanding among nations. Initiatives such as the Olympic Truce encourage countries to cease hostilities and engage in dialogue during the Games.
- **Protecting the Integrity of Sport:** The IOC leads the fight against doping, competition manipulation, and other forms of cheating. It collaborates with organizations like the World Anti-Doping Agency (WADA) to establish anti-doping regulations and conduct testing. The IOC also works to prevent match-fixing and other forms of corruption in sports.

Structure

The IOC's organizational structure is designed to facilitate effective governance and decision-making within the Olympic Movement. It is composed of the following key components:

- **The Session:** The Session is the general assembly of the IOC members and serves as the supreme decision-making body. It meets once a year to discuss and vote on important matters such as the election of IOC members, the selection of host cities for the Olympic Games, and amendments to the Olympic Charter.
- **The Executive Board:** The Executive Board is responsible for the administration and management of the IOC's affairs. It consists of the President, four Vice-Presidents, and ten other members elected by the Session. The Board meets regularly to make decisions on a

wide range of issues, including finance, marketing, and development programs.
- **The President:** The President represents the IOC and is responsible for ensuring that its activities align with the principles of Olympism. The President is elected by the Session for an initial term of eight years, with the possibility of a four-year renewal.
- **Commissions and Working Groups:** The IOC has various commissions and working groups that address specific areas such as ethics, athletes' rights, sustainability, and the coordination of the Olympic Games. These bodies provide expert advice and recommendations to the Executive Board and the Session.

The IOC recognizes 206 National Olympic Committees (NOCs) and eighty-two International Sports Federations (IFs). NOCs are responsible for the development and promotion of Olympism within their respective countries, while IFs govern their respective sports on a global scale. Both NOCs and IFs play crucial roles in ensuring compliance with the Olympic Charter and the smooth operation of the Olympic Games.

One of the most tragic failures of the Olympic movement occurred during the 1972 Munich Games, where eleven Israeli athletes and coaches were taken hostage and killed by the Palestinian terrorist group Black September. This incident highlighted severe security lapses and had a lasting impact on the IOC's approach to security. The IOC has also grappled with numerous doping scandals that have marred the credibility of the Games. The systematic doping program in East Germany during the 1970s and 1980s and the more recent Russian doping scandal exposed during the 2014 Sochi Winter Games have been significant blows to the integrity of Olympic competition. Additionally, the 2002 Winter Games in Salt Lake City were overshadowed by revelations of corruption in the bidding process. Several IOC members were found to have accepted bribes from the Salt Lake Organizing Committee. Tokyo's bid for the 2020 Summer Olympics was also marred by bribery scandals, with trials revealing that several companies, including the advertising giant Dentsu, were involved in bid-rigging and bribery to secure contracts. These scandals tarnished the reputation of the Olympic Games and led to calls for more transparency and accountability in the bidding process.

Current challenges for the IOC include the contentious topic of gender classification in sports. The participation of transgender athletes and athletes with differences in sex development (DSD) has sparked intense debates over fairness and inclusivity. A recent example is the controversy surrounding the Paris Olympics boxing competition, where two intersex athletes, Algerian boxer Imane Khelif and Taiwanese boxer Lin Yu-ting, competed and won gold medals in the women's Olympic welterweight and flyweight divisions, respectively. This situation has led to significant criticism from leading women's sports activists, including Martina Navratilova, who argued that the IOC's decision to allow these athletes to compete based solely on their passports and birth certificates, which identified them as female, was flawed. Critics contend that the IOC should have required objective scientific criteria, such as specific hormonal levels, to ensure a fair competition. Adding to the controversy, Imane Khelif filed cyberbullying complaints against Elon Musk and *Hunger Games* author J. K. Rowling, who publicly questioned her gender in online comments. This incident underscores the ongoing challenges the IOC faces in balancing competitive fairness with human rights, as any current international federation or IOC guidelines on testosterone levels for female athletes continue to draw condemnation from some quarters.

Advancements in technology and equipment present both opportunities and challenges for the International Olympic Committee (IOC). While innovations like VAR (Video Assistant Referee) and new materials for athletic gear can enhance performance and fairness, they also raise concerns about accessibility, fairness, and the spirit of the sport.

A notable example of technological impact in sports is the controversy surrounding the Speedo LZR Racer swimsuit, introduced before the 2008 Beijing Olympics. This high-tech swimsuit incorporated polyurethane panels that significantly reduced drag, improved buoyancy, and allowed swimmers to break fifty-five world records in 2008 alone, including twenty-five during the Olympics. The suit was so effective that it led to an "arms race" in swimwear technology, with other manufacturers creating even more advanced suits, resulting in sixty-seven world records being broken in 2009. However, concerns about the fairness of these suits, which essentially provided swimmers with a technological boost, led to their ban by World Aquatics in 2010. Since then, only textile-based suits are allowed in competition, and many of the records set during the "super-suit" era remain among the fastest times in swimming history.

In another example of technology pushing ethical boundaries, the Canadian women's soccer team was embroiled in a scandal at the 2024

Paris Olympics when two of their staff members were dismissed for using a drone to spy on New Zealand's practice sessions. This incident raised ethical concerns about the use of technology to gain an unfair advantage, further complicating the balance between innovation and sportsmanship.

These examples highlight the ongoing challenges that technological advancements pose to maintaining the integrity of competition in the Olympics, prompting the IOC and other sports governing bodies to continuously adapt their regulations to preserve the spirit of fair play in sports.

Besides technological advancements and related ethical fairness challenges, hosting the Olympic Games has significant environmental impacts, from construction to waste management. The IOC faces the ongoing responsibility of ensuring that future Games are sustainable, minimizing carbon footprints, and promoting environmentally friendly practices. For example, the carbon footprint associated with international travel for athletes and spectators remains a major concern, with efforts being made to reduce emissions through more efficient transportation and offset programs. Waste management is another critical issue, as seen in the challenges of disposing of the massive amounts of trash generated during the Games.

The 2008 Beijing Games highlighted issues related to air quality, where the city's notorious pollution levels required extensive measures to ensure cleaner air for athletes, including temporarily shutting down factories and limiting vehicle use. Similarly, the 2024 Paris Games faced the not particularly successful challenge of ensuring clean water for open water swimming and triathlon events in the Seine River, which has long been plagued by pollution. The 2028 Los Angeles Games present their own set of environmental challenges, particularly concerning air quality and water resources in a city already grappling with pollution and drought and a homeless population presenting human rights and health and safety issues. Additionally, concerns about the impact on local ecosystems from the construction of new venues and infrastructure are significant, with the city needing to balance its iconic car culture with sustainable transport options to reduce emissions.

The IOC's Olympic Agenda 2020 aims to address these concerns, but implementation remains a complex issue. The selection of host cities often brings to light human rights issues. For example, the 2008 Beijing Games and the 2022 Beijing Winter Games were criticized for China's human rights record. The IOC must continue to address the delicate balance between promoting international sports, environmental challenges, and addressing ethical concerns, free speech, and human rights related to the conduct of host nations.

Despite these challenges, the IOC remains committed to evolving and improving the Olympic Movement. By learning from past failures and addressing current issues head-on, the IOC aims to continue fostering a global sporting environment that reflects the highest values of Olympism. Initiatives to enhance transparency, ensure fairness, and promote sustainability are central to the IOC's strategy moving forward. The continued success of the Olympic Games depends on the IOC's ability to adapt to an ever-changing world while staying true to the principles that have defined the Games since their inception.

Key Olympic Rules and Regulations

As discussed earlier, the Olympic Games operate under a comprehensive set of rules and regulations designed to ensure fair competition, uphold the values of Olympism, and maintain the integrity of the Games. These guidelines cover a wide range of aspects, from which sports are recognized to the operational protocols for host cities and the conduct of athletes and coaches.

The IOC determines which sports are included in the Olympic program. This decision is based on factors such as global popularity, universality, and the sport's adherence to the Olympic Charter. The IOC periodically reviews the list of sports, allowing for the inclusion of new disciplines and the removal of others. Each host city has the opportunity to propose the addition of new temporary sports, which must be approved by the IOC. For example, the Los Angeles 2028 Olympics features sports like surfing, skateboarding, flag football, and sport climbing, reflecting contemporary interests and trends.

To manage the scale of the Games and ensure a high level of competition, the IOC sets limits on the number of athletes per sport and nation. Athletes must meet minimum qualifying standards, such as achieving specific times or scores in their respective disciplines. This system ensures that only the best athletes compete, maintaining the Games' prestige and competitive integrity. However, this system favors wealthier nations that can provide superior training facilities, coaching, nutritional, physical, and psychological support. Media coverage often emphasizes the medal count, turning it into a competition among nations rather than a celebration of individual and collective athletic achievements. This focus on national dominance runs counter to the original spirit of the Games, which aims to promote unity, peace, and the joy of sport for all participants.

Gender equity is a fundamental principle of the Olympic Movement. The IOC strives for equal participation of men and women across all sports. Significant progress has been made, with women now competing in all sports on the Olympic program since the 2012 London Games. The inclusion of mixed-gender events, such as mixed relay races in triathlon, track and field, and swimming, as well as mixed team events in archery, tennis, judo, and table tennis, further promotes gender equality. These events also enhance the camaraderie and enjoyment for competitors who frequently train together and now get the opportunity to compete as a team, showcasing their combined skills and teamwork on the global stage.

The IOC recognizes that athletes from less economically developed countries generally lack the resources and support available to their counterparts from wealthier nations. To address this, the IOC provides financial assistance through programs like Olympic Solidarity, which funds training, coaching, and facilities for athletes from underrepresented nations. These initiatives help ensure a more inclusive and diverse Olympic Games.

For example, countries such as Bhutan, which has never won an Olympic medal, often struggle with limited sports infrastructure and funding. Through Olympic Solidarity, athletes from such nations receive scholarships to train at better-equipped facilities and gain access to expert coaching. Similarly, nations like Niger and Cambodia, which have had very few participants in the Games, benefit from tailored programs that provide resources and opportunities for their athletes to compete at a higher level.

Despite these efforts, it remains an enormous challenge for athletes from these countries to compete on equal footing with those from wealthier nations. They face obstacles such as inadequate training environments, lack of exposure due to lack of financial resources to travel to international competition, and limited access to advanced sports science and medical support. The financial assistance and programs provided by the IOC are crucial in bridging this gap, but the journey to the podium remains a formidable one for many athletes from less privileged backgrounds.

However, there have been inspiring success stories. For instance, Julius Yego from Kenya, known as the "YouTube Man" for learning javelin techniques online, won a silver medal in the men's javelin throw at the 2016 Rio Olympics. His achievement highlighted how determination and IOC support can lead to remarkable success despite limited resources. Another example is Majlinda Kelmendi from Kosovo, who also won a gold medal in judo at the Rio Olympics, bringing her country its first-ever Olympic medal. Her victory demonstrated the impact of focused support and the potential for athletes from small or economically disadvantaged nations to excel on the world stage.

The opening and closing ceremonies are significant cultural events that symbolize the unity and diversity of the Olympic Movement. The opening ceremony includes the Parade of Nations, where athletes from each country march into the stadium, fostering at least the appearance of a sense of global community in the midst of hostilities throughout the world. The closing ceremony celebrates the achievements of the athletes and marks the official end of the Games. Both ceremonies feature artistic performances that highlight the host country's culture and heritage.

The Olympic Village is a key component of the Games, providing accommodation and facilities for athletes and coaches. Dating back to the ancient Olympic Games, where athletes from various Greek city-states gathered in a sacred grove near Olympia, the concept of a communal living space was designed to foster unity and camaraderie among competitors. The modern Olympic Village operates as a self-contained community, offering dining, medical services, recreational activities, and training facilities. This environment not only ensures that athletes have a comfortable and supportive place to stay but also promotes interactions and friendships among athletes from different countries, reinforcing the Olympic values of peace and mutual understanding.

Coaches and support staff play a crucial role in the success of athletes. They are allowed to attend the Games, providing technical guidance, strategic planning, and moral support. Their presence is viewed as essential for the athletes' performance and well-being. Coaches develop tailored training regimens and strategies specific to each competition, helping athletes refine their techniques and optimize their performance. Support staff, including physiotherapists, nutritionists, and sports psychologists, ensure that athletes are physically and mentally prepared for their events. This comprehensive support system is vital for athletes to perform at their best and handle the physical, mental, and social expectations and pressures of competing on the world stage. The close-knit team environment also helps foster a sense of community and confidence, which is crucial for success in high-stakes competitions like the Olympics.

Promotional Limitations

Rule 40 of the Olympic Charter restricts athletes from participating in advertising during the Games unless it is with official sponsors. This rule aims to protect the exclusivity of Olympic sponsors and maintain the amateur spirit of the Games. While controversial, Rule 40 ensures that the focus remains on the competition and not commercial interests.

Complementing Rule 40, Rule 41 of the Olympic Charter governs the eligibility of athletes to compete in the Olympic Games. Specifically, it states that athletes must be nationals of the country they represent and comply with any additional eligibility requirements set by their respective International Federations. Rule 41 is crucial in preserving the integrity of the Games, ensuring that athletes compete fairly under their national banners. Together, Rules 40 and 41 reinforce the Olympic values of fair play and unity, balancing the commercial aspects with the fundamental principles of the Olympic Movement.

However, Rule 40 has sparked immense controversy and creative attempts by athletes to circumvent its restrictions. Athletes, who often rely on personal sponsorships for their livelihood, find this rule particularly challenging. For instance, during the 1992 Barcelona Olympics, the USA men's basketball "Dream Team" (considered the greatest assembly of basketball talent ever, including NBA players Magic Johnson, Larry Bird, Charles Barkley, Karl Malone, John Stockton, Patrick Ewing, Scottie Pippen, David Robinson, Clyde Drexler, Chris Mullin, and the only college athlete Christian Laettner) famously draped themselves in the American flag during medal ceremonies to obscure logos of their personal sponsors that were not official Olympic sponsors. This move allowed them to honor their contractual obligations without blatantly violating Olympic rules.

Similarly, during the 2016 Rio Olympics, several US women's track and field athletes wore Nike necklaces at medal ceremonies despite Nike not being an official sponsor of the Games. These subtle yet deliberate acts highlighted the ongoing tension between athletes' personal endorsements and the IOC's strict sponsorship guidelines.

Michael Phelps, the most decorated Olympian of all time, faced similar challenges. Phelps had lucrative endorsement deals with brands like Under Armour, Aqua Sphere, and Master Spas that were not official Olympic sponsors, and working around Rule 40 during the Games was a constant balancing act. While athletes are allowed to wear their sponsored gear during competition if it meets certain criteria, they cannot engage in any form of promotional activities that highlight these sponsors during the "Games Period." This period typically starts nine days before the opening ceremony and ends three days after the closing ceremony.

For example, athletes cannot post social media messages that feature or mention non-Olympic sponsors, even if they have long-standing endorsement deals with these companies. Rule 40 violations can result in sanctions against the athlete, ranging from warnings to disqualification, though enforcement can be challenging and inconsistent. The rule has also faced legal challenges, with athletes arguing that it unfairly restricts their earning potential during a time when they are most visible to the public. For example, British sprinter Adam Gemili and Canadian pole vaulter Shawn Barber have been vocal about the financial hardships caused by this rule, highlighting the difficulties athletes face when their personal sponsors cannot capitalize on the peak visibility the Olympics provide.

The tension between Rule 40 and athletes' sponsorship obligations underscores the broader challenge of balancing commercial interests with the Olympic spirit. While the rule is intended to maintain the purity and focus of the Games, it also places athletes in a difficult position, channeling complex endorsement landscapes while striving to achieve peak performance on the world stage. This balancing act is further complicated by the significant financial investments athletes often require to reach the Olympic level, making personal sponsorships a vital part of their careers.

In response to growing pressure, the IOC has made some amendments to Rule 40, allowing for limited athlete marketing during the Games, provided it does not use Olympic properties and adheres to specific guidelines. Despite these changes, the rule remains a contentious issue, reflecting the ongoing struggle to align the commercial realities of modern sports with the traditional values of the Olympic Movement.

Athlete Safety and Welfare

Ensuring the safety and welfare of athletes is a paramount responsibility for the IOC and national bodies like the USOPC. These organizations have established comprehensive policies and protocols to protect athletes' physical and mental well-being, aiming to create a safer and more supportive environment for all participants.

The IOC has implemented guidelines and procedures to safeguard athletes' physical health. These include providing extensive medical facilities and services at all Olympic venues, including emergency care, routine medical checks, and specialized treatments. Injury prevention programs are promoted through education and training, ensuring athletes are aware of the latest techniques and technologies to minimize risk. Additionally, the IOC seeks to enforce anti-doping regulations, albeit not always evenly, to ensure fair competition and protect athletes' health from the harmful effects of performance-enhancing drugs.

Recognizing the critical importance of mental health, the IOC and national committees have prioritized psychological support for athletes. Key initiatives include offering access to mental health professionals, including psychologists and counselors, who provide support and therapy to athletes experiencing stress, anxiety, or other mental health issues. Workshops and seminars are conducted to educate athletes about mental health, encouraging them to seek help when needed and destigmatizing mental health challenges. Crisis intervention protocols are also implemented to address urgent mental health issues promptly, ensuring athletes receive immediate care and support.

A prime example of prioritizing mental health is Simone Biles' decision to withdraw from several events during the Tokyo 2020 Olympic Games. Biles, a decorated gymnast, cited concerns about her mental health and "the twisties"—a condition that affects spatial awareness—which posed a serious risk to her physical safety during high-stakes routines. Her decision highlighted the intense pressure athletes face and underscored the importance of mental health in competitive sports. Biles' openness about her struggles sparked a global conversation about athlete welfare and the necessity of mental health support.

Similarly, Michael Phelps, the most decorated Olympian of all time, has openly discussed his battles with depression and anxiety, particularly after the 2012 Olympics. Phelps has shared how he struggled with the overwhelming pressures of success, which led to bouts of severe depression, even contemplating suicide at one point. His decision to seek therapy and his advocacy for mental health awareness have been pivotal in breaking the stigma surrounding mental health issues in sports. Phelps' work with the Michael Phelps Foundation, which promotes mental health awareness, and his partnership with organizations like Talkspace have further amplified the importance of prioritizing mental health in the athletic community. His candidness about his struggles has encouraged many athletes to speak out and seek help, emphasizing that mental health is as critical as physical health for overall well-being and performance.

To further safeguard athletes, the IOC and the USOPC, in particular, have established policies to prevent and address sexual harassment and abuse. These policies include comprehensive education, training, and resources designed to prevent abuse and misconduct. Key initiatives feature mandatory reporting procedures and comprehensive support systems for victims, ensuring that those affected by abuse receive the necessary care and justice. Additionally, a strict code of conduct is enforced for coaches, staff, and athletes to maintain a respectful and safe environment across all levels of competition. Independent bodies like SafeSport in the United States—frequently overwhelmed by the sheer number of complaints—are set up to investigate allegations of abuse and misconduct, ensuring some level of transparency and accountability.

However, despite these efforts, there is currently no global standard or international adjudicatory body equivalent to the United States' SafeSport to address and prevent abuse in sports worldwide. The absence of a unified framework leaves a consequential gap in the consistent protection of athletes, particularly in regions where such protections may be less developed or enforced. Without a global equivalent, efforts to protect athletes from abuse remain fragmented, and the effectiveness of these safeguards can vary significantly across different countries and sports organizations. This lack of international standards and control highlights the pressing need for international collaboration to establish robust, universally recognized standards and mechanisms that can protect athletes' well-being on a global scale.

There have been several high-profile cases of abuse at the Olympic level. One notorious example is the scandal involving former Team USA Gymnastics team doctor Larry Nassar, who was found guilty of sexually abusing 265 women, including prominent Olympic gymnasts such as Simone Biles, Aly Raisman, McKayla Maroney, and Jordyn Wieber. Nassar sexually assaulted athletes under the guise of providing medical treatment. The abuse spanned over two decades and in many cases involved minors, demonstrating a major failure to prevent and stop these abuses by Michigan State University and the USOPC. This horrendous case brought global attention to the issue of sexual abuse in sports and led to serious changes in how abuse allegations are handled in the United States. Additionally, in another form of abuse, during the 2022 Beijing Winter Olympics, Russian figure skater Kamila Valieva's poor performance and the subsequent outrageous public treatment by her coaches raised concerns about the emotional and psychological abuse athletes should not have to endure. The harsh public criticism and pressure Valieva faced from her coaches brought to light the intense and sometimes harmful environment in competitive sports.

There have also been instances of harassment and abuse at the Games. For example, during the 2008 Beijing Olympics, a coach was expelled from the Games after being accused of sexually harassing an athlete. At the Rio Olympics, Cuban volleyball player Ariel Saúl Rámirez was accused of sexually assaulting a Brazilian housekeeper in the Olympic Village. He was subsequently arrested and faced legal proceedings in Brazil. These cases underscore the ongoing need for stringent policies and proactive measures to protect all individuals involved in the Olympic movement from abuse and misconduct that are still lacking.

Anti-Doping and Performance-Enhancing Drug Restrictions

The idealistic vision of the Olympic Games—a celebration of athletic prowess achieved through dedication and skill—has long been shadowed by concerns over the use of performance-enhancing drugs (PEDs). Even as far back as the original Olympic Games in ancient Greece, there were charges of doping, with competitors allegedly using substances like mushrooms and other psychedelic herbs to either enhance their performance or sabotage their opponents. These early instances of doping eventually led to the creation of the Olympic Village, a controlled environment where athletes' food and beverages could be closely monitored to prevent tampering and ensure fair competition.

In modern times, the regulation of PEDs and other anti-doping measures represents an ongoing issue within the sports law arena, touching all levels of athletic competition, from amateur sports to the professional ranks. Defining what substances or techniques are considered performance-enhancing and illegal, developing effective testing protocols, enforcing rules, respecting some modicum of privacy and due process, and adjudicating violations in a fair and objective manner are among the many challenges facing the bodies entrusted with keeping competitive sports fair and legal. These complexities are further amplified by the differing rules and enforcement mechanisms adopted by various regulatory bodies, such as the National Collegiate Athletic Association (NCAA), the IOC, USOPC, and professional sports leagues. Our focus in this chapter is primarily on the IOC and USOPC rules and regulations.

Drug testing in sports began in earnest during the 1960s as concerns over the health and fairness implications of performance-enhancing drugs grew. The widespread use of stimulants and other substances in competitive sports has raised alarms about the potential for serious health risks and the erosion of fair play. Athletes sought ways to enhance their performance, often at the expense of their health and the integrity of the competition.

The first known drug testing at the Olympic Games occurred during the 1968 Winter Olympics in Grenoble, France. This initial step marked the first of its kind in the fight against doping, although the efforts were rudimentary. The focus was primarily on detecting stimulants and narcotics, which were known to be widely abused by athletes seeking to gain a competitive edge. The testing methods used at that time were relatively simple, and the range of detectable substances was limited, focusing on basic chemical analysis techniques like thin-layer chromatography and colorimetric assays. These methods could detect only a narrow range of substances by identifying their presence through changes in color or movement on a chromatography plate. The sensitivity and specificity of these tests were limited, making it difficult to identify more complex or less common doping agents.

Anabolic Steroids

As the understanding of performance-enhancing drugs evolved, so did the methods employed by athletes to enhance their performance. By the late 1960s and early 1970s, anabolic steroids had become a major concern. These substances, which promote muscle growth and improve strength, posed significant health risks and offered a considerable advantage to users. The prevalence of steroid use highlighted the need for more comprehensive and sophisticated testing protocols.

Anabolic steroids, synthetic derivatives of testosterone, were initially developed in the 1930s to treat conditions like delayed puberty and diseases that cause muscle loss. However, their potential for enhancing athletic performance quickly became apparent. Athletes began using these substances to increase muscle mass, strength, and endurance, leading to widespread abuse across various sports.

Several high-profile cases have underscored the extent of steroid use in competitive sports and the urgency of developing effective testing methods. For example, American swimmer Angel Martino, initially known as Angel Myers, won multiple events at the US Olympic Trials and went on to compete successfully in the 1992 and 1996 Olympics, but she was once suspended for two years in 1988 after testing positive for the anabolic steroid nandrolone and was banned from competing in the 1988 Olympic Games. Her case drew significant media attention and highlighted the need for more rigorous testing procedures across sports, along with enhanced due process rights for those accused of doping.

Moreover, the issue of doping was not limited to individual athletes; it was systematically entrenched in some countries' sports programs. The most notorious example is the East German Olympic teams during the 1970s and 1980s, where the government orchestrated a comprehensive, state-sponsored doping program. Athletes were given anabolic steroids and other performance-enhancing drugs, often without their informed consent, to dominate international competitions and enhance the nation's prestige. The success of this program was evident in the significant number of medals won by East German athletes during this period.

Despite widespread knowledge of this doping program, the IOC and other global sports bodies did little to address the issue at the time. Even today, many athletes who were part of this program retain their medals, while those who lost out on recognition due to these unfair advantages remain without the Olympic honors they rightfully deserved.

Another infamous case is that of Canadian sprinter Ben Johnson, who won the gold medal in the 100 meters at the 1988 Seoul Olympics, setting a world record. However, Johnson tested positive for stanozolol, an anabolic steroid, just days after his victory. The scandal not only stripped Johnson of his medal but also cast a shadow over the entire athletics community, especially in track and field events, revealing the pervasive nature of doping in the sport. To this day, the legacy of these doping scandals continues to haunt the Olympic movement, raising questions about the integrity of past competitions and the fairness of current anti-doping measures.

The Bay Area Laboratory Co-operative (BALCO)

The Bay Area Laboratory Co-operative (BALCO) scandal in the early 2000s brought to light the use of "designer drugs"—substances specifically engineered to evade detection by standard drug tests. BALCO, founded by Victor Conte, was at the center of a doping ring that supplied performance-enhancing drugs to numerous high-profile athletes. Designer drugs, such as tetrahydrogestrinone (THG), were created to be chemically distinct from known steroids, making them undetectable by existing testing methods. These substances could enhance performance without being identified during routine drug tests, presenting a significant challenge for anti-doping agencies.

The BALCO scandal unraveled after a syringe containing THG was anonymously sent to USADA in 2003. This led to the development of new tests capable of detecting THG, revealing widespread use among elite athletes. The subsequent investigation implicated numerous Olympians and professional athletes, exposing the extent of designer drug use. Several prominent athletes were linked to BALCO and its doping program, including Marion Jones, the American sprinter and long jumper, who won five medals at the 2000 Sydney Olympics and later admitted to using steroids provided by BALCO. Tim Montgomery, the American sprinter and former 100 meters world record holder, was banned from competition for two years for doping. Dwain Chambers, the British sprinter, was banned for two years and stripped of his records and medals after testing positive for THG.

Beyond anabolic steroids, the use of erythropoietin (EPO) and human growth hormone (HGH) became prominent in the late twentieth and early twenty-first centuries. EPO, a hormone that stimulates red blood cell production, was widely used in endurance sports to enhance aerobic capacity. The Tour de France, cycling's most prestigious event, was plagued by EPO scandals. In 1998, the Festina team was expelled from the Tour after a team car was found with large quantities of EPO. This incident, known as the Festina Affair, exposed the extensive use of EPO in professional cycling.

The long saga of Lance Armstrong epitomizes the battle against doping in sports. Armstrong, a seven-time Tour de France winner, was a symbol of triumph over cancer until an investigation revealed a sophisticated doping program involving EPO, HGH, and blood transfusions. Investigations and reports have revealed that cycling's international federation, Union Cycliste Internationale (UCI), colluded with Lance Armstrong to bypass doping accusations and provided him with preferential treatment over a lengthy period. The Cycling Independent Reform Commission (CIRC) report found that the UCI leadership turned a blind eye to doping allegations against Armstrong, accepted $100,000 from Armstrong under the guise of improving doping protocols, and allowed him to back medical certificates to cover up positive test results. Armstrong was stripped of his titles and banned from professional cycling for life. His fall from grace highlighted the lengths to which athletes would go to avoid detection and the importance of relentless anti-doping efforts.

Blood Doping

In addition to anabolic steroids, another significant development in the realm of PEDs was the practice of blood doping. This technique involves increasing the number of red blood cells in the bloodstream to enhance aerobic capacity and endurance. Athletes would either transfuse their own stored blood (autologous transfusion) or use blood from a donor (heterologous transfusion). Blood doping provided a substantial performance boost, particularly in endurance sports such as cycling and long-distance running.

Blood doping was once legal, and its use was widespread among competitive cyclists. The US Olympic cycling team won several championships in the 1980s, with many cyclists later admitting to blood doping. This method allowed them to improve their oxygen-carrying capacity, thereby enhancing their performance and endurance. The process typically involved athletes training at high altitudes to increase their red blood cell count naturally, then storing the blood for reinfusion before competition.

Detecting blood doping presented a formidable challenge for anti-doping authorities. Unlike chemical substances, blood doping involved the manipulation of the athlete's own physiology, making it difficult to identify. The development of reliable testing methods for blood doping lagged behind the techniques used to detect anabolic steroids and other substances. Advances in hematological testing, including the measurement of blood parameters like hemoglobin and hematocrit levels, eventually provided tools to identify suspicious changes indicative of blood doping.

Lance Armstrong, once more, and his US Postal Service team were notorious for their use of blood doping, among other PEDs. Armstrong's team, as described above, used a sophisticated regimen that included EPO, HGH, and blood transfusions. They took advantage of the difficulty in detecting autologous transfusions because the reinfused blood was the athlete's own. This method allowed them to compete at a high level without immediate detection. Armstrong trained at high altitudes to boost his red blood cell count and stored the blood for reinfusion before major races.

However, not all blood doping schemes were foolproof. During the 2006 Tour de France, cyclist Floyd Landis was caught doping after substituting someone else's blood for his own when he ran out of his stored blood supply. This substitution led to elevated red blood cell counts that did not match his biological passport, resulting in his disqualification and stripping of the Tour de France title.

Blood doping was officially banned by the IOC in 1986, but it took years for effective detection methods to be developed. Today, techniques such as the Athlete Biological Passport (ABP) monitor athletes' blood profiles over time to detect any physiological changes indicative of doping. Despite the ban, some athletes have sought legal methods to achieve similar benefits. Techniques like high-altitude training, which naturally increases red blood cell production, are widely used and legal. Additionally, the use of hypoxic tents and chambers simulates high-altitude conditions, offering a legal way to enhance performance.

Uneven Enforcement

Despite efforts to police, deter, and punish those who use performance-enhancing drugs, even today the enforcement mechanisms are not always perfect. According to a published story in *The New York Times*, twenty-three Chinese swimmers tested positive for PEDs at the Tokyo Olympics. Some of these athletes were medal winners. When the positive test findings were presented to the Court of Arbitration for Sport (CAS), it ruled that there was insufficient evidence to warrant stripping them of their medals.

The Chinese government successfully argued that the twenty-three swimmers who tested positive for trimetazidine before the Tokyo Olympics did so due to contaminated food. According to Chinese authorities, the positive tests were attributed to contaminated food consumed by the swimmers at a training camp. Trimetazidine, a heart medication banned in sports because it can enhance endurance, was detected in the athletes' systems. However, this explanation was met with skepticism. Critics doubted the plausibility of food contamination being the source, arguing that the likelihood of all twenty-three swimmers ingesting the same contaminant was statistically improbable. This controversy cast further doubt on the effectiveness of anti-doping measures and the transparency of the testing process, especially when powerful nations are accused of rule breaking.

A similar controversy arose a few years earlier involving widespread systematic doping by Russian athletes. During the Winter Olympic Games held in Sochi in 2014, a state-sponsored doping program was uncovered, revealing that Russia had manipulated drug tests and provided banned substances to its athletes on a massive scale. This blatant cheating, exposed after a prominent Russian scientist familiar with techniques Russia used to avoid detection defected to the United States and became a whistleblower, led to significant international outcry and subsequent investigations by the WADA and the IOC.

As a result of these findings, a small handful of Russian athletes faced severe sanctions. At the following Summer Olympics, however, Russian athletes were allowed to compete only as individuals under a neutral flag, without any association with the Russian Olympic delegation. Additionally, during medal ceremonies, the Russian national anthem was not played. Not surprisingly, many observers were dismayed and angry over what they perceived as lenient treatment, arguing that allowing Russian athletes to compete at all sent a negative message and undermined efforts to ensure fairness in sports. They felt this decision was unfair to athletes from other countries who had adhered to the rules and competed without doping. This situation highlights the ongoing exhaustive challenges in enforcing anti-doping regulations and maintaining a level playing field in international sports competitions.

In the aftermath of the Russian systematic doping scandal, there was a recognized need for an independent organization to more effectively manage and enforce anti-doping regulations across international sports. This led to the formation of the International Testing Agency (ITA), which operates separately from the WADA. While WADA remains the global leader in the fight against doping, setting the standards for anti-doping, coordinating the World Anti-Doping Code (the Code), and managing the Anti-Doping System, the ITA was created to manage anti-doping programs on behalf of International Federations (IFs), Major Event Organizers (MEOs), and other Anti-Doping Organizations (ADOs).

WADA's role is primarily that of a rule-maker. It establishes the rules and standards for anti-doping worldwide, ensuring a uniform approach to doping control across all sports and countries. On the other hand, the ITA serves as the rule-enforcer. It implements the rules and standards set by WADA, acting as the operational arm that manages the day-to-day anti-doping programs, including testing and investigation.

In essence, while WADA functions as the governing body creating the framework and regulations for anti-doping, the ITA operates like the police force, ensuring that these rules are enforced and adhered to by athletes and organizations globally. This division of responsibilities aims to enhance the integrity of anti-doping efforts by separating the rule-making and rule-enforcement functions, thereby reducing potential conflicts of interest and increasing the effectiveness of the global fight against doping in sports.

Many had hoped the days of systematic, government-organized, and implemented drug cheating, as occurred with the East Germans in the 1970s, were over. The East German doping program systematically provided athletes with performance-enhancing drugs to dominate international sports, with the full support and orchestration of state authorities. Unfortunately, recent events, such as the Russian doping scandal, reveal that such cheating continues in modern times.

These cases underscore that doping in sports is not merely a relic of the past but a persistent and pressing issue. The continued prevalence of such illegal practices highlights the urgent need for stronger anti-doping measures and more consistent enforcement to protect the integrity of competitive sports. Without adequately addressing these concerns, the public's confidence in the fairness of sports will erode. A glaring disparity exists where some elite athletes train and compete within state-sponsored doping regimes, while others, particularly those from the United States, are subject to random drug testing at any time, both in and out of competition. This uneven playing field leaves many feeling cheated. The global sports community must commit to creating a vigilant, transparent, and level playing field. Failing to do so will inevitably lead to widespread doubts about the fairness of international sports competitions, raising the question of whether sports, as we know them, are even worth competing in. If this trend continues unchecked, we may need to reconsider the rules, potentially allowing performance-enhancing drugs (PEDs) under strict medical observation and control to ensure everyone is playing by the same rules.

Gender Classification

The IOC has recently updated its guidelines to create a more inclusive environment for transgender and intersex athletes, moving away from stringent testosterone level requirements. This shift, encapsulated in the IOC's "Framework on Fairness, Inclusion and Non-Discrimination on the Basis of Gender Identity and Sex Variations," emphasizes respect for human rights and inclusion. The new guidelines, developed after extensive consultations with athletes, sports organizations, and experts in human rights, law, and medicine, aim to ensure that athletes can engage in sports without the need for hormone level adjustments or medically unnecessary procedures.

This approach marks a significant departure from previous policies that required athletes to undergo invasive examinations and sex testing, which were criticized for causing harm and violating athletes' rights. However, the updated guidelines have sparked debates about fairness in competition. Critics argue that even with testosterone suppression, transgender women may retain physical advantages from male puberty, such as increased muscle mass and bone density, which could provide an unfair competitive edge over cisgender women. This concern is particularly pronounced in sports where physical strength, speed, and endurance are critical. For example, the participation of New Zealand weightlifter Laurel Hubbard in the Tokyo Olympics brought attention to this issue, as some argued that her previous male puberty gave her an advantage despite meeting the testosterone suppression requirements. The IOC's new framework acknowledges these concerns but leaves the responsibility of establishing specific guidelines to individual sports federations, recognizing that the impact of testosterone and other factors can vary significantly across different sports.

The case of Caster Semenya, a South African runner with naturally high testosterone levels due to Differences of Sex Development (DSD), further illustrates the complexities of gender classification in sports. Despite winning a discrimination case in the European Court of Human Rights, Semenya and other athletes with similar conditions continue to face restrictions under World Athletics (the international federation governing track and field) regulations, which require them to undergo hormone treatments to compete in women's events. This situation underscores the tension between upholding competitive fairness and respecting athletes' rights to bodily integrity and non discrimination. Additionally, cultural and religious concerns add another layer of complexity, as different societies have varying views on gender identity and the inclusion of transgender athletes in sports. Balancing these diverse perspectives while ensuring fair and inclusive competition remains a constant challenge for the IOC and other sports governing bodies.

As described in the earlier chapter on Gender Equity, in the United States, the debate over transgender participation in sports has led to a patchwork of state laws and policies by high school associations and the NCAA. More than twenty states have enacted laws restricting transgender athletes' participation in school sports based on their gender identity, often citing concerns over fairness and competitive balance. These laws have sparked legal battles and are expected to be reviewed by the Supreme Court eventually.

The scientific community remains divided on the issue. While some experts argue that testosterone suppression can mitigate physical advantages, others contend that certain benefits, such as height and hand size, cannot be fully reversed, thus maintaining a competitive disparity. The broader cultural and religious concerns also play a role, as different societies have varying views on gender identity and the inclusion of transgender athletes in sports, further complicating the development of universally accepted policies.

Overall, the issue of gender classification in sports continues to evolve, with ongoing debates and varying approaches to balancing inclusivity and fairness in competition.

The Mission and Structure of the USOPC

The United States Olympic & Paralympic Committee (USOPC) is the national Olympic and Paralympic governing body for the United States. Its mission is to support US athletes in achieving sustained competitive excellence while promoting and growing the Olympic and Paralympic movements. The USOPC is responsible for overseeing the training, funding, and development of American athletes competing in the Olympic, Pan American, and Paralympic Games.

The USOPC operates under a board of directors and is led by a CEO. It includes various committees and divisions dedicated to athlete support, sport performance, marketing, and administration. The USOPC works with National Governing Bodies (NGBs) for each sport, which handle the day-to-day management and development of their respective sports.

The USOPC is funded through a combination of sponsorships, fundraising, and broadcast rights, rather than government funding. This model allows it to maintain autonomy and financial independence. Sponsorship deals with major corporations, revenue from broadcasting the Games, and private donations form the backbone of its funding.

Athletes benefit from the USOPC through financial support, access to training facilities at Colorado Springs for summer sports and Lake Placid for winter sports, medical care, and performance services. The USOPC provides stipends, health insurance, tuition grants, and other forms of assistance to help athletes focus on their training and competition without undue financial stress.

The Ted Stevens Olympic and Amateur Sports Act

The Ted Stevens Olympic and Amateur Sports Act, passed in 1978 and amended in 1998, was instrumental in shaping the current structure of the USOPC. The Act was named after Senator Ted Stevens of Alaska and granted the USOPC exclusive jurisdiction over all Olympic-related activities in the United States. It aimed to ensure athletes' rights and enhance the support system for elite athletes.

The Act guarantees athletes the right to participate in Olympic, Paralympic, and Pan American Games trials and competitions. It also ensures due process for athletes in matters of eligibility and disciplinary actions. The Act provides athletes with a voice in governance through the establishment of the Athletes' Advisory Council, which represents athletes' interests within the USOPC.

Before the Ted Stevens Act, the Amateur Athletic Union (AAU) was the primary governing body for amateur sports in the United States. However, the AAU was criticized for its bureaucratic and inconsistent administration, which often led to conflicts and inequities. Elite athletes, such as Steve Prefontaine, faced restrictions on receiving prize money, limiting their ability to support themselves financially while training.

The Ted Stevens Act addressed these issues by shifting governance from the AAU to the USOPC, which was designed to be more athlete-centered and efficient. The Act also introduced due process protections for athletes, ensuring fair treatment in eligibility and disciplinary matters.

The Dr. Larry Nassar Scandal and SafeSport

The USOPC faced a significant crisis with the Dr. Larry Nassar scandal, where the former USA Gymnastics team doctor was convicted of sexually abusing numerous athletes over decades. This scandal exposed severe failures in athlete protection and oversight, nearly leading to the demise of the USOPC.

In response to the Nassar scandal and other abuse cases, the US Center for SafeSport was established in 2017. SafeSport's role is to investigate and resolve allegations of sexual misconduct and other forms of abuse within the US Olympic and Paralympic movements.

SafeSport has broad investigative powers over athletes, coaches, and other personnel involved in the Olympic and Paralympic movements. It can impose sanctions, including suspensions and bans, on individuals found guilty of misconduct. SafeSport aims to create a safer environment for athletes by enforcing strict policies and providing education on abuse prevention. It has also served as a model at the international sports governing level under a program known as Safeguarding.

Pros and Cons of SafeSport

Pros:

- Centralized authority for handling abuse allegations.
- Provides a clear and consistent process for investigations.
- Focuses on athlete safety and well-being.
- Independent from sports organizations, reducing conflicts of interest.

Cons:

- Some critics argue that the investigative process can be slow and lacks transparency.
- There are concerns about due process for the accused, as some feel the procedures may be overly punitive without sufficient evidence.
- Limited resources and funding can constrain the scope and effectiveness of SafeSport's activities.

USADA

The USOPC also collaborates with the USADA to promote clean sport. USADA, as addressed earlier, is responsible for testing American athletes and enforcing anti-doping rules domestically. It operates independently from the USOPC and works in collaboration with WADA to maintain the integrity of international competitions, such as the Olympics, Paralympics, Pan American Games, and world championships in individual Olympic-recognized sports.

Banned Substances and Techniques

The WADA maintains the Prohibited List, which is updated annually and includes substances and methods banned both in and out of competition. This list seeks to be comprehensive, encompassing various categories of substances and methods used to enhance performance illegally. The USADA follows the WADA Prohibited List, ensuring consistency and adherence to international standards. This alignment is crucial for maintaining a level playing field in global competitions and reflects the collaborative effort required to combat doping in sports in a never-ending challenge.

Categories of Banned Substances

- **Anabolic Agents**: Steroids that promote muscle growth, commonly used to increase strength and endurance.
- **Hormone and Metabolic Modulators**: Substances like erythropoietin (EPO) that enhance oxygen delivery to muscles, significantly boosting endurance.
- **Beta-2 Agonists**: Medications typically used to treat asthma that can also enhance performance by opening the airways and increasing oxygen intake.
- **Stimulants**: Substances that increase alertness and reduce fatigue, offering a competitive edge in focus and energy.
- **Narcotics**: Pain relief medications that can mask injuries, allowing athletes to perform beyond their natural physical limits.
- **Cannabinoids**: Including marijuana and synthetic cannabinoids, which are banned for their potential to affect concentration and performance.
- **Glucocorticoids**: Anti-inflammatory substances that can enhance recovery, reducing downtime between training sessions.
- **Methods**: Techniques like blood doping and gene doping, which manipulate the body's natural processes to enhance performance.

Therapeutic Use Exemptions (TUEs)

Therapeutic Use Exemptions (TUEs) allow athletes to use prohibited substances for legitimate medical reasons. To obtain a TUE, athletes must receive approval from their sport's governing body, ensuring that the medication is necessary for health and not for performance enhancement. High-profile athletes, such as Venus and Serena Williams, have received TUEs for medications including steroids used to treat chronic conditions, allowing them to compete at various Olympic Games. The TUE process aims to balance the need for medical treatment with the principles of fair competition, but it is often viewed as a "dirty little secret" way to lawfully work around prohibitions against doping.

Testing Protocols and Due Process

Anti-doping testing involves rigorous protocols to ensure accuracy and fairness. The typical process includes:

- **Sample Collection**: Athletes provide urine and/or blood samples, which are divided into "A" and "B" samples to ensure reliability and allow for retesting if needed.
- **Laboratory Analysis**: Accredited laboratories analyze the "A" sample. If it tests positive, the athlete can request that the "B" sample be tested for confirmation.
- **Due Process**: Athletes are entitled to a fair hearing, representation, and the opportunity to present evidence. Disputes are often resolved by the Court of Arbitration for Sport (CAS), an independent body that ensures impartial adjudication of doping cases.

The Role of CAS

CAS provides a neutral forum for resolving disputes in sports, including doping violations. Although it operates under the auspices of the IOC, it maintains independence to ensure fair outcomes. CAS handles a wide range of cases, from individual doping violations to complex cases involving national anti-doping policies. Its decisions are binding, making it a critical component of the global anti-doping framework.

While there are many CAS decisions to choose from, these two cases serve as illustrations of the scope of its jurisdiction and powers to adjudicate doping cases. Simona Halep, a professional tennis player from Romania, tested positive for Roxadustat, a prohibited substance, during the US Open on August 29, 2022. Her Athlete Biological Passport (ABP) also indicated the use of a prohibited substance or method. The International Tennis Federation (ITF) initially imposed a four-year period of ineligibility on Halep. However, upon appeal, the CAS reduced her ineligibility to nine months. The CAS Panel also ordered the disqualification of all her competitive results for the period in question including the forfeiture of any medals, titles, ranking points, and prize money.

Kanak Jha, an American table tennis player, faced a doping case related to whereabouts failures after missing three doping tests, prompting an investigation by USADA. The CAS reviewed the case and imposed a twelve-month period of ineligibility on Jha, starting from the date of his provisional suspension. This decision was based on the cumulative effect of his missed tests and the investigation into his whereabouts failures.

The whereabouts requirement is a crucial part of the global anti-doping system, ensuring athletes are available for unannounced, out-of-competition drug testing. It applies to athletes in the registered testing pool (RTP) managed by their International Federation (IF) or National Anti-Doping Organization (NADO), like the USADA.

Athletes in the RTP must provide detailed daily information about their location, training schedule, and travel plans. This enables doping control officers to conduct surprise tests, maintaining the integrity of anti-doping efforts. The requirement primarily targets athletes competing at the national or international level, especially in Olympic-related sports.

However, the whereabouts requirement is controversial among athletes, particularly older ones with families, who see it as a hardship and a privacy violation. They must inform their national governing body of their whereabouts daily, and failing to appear with as little as twenty-four hours' notice can lead to sanctions.

Broadcasting and Media in the Olympics

Broadcasting and media play a critical role in the IOC and the Olympic Games, serving as the primary means through which people worldwide experience the event. The IOC owns the global media rights for the Olympic Games, encompassing television, radio, and digital platforms. These rights are allocated to media companies across the globe through negotiated agreements. Olympic Broadcasting Services (OBS), established by the IOC in 2001, is responsible for producing the international television and radio signals from the Games. This ensures consistent high standards of coverage across different editions of the Games.

Major broadcasters like NBCUniversal in the United States, Eurosport in Europe, and various national broadcasters such as BBC in the UK and NHK in Japan play pivotal roles in bringing the Olympics to audiences worldwide. The financial stakes involved in broadcasting the Olympics are enormous. For instance, NBCUniversal secured the American broadcasting rights for the Olympics through 2032 with a contract worth $7.75 billion. This deal underscores the major investment media companies and risks, make to secure exclusive broadcasting rights. The revenue generated from these deals is a substantial part of the IOC's income, which is used to fund the Olympic Movement and support athletes globally.

In addition to broadcasting rights, the IOC's Olympic Partner (TOP) program attracts major multinational sponsors like Coca-Cola, Samsung, Visa, and Procter & Gamble. These sponsors contribute billions of dollars, with the TOP program alone generating around $2 billion per four-year cycle. The combined revenue from broadcasting rights and sponsorships is necessary for the financial viability of the Games and the development of sports worldwide.

Despite the financial success, broadcasting the Olympics faces several challenges. Viewership patterns have shifted significantly due to the rise of digital platforms and streaming services. For example, NBC's traditional TV viewership for the Tokyo 2020 Olympics saw a notable decline compared to previous Games, averaging 15.5 million viewers in primetime, down from the 2016 Rio Olympics. However, digital engagement surged, with over 5.5 billion streaming minutes, making Tokyo 2020 the most streamed Olympics ever. This shift reflects broader changes in media consumption habits, where audiences increasingly prefer on-demand and digital content over traditional TV broadcasts.

Additionally, the Covid-19 pandemic and geopolitical issues, such as the ongoing Russo-Ukrainian War affecting broadcasters in Russia and Belarus, have further complicated the broadcasting landscape. These challenges necessitate continuous adaptation by broadcasters and the IOC to meet evolving audience preferences and ensure the broadest possible reach for the Olympic Games.

Paralympics

The Paralympics are organized by a different organization than the IOC known as the International Paralympic Committee (IPC). The IPC is responsible for overseeing the Paralympic Games and promoting the Paralympic Movement worldwide. While the IPC and the IOC collaborate closely, particularly in coordinating the Olympic and Paralympic Games in the same host city, they are distinct entities with separate governance structures.

Key Points

- **International Paralympic Committee (IPC)**: The IPC is the global governing body for the Paralympic Movement. It organizes the Summer and Winter Paralympic Games and acts as the international federation for several sports.
- **Collaboration with the IOC**: Although separate, the IPC and IOC have a strong partnership. The IOC supports the IPC, and both organizations work together to ensure the success and smooth operation of the Paralympic Games following the Olympic Games in the same venues.
- **Governance**: The IPC has its own president, executive board, and assembly, which are responsible for the administration and development of Paralympic sports.

The distinction between the IPC and IOC allows for specialized focus on the unique aspects and needs of Paralympic athletes and competitions while maintaining a collaborative relationship to enhance the overall impact of the Olympic and Paralympic Movements.

The Paralympics were first held in 1960 in Rome, Italy. Since then, the event has seen steady growth in both the number of athletes participating and the variety of sports included. The first Paralympics featured 400 athletes from twenty-three countries, primarily competing in wheelchair events. In the most recent summer Paralympics, the number of athletes had grown to over 4,400 from 162 nations, competing in more than twenty sports.

The Paralympics have expanded to include athletes with various disabilities, including physical impairments, visual impairments, and intellectual disabilities. This growth has not only increased the visibility of Paralympic sports but also fostered greater inclusion and recognition of athletes with disabilities.

One immediate area of controversy in the Paralympics involves the use of adaptive equipment, particularly in running events. The use of "blades," or prosthetic limbs designed for running, has sparked debates about whether they provide an unfair advantage. The case of South African sprinter Oscar Pistorius brought this issue to the forefront. Pistorius, a double amputee, successfully campaigned to compete in both the Paralympics and the Olympics, but questions about the fairness of his blades persisted. Critics argue that such prosthetics could offer mechanical advantages, such as reduced energy expenditure and increased stride length, while supporters contend that they level the playing field for athletes with disabilities.

Another area of contention is the classification system used to ensure fair competition among athletes with different types of impairments. The classification process aims to group athletes by the impact of their disability on performance. However, the system has faced criticism for being subjective and inconsistent, leading to disputes and appeals. Athletes and coaches have called for more transparency and scientific rigor in the classification process to ensure fairness.

Paralympic athletes are subject to the same anti-doping rules as their Olympic counterparts, with the International Paralympic Committee (IPC) adhering to the WADA guidelines to seek to maintain clean sport.

However, enforcing these rules presents ongoing obstacles, as demonstrated by the case of Russian rower Igor Bespaliy, who competed in the Tokyo 2020 Paralympic Games. Bespaliy tested positive for dehydrochlormethyltestosterone (DHCMT), an anabolic steroid, during an out-of-competition test conducted by the IPC. As a result, he was suspended from competition.

In the United States, financial rewards for winning Paralympic medals have historically been lower than those for Olympic medals, with payments coming from the national governing bodies of each sport rather than the USOPC. Although efforts have been made to close this gap, discrepancies still exist depending on the sport and the resources of its national federation. For instance, US Olympic gold medalists in sports like swimming or track and field receive $37,500, while silver and bronze medalists earn $22,500 and $15,000, respectively. Recently, US Paralympic swimmers have begun receiving the same amounts for their medals, marking progress toward equity. However, in other sports, Paralympic athletes may still receive lower financial awards, depending on the resources and sponsorships available to their respective federations.

While both Paralympic and Olympic athletes have access to training facilities, coaching, and sports science support through the USOPC's elite athlete programs, Paralympians often face more limited access to specialized training facilities and coaching tailored to their specific needs. Despite the narrowing financial gap for medals, disparities persist in sponsorship opportunities, media exposure, and the quality of training equipment and support available, which can be more readily accessible to Olympic athletes.

Summary

The International Olympic Committee (IOC) is a cornerstone of global sports governance, responsible for organizing the Olympic Games and promoting Olympism worldwide. Its mission is to foster a spirit of friendship, solidarity, and fair play across nations. However, the IOC faces formidable challenges, including selecting host cities, dealing with corruption scandals, helping athletes develop and maintain mental strength and physical health, and preventing and policing sexual abuse and harassment. Despite these legal and practical issues, the IOC continues to strive for improved transparency and accountability in its operations.

The United States Olympic & Paralympic Committee (USOPC) supports athletes, enforces regulations, and promotes sports development at all levels within the United States. The USOPC faces its own set of demanding challenges, such as managing athletes' well-being and responding to the fluid environment of sports governance. The organization plays a vital role in upholding the integrity of sports and ensuring that American athletes compete fairly on the global stage at the Pan American Games, world championships, and the Olympic Winter and Summer Games.

The World Anti-Doping Agency (WADA) and the United States Anti-Doping Agency (USADA) are crucial in the fight against doping in sports. WADA sets international standards for anti-doping policies and procedures, while USADA enforces these standards within the United States. Both agencies work to ensure that athletes compete on a level playing field, free from the influence of performance-enhancing drugs. Despite their efforts, doping scandals continue to challenge the effectiveness of anti-doping measures, highlighting the need for ongoing vigilance and improvement in education, policing, protecting, and enforcing regulations.

The Court of Arbitration for Sport (CAS) serves as a neutral platform for resolving disputes in the sports world. Its jurisdiction covers a wide range of issues, from doping violations to governance disputes. CAS plays a crucial role in maintaining the credibility and integrity of global sports events by providing a process for resolving conflicts. However, the increasing complexity and volume of cases present ongoing challenges for the CAS.

The chapter also addresses the controversial topic of gender classification in Olympic sports, particularly the participation of transgender and intersex athletes. The IOC's recent updates to its guidelines aim to balance inclusion with fairness, but the debate over competitive advantages and human rights continues. Cases like that of Caster Semenya highlight the ethical and cultural dimensions of this issue, underscoring the need for policies that respect both the rights of athletes and the integrity of competition.

In summary, the intricate network of global sports bodies, including the IOC, USOPC, WADA, USADA, and CAS, plays an indispensable role in upholding the principles of fair play and integrity in sports. Through continuous efforts to improve transparency, accountability, and inclusivity, these bodies strive to create a fair and equitable environment for athletes worldwide.

Discussion Questions

1. What are the primary roles and responsibilities of the International Olympic Committee (IOC) in global sports governance?
2. How do the challenges faced by the IOC, such as corruption scandals and the selection of host cities, impact its mission and effectiveness?
3. In what ways does the United States Olympic & Paralympic Committee (USOPC) support American athletes, and what unique challenges does it face compared to international bodies?
4. Discuss the role of the World Anti-Doping Agency (WADA) and the United States Anti-Doping Agency (USADA) in maintaining fair competition. What are the main challenges these organizations encounter in their anti-doping efforts?
5. How does the Court of Arbitration for Sport (CAS) contribute to resolving disputes in the sports world?
6. Evaluate the effectiveness of the current anti-doping measures enforced by WADA and USADA. What improvements could be made to enhance their impact?
7. Examine the ethical and cultural dimensions of gender classification in sports, particularly concerning transgender and intersex athletes. How should sports' governing bodies balance inclusion and fairness?
8. Do you believe the entire Olympic movement places too much pressure on the need to win at the expense of athletes' well-being?
9. How do global sports bodies like the IOC and national organizations like the USOPC collaborate to uphold the principles of Olympism and fair play?

10. Lance Armstrong famously said: "If you think I cheated to win the Tour de France, they're f-----g dumb. All two hundred guys that started the race broke the rules. We all would have lied. You would have lied." Would you have lied to cover up a win tainted by illegal doping?

5

The Business of Sports
Labor Relations and Antitrust Issues and the Role of Contracts

Chapter Outline

Labor and Antitrust Law in Sports	148
The Role of Contracts	149
Brief History of Professional Sport Leagues	152
Antitrust Law, Labor Law, and Collective Bargaining	156
Impact of the NLRB on Professional Sports	160
The Sports Broadcasting Act of 1961	166
The Americans with Disabilities Act (ADA)	167
Role and Power of the Commissioner in Professional Sports	173
Professional Sports Leagues	178
Summary	182
Discussion Questions	184

Labor and Antitrust Law in Sports

Labor, antitrust, and collective bargaining issues form a dynamic and complicated part of professional team sports in America, creating a fascinating interplay between athletes, management, and legal frameworks. At the core of this relationship lies the tension between antitrust laws, designed to foster competition, and labor laws, which govern the collective bargaining process. Antitrust laws generally prohibit business practices that restrain trade and reduce competition. However, in the realm of professional sports, these laws intersect with labor laws, crafting a unique legal landscape that balances competitive integrity with the rights of athletes to organize collectively.

Professional athletes, organized through unions or players' associations, engage in collective bargaining with team owners and league management to negotiate agreements that cover a wide array of critical issues. These collective bargaining agreements (CBAs) address salaries, working conditions, free agency, revenue sharing, and health and safety protocols. The collective bargaining process is essential for balancing the interests of athletes and management, ensuring fair labor practices, and maintaining labor peace within the leagues. The outcomes of these negotiations are crucial for the stability and functioning of professional sports leagues, as they establish the rules and standards that govern the sport.

Intriguingly, the results of the collective bargaining process enjoy a certain immunity from antitrust scrutiny under the federal labor law exemption, provided they are the product of bona fide collective bargaining. This exemption allows players' associations and league management to negotiate terms that might otherwise be considered anti-competitive, such as salary caps, draft systems, and other mechanisms that limit competition among teams for players. Moreover, the byproduct of good faith contract negotiations is also exempt from antitrust scrutiny under labor law. However, this interplay between labor and antitrust law is not without controversy. It has led to numerous legal battles, strikes, and lockouts over the years, as both sides seek to maximize their interests within the confines of the law. Understanding this complex relationship is essential for comprehending the economic and legal dynamics that shape professional team sports, highlighting the delicate balance achieved through collective bargaining and the legal protections afforded by the labor exemption.

The Role of Contracts

Contracts are the backbone of professional sports, shaping every facet of the industry—from player-team relationships to league-wide media rights, merchandise licensing, and corporate sponsorships. These agreements establish a predictable, enforceable framework that ensures fair treatment, financial security, and the preservation of competitive balance. Within professional leagues, contracts extend beyond just player agreements to encompass a range of business arrangements that make sports one of the most structured and lucrative industries worldwide.

In leagues governed by collective bargaining agreements (CBAs), such as the NFL, NBA, MLB, and NHL, standard player contracts are essential. These contracts create consistency across teams, defining minimum salary, terms of employment, and conditions of performance. For instance, the NFL's standard contract requires players to adhere to rigorous training standards, participate in league and team events, and maintain a high level of fitness. In return, the team provides salary, injury protections, and benefits, such as post-retirement healthcare.

The importance of standard player contracts extends to handling issues like player termination, trade clauses, and grievance procedures. The NFL's standard contract, for example, contains an "injury waiver" that allows teams to release players if they cannot physically perform due to injury. However, CBAs often include protections that limit the scope of these waivers, ensuring fair treatment. NBA contracts include specific clauses on player conduct, specifying fines and suspensions for behaviors detrimental to the league's image, thus safeguarding both financial interests and league reputation.

Endorsement contracts allow players to monetize their public personas by associating with brands. These agreements are mutually beneficial, with athletes gaining revenue and brands increasing their visibility through association with popular sports figures. For example, LeBron James' lifetime endorsement contract with Nike is reportedly worth over

$1 billion, making it one of the most lucrative deals in sports history. Such contracts often include specific clauses that outline exclusivity rights, prohibiting the athlete from promoting competing brands within the same product category.

Sponsorship contracts extend to leagues and teams as well. The NFL's deal with Pepsi as its official beverage sponsor is worth millions annually and grants Pepsi exclusive rights to advertise its products during NFL games and events. Similarly, Formula 1 (F1) teams like Ferrari and Mercedes rely heavily on sponsorship contracts with brands like Shell and Petronas, respectively, to fund team operations. These contracts often feature complex arrangements for brand placement on cars, team uniforms, and digital content, maximizing brand exposure on a global scale.

Broadcasting contracts are among the most lucrative agreements in professional sports, providing leagues and teams with billions in revenue. For example, the NFL's multi-billion-dollar deal with CBS, NBC, and Fox is foundational to the league's financial structure, as it not only funds player salaries and team operations but also determines game schedules and broadcast exclusivity. These contracts often include provisions for digital rights, allowing networks to stream games on platforms like Amazon Prime or Peacock, and expanding viewership.

Similarly, global events like the Olympics and FIFA World Cup generate immense revenue through broadcasting contracts. FIFA's World Cup broadcasting rights are sold years in advance, with networks like Fox in the UnitedStates paying substantial sums for exclusive coverage. Such contracts are critical in international sports, where fan engagement across different time zones and cultures demands a highly organized and profitable media strategy.

Licensing agreements allow businesses to use team logos, player images, and league branding on products, generating substantial revenue for sports organizations. For instance, the NBA's agreement with Nike to produce official jerseys provides a significant income stream for both the league and its players, who receive a share of merchandise sales. Similarly, MLB's licensing deals for team caps, jerseys, and memorabilia extend the reach of the brand, creating a lasting impact on fan loyalty and team revenue.

Athletes with strong individual brands also sign personal licensing deals. Michael Jordan's long-standing partnership with Nike, which created the Air Jordan brand, generated billions and set the standard for personal licensing in sports. These agreements often include royalty clauses, with athletes earning a percentage of each item sold, adding a powerful financial incentive to maintain a positive public image.

As discussed in an earlier chapter, in recent years, name, image, and likeness (NIL) contracts have transformed the sports landscape, especially in college athletics. With the NCAA's decision to allow college athletes to sign NIL agreements, student-athletes can now profit from endorsements, social media promotions, and personal branding. This shift has led to contracts like the one signed by gymnast Olivia Dunne with multiple brands, reportedly worth millions. NIL agreements, though beneficial for athletes, are also complex, with clauses that prevent conflicts of interest with team sponsorships and protect the university's branding.

Contracts for naming rights and venue sponsorships are significant revenue sources for sports organizations. These agreements grant companies the right to name a stadium or arena, ensuring high-profile brand exposure. For example, SoFi Stadium in Los Angeles is named after a financial services company that signed a multi-million-dollar contract with the venue. Similarly, Citi Field, home of the New York Mets, exemplifies how naming rights contribute to both the venue's upkeep and the team's revenue.

In addition to naming rights, venue contracts cover agreements with food and beverage vendors, security services, and entertainment providers. These agreements ensure that venues operate smoothly and enhance fan experience, generating additional revenue through food sales, merchandise, and VIP seating arrangements. Contracts with vendors also include detailed service standards, ensuring consistent quality and service that align with the team's brand.

Many professional leagues expand their brand globally by hosting exhibition games in other countries, often through complex contracts with international venues and sponsors. The NFL's International Series, which includes regular-season games in London and Mexico City, involves agreements with local governments, stadiums, and international broadcasters. These contracts specify revenue-sharing terms, security measures, and logistical details, allowing the NFL to reach global audiences and generate additional revenue streams.

Similarly, NBA teams play exhibition games in cities like Paris, Shanghai, and Tokyo, fostering international fan engagement. These games rely on contracts that secure sponsorships, broadcasting rights, and venue partnerships, showcasing how leagues leverage contracts to expand their brand beyond national borders.

Coaching and staff contracts are crucial for defining the responsibilities and expectations of those guiding and supporting athletes. Coaches often sign multi-year agreements that include performance-based incentives, such as bonuses for reaching playoffs or winning championships.

These contracts also cover termination clauses, outlining compensation if the coach or staff member is fired before the contract term ends. In many sports, these buyout clauses are substantial, ensuring financial security for coaches even if they are released early. Such contracts are often a point of negotiation, as colleges and professional teams aim to attract top coaching talent while managing the financial implications of long-term agreements.

Brief History of Professional Sport Leagues

The development of professional sports in the United States has a rich history, marked by watershed moments, influential figures, and strategic expansions. From the early days of baseball in the mid-nineteenth century to the modern era's multi-billion-dollar sports industry, the evolution of sports leagues and teams reflects broader societal changes and technical advancements. This section explores the origins and growth of major sports leagues and the impact of game-changing figures, leading into players forming unions or player associations and bargaining for better wages and other terms and conditions of meaningful employment.

Baseball, often referred to as America's pastime, has a storied history dating back to the mid-nineteenth century. The National League (NL) was established in 1876, followed by the American League (AL) in 1901. These two leagues formed Major League Baseball (MLB) in 1903 through the National Agreement, creating a structured and competitive environment for professional baseball. The Negro Leagues, formed in 1920 under the leadership of Andrew "Rube" Foster, provided a platform for Black players excluded from MLB due to racial segregation. The integration of baseball began with Jackie Robinson breaking the color barrier playing for the Brooklyn Dodgers. This historic moment not only paved the way for other Black players but also profoundly impacted the civil rights movement.

American football evolved from soccer and rugby, with the first professional game played in 1892. The National Football League (NFL) was established in 1920 as the American Professional Football Association, later adopting its current name in 1922. The NFL faced competition from the American Football League (AFL) in the 1960s, leading to a merger in 1970 that created a unified league with two conferences. Pioneer figures like George Halas, who founded the Chicago Bears, played a pivotal role in the NFL's development. The NFL has since grown into the most popular sport in the United States, with the Super Bowl becoming a major cultural event. The league's expansion, media exposure, and high attendance rates have solidified its dominance in American sports.

Basketball was invented by James Naismith in 1891, and the professional game took off with the formation of the National Basketball League (NBL) in 1898. The Basketball Association of America (BAA) was established in 1946, merging with the NBL in 1949 to form the National Basketball Association (NBA). The NBA grew rapidly in popularity, especially during the 1980s and 1990s and beyond, with stars like Magic Johnson, Larry Bird, and later Michael Jordan followed by LeBron James and Stephen Curry elevating the sport's profile. The Women's National Basketball Association (WNBA) was founded in 1996 as the women's counterpart to the NBA, providing a professional platform for female athletes. The WNBA has faced challenges in attracting a large mainstream audience that is rapidly growing thanks to the entrance of game-changing college players like Caitlin Clark and A'ja Wilson.

Ice hockey's professional roots in the United States date back to the early twentieth century, with the establishment of the International Professional Hockey League in 1904. The National Hockey League (NHL) was founded in 1917 and expanded into the United States in 1924 with the Boston Bruins. The NHL has grown to include thirty-two teams, with significant expansion into nontraditional markets in the Sun Belt. The league's popularity has been bolstered by international competitions and the inclusion of professional players in the Olympics. The NHL is now one of the four major professional sports leagues in the United States, with a strong following especially in regions with cold climates.

Soccer in the United States has seen steady progression, particularly since the 1994 FIFA World Cup, which the country hosted, and the 2026 FIFA World Cup hosted with Canada and Mexico. Major League Soccer (MLS) was founded in 1993 in the aftermath of the demise years earlier of the North American Soccer League (NASL) led by superstars Pele and Salif Keita and began play in 1996 with ten teams. Despite early financial struggles, MLS has expanded to twenty-nine teams and become profitable, thanks to soccer-specific stadiums, the Designated Player Rule often referred to as the Beckham Rule (a regulation in MLS that allows teams to sign up to three players whose total compensation and acquisition costs exceed the league's salary cap), and national TV contracts. The league has the fourth-highest average attendance among major professional sports leagues in the United States and Canada.

Women's professional sports in the United States have a rich history marked by the formation of various teams and leagues. The All-American Girls Professional Baseball League (AAGPBL), established in 1943, was one of the first professional women's sports leagues, providing opportunities for female athletes during the Second World War. The Women's Professional Basketball League (WBL), formed in 1978, was the first professional women's basketball league in the United States, although it only lasted three seasons. The Women's National Basketball Association (WNBA), founded in 1996, has become the premier women's basketball league globally, providing a platform for female athletes to showcase their talents.

In international soccer, the US Women's National Team has played a crucial role in popularizing the sport, achieving multiple World Cup victories and Olympic gold medals, a level of success not matched by the men's team. However, the journey of women's professional soccer leagues in the United States has been marked by ups and downs. The Women's United Soccer Association (WUSA), launched in 2001, was the first professional women's soccer league in the country but folded after three seasons. Its successor, Women's Professional Soccer (WPS), also struggled financially and ceased operations in 2012. Despite these challenges, the National Women's Soccer League (NWSL), established in 2013, has found stability and continues to grow, providing a platform for elite female soccer players in the United States and worldwide.

Several noteworthy figures have left an indelible mark on the development of professional sports in the United States. Jackie Robinson's integration into Major League Baseball (MLB) in 1947 was a groundbreaking moment for both civil rights and sport. His impact on race relations and society's perception of Black athletes cannot be overstated. When Robinson broke Major League Baseball's color barrier, he did more than just integrate a sport; he catalyzed a broader movement toward racial equality in America. Robinson's entry into MLB occurred seven years before the Supreme Court's historic decision in *Brown v. Board of Education*, which declared state laws establishing separate public schools for Black and white students to be unconstitutional.

Robinson's presence on the field challenged the deeply ingrained racial prejudices of the time and demonstrated that talent and determination transcended race. Despite facing racial slurs from fans, threats from opposing players, and even resistance from some teammates, Robinson maintained his composure and excelled on the field. His success—winning the Rookie of the Year award in 1947, the National League MVP in 1949, and leading the Dodgers to six World Series appearances—proved that Black athletes could compete and excel at the highest levels of professional sports. This not only opened doors for other players of color, but also began to shift public opinion, showing that integration could succeed in other areas of American life as well.

Babe Ruth, known as "The Sultan of Swat," revolutionized baseball with his prodigious home run hitting and larger-than-life persona. Playing primarily for the New York Yankees, Ruth's ability to draw crowds and his charismatic personality helped popularize the sport during the 1920s and 1930s. His influence extended beyond the diamond, as he became a national icon and a symbol of the American spirit during the Roaring Twenties. When asked why he made more money than the President of the United States ($100,000 at the time), Ruth famously quipped, "I had a better year." This remark encapsulates his confidence and the immense popularity he enjoyed during his career.

In football, George Halas, one of the founding fathers of the National Football League (NFL), played a crucial role in shaping the league's early years. As a player, coach, and owner of the Chicago Bears, Halas was instrumental in the NFL's growth and development. His contributions to the sport, including innovations in coaching and team management, helped establish the NFL as a major professional sports league in the United States.

Billie Jean King, a tennis legend, has been a tireless advocate for gender equality in sports and the development of women's professional sports.

She fought for equal prize money and co-founded the Women's Tennis Association (WTA) and the Women's Sports Foundation. Her victory in the 1973 "Battle of the Sexes" match against Bobby Riggs was an instrumental moment that showcased the prowess of female athletes. Annika Sörenstam, one of the greatest female golfers, broke barriers by competing in a PGA Tour event in 2003, showcasing her skill and determination. Lorena Ochoa, from Mexico, was another exceptional golfer. She was the world number one ranked female golfer for 158 consecutive weeks. Their successes have inspired countless young girls and women athletes and helped elevate the profile of their respective sporting endeavors.

Antitrust Law, Labor Law, and Collective Bargaining

Antitrust laws, such as the Sherman Act, enacted by the federal government are designed to promote competition and prevent monopolistic practices. These laws aim to protect consumers and ensure a competitive market by prohibiting activities that restrain trade or create unfair monopolies. In most industries, antitrust scrutiny ensures that no single entity can dominate a market to the detriment of competition and consumer choice.

The Sherman Antitrust Act, passed in 1890, is the cornerstone of antitrust legislation in the United States. It prohibits any contract, combination, or conspiracy that unreasonably restrains interstate and foreign trade. The Act also makes it illegal to monopolize, or attempt to monopolize, any part of trade or commerce. Violations of the Sherman Act can result in severe penalties, including fines and imprisonment for individuals and substantial fines for corporations.

In the context of sports, the Sherman Act has been applied to various professional leagues to prevent anti-competitive practices. For example, the Supreme Court's decision in *American Needle, Inc. v. National Football League,* described further within this chapter, clarified that NFL teams are separate economic actors and thus subject to antitrust laws when they collectively license their intellectual property.

The Clayton Act, enacted in 1914, builds on the Sherman Act by addressing specific practices that could lead to anti-competitive behavior. It prohibits mergers and acquisitions that may substantially lessen competition or tend to create a monopoly. The Act also allows private parties to sue for triple damages when they have been harmed by conduct that violates either the Sherman Act or the Clayton Act. In sports, the Clayton Act has been used to challenge mergers and acquisitions that could reduce competition. For instance, the Federal Trade Commission (FTC) and the Department of Justice (DOJ) scrutinize mergers between sports teams or media companies that hold broadcasting rights to ensure they do not create monopolistic entities.

Collusion among league owners and price fixing are obvious concerns in the sports industry. Collusion occurs when team owners or league officials conspire to set prices, wages, or other competitive terms, thereby restricting competition. Price fixing involves an agreement among competitors to raise, lower, or stabilize prices or competitive terms. The Sherman Act explicitly prohibits such collusive behavior. For example, the NFL has faced lawsuits alleging that its teams colluded to suppress player salaries and restrict free agency, which would be a violation of antitrust laws. Similarly, Major League Baseball (MLB) has been accused of colluding to fix minor league player wages below minimum wage standards.

The Norris-LaGuardia Act of 1932, another federal antitrust legislation, specifically limits the power of courts to issue injunctions against nonviolent labor disputes, fostering an environment where collective bargaining could thrive. This legislative framework allowed players' unions to negotiate terms without fear of antitrust repercussions, provided the outcomes were a product of good faith negotiations.

Unionization and Collective Bargaining in Professional Sports

Professional athletes began to unionize primarily in response to the restrictive and often exploitative practices of team owners and league management. These efforts were driven by the need to address issues such as less than market value compensation, inability to move freely to another team, and lack of job security. Here are some examples from various sports:

The Major League Baseball Players Association (MLBPA) was formed in 1953, but it gained significant power under the leadership of Marvin Miller in the 1960s. Players were frustrated with the reserve clause, which bound them to their teams indefinitely and severely restricted their earning potential and mobility. The MLBPA negotiated the first collective bargaining agreement (CBA) in professional sports in 1968, which included increases in the minimum salary and the establishment of a formal grievance procedure. The MLBPA's efforts culminated in the Curt Flood Act of 1998, which partially removed baseball's antitrust exemption concerning labor relations, allowing players to challenge MLB practices under antitrust laws. This exemption originated from the *Baltimore Federal Baseball* Supreme Court case, where baseball was granted immunity because the sport was not viewed as interstate commerce.

The NFL Players Association (NFLPA) was established in 1956 by players from the Green Bay Packers and Cleveland Browns. The union was formed in response to the brutal and short careers of NFL players, who lacked adequate pensions and healthcare. The NFLPA achieved significant victories, including free agency rights and better pension benefits, through collective bargaining. The landmark case *Mackey v. NFL* (1976) struck down the NFL's "Rozelle Rule," which required a team signing a free agent to compensate the player's former team, as a restraint of trade in violation of antitrust laws.

The National Basketball Players Association (NBPA), founded in 1954 by renowned Boston Celtics player Bob Cousy, became the first trade union in the major North American sports leagues. Initially, players threatened to skip the All-Star game to gain recognition for their union and secure a series of raises. The NBPA has successfully negotiated numerous CBAs, addressing issues like salary caps, player mobility, and health benefits. The average NBA salary has seen a dramatic increase from $8,000 before the union's formation to more than $9 million per year, with star players like Jason Tatum earning $60 million annually.

In the late 1950s, NHL players began to attempt to form a union after injuries left star players broke and others working side jobs. League officials and team owners resisted these efforts, often trading, cutting, or demoting players involved in unionization. However, by 1967, players united in sufficient numbers to convince owners to recognize the NHLPA and stop punishing players for being members. The NHLPA has since negotiated CBAs that have improved player salaries, benefits, and working conditions.

Recent legal battles have challenged the NCAA's long-held amateurism principle, with cases addressing name, image, and likeness (NIL) deals and athlete compensation restrictions. For instance, a US appeals court ruled that college athletes in Division I revenue-generating sports, such as football and basketball, might qualify as employees under labor laws. This decision challenges the NCAA's long-standing argument that these athletes are amateurs and not entitled to worker protections. The Third US Circuit Court of Appeals denied the NCAA's attempt to dismiss a lawsuit filed by former Villanova football player and other athletes. The lawsuit argues that athletes should be covered by the Fair Labor Standards Act (FLSA), which mandates minimum wage and overtime pay. The court criticized the term "student-athlete" as a marketing tool by the NCAA and stated it shouldn't define the athletes' economic relationship with their schools. The ruling allows athletes who perform services for their schools and receive compensation to seek labor protections.

The decision could lead to some athletes in high-profile sports at wealthy schools gaining minimum wage and other benefits. The NCAA argues that treating athletes as employees could harm various sports programs, particularly women's sports, Olympic sports, and smaller schools' teams, along with raising serious violations of Title IX concerns. The NCAA continues to lobby Congress to prevent athletes from being classified as employees, fearing it would make sports programs unsustainable.

The National Labor Relations Act and NLRB Certification

The National Labor Relations Act (NLRA) of 1935, also known as the Wagner Act, provided the legal foundation for collective bargaining in the United States. It established the National Labor Relations Board (NLRB) to oversee the process of unionization and certify unions as the official representatives of employees.

The NLRB, established by the NLRA, plays a crucial role in the unionization process. It is responsible for overseeing union elections, investigating unfair labor practices, and ensuring that employees can exercise their rights to organize and bargain collectively. The NLRB certification process involves several steps:

1. **Union Campaign**: Athletes interested in forming a union begin by organizing a campaign to gather support from their peers.
2. **Petition for Election**: Once sufficient interest is demonstrated, the union files a petition with the NLRB to hold a representation election.
3. **Election**: The NLRB conducts an election where athletes vote on whether to unionize. A majority vote in favor is required for certification.
4. **Certification**: If the vote passes, the NLRB certifies the union, granting it the right to negotiate on behalf of the players as their bargaining agent.

Athletes sought to unionize for several reasons:

- **Fair Compensation**: To negotiate better salaries and benefits collectively, rather than individually, in response to increased game attendance and media exposure revenue benefiting management.
- **Working Conditions**: To improve health and safety standards, including medical care and injury prevention, especially as they relate to concussion protocols and mental health concerns.
- **Job Security**: To address issues like the reserve clause in baseball, which restricted player movement and free agency, in the absence of this clause, players will have more mobility to change teams and increase their market value.

Impact of the NLRB on Professional Sports

The NLRB has played a significant role in resolving disputes between management and players' unions or associations in various professional sports. By intervening in strikes and securing settlements, the NLRB helps maintain a balance of power between players and management, ensuring that collective bargaining processes are respected and that players are treated fairly. These actions not only resolve immediate conflicts but also set important precedents for future labor relations in professional sports.

Here are some key examples:

The NLRB was instrumental in ending the 1995 Major League Baseball strike. The strike, which began in August 1994, led to the cancellation of the World Series for the first time in ninety years. The NLRB secured an injunction under Section 10(j) of the *National Labor Relations Act* (NLRA), requiring baseball club owners to withdraw their unilaterally imposed changes to the wage-setting system. This intervention by the NLRB, with the injunction issued by then-U.S. District Court Judge Sonia Sotomayor, was crucial in bringing the strike to an end and resuming the baseball season.

During the 1987 NFL players' strike, the NLRB played a critical role in securing a $30 million back pay settlement in 1994. The central charge by the National Football League Players Association (NFLPA) was that the teams had unlawfully refused to allow the 1,300 returning striking players to participate in the games immediately following the end of the strike. The NLRB's intervention ensured that the players were compensated for the games they were barred from playing, addressing the unfair labor practices by the NFL teams.

The NLRB has also sought temporary Section 10(j) injunctions against regional soccer and hockey leagues for engaging in unfair labor practices that undermined bargaining with unions representing players. These injunctions are used to prevent ongoing unfair labor practices while the case is being litigated, ensuring that the bargaining process is not compromised and that players' rights are protected during negotiations.

Key Cases and Legislative Acts

Federal Baseball Club of Baltimore v. National League of Professional Baseball Clubs (1922)

In the landmark case of *Federal Baseball Club of Baltimore v. National League of Professional Baseball Clubs*, the US Supreme Court addressed the applicability of antitrust laws to professional baseball. The controversy began when the Federal League, a competitor to the established National and American Leagues, collapsed, prompting the Baltimore Terrapins, a former Federal League team, to sue the National League. They alleged that the National League had violated the Sherman Antitrust Act by conspiring to monopolize the business of baseball. In a decisive ruling written by Justice Oliver Wendell Holmes, the Supreme Court concluded that baseball games were not interstate commerce and therefore not subject to federal antitrust laws. Holmes reasoned that baseball was merely a series of local exhibitions and did not constitute a business engaged in commerce across state lines. Despite widespread criticism and the evident interstate nature of professional baseball, this decision set a precedent by establishing baseball as an exception to antitrust laws, a precedent that has remarkably endured over the years.

Flood v. Kuhn (1972)

The Supreme Court revisited the issue of baseball's antitrust exemption in the 1972 case of *Flood v. Kuhn*. Curt Flood, a star outfielder, challenged Major League Baseball's reserve clause, which bound players to their teams indefinitely, arguing that it violated antitrust laws by restricting his ability to negotiate with other teams. However, the Supreme Court upheld its earlier decision in *Federal Baseball*, citing the principle of stare decisis, which emphasizes the importance of adhering to precedent. The Court acknowledged that the original reasoning might have been flawed, but it maintained the exemption due to baseball's long-standing reliance on the precedent. This decision underscored the unique legal status of baseball in American jurisprudence, affirming its antitrust exemption despite the Court's recognition of the exemption's contentious basis. The ruling highlighted the tension between legal consistency and evolving interpretations of justice, illustrating how deeply ingrained practices in sports law can persist despite evolving societal and legal standards. Flood's case brought significant attention to players' rights and the restrictive nature of the reserve clause, ultimately contributing to the gradual evolution of free agency in professional baseball.

The Curt Flood Act (1998)

In response to the issues highlighted by the *Flood* case, the Curt Flood Act was enacted in 1998. This legislation partially removed baseball's antitrust exemption, specifically allowing players to challenge Major League

Baseball practices under antitrust laws concerning employment terms. The Act was a significant step in addressing player grievances but maintained substantial portions of the original exemption, particularly regarding franchise relocation and broadcast rights. This selective application of antitrust laws continued to reflect the unique legal landscape in which professional baseball operates.

McNally v. United States (2006)

In *McNally v. United States*, the court examined the arbitration procedures used in Major League Baseball. Players argued that these procedures restricted their ability to negotiate freely. The court, however, upheld the arbitration system, emphasizing that it was part of the collective bargaining agreement negotiated in good faith between players and owners. This decision affirmed the legitimacy of arbitration within the context of baseball's labor relations, underscoring its role as a valid and essential method for resolving disputes. The ruling highlighted the importance of adhering to agreed-upon procedures within collective bargaining agreements, thereby reinforcing the stability and predictability of labor relations in professional sports. The case serves as a pivotal reference for the acceptance and enforcement of arbitration as a means to manage conflicts and maintain harmony between players and team management.

Mackey v. National Football League (1976)

The *Mackey* case, centered on the National Football League's "Rozelle Rule," addressed the requirement that a team signing a free agent had to compensate the player's former team. This rule often hindered player movement and was seen as a significant obstacle to free agency. The court ruled that the "Rozelle Rule" constituted a restraint of trade, violating antitrust laws, as it effectively limited the players' ability to freely negotiate with new teams. This decision underscored that even collectively bargained agreements must comply with antitrust laws if they unduly restrict competition. The ruling marked a pivotal moment in the legal oversight of professional sports leagues, emphasizing that the rights of players to move freely between teams could not be unreasonably constrained by league rules. This case paved the way for greater player mobility and highlighted the need for sports leagues to balance their operational rules with the broader principles of fair competition enshrined in antitrust law.

Smith v. Pro-Football, Inc. (1978)

In *Smith v. Pro-Football, Inc.*, the court examined the NFL draft system, where players contended it violated antitrust laws. This pivotal case arose when John Mackey, a professional football player, argued that the NFL's draft, combined with other restrictive practices like the "Rozelle Rule," unreasonably restrained trade and restricted players' freedom to contract. The Rozelle Rule required a team signing a free agent to provide compensation to the player's former team, effectively limiting player mobility. The court acknowledged the antitrust implications but ultimately ruled that the draft was a reasonable method to maintain competitive balance within the league. It emphasized that while the draft system did impose some restrictions on player movement, it was essential for ensuring parity among teams, which benefited the overall competitive nature of the league. This decision underscored the necessity for courts to strike a delicate balance between allowing league rules that promote competition and ensuring they do not excessively restrain individual players' rights. The case reinforced the legal framework within which sports leagues operate, highlighting the intersection of antitrust principles and the unique nature of professional sports leagues.

Powell v. National Football League (1989)

The *Powell v. National Football League* case, decided in 1989, centered on the NFL's ability to maintain its non-statutory labor exemption from antitrust laws even after a collective bargaining agreement (CBA) had expired. This landmark decision had profound implications for labor relations in professional sports. The dispute arose when the NFL Players Association (NFLPA) challenged the league's continued imposition of player contract terms after the expiration of the CBA. The NFL had been imposing terms related to player movement and salaries, which the NFLPA argued violated antitrust laws. The central legal question was whether the NFL's actions were protected under the non-statutory labor exemption, which shields certain union-related activities from antitrust scrutiny.

The Eighth Circuit Court of Appeals ruled that the non-statutory labor exemption continued to apply even after the expiration of the CBA, as long as the parties were still negotiating or the terms were related to the collective bargaining process. This ruling allowed the NFL to continue imposing terms from the expired agreement, significantly impacting the balance of power in negotiations. It gave the league considerable leverage over players, who could no longer use antitrust law to challenge the terms.

The decision influenced the strategies of both leagues and players' unions in future collective bargaining negotiations, as both sides had to consider the implications of the non-statutory labor exemption on their negotiating positions. The case set a precedent for how courts interpret the non-statutory labor exemption in the context of professional sports, providing a reference point for subsequent legal challenges and negotiations.

American Needle Inc. v. National Football League (2010)

In *American Needle Inc. v. National Football League*, the US Supreme Court ruled that the NFL's collective licensing agreements were subject to antitrust scrutiny. The decision determined that the NFL was not a single entity but a collection of thirty-two independent businesses, each capable of competing in the marketplace. This ruling had profound implications for how antitrust laws apply to the operations of professional sports leagues, emphasizing the need for careful legal examination of their business practices. An interesting facet of this case is how it highlights the struggle of a small apparel company, American Needle, in battling the giants of the sports industry. American Needle, which had been producing headwear for NFL teams for decades, found itself shut out when the NFL granted an exclusive license to Reebok. The Supreme Court's decision allowed American Needle to challenge this exclusive deal, marking a significant win for smaller companies fighting for fair competition in a market dominated by large corporations. This case underscored the importance of antitrust laws in preserving competitive markets, ensuring that even smaller entities have a chance to thrive against powerful conglomerates.

The Sports Broadcasting Act of 1961

Before the Sports Broadcasting Act, professional sports leagues faced antitrust challenges with their collective broadcasting agreements. A federal court had ruled that the NFL's collective television contract violated antitrust laws, which threatened the ability of leagues to negotiate national television contracts. This posed a risk to the financial stability and growth of professional sports.

To address these issues, the Sports Broadcasting Act of 1961 was enacted. The Act allowed professional sports leagues to pool their broadcasting rights and sell them as a package to television networks without violating antitrust laws. This exemption applied to the NFL, MLB, the NBA, and the NHL.

The Act had several important impacts on professional team sports:

1. **Financial Stability and Revenue Sharing**: Leagues could negotiate lucrative national television contracts, generating significant revenue for all teams, not just the most popular ones. This revenue sharing helped maintain competitive balance by providing financial stability to smaller-market teams.
2. **Growth of Television Broadcasts**: Collective bargaining for broadcast rights led to more games being televised, enhancing the visibility and popularity of professional team sports nationwide.
3. **Enhanced Negotiating Power**: Leagues gained greater negotiating power with television networks, securing better deals with more favorable terms and higher payments for broadcasting their games.
4. **Impact on Local and Regional Broadcasting**: Although the Act primarily addressed national contracts, it also influenced local and regional broadcasting. Teams and leagues developed regional sports networks, increasing their revenue streams.
5. **Innovations in Broadcasting**: The financial stability provided by the Act allowed leagues to invest in broadcasting innovations, such as instant replay, enhanced camera angles, and the development of dedicated sports channels like ESPN.
6. **Antitrust Considerations and Limitations**: The Act specifically exempted pooled broadcasting agreements from antitrust laws but

did not extend this exemption to other aspects of league operations. Leagues could collectively negotiate broadcast rights but were still subject to antitrust scrutiny in other business practices.

The Sports Broadcasting Act of 1961 played a crucial role in shaping the modern scope and environment of professional sports broadcasting. By allowing leagues to collectively negotiate television contracts, the Act ensured financial stability for professional team sports, promoted competitive balance, and facilitated the widespread availability of sports broadcasts. This legislative intervention helped transform professional sports into a major industry deeply integrated with American culture and media.

The Americans with Disabilities Act (ADA)

The Americans with Disabilities Act (ADA) of 1990 is a landmark civil rights law that bans discrimination based on disability. While it primarily aims to protect individuals with disabilities in public spaces and workplaces, its implications extend to professional sports. The ADA ensures that professional athletes with disabilities receive reasonable accommodations, enabling them to compete on an equal footing.

A notable case highlighting the ADA's impact on professional sports is *PGA Tour, Inc. v. Martin* (2001). In this case, the Supreme Court ruled that the PGA Tour must allow golfer Casey Martin, who had a degenerative leg condition, to use a golf cart during tournaments. This decision underscored the ADA's applicability to professional sports, ensuring that athletes with disabilities are not unfairly excluded from competition.

Professional sports stadiums and arenas must also comply with ADA requirements to accommodate fans with disabilities. This includes providing accessible seating, restrooms, concession stands, and parking. For example, modern stadiums like AT&T Stadium in Arlington, Texas, and Levi's Stadium in Santa Clara, California, are designed with extensive ADA-compliant features, such as wheelchair-accessible seating areas, elevators, ramps, and assistive listening devices for the hearing impaired.

Concussion Protocol

Concerns over health and safety among professional football players have been mounting for years, particularly regarding the long-term effects of repetitive head trauma. The groundbreaking film *Concussion* brought these issues into the public eye. The film focused on Dr. Bennet Omalu, a Nigerian-American forensic pathologist who discovered Chronic Traumatic Encephalopathy (CTE). Dr. Omalu's research underscored the severe impacts of repeated head injuries in football and played a crucial role in raising awareness about the dangers of CTE. Despite this, the NFL faced significant criticism for burying or refusing to acknowledge the mounting evidence about the dangers of concussions. For years, the league downplayed the risks, often dismissing external research that contradicted their stance. It wasn't until Dr. Omalu's findings, coupled with increasing public scrutiny and pressure from the medical community, that the NFL began to take meaningful action. This shift led to the implementation of stricter concussion protocols and a broader acceptance of the need for comprehensive player safety measures. The league's delayed response highlighted the importance of independent research and advocacy in driving change within powerful organizations resistant to confronting uncomfortable truths.

The legal battle against the NFL, known as the NFL Concussion Settlement, was filed in federal court in the United States District Court for the Eastern District of Pennsylvania. This class-action lawsuit, settled in 2015, established a fund to provide monetary awards to former players suffering from various neurological conditions, including CTE. The settlement, with payouts expected to exceed $1.4 billion, aimed to compensate for the long-term impacts of brain injuries sustained during their careers.

The implications of the NFL concussion litigation have been extensive, influencing health and safety protocols across various levels of sports. In professional sports, the case set a precedent for other leagues like the NHL and FIFA, which have also faced scrutiny and legal challenges over their handling of player head injuries. The increased awareness of concussion risks has led to significant policy changes at the collegiate and high school levels. The NCAA, for instance, has implemented stricter concussion protocols, and numerous states have enacted laws to improve concussion management and prevention in youth sports.

Additionally, the case spurred significant increases in research funding and studies focused on understanding and mitigating the effects of head injuries. Institutions like the Concussion Legacy Foundation and various universities have intensified their efforts to study CTE and develop better protective measures for athletes. The litigation also highlighted the potential for using antitrust laws to protect individual rights. Players and stakeholders have leveraged antitrust arguments to challenge sports organizations that fail to address health and safety concerns adequately. This legal approach has opened the door for further lawsuits aimed at enforcing higher standards and protections across sports.

Key Components of CBAs

CBAs cover a wide array of critical issues, including:

Basic Athlete Benefits: Health benefits, safety standards, and pension security are fundamental components of CBAs. These provisions ensure that athletes receive adequate medical care during and after their careers and have financial security upon retirement. For example, the NFL CBA includes comprehensive health insurance for players and their families, annual physical exams, and extended health coverage post-retirement. The MLB CBA mandates that clubs provide the best medical care and facilities, and the NBA CBA includes mental health and wellness programs, emphasizing holistic athlete care.

Wages and Hours: Collective Bargaining Agreements (CBAs) establish salary structures, minimum salaries, and working hours. For example, the MLB CBA includes provisions for salary arbitration and minimum salary increases, providing a structured approach to player compensation. The NBA CBA sets salary caps and defines maximum and minimum player salaries, implementing a "soft" salary cap that allows teams to exceed the cap to retain their own players, but with penalties for exceeding certain thresholds. This system aims to maintain competitive balance while accommodating the financial capabilities of different teams. Defined revenue in this context refers to the total income generated by the league, including ticket sales, broadcasting rights, and merchandise. The NFL employs a "hard" salary cap, which strictly limits the total amount teams can spend on player salaries based on a percentage of the league's revenue. This approach enforces a more uniform spending structure across all teams, promoting parity within the league. In contrast, MLB does not have a salary cap but uses a luxury tax system. Teams that exceed a specified payroll threshold must pay a tax to the league, which discourages excessive spending and encourages competitive balance. Salary caps are determined based on a percentage of the league's defined revenue. For instance, the NFL's salary cap is calculated by dividing the players' share of revenue by the number of teams, ensuring each team has an equal spending limit. The NBA's salary cap is similarly tied to the league's revenue but includes mechanisms like the "Bird rights" exception, allowing teams to exceed the cap to re-sign their own players. The NHL also uses a hard salary cap, with the cap amount set annually based on the league's revenue from the previous season. Luxury taxes are additional financial penalties imposed on teams that exceed certain payroll thresholds. In the NBA, the luxury tax threshold is set above the salary cap, and teams that exceed this threshold must pay escalating penalties based on how much they overspend. The MLB's luxury tax system imposes a tax rate that increases with the amount by which a team exceeds the payroll threshold, with the collected tax used for player benefits and other league-wide initiatives. Each league's approach to salary caps and spending limits reflects its unique economic structure and competitive philosophy. The NHL uses a hard salary cap similar to the NFL, aiming for financial stability and competitive balance by preventing wealthy teams from outspending smaller-market teams. The NBA's soft cap allows for more flexibility, fostering team loyalty and player retention while still imposing financial discipline through luxury tax penalties. In soccer, different leagues and governing bodies implement varying financial regulations, such as UEFA's Financial Fair Play (FFP) regulations, which aim to prevent clubs from spending beyond their means and encourage financial sustainability.

Injury Protection: CBAs include clauses for injury protection, ensuring that players receive compensation and medical care for injuries sustained during their careers. This includes protocols for concussion management and other health-related issues. For example, the NFL has specific protocols for diagnosing and managing concussions, including mandatory baseline testing and return-to-play guidelines. The NHL's CBA also includes provisions for long-term disability benefits and rehabilitation services for players with career-ending injuries.

Revenue Sharing: Revenue-sharing agreements are crucial for maintaining competitive balance within leagues. These agreements dictate how league revenues are distributed among teams and players. For instance, the NFL's revenue-sharing model ensures that all teams receive a portion of the league's national broadcasting and sponsorship deals, promoting financial parity. The MLB's revenue-sharing plan involves distributing a percentage of each team's local revenues to a central fund, which is then redistributed to support lower-revenue teams.

Draft and Free Agency: CBAs outline the rules for player drafts and free agency, including eligibility criteria and compensation for teams losing free agents. The NFL and NBA have specific draft systems that allocate new talent to teams, while free agency rules allow players to negotiate contracts with new teams after a certain period. The reserve clause, historically used to bind players to their teams, has been replaced by free agency rules allowing players to move between teams after fulfilling certain contract conditions, exemplified by the Curt Flood case leading to modern free agency in MLB. The NHL's draft system is designed to distribute young talent equitably among teams, while its free agency rules allow players to seek new opportunities once they have accrued a certain number of professional seasons.

Social Media and Publicity Rights: Modern CBAs address the use of social media and players' publicity rights, ensuring that athletes can leverage their personal brands while protecting the league's interests. For instance, the NBA's CBA includes provisions that allow players to engage in social media activities but with guidelines to prevent conflicts of interest or actions detrimental to the league's image. The NFL's CBA also includes clauses that protect players' rights to monetize their name, image, and likeness through endorsements and social media platforms.

Training Camps and Termination: CBAs define the terms for training camps, including schedules and compensation, and outline the procedures for contract termination and player discipline. The NFL's CBA, for example, specifies the duration and structure of training camps, including mandatory rest periods and limits on full-contact practices to reduce the risk of injuries. The NHL's CBA includes detailed procedures for handling contract disputes, grievances, and disciplinary actions, ensuring a fair process for all parties involved.

Mental Health Protections: Due to a rise in athlete suicides and mental health issues, recent agreements emphasize access to mental health professionals, confidential counseling, and comprehensive mental health programs. The NBA's CBA, for instance, includes provisions for mental health screenings, education, and support services for players and their families. The NFL's CBA has also introduced mental health initiatives, including mandatory mental wellness training for players, coaches, and staff.

Political Activities: Political activities by players, such as Colin Kaepernick's protests during the national anthem and the widespread support for Black Lives Matter, have led to CBAs incorporating clauses that protect players' rights to engage in political activism, ensuring they can express their views without facing retribution from team owners or the league. The NBA's CBA explicitly supports players' rights to speak out on social and political issues, while the NFL's CBA includes guidelines that balance players' freedom of expression with the league's desire to maintain a unified image.

The negotiation process for CBAs involves extensive discussions between players' unions and league management, often becoming contentious as both sides seek to maximize their interests. Negotiations can lead to lockouts or strikes if an agreement cannot be reached. For example, the 2011 NFL lockout and the 2011 NBA lockout were both the result of failed negotiations over revenue sharing, salary caps, and player benefits. When a CBA expires, unions can strike, exemplified by the 1994 MLB strike, while team owners can lock out players, seen in the 2011 NBA lockout. Once a CBA is in place, strikes and lockouts are prohibited.

Mandatory and permissive subjects in collective bargaining represent two distinct categories that significantly influence negotiations between employers and employees. **Mandatory subjects** are essential issues that both parties are legally required to negotiate in good faith. These topics include core aspects of the employment relationship, such as wages, hours, and employment conditions. For example, in the sports industry, this encompasses salary caps, health standards, player safety protocols, and grievance procedures. Negotiating these issues is crucial for maintaining equitable labor relations and ensuring that both parties' fundamental needs and concerns are addressed.

In contrast, **permissive subjects** are optional topics that parties may choose to negotiate but are not legally obligated to discuss. These subjects typically relate to less critical aspects of the employment relationship and can include matters such as the type of playing surface in stadiums, rules regarding player conduct outside of official activities, and promotional activities. While these topics may still hold significant importance for either party, their negotiability depends on mutual agreement and discretion. The distinction between mandatory and permissive subjects ensures a structured and fair system governing the relationship between athletes and team owners. By clearly delineating these categories, both parties can focus their negotiations on essential matters that affect the core of their working relationship, thereby promoting a stable and competitive environment in professional sports. Understanding these components is vital for fostering productive and balanced labor negotiations, ultimately contributing to the overall health and success of the industry.

Role and Power of the Commissioner in Professional Sports

The role of the commissioner in professional sports is pivotal, encompassing a broad range of responsibilities and powers that are often enshrined in the league's constitution, bylaws, and CBAs. The commissioner is typically hired by the team owners and is responsible for maintaining the integrity of the sport, overseeing league operations, and enforcing disciplinary measures. This role was first prominently established in MLB with the appointment of Kenesaw Mountain Landis in 1920, following the Black Sox Scandal, to restore public trust in the game. Landis used his authority to ban eight players for fixing the World Series.

The commissioner's authority includes the ability to discipline players for conduct deemed detrimental to the sport. This power is often justified under the broad mandate to act in the "best interests" of the game, a principle that has been upheld and expanded over the years. For instance, the MLB commissioner can investigate and impose penalties for actions that harm the sport's integrity, including suspensions and fines. Similarly, the NFL commissioner has significant disciplinary powers under the league's CBA and Personal Conduct Policy, allowing for the imposition of sanctions and the oversight of appeals. A notable initiative led by the NFL commissioner is the implementation of the Rooney Rule, which requires teams to interview minority candidates for head coaching and senior football operation positions. This rule has been influential, with other leagues adopting similar measures to promote diversity.

Despite the extensive powers of commissioners, players' unions have frequently pushed back against what they perceive as overreach or lack of due process. One notable example is the NFL Players Association's (NFLPA) response to the disciplinary actions taken by NFL Commissioner Roger Goodell. The NFLPA has often contested Goodell's dual role in imposing and adjudicating penalties, arguing that it undermines impartiality and fairness. A prominent case illustrating this tension is the "Deflategate" scandal involving Tom Brady. In 2015, Brady was suspended for four games by Goodell for his alleged involvement in deflating footballs to gain a competitive advantage. Brady and the NFLPA challenged the suspension, arguing that the process violated his due process rights. Although the suspension was initially overturned by a federal judge, it was later reinstated by an appellate court, highlighting the contentious nature of the commissioner's disciplinary powers and the ongoing struggle for fair treatment.

The issue of due process in the context of commissioner-imposed discipline is a recurring theme in professional sports. Players and their unions have argued that the current systems often lack adequate protection and impartiality. For instance, a study by the University of Texas highlighted several ways in which major sports leagues might violate players' due process rights, such as the exclusion of certain players from arbitration processes and the lack of transparent procedures for handling off-field misconduct. To address these concerns, some have proposed reforms to ensure fairer disciplinary processes. These include the introduction of impartial arbitration panels to hear appeals, rather than allowing the commissioner to oversee appeals of their own decisions. This approach aims to provide a more balanced and just system, protecting the rights of players while maintaining the integrity of the sport.

Several high-profile incidents have underscored the complexities and controversies surrounding the commissioner's disciplinary powers. Beyond "Deflategate," other notable examples include:

Gambling and Drug Use: Players caught gambling or using illegal drugs have often faced severe penalties from commissioners. For example, MLB's lifetime ban on Pete Rose for gambling on baseball games remains one of the most significant disciplinary actions in sports history. Similarly, commissioners in other major professional sports leagues in the United States have acted unilaterally to enforce strict penalties for such violations.

In the NFL, Commissioner Roger Goodell has imposed substantial penalties for gambling and substance abuse violations. Recently, several NFL players, including Calvin Ridley, faced suspensions for betting on NFL games, underscoring the league's zero-tolerance policy. Similarly, Goodell has handed down lengthy suspensions for violations of the league's substance abuse policy, such as the indefinite suspension of Josh Gordon, who struggled with repeated violations over several seasons.

The NBA has also seen its commissioner take decisive actions. In 2006, then-NBA Commissioner David Stern banned Chris Andersen for two years for violating the league's anti-drug policy. This move demonstrated the league's firm stance against drug abuse and its commitment to maintaining a drug-free environment, while recognizing the need for education and counseling for those players who come forward voluntarily.

In the realm of tennis, while not overseen by a single commissioner, the sport's governing bodies have similarly enforced stringent penalties. The International Tennis Federation (ITF) imposed a two-year suspension on Martina Hingis in 2007 after she tested positive for cocaine, highlighting the global commitment to upholding the sport's integrity.

Soccer, under the governance of FIFA, has witnessed significant disciplinary actions as well. Diego Maradona's fifteen-month ban for cocaine use in 1991 was a landmark decision, reinforcing the organization's strict anti-drug policies.

Moreover, Major League Baseball (MLB) has seen commissioners act decisively beyond the Pete Rose case. In 2013, MLB Commissioner Bud Selig suspended Alex Rodriguez for the entire 2014 season due to his involvement in the Biogenesis scandal (often compared to the BALCO scandal), which implicated several players in the use of performance-enhancing drugs. The BALCO scandal itself had far-reaching consequences, with numerous high-profile athletes, including Barry Bonds, being linked to the Bay Area Laboratory Co-operative. This scandal led to a massive fallout, including Congressional investigations and hearings where athletes were subpoenaed to testify about their involvement with performance-enhancing drugs. The intense scrutiny culminated in the Mitchell Report, an extensive document released in December 2007 by former Senator George Mitchell, detailing the widespread use of steroids and other performance-enhancing substances in baseball. The report named eighty-nine MLB players, providing evidence of their drug use and highlighting the failure of the MLB's drug prevention policies at the time. The revelations from BALCO and the subsequent investigations profoundly impacted the sport, leading to stricter drug testing policies and significant changes in how MLB handled doping allegations, setting a precedent for future cases like that of Alex Rodriguez.

Domestic Violence and Off-Field Conduct: The handling of domestic violence cases in the NFL has been a flashpoint issue, particularly highlighted by the Ray Rice incident. In 2014, a video surfaced showing Ray Rice, then a running back for the Baltimore Ravens, assaulting his fiancée in an elevator. Initially, NFL Commissioner Roger Goodell suspended Rice for two games, a decision that was widely criticized as too lenient given the severity of the incident.

The backlash was swift and intense. Critics accused Goodell and the NFL of not taking domestic violence seriously enough, arguing that the league's disciplinary measures were insufficient and inconsistent. The public outcry led to widespread discussions about the NFL's policies and their enforcement.

In response to the criticism, the NFL revised its domestic violence policy, implementing stricter penalties for players involved in such incidents. The new policy mandated a six-game suspension without pay for a first offense and a lifetime ban for a second offense, though there would be opportunities for reinstatement. Additionally, the NFL committed to increasing transparency in its disciplinary processes and to providing better support for victims.

Performance-Enhancing Drugs: The use of performance-enhancing drugs (PEDs) has been a persistent issue in professional sports, leading to numerous suspensions and significant controversies. Major League Baseball (MLB), in particular as also described above, has had to navigate the complexities of PED use, balancing the need for strict enforcement with the rights of players to fair hearings and appeals. Recent developments in collective bargaining agreements (CBAs) across various sports leagues have introduced new measures focusing on education, counseling, and revised testing protocols to address these challenges more effectively.

MLB has a long history of dealing with PEDs, with policies evolving over the years to become more stringent. The current penalties for PED violations in MLB are severe, with an eighty-game suspension for a first offense, 162 games for a second offense, and a permanent suspension for a third offense. These measures are intended to deter players from using banned substances and maintain the integrity of the sport. Recent changes to MLB's Joint Drug Agreement (JDA) reflect a nuanced approach to PEDs. For instance, MLB has adjusted the thresholds for certain banned substances like Nandrolone and Clenbuterol to account for potential contamination and inadvertent ingestion. Additionally, there have been discussions about setting minimum thresholds for long-term metabolites of substances like Dehydrochlormethyltestosterone (DHCMT), commonly known as Oral Turinabol, to prevent false positives and ensure fair treatment of players. These changes aim to balance strict enforcement with fairness and due process.

The NFL has also made significant strides in its approach to PEDs. Under the NFL's Performance Enhancing Substances (PES) policy, players are subject to random testing throughout the year, with specific testing protocols during the offseason and training camp. The NFL Players Association (NFLPA) has been actively involved in negotiating these policies to ensure they are fair and transparent. Recent updates to the NFL's CBA have emphasized the importance of education and counseling for players who test positive for PEDs. Players are now provided with resources to understand the substances they are being tested for and the potential consequences of a positive test. This educational approach is designed to prevent PED use through awareness and support, rather than solely relying on punitive measures.

The NBA has taken a progressive stance on certain substances, particularly cannabis. Under the new CBA effective from July 1, 2023, cannabis has been removed from the banned substances list, and players are now allowed to invest in companies that sell CBD or marijuana. This change reflects a broader societal shift toward the acceptance of cannabis and acknowledges its limited performance-enhancing effects. However, the NBA continues to enforce strict policies against traditional PEDs. Players who test positive for such substances are subject to suspension and mandatory counseling programs. The league's focus on education and rehabilitation aims to support players in making informed decisions about their health and performance.

The NHL has implemented a drug policy that includes random testing for PEDs and significant penalties for violations. The league's approach is aligned with the standards set by the World Anti-Doping Agency (WADA), which regularly updates its prohibited list to include new substances and methods that could enhance performance unfairly. The NHL's policy emphasizes both deterrence and education, providing players with the information they need to comply with anti-doping regulations.

The role of the commissioner in professional sports is both powerful and controversial. While commissioners are tasked with upholding the integrity of their respective sports, their broad disciplinary powers often lead to conflicts with players and their unions. Ensuring due process and fairness in disciplinary actions remains a critical challenge, necessitating ongoing dialogue and potential reforms to balance the interests of all stakeholders involved.

Professional Sports Leagues

Professional sports leagues are typically organized around a franchise system, where individual teams are owned by separate entities but operate under the league's governance. This system was first introduced in baseball with the formation of the National League in 1876 and has since been adopted by other major North American sports leagues, including the NFL, NBA, NHL, and MLS. Each franchise has territorial rights, which usually cover major metropolitan areas to avoid local competition. New teams can only join the league through a vote by existing members, often involving a substantial expansion fee. Leagues operate within a closed membership system, meaning teams do not face relegation or promotion based on their performance. This structure ensures the stability and continuity of the teams within the league. For instance, the NHL's Montreal Canadiens are the only team that existed before joining the NHL; all others were created as expansion teams or through mergers. This model contrasts with European sports leagues, which often use a promotion and relegation system.

Ownership of franchises in these leagues is typically restricted to individuals or groups who pass rigorous vetting processes. Potential owners must demonstrate financial stability, a commitment to the sport, and sometimes a connection to the local community. The board of directors or other existing owners often vote on new owners. It's possible to own franchises in different leagues simultaneously, as seen with owners like Stan Kroenke, who owns teams in the NFL, NBA, NHL, and MLS.

The value of franchises has soared in recent decades, driven by lucrative broadcasting rights, sponsorship deals, and the overall commercial appeal of sports. The most valuable franchises, such as the Dallas Cowboys in the NFL estimated to be worth over $10 billion, purchased for $140 million in 1989, and the New York Yankees in MLB worth about $8 billion, after being purchased for $8.8 million in 1973, according to Sportico. This significant increase in franchise values has attracted investment from hedge funds and private equity firms, which seek to capitalize on the robust and growing revenue streams associated with professional sports.

Historically, sports franchises were often family-owned and operated, reflecting more local and community-focused ownership structures. However, the modern landscape has shifted toward more corporate and investor-driven ownership models, focusing on maximizing profitability and leveraging brand value. This transition has led to greater commercialization and a more business-oriented approach to running sports teams, impacting everything from team operations to fan engagement strategies.

Broadcasting rights are a significant revenue source for sports leagues. For instance, the NBA recently secured an eleven-year media rights deal worth $77 billion, which includes partnerships with ESPN, ABC, NBC, and Amazon Prime. This deal not only boosts the league's revenue but also ensures that player salaries will increase in line with the revenue growth. Similarly, the NFL generates substantial income from its broadcasting deals, contributing to its overall revenue of over $20 billion annually. The English Premier League (EPL) also exemplifies the value of broadcasting rights, having secured an excess of $12 billion deal for domestic and international rights for one year of broadcasting. These deals emphasize how critical broadcasting rights are to the financial health and competitive balance of leagues. In addition to traditional broadcasting, sports leagues are increasingly leveraging social media and streaming platforms to reach wider audiences. Platforms like Twitch and social media sites have become popular for broadcasting games and engaging with fans, although the financial conversion of social media followers into revenue remains a challenge. For example, the NFL's partnership with Amazon to stream "Thursday Night Football" on Prime Video highlights the shift toward digital platforms. This shift reflects the changing consumption habits of sports fans, particularly among younger demographics, who prefer to consume content on-demand and interactively.

Expanding a sports league involves significant financial and logistical considerations. Expansion fees have risen dramatically in recent years, with MLS's latest expansion team, Charlotte FC, paying $325 million to join the league. Similarly, the NHL's recent expansion team, the Seattle Kraken, paid a $650 million expansion fee, illustrating the escalating costs associated with league expansion. The NFL, which last expanded in 2002 with the Houston Texans, now considers expansion costs that could reach several billion dollars, particularly if expanding internationally. The NBA is also contemplating expansion, with cities like Seattle and Las Vegas frequently mentioned as potential candidates, highlighting the lucrative nature of expanding a major sports league.

The relocation of franchises can also be contentious. For example, the NFL's St. Louis Rams relocated to Los Angeles in 2016, becoming the Los Angeles Rams. This move was driven by financial incentives, including a new stadium in Inglewood, California, which is part of a $5 billion sports and entertainment complex. Similarly, the Oakland Raiders relocated to Las Vegas, becoming the Las Vegas Raiders, and moved into Allegiant Stadium. These moves often lead to legal battles, protests from fans, and significant economic impacts on the cities involved. The relocation of the Cleveland Browns to Baltimore in 1995 to become the Ravens is another example, highlighting the complexities and emotional stakes of franchise relocations. In this case, a settlement allowed the Browns' legacy to remain in Cleveland, while the team personnel moved to Baltimore. Another example is the NHL's Quebec Nordiques moving to Colorado to become the Avalanche in 1995, causing a significant emotional and economic impact on the Quebec City fan base but resulting in financial success in Colorado. These relocations reflect the intricate balance between financial opportunities and community loyalty.

Revenue Streams

Professional sports leagues have continuously explored new revenue streams, adapting to changing market dynamics and technological advancements. Beyond traditional sources like ticket sales, broadcasting rights, and merchandise, leagues and teams have diversified their revenue models to include innovative and creative avenues.

Sponsorship deals have become increasingly lucrative, with companies eager to associate their brands with popular sports teams and events. For instance, the NFL has partnerships with major corporations like Pepsi, Nike, and Microsoft, which contribute substantial revenue. The NBA also benefits from significant sponsorship deals, including a landmark agreement with Nike to produce official uniforms. Naming rights for stadiums and arenas are another major revenue source. Deals like the $400 million agreement for SoFi Stadium and the $400 million deal for Citi Field exemplify the high value of these partnerships.

The NBA's Jersey Patch Program, introduced in 2017, has become a significant revenue stream. This program allows companies to place their logos on the jerseys of NBA teams, offering them prime visibility during games and broadcasts. Initially met with skepticism, the program now brings in over $250 million annually, comprising nearly 15 percent of the NBA's overall sponsorship revenue. Teams like the Utah Jazz and Charlotte Hornets have leveraged these patches to foster connections with local and younger audiences, respectively. The integration of technology, such as QR codes on jerseys, further enhances fan engagement and offers innovative marketing opportunities.

The legalization of sports betting in many US states has opened up new revenue streams for professional sports leagues. Partnerships with sports betting companies like DraftKings and FanDuel generate millions in ad revenue and sponsorship deals. The NFL, for example, has embraced this shift, with teams and the league itself benefiting financially from these partnerships. This marks a significant change from the past when professional sports leagues avoided any association with gambling.

The rise of social media and streaming platforms has transformed how sports content is consumed and monetized. Leagues and teams now use platforms like Twitch, YouTube, and Instagram to reach global audiences, particularly younger demographics. These platforms offer new advertising opportunities and direct-to-consumer revenue models, such as subscription services and pay-per-view events. The NBA, for instance, has seen substantial engagement and revenue growth through its digital presence.

Podcasts have emerged as another potential revenue source. Athletes and teams have launched popular podcasts, generating income through sponsorships, advertisements, and listener subscriptions. For example, the "All the Smoke" podcast, hosted by former NBA players Matt Barnes and Stephen Jackson, has garnered a large following and attracts high-profile guests, creating significant revenue opportunities.

Licensing deals allow businesses to use team logos and athlete likenesses on their products, generating royalty fees for the teams. This extends the sports brand beyond the game and provides a continuous income stream. Merchandise sales, including apparel, accessories, and memorabilia, remain a vital revenue source, with teams constantly innovating to keep products appealing to fans.

Teams that own and operate their venues can generate additional revenue by hosting non-sporting events such as concerts, conferences, and other entertainment activities. For example, the Los Angeles Kings benefit from operating the Crypto.com Arena, which hosts a variety of high-profile events, including the Grammy Awards and the 2028 Summer Olympics.

Interactive media has become an exciting frontier for fan engagement and revenue. Augmented reality (AR) and virtual reality (VR) experiences allow fans to interact with their favorite teams and players in immersive ways, creating new sponsorship and advertising opportunities. For instance, the NBA has experimented with VR broadcasts of games, offering a unique viewing experience that fans can pay to access. Additionally, interactive fan experiences, such as live Q&A sessions with players or virtual meet-and-greets, can be monetized through platforms like Cameo or custom-built team apps.

Professional sports leagues' exploration of these diverse and innovative revenue streams demonstrates their adaptability and commitment to maximizing financial potential while enhancing fan engagement and experience.

Summary

The chapter on the business aspects of professional sports and collective bargaining delivers a comprehensive overview of the complex interplay between antitrust and labor law issues, key legal cases, the role of the league commissioner, the franchise system, contentious issues, and the various revenue streams in professional sports. It begins by discussing the organizational structure of sports leagues, highlighting the franchise model where individual teams operate under league governance. This model ensures stability and continuity within the league, allowing for a controlled and strategic approach to expansion and operations. The chapter emphasizes the oversized role of the league commissioner, who oversees operations, enforces rules, negotiates broadcasting and sponsorship deals, and represents the league in various capacities. The commissioner's role is invaluable in maintaining the integrity and financial health of the league.

The chapter reviews the leading legal cases that have shaped the sports landscape, such as *Federal Baseball Club of Baltimore v. National League*, *Flood v. Kuhn*, and *PGA Tour, Inc. v. Martin*. These cases illustrate the application of antitrust laws and the Americans with Disabilities Act (ADA) in professional sports. For instance, the *Federal Baseball* case established baseball's exemption from antitrust laws, a precedent that still impacts the sport today. *Flood v. Kuhn* reaffirmed this exemption despite acknowledging its flawed basis, while *PGA Tour, Inc. v. Martin* highlighted the ADA's role in ensuring that athletes and fans with disabilities receive reasonable accommodation.

Collective bargaining agreements (CBAs) are explored in depth, highlighting their vital role in determining revenue sharing, salary caps, player transfers, health benefits, and other essential aspects of player-management relations. The negotiation of CBAs can lead to disputes, resulting in lockouts or strikes, as seen in the NFL and NBA. These agreements are decisive in maintaining a balance between the interests of players and management, ensuring fair compensation and working conditions for athletes.

The chapter also examines the impact of broadcasting rights, sponsorship deals, and new revenue streams on the financial health of sports leagues. Broadcasting rights, such as the NBA's $76 billion media rights deal, generate substantial income and ensure that player salaries increase in line with revenue growth. Sponsorship deals with major corporations contribute significantly to league revenues, while the rise of social media and streaming platforms provides new avenues for engaging with fans and generating income.

Contentious issues such as franchise expansion and relocation are addressed, submitting examples like the relocation of the St. Louis Rams to Los Angeles and the Oakland Raiders to Las Vegas. These moves often involve substantial financial considerations, legal battles, and emotional impacts on fans and local communities. The complexities and stakes involved in these decisions are highlighted, showcasing how they affect the league's dynamics and financial health.

Through this multifaceted examination, the chapter underscores the knotty legal and business frameworks that sustain the professional sports industry. It supplies a thorough understanding of how legal rulings, collective bargaining, revenue generation, and management practices interact to shape the modern world of professional sports. This comprehensive approach offers valuable insights into the challenges and opportunities faced by leagues, teams, and players in the ever-advancing sports business environment.

Discussion Questions

1. How does the franchise model contribute to the stability and continuity of professional sports leagues?
2. What is the role of the league commissioner in professional sports, and how does it impact the overall functioning and financial health of a league?
3. Examine the impact of the *Federal Baseball Club of Baltimore v. National League* case on the application of antitrust laws in professional sports. How has this precedent affected other sports beyond baseball?
4. Discuss the significance of the *Flood v. Kuhn* case in reaffirming baseball's antitrust exemption. Why did the Supreme Court decide to uphold this exemption despite acknowledging its flawed basis?
5. Analyze the implications of the *PGA Tour, Inc. v. Martin* case for the application of the Americans with Disabilities Act (ADA) in professional sports. How does this case illustrate the challenges and opportunities for athletes with disabilities?
6. How do collective bargaining agreements (CBAs) shape the relationship between players and management in professional sports? Discuss the key elements of CBAs and their impact on revenue sharing, salary caps, and player rights.
7. What are the economic and emotional stakes involved in franchise relocation? Discuss the examples of the St. Louis Rams moving to Los Angeles and the Oakland Raiders moving to Las Vegas.

What factors drive these decisions, and how do they affect local communities and fan bases?

8. Evaluate the role of broadcasting rights and sponsorship deals in the financial health of professional sports leagues. How do these revenue streams impact player salaries and league operations? Provide specific examples from recent deals.

9. How have social media and streaming platforms changed the way sports are consumed and monetized? Discuss the opportunities and challenges these new media present for sports leagues and teams.

10. What are the primary legal and business challenges facing professional sports leagues today? How can leagues balance the need for financial stability, competitive balance, and player rights in an increasingly complex and globalized sports industry?

6

Power Brokers

The Role of Agents in Sports Law

Chapter Outline

History, Evolution, and Influence	187
Modern Day Agents	189
Pressure Cooker Field	191
Contract Negotiations	194
Agent Certification Process and Legal Relationship	195
State and Federal Regulation	199
Fiduciary Duties and Responsibilities of a Sports Agent	200
Financial Mismanagement and Conflicts in Sports	205
NIL Rights and Digital Transformation	207
Summary	210
Discussion Questions	211

History, Evolution, and Influence

The use of professional representatives or sports agents to negotiate contracts for professional athletes and entertainers is now commonplace. It has not always been this way. Historians point to the American entrepreneur Charles Pyle as one of the first sports agents. In the 1920s, this Chicago-based theater owner negotiated the first professional sports contract. His client, "Red" Grange, was a star running back for the University of Illinois when he elected to turn professional. Pyle convinced George Halas, owner of the Chicago Bears, to guarantee Grange up to $3,000 per game plus a share of the gate. Grange, who is considered one of the most talented running backs in the history of football, brought prominence and legitimacy to a league that was struggling for public recognition and acceptance. Pyle also is credited with starting the first professional tennis tour. The flamboyant French tennis player Suzanne Lenglen was the world's original female celebrity-athlete when Pyle signed her to a $50,000 contract to tour the United States and play against the leading female tennis players. Her decision to turn professional was widely criticized by the tennis establishment, including the All-England Club at Wimbledon, which revoked her honorary membership even after she had won six single championships.

By the 1960s and 1970s, as professional sports teams gained in popularity, streams of revenue increased, and players became cultural icons, players' unions were recognized by the NLRB and leagues gained a greater role in collectively negotiating higher salaries and better benefits. However, the need for individual player representation in the form of player agents rose as salaries increased, and outside endorsement and sponsorship income opportunities improved. Athletes who were now generating more revenue required expert tax, investment, and financial advice. Notwithstanding the early success of Charles "Cash and Carry" Pyle, most team owners and managers refused to negotiate with player agents.

A poignant example of this animosity is illustrated by an experience of Michael Jones, your author and a former player agent. Jones once represented a basketball player drafted by the Boston Celtics. The coach and general manager of the Celtics at the time was the legendary Red Auerbach, well-known for his dislike of agents. Jones had sent Coach Auerbach a letter informing him of his representation of this player and at his convenience, they could begin contract negotiations. However, Auerbach repeatedly contacted the player directly, inviting him to the Boston Garden to show him around the facility. In his office, Auerbach would push a player's contract in front of the player and tell him to sign.

Following Jones' advice, the player politely informed Coach Auerbach that he needed to consult with his agent, Jones, but could discuss basketball training. Despite multiple attempts by Auerbach to get the player to sign the contract, the player stood firm. After several such encounters and persistent reminders from Jones about the rules regarding contract discussions, Auerbach sent Jones a terse note: "If I wanted to talk basketball contracts with you, then I would have drafted you, not your player."

This story symbolizes the resistance between player agents and club negotiators during that era. It underscores the challenging dynamics faced by agents striving to protect and advance their clients' interests amid an environment where many team owners and managers were unwilling to acknowledge their role.

Modern Day Agents

One notable example of the financial impact of player agents during this time is the landmark contract negotiated by Bob Woolf for Larry Bird. Woolf secured a five-year, $5 million contract for Bird with the Boston Celtics in 1979, making Bird the highest-paid rookie in NBA history at that time. This deal set a precedent for future negotiations, highlighting the role agents played in elevating athletes' financial status.

Years before negotiating Bird's NBA contract, Woolf represented Boston Red Sox pitcher Earl Wilson. Wilson came to Woolf after a car accident, seeking legal advice. Woolf ended up serving as his player agent, marking the beginning of his career in sports representation. Woolf's success with Wilson and other athletes underscored the growing importance of professional agents in securing lucrative deals and managing athletes' careers and served as a model for other prospective agents.

The evolution of sports agencies from single-firm operations like Bob Woolf's foray into the field to multifaceted organizations has dramatically transformed the sports management landscape. This journey began with Mark McCormack, widely regarded as one of the pioneers of modern sports management. In 1960, McCormack founded International Management Group (IMG), starting by representing two golfers, Arnold Palmer and Gary Player. The early successes of Palmer and Player, followed by the addition of Jack Nicklaus to his roster, established McCormack as a leading sports agent. These iconic figures in golf, coupled with McCormack's innovative approach to sports marketing, set the stage for the expansion of sports management and marketing. McCormack's vision was to create a full-service agency capable of handling all aspects of an athlete's career, including contract negotiation, endorsements, and media appearances, which revolutionized the industry.

Following McCormack's groundbreaking work, the industry saw significant expansion and diversification. Founded in 1975, Creative Artists Agency (CAA) quickly ventured into sports management, representing a wide array of athletes across various sports, including Dwyane Wade, Cristiano Ronaldo, and Aaron Rodgers. CAA is particularly known for securing lucrative endorsement deals, such as Cristiano Ronaldo's lifetime deal with Nike, valued at over $1 billion.

Wasserman, founded by Casey Wasserman, has grown to become one of the largest sports agencies globally. The agency represents top-tier athletes like Russell Westbrook, Anthony Davis, and Klay Thompson. Wasserman's comprehensive approach includes marketing, endorsements, and media rights, exemplified by the $85 million deal they secured for Russell Westbrook with the NBA's Oklahoma City Thunder.

Octagon, established in 1983, represents a diverse range of athletes, including Olympians. One of its most notable clients is Michael Phelps, the most decorated Olympian of all time. Octagon managed Phelps' endorsements and media appearances, dramatically boosting his income through deals with companies like Speedo, Under Armour, and Visa, contributing to his estimated net worth of $80 million.

Excel Sports Management, founded by Jeff Schwartz, has also risen to prominence in the sports agency world. The agency represents high-profile clients like Tiger Woods, Kevin Love, and Kris Bryant. Tiger Woods' endorsement deals, including his once relationship with Nike, have made him one of the highest-paid athletes in the world.

IMG has expanded and diversified its services beyond athlete management. IMG represents a wide range of athletes, including tennis stars Maria Sharapova and Serena Williams. The agency's strategy includes managing sports careers, producing sports events, and managing media rights.

A testament to IMG's continued influence in sports management is its partnership with The All-England Lawn Tennis Club (AELTC). Together, they recently announced a long-term extension of their exclusive media rights and commercial representation partnership for The Championships,

Wimbledon. IMG has been working with the club for more than fifty years, helping to maximize engagement, reach, and revenues for the world-famous Grand Slam through international media rights management and sales, including a media relationship with ESPN, which was renewed through 2035. Additionally, the AELTC and IMG have established an expanding portfolio of official partnerships with leading brands around the world, such as a new multi-year deal with Barclays to become the Official Banking Partner of The Championships.

Finally, the influence of sports agents in shaping iconic deals and careers is exemplified in the story of David Falk and his role in Michael Jordan's groundbreaking deal with Nike, as depicted in the film *Air*. In the film, Falk, depicted as Michael Jordan's agent, plays a pivotal role in the incredible licensing contract that revolutionized sports marketing and athlete endorsements. The narrative follows Nike's ambitious move into the basketball shoe market, then dominated by Asics, Puma, and Converse. Led by Sonny Vaccaro and Nike co-founder Phil Knight, the company sought to make a bold entrance by signing the up-and-coming NBA rookie, Michael Jordan. The film highlights Falk's challenging negotiations with Nike, recognizing the potential for a groundbreaking deal that could influence both Jordan's career and Nike's market position. Falk envisioned not just a contract but a brand built around Jordan's talent and charisma.

The signing of Jordan by Nike was both imaginative and transformative, largely thanks to his sports agent's efforts. Nike offered a $2.5 million, five-year contract with 25 percent royalties on all shoes sold with Jordan's likeness, an unprecedented deal at the time. This equity push, driven by Falk's negotiation skills, set new standards for athlete endorsements and reshaped sports marketing. His representation of Jordan and innovative approach to athlete endorsements left a lasting impact on the industry, illustrating the trailblazing role agents play in shaping iconic deals and careers.

Pressure Cooker Field

The world of sports agencies is a pressure cooker of ambition and deal-making. Aspiring agents jostle for position, all vying to represent the next generation of athletic superstars. This fierce competition is fueled by the immense potential rewards. Landing a top athlete can translate to significant wealth for the agent. Commissions on multi-million-dollar contracts, typically ranging from 4 to 10 percent capped by the various players' associations, can quickly add up. Add to that a slice (10–20 percent) of endorsement deals negotiated on behalf of the athlete, and the financial stakes become clear. Imagine securing a record-breaking contract for your client, a deal that guarantees them financial security for years to come. That's the kind of life-changing impact a successful sports agent can have.

The job of a sports agent extends far beyond basic contract negotiations with teams; they are multifaceted strategists adept at traversing the complex world of professional sports. Leveraging their extensive networks, which are critical to their success, sports agents cultivate relationships with team owners, coaches, and corporate sponsors over the years. They handle media attention and distractions, manage athletes' branding, and understand the impact of both positive and negative publicity, using it to their clients' advantage. Effective sports agents not only negotiate contracts but also craft and maintain their clients' public image, ensuring their brand remains strong and marketable in the ever-evolving landscape of professional sports.

Sports agents are not merely cheerleaders for their clients; the best are shrewd negotiators with deep knowledge of contract law, collective bargaining agreements, licensing and endorsement opportunities, social media management, financial planning, and even artificial intelligence (AI). This expertise allows them to analyze the intricacies of every contract clause, ensuring their clients receive the best possible terms and conditions. They possess the financial wizardry to skillfully negotiate deals that include signing bonuses, performance incentives, and lucrative brand partnerships, demonstrating their role in their clients' careers.

While a law degree can be a valuable asset, it's not the sole passport to success. The field welcomes individuals from various backgrounds, including business, marketing, finance, taxation, social media, data analytics, and sports management. As long as they meet the certification requirements set by players' associations, they have a shot at the big leagues of client representation. This diversity brings a wealth of perspectives and skill sets to the table, further enriching and energizing the field.

To ensure fair representation and protect athletes' interests, there's a regulatory layer in place. In major professional sports like the NFL, NBA, MLB, MLS, NHL, and WNBA, agents must be certified sub-agents of the respective players' associations for these leagues. This certification process includes background checks, exams, and adherence to strict ethical codes that will be described further within this chapter.

The sheer number of agents compared to athletes underscores the intensity of competition. Take the NBA, where over 400 registered NBPA agents fight over a pool of just 450 active players. The odds are stacked against aspiring agents, highlighting the need for a strategic approach and a standout track record. Similarly, in the NFL, where roughly 800 certified contract advisors compete for around 1,700 active players, the fight for representation is fierce.

Legends like Scott Boras, known for securing record-breaking contracts for MLB stars like Gerrit Cole and Bryce Harper, exemplify the impact a top agent can have. Boras's approach is meticulously analytical, often using comprehensive data to justify record-setting deals for his clients, while remaining in constant communication with his clients literally on a day-to-day basis. This method has earned him billions in contracts for his players, making him one of the most influential figures in baseball.

Rich Paul, founder of Klutch Sports Group and the man behind LeBron James and Anthony Davis's deals, showcases the importance of strategic negotiation and a stellar reputation in the industry. His client-first approach and keen understanding of market dynamics have allowed him to negotiate some of the most lucrative deals in NBA history. These high-profile agents pave the way for the next generation, demonstrating the power of expertise, networking, and a relentless drive to succeed.

The field of sports agency is fiercely competitive, with agents striving to represent elite talent and secure lucrative contracts. This intense rivalry has given rise to prominent figures like Leigh Steinberg, while also exposing the challenging and often harsh realities of the profession. During his fifty-year plus career, Steinberg has represented over 300 professional athletes in football, baseball, basketball, boxing, and Olympic sports. He has represented the No. 1 overall pick in the NFL draft a record eight times. Steinberg is often credited as the real-life inspiration for the sports agent in Cameron Crowe's film *Jerry Maguire* in 1996, where the fictional NFL player Rod Tidwell famously screamed at his agent played by Tom Cruise: "Show me the money!" Steinberg has successfully negotiated over $3 billion in contracts for athletes including Troy Aikman, Steve Young, Tom Brady, Lennox Lewis, and Oscar de la Hoya. Steinberg's success, however, was tempered by an addiction that resulted in bankruptcy and the loss of his license to practice law and represent athletes. However, after addressing his addiction and sharing his story publicly, Steinberg made a remarkable comeback representing top-tier NFL talents like Patrick Mahomes.

Contract Negotiations

A contract is a legally binding agreement between two or more parties, outlining the terms and conditions of their relationship and obligations. In the context of sports, contracts are crucial as they define the financial and professional terms under which athletes operate. These contracts are formed through a process of negotiation, where the sports agent represents the athlete's interests, ensuring that the terms are favorable and legally sound. This process involves several key elements: offer, acceptance, consideration, lawful purpose, and meeting of the minds.

The formation of a contract begins with an offer, where one party proposes specific terms to the other. For example, a sports team might offer an athlete drafted out of college a contract outlining salary, duration, and performance bonuses. Acceptance occurs when the athlete, through their agent, agrees to the terms without modification. If any terms are changed, it becomes a counteroffer, which must then be accepted by the other party.

Consideration refers to the value exchanged between the parties. In a sports contract, consideration is often monetary compensation for the athlete's services. Both parties must provide something of value for the contract to be binding; the athlete provides their skills and performance, while the team offers financial compensation and other benefits.

The purpose of the contract must be legal, meaning it cannot involve illegal activities such as performance-enhancing drugs. All terms must comply with relevant laws and regulations, including league rules and collective bargaining agreements.

Meeting of the minds ensures that both parties have a mutual understanding and agreement on the terms. It involves clear communication and documentation of all contract details. Any ambiguities can lead to disputes, so it is crucial that all terms are explicitly agreed upon and understood by both the athlete and the team.

Sports agents negotiate various types of contracts, each with unique considerations. Player contracts specify the terms of the athlete's engagement with a team, including salary, duration, performance incentives, and conditions for termination. For example, a player's contract, which follows the union's mandatory standard player's contract, might include clauses for injury protection, bonuses for achieving specific performance metrics, and options for contract renewal.

Endorsement deals involve athletes promoting brands or products. An endorsement contract might require an athlete to wear specific apparel, participate in advertising campaigns, make public appearances, or engage with fans on social media. Such arrangements can favorably enhance an athlete's income and public profile. A notable example is LeBron James' endorsement contract with Nike, which has not only provided immense financial rewards but also bolstered his global brand presence.

Many endorsement relationships include a morality clause, which allows the sponsoring company to terminate the contract if the athlete engages in conduct that could damage the brand's reputation. For instance, Tiger Woods faced significant consequences after his personal scandals, leading to the termination of several endorsement deals. Similarly, Lance Armstrong's doping scandal resulted in the loss of numerous sponsorships, severely impacting his financial standing and public image. These morality clauses ensure that athletes maintain a standard of behavior that aligns with the brand's values, protecting the company's interests.

Media agreements involve athletes in various media ventures, such as television appearances, film roles, or participation in digital content. These agreements can boost an athlete's visibility and earning potential. For instance, Simone Biles' media deals include endorsements and appearances that extend her influence beyond gymnastics, showcasing her as a talented and trustworthy public figure.

Agent Certification Process and Legal Relationship

Once the National Labor Relations Board (NLRB) recognizes a player's association or union as the official collective bargaining agent for players in a league, that union is recognized as the exclusive bargaining representative. Ideally, a players' union negotiates for stronger rights, free agency, pension plans, injury protection, and higher salaries for its players. In practice, leading sports agents have been strong advocates for unionization and play a primary role in individual contract negotiations. Today, typical sports collective bargaining agreements (CBAs) recognize the right of players to negotiate contracts with the assistance of their own agents. In essence, unions delegate their exclusive authority to negotiate individual player agreements to agents.

However, each player's association has established specific rules and regulations for the certification of sports agents or contract advisors, as the NFLPA refers to them, before they are authorized to negotiate. Legally, sports agents are sub-agents of players' associations, meaning individual players can select agents to represent them in negotiating compensation packages within the league's collective bargaining framework. Complaints from athletes about agents mismanaging funds, inducing them to accept gratuities jeopardizing college eligibility, or other misconduct have led to stricter regulations by players' associations to protect players.

Certification Procedures

National Football League Players Association (NFLPA):

- **Application Fee:** Non-refundable fee of $2,500.
- **Educational Background:** An undergraduate and postgraduate degree (Master's or Law) from an accredited institution, or at least seven years of sufficient negotiating experience as an alternative.
- **Background Check:** Authorization for a thorough background investigation, including education, professional certificates, work experience, civil and criminal history, financial matters, and social media review.
- **Virtual Seminar:** Mandatory attendance at a two to three-day virtual seminar, followed by an additional day for the administration of the exam.
- **Examination:** Successful completion of a sixty-question, multiple-choice, computer-based exam covering the CBA, salary cap, NFL

player benefits, NFLPA regulations, and policies on substances of abuse and performance-enhancing substances.
- **Professional Liability Insurance:** Requirement to obtain professional liability insurance from an approved carrier annually.
- **Annual Fee:** Payment of an annual fee and attendance at one of three NFLPA seminars held each year.
- **Contract Negotiation:** Requirement to negotiate at least one player contract within a three-year period (excluding practice squad contracts).

National Basketball Players Association (NBPA):
- **Application Fee:** Non-refundable fee of $2,500.
- **Educational Background:** A degree from an accredited four-year college or university. Relevant negotiating experience may substitute for formal education.
- **Background Check:** Completion of a background investigation.
- **Examination:** Passing a written exam administered by the NBPA, focusing on key provisions of the CBA, NBPA regulations, and other relevant matters. Educational resources are provided, but there are no official practice exams.
- **Agent Seminar:** Attendance at one of three agent seminars offered toward the end of the current season for the first three years of certification, typically held in Los Angeles, Chicago, and New York City.
- **Annual Dues:** Payment of annual dues by July 1 each year, with the amount varying based on the number of players represented (ranging from $2,500 to $7,500).
- **Compliance:** Continued compliance with NBPA regulations, including attending seminars and paying annual dues.

Major League Baseball Players Association (MLBPA):
- **Application Fee:** Varies based on representation type.
- **Educational Background:** A college degree and significant professional experience.

- **Background Check:** Mandatory background check.
- **Examination:** Passing a written exam on the CBA and MLBPA regulations.
- **Professional Liability Insurance:** Required.
- **Annual Seminar:** Mandatory attendance at MLBPA seminars.
- **Contract Negotiation:** Demonstrated experience in negotiating player contracts.

National Hockey League Players Association (NHLPA):

- **Application Fee:** Set fee for agent certification.
- **Educational Background:** Relevant educational qualifications and experience.
- **Background Check:** Required.
- **Examination:** Must pass an exam on the CBA and NHLPA regulations.
- **Seminars:** Participation in NHLPA seminars.
- **Contract Negotiation:** Proven negotiation experience.

FIFA and US Soccer

Not long ago, FIFA changed its licensing system, requiring US Soccer to implement a licensing process for player agents. Licensure, similar to certification, requires:

- **Indemnity Insurance:** Agents must obtain indemnity insurance.
- **Examination:** Passing an exam.
- **Contractual Agreement:** Agents must have a written contract with the player.
- **Reputation:** Agents must have an impeccable reputation.
- **FIFA Regulations:** Compliance with FIFA regulations, including a ban on having direct relationships with FIFA.

These rigorous certification processes ensure agents are well-qualified and adhere to high ethical standards, safeguarding athletes and maintaining the integrity of the representation process.

State and Federal Regulation

Beginning in the early 1980s, states with prominent college athletic programs began to regulate sports agents to protect their interests. California, a state known for its prestigious academic institutions such as UCLA, USC, Cal-Berkeley, Stanford, and San Diego State, pioneered this regulatory movement by enacting the first statute requiring non-lawyer agents to comply with stringent measures. These included mandatory registration with the state, payment of a licensing fee, posting a surety bond, filing a fee schedule, maintaining detailed accounting records, and agreeing to arbitrate any disputes with players. The primary objective of these statutes was to safeguard colleges from losing their elite athletes before their eligibility expired and to prevent the forfeiture of wins due to NCAA bylaw violations, which could occur if ineligible players participated in games.

To ensure a more uniform regulation of sports agents across various states, the National Conference on Uniform State Laws and the NCAA advocated for the adoption of the Uniform Athlete Agents Act (UAAA). The UAAA, now adopted by over forty states and the District of Columbia, establishes civil and criminal penalties for agents who engage in impermissible conduct, such as failing to inform student-athletes about the potential loss of amateur eligibility when signing an agency contract. Additionally, the UAAA empowers schools to sue agents for financial losses incurred due to NCAA penalties, should ineligible student-athletes be found participating in games. Despite the UAAA's comprehensive provisions, the enforcement of civil penalties and criminal indictments under the act remains infrequent. Nevertheless, states like Florida, Louisiana, and Texas have taken action against agents for non-compliance, such as failing to register or not promptly notifying the school's athletic director after engaging with student-athletes regarding representation.

On the federal level, regulation of sports agents was significantly enhanced in 2004 when President George W. Bush signed the *Sports Agent Responsibility and Trust Act* (SPARTA) into law. SPARTA's provisions closely align with those of the UAAA, aiming to protect student-athletes from exploitation and misconduct by agents. The act mandates that agents conspicuously notify student-athletes about the potential loss of eligibility when signing an agency agreement, prohibits illegal inducements, and requires both the agent and the student-athlete to inform the athletic director upon signing the agreement. The Federal Trade Commission (FTC) oversees compliance with SPARTA, focusing on key areas such as disclosure, truthfulness, and the prohibition of buying student-athletes. It is important to note that both SPARTA and the UAAA cease to apply once a student-athlete's college eligibility has expired, thus marking a transition to different regulatory frameworks for professional athletes.

Fiduciary Duties and Responsibilities of a Sports Agent

The relationship between a sports agent and their client is fundamentally rooted in trust and confidence, characterized by the legal concept of fiduciary duty. This fiduciary relationship imposes the highest standard of care and loyalty on the agent toward their client. Here's a detailed look at the fiduciary duties sports agents owe to their clients:

1. Duty of Loyalty

The duty of loyalty requires sports agents to act in the best interests of their clients, placing the client's interests above their own. This duty prohibits agents from engaging in activities or transactions that could create a conflict of interest. For example, an agent must not represent competing interests or accept deals that benefit them more than their client.

2. Duty of Care

The duty of care mandates that agents perform their responsibilities with the necessary level of competence and diligence. This includes thoroughly researching and negotiating contracts, ensuring all terms are favorable to the client, and providing sound advice on career decisions. Agents are expected to use their expertise to protect their clients from unfavorable deals and to maximize their professional opportunities.

3. Duty of Good Faith and Fair Dealing

Sports agents must conduct themselves with honesty and fairness in all dealings with their clients. They must communicate openly and transparently, disclosing all relevant information and avoiding any misrepresentation or deceit. This duty also entails keeping the client informed about negotiations and any significant developments affecting their career.

4. Duty to Avoid Conflicts of Interest

Agents must avoid situations where their interests might conflict with those of their clients. This includes refraining from representing both a player and a team in the same negotiation or accepting commissions from third parties that could influence their impartiality. Agents should fully disclose any potential conflicts and seek the client's informed consent before proceeding.

5. Duty of Confidentiality

The duty of confidentiality obligates agents to keep their client's personal and professional information private. This includes financial details, contract terms, and any other sensitive information shared during their professional relationship. Unauthorized disclosure of such information can severely damage the client's interests and trust.

6. Duty to Act Within Scope of Authority

Agents must act within the scope of the authority granted by their clients. They cannot make binding decisions or agreements on behalf of their clients without explicit authorization. This duty ensures that the client retains control over major career decisions and contractual agreements.

7. Duty to Provide Full Disclosure

Agents are required to provide full disclosure of any material facts that might affect the client's decisions. This includes revealing all terms of a contract, potential endorsement deals, or any issues that might arise during negotiations. Full disclosure allows clients to make informed decisions about their careers.

8. Duty of Accountability

Agents must be accountable for their actions and decisions. This includes keeping accurate records of all financial transactions, contract negotiations, and communications on behalf of the client. Agents should be prepared to provide detailed reports and explanations of their activities to their clients.

Practical Examples

- **Contract Negotiations:** A sports agent must negotiate contracts that secure the best possible terms for their client, including salary, bonuses, and other benefits. This involves leveraging their knowledge of the industry and the client's market value to ensure favorable outcomes, while keeping their client informed throughout the negotiations.
- **Endorsements and Sponsorships:** When securing endorsement deals, agents must ensure the terms align with the client's brand and career goals. They must also disclose any personal benefits they might receive from these deals to avoid conflicts of interest.
- **Financial Management:** Agents often advise clients on financial matters, including investment opportunities and tax obligations. They must provide sound, unbiased advice and avoid steering clients toward investments where they have a personal stake.

In addition to statutory and union-imposed agency standards of conduct, a fiduciary relationship exists between a sports agent and an athlete upon the signing of a representation agreement. This contract is separate from the player-team standard contract and endorsement contracts. Each player's association has its own basic player-agent agreement that agents must use to represent an athlete in team contract negotiations. Agents are free to draft their own agreements for non-team affairs, such as licensing and merchandising the athletes' publicity rights.

Case Examples
Mark McCormick's IMG and LaDainian Tomlinson
In the case involving Mark McCormick's IMG and NFL running back LaDainian Tomlinson, an IMG agent breached his fiduciary duty by negotiating a $500,000 memorabilia deal for Tomlinson while secretly receiving a $50,000 kickback. Tomlinson discovered the undisclosed kickback during a financial review, prompting an internal investigation by IMG. This breach of trust led Tomlinson to seek legal counsel for future agreements. In response, IMG dismissed the agent and implemented stricter internal controls and compliance training.

Legally, the agent's failure to disclose the kickback constituted a breach of fiduciary duty, fraud, and misrepresentation. His actions violated ethical standards set by IMG and the NFL Players Association (NFLPA). Tomlinson had the right to pursue legal action for damages, including claims for breach of fiduciary duty, fraud, and misrepresentation. Under agency law, agents must disclose conflicts of interest, and the undisclosed kickback clearly violated this principle. IMG's termination of the agent was justified by his ethical and contractual violations.

Tank Blank and the NFLPA
Tank Blank, a certified NFL agent, was involved in illegal activities, including supplying money to college athletes and laundering money for drug dealers. He was decertified by the NFLPA and served time in federal prison. Blank's involvement extended to manipulating college football games through bribes, aiming to sway the outcomes for betting advantages. Additionally, he used his connections within the NFL to facilitate under-the-table deals, skirting salary cap regulations for certain players. His actions violated fiduciary duties and legal standards, highlighting the importance of ethical behavior in agent-client relationships. The scandal not only tarnished his reputation but also brought increased scrutiny and regulatory measures from the NFLPA to prevent future misconduct.

Carlos Daniels v. AAG Sports & Kenneth Edelin
Former NFL wide receiver Carlos Daniels sued his agent AAG Sports and Kenneth Edelin, alleging breach of fiduciary duty and fraud. Daniels

claimed they misled him into signing a below-market contract extension with the Cincinnati Bengals and mismanaged his finances. The legal issue centered on the breach of fiduciary duty and fraud, as Daniels argued his agents pressured him into the extension without fully explaining its terms and failed to properly manage his endorsement deals. A jury ruled in favor of Daniels, awarding him $23 million in damages.

Zion Williamson v. Prime Sports Marketing

Zion Williamson, a prominent NBA player, filed a lawsuit against his former marketing agency, Prime Sports Marketing, and its agent Gina Ford. Williamson sought a declaratory judgment that the contract he signed with Prime was void under the North Carolina Uniform Athlete Agents Act. Ford was not registered as an athlete agent in North Carolina, and the contract did not include the required warnings and disclosures. Williamson terminated the contract a month after signing it and subsequently signed with CAA. The legal issues revolved around the validity of the contract under the North Carolina Uniform Athlete Agents Act, specifically whether Ford's lack of registration as an athlete agent in North Carolina rendered the contract void and whether the absence of required warnings and disclosures in the contract invalidated it. The US Court of Appeals for the Fourth Circuit ruled in favor of Williamson, affirming that the contract was void due to Ford's failure to register as an agent and the contract's lack of necessary warnings. The court upheld the district court's decision, and Williamson was not liable for the $100 million in damages that Prime sought for the alleged breach of contract.

Gervon Dexter v. Big League Advance Fund II

Former Florida football player Gervon Dexter filed a lawsuit against Big League Advance Fund II (BLA) after signing a contract that entitled the firm to 15 percent of his pre-tax NFL earnings for twenty-five years. Dexter claimed he was misled about the terms and consequences of the agreement, which he signed while still in college. The legal issues in this case included whether the contract constituted an unfair and deceptive trade practice, whether Dexter was adequately informed about the terms and long-term implications of the agreement, and whether the contract was enforceable under state and federal laws governing athlete-agent relationships and financial agreements. The court sided with Dexter, ruling that the contract was unconscionable and unenforceable. The decision emphasized the importance of transparency and fairness in agreements between athletes and financial firms, particularly when the athlete is still in college and may lack the experience to fully understand complex financial arrangements.

Financial Mismanagement and Conflicts in Sports

Many athletes face financial ruin due to the mismanagement of their funds by unscrupulous agents and poor financial decisions. According to *Sports Illustrated*, nearly 80 percent of former NFL players are bankrupt or nearly bankrupt within two years of retirement, and 60 percent of NBA players face similar issues within five years. High-profile cases, such as those of Warren Sapp and Antoine Walker, underscore the severe impact of poor financial management and in many cases questionable lifestyle decisions.

A factor contributing to athletes' financial difficulties is the pressure to support extended families and friends due to newfound wealth. This financial burden can be overwhelming and lead to unsustainable spending patterns. Therefore, it is essential for agents to act in an advisory capacity, often collaborating with tax accountants and financial planners to ensure responsible management of an athlete's finances. Sports agents should:

- **Provide Comprehensive Financial Planning:** Agents should guide athletes in budgeting, saving, and investing wisely to secure their financial future.
- **Collaborate with Experts:** By working with tax accountants and financial planners, agents can offer a holistic approach to financial management, addressing all aspects of an athlete's financial life.
- **Educate Athletes:** Agents should educate athletes about the importance of financial literacy, helping them understand the long-term implications of their financial decisions.

- **Protect Athletes' Interests:** Agents must act ethically and in the best interests of their clients, ensuring that their advice and actions contribute to the athlete's financial stability.

Player associations also play a weighty role in mitigating these issues. They provide education seminars at prestigious institutions like Harvard Business School, equipping athletes with the knowledge to make informed financial decisions and avoid common pitfalls. These programs aim to enhance financial literacy among athletes, teaching them the importance of budgeting, investing wisely, and planning for the future.

Warren Sapp, a former NFL defensive tackle, filed for bankruptcy despite earning over $40 million during his career. His financial downfall was attributed to several factors:

- **Extravagant Spending:** Sapp reportedly spent excessively on luxury items, including a $6.45 million mansion and expensive watches.
- **Child Support Payments:** He had significant financial obligations, including child support for multiple children.
- **Failed Investments:** Sapp made poor investment choices, including sinking money into ventures that did not yield returns.
- **Unpaid Debts:** By the time he filed for bankruptcy, Sapp owed millions to various creditors, including $876,000 in alimony and child support.

Antoine Walker

Antoine Walker, a former NBA player, faced financial ruin despite earning over $108 million during his career. Walker's financial troubles were similarly attributed to:

- **Lavish Lifestyle:** Walker lived an opulent lifestyle, purchasing multiple homes, cars, and other luxury items.
- **Gambling:** He had a known gambling problem, which exacerbated his financial issues.
- **Bad Investments:** Walker invested heavily in real estate, but a market crash left him with significant losses.
- **Mismanagement by Advisors:** Walker trusted financial advisors who did not act in his best interest, leading to further financial losses.

Common Issues Leading to Financial Ruin

Several common issues lead to the financial downfall of athletes:

1. **Poor Financial Education:** Many athletes lack financial literacy, making them vulnerable to poor decisions and exploitation.
2. **Extravagant Lifestyles:** Athletes often spend excessively, not accounting for the limited duration of their high earnings.
3. **Trusting the Wrong Advisors:** Unscrupulous agents and advisors can mismanage funds or act fraudulently.
4. **Family and Friends:** Athletes often feel pressured to support extended family and friends, leading to unsustainable financial burdens.
5. **Short Career Spans:** The average career span of professional athletes is short, necessitating careful financial planning to sustain their post-career lives.

Together, regulatory oversight, financial education forums, and stringent fiduciary duty requirements form a comprehensive framework aimed at safeguarding athletes from financial exploitation and mismanagement. These measures are designed to protect athletes' financial interests, prevent exploitation, and promote sound financial management. This holistic approach not only secures athletes' current financial well-being but also contributes to their long-term financial stability and success, while allowing athletes to focus on their professional sports careers.

NIL Rights and Digital Transformation

The advent of Name, Image and Likeness (NIL) rights has revolutionized the relationship between college athletes and agents. With the NCAA's new NIL policy, college athletes can now legally profit from their name, image, and likeness without jeopardizing their athletic eligibility. This has led to a surge in partnerships between athletes and sports agents who can lawfully negotiate NIL deals on their behalf. Agents play a major role in securing endorsements, sponsorships, and other lucrative opportunities, ensuring that athletes maximize their earning potential while maintaining compliance with NCAA rules and state regulations.

College athletes, with the assistance of sports agents, have been able to negotiate high-profile endorsement deals under the NIL regulations. For instance, a gymnast from Louisiana State University has leveraged her massive social media following to secure deals with brands such as American Eagle and Vuori, while a quarterback from the University of Alabama has reportedly earned over a million dollars through various endorsements. These examples highlight how agents help athletes navigate the complexities of NIL agreements, ensuring they benefit financially while adhering to NCAA guidelines. Additionally, a basketball player at the University of Southern California, with an estimated NIL value of $4.9 million, has secured deals with major brands such as Nike, Google, and PSD Underwear, leveraging his substantial social media following and high-profile legacy. Another notable athlete is a basketball player from the University of Iowa, who has earned approximately $3.1 million through endorsements with Gatorade, State Farm, and Nike. Her impressive performance on the court and strong social media presence have made her a top NIL earner among female athletes. Similarly, a quarterback at the University of Colorado, with an NIL valuation of $4.7 million, has secured endorsements with Google, Beats by Dre, and Under Armour, showcasing how his athletic prowess and family legacy have attracted lucrative sponsorships. Furthermore, the quarterback for the University of Georgia has NIL deals with EA Sports, The Players' Lounge, and Leaf Trading Cards, contributing to his $1.5 million valuation. These examples illustrate the significant financial opportunities available to college athletes through NIL deals, with agents playing a crucial role in securing these endorsements, ensuring compliance with NCAA regulations, and maximizing the athletes' earning potential.

The digital transformation of sports marketing has further expanded the role of agents. Beyond traditional endorsements, agents must now manage athletes' digital branding, social media presence, and online endorsements. This requires proficiency in leveraging platforms like Instagram, Twitter, TikTok, and YouTube to enhance athletes' visibility and engagement with fans. For example, some elite high school basketball players have leveraged social media to amass a following of tens of thousands of fans. Their agents strategically negotiate deals with major brands, demonstrating the potential for amazing revenue through digital platforms for teenage athletes.

The integration of AI and advanced analytics in sports marketing has become a game-changer. Agents can now use AI tools to analyze market trends, audience demographics, and engagement metrics to create tailored marketing strategies for their clients. This data-driven approach helps in optimizing endorsement deals and identifying the most impactful brand partnerships. AI can also predict the best times for posting content and the types of posts that will generate the most engagement, maximizing an athlete's online presence and marketability.

However, this digital landscape also presents several concerns. Agents must anticipate issues related to data privacy, the ethical use of AI, and the potential for misinformation or negative publicity spreading rapidly on social media. Ensuring that athletes' digital content remains authentic and aligns with their personal brand is necessary to maintaining fan trust and loyalty.

Agents play an important role in protecting athletes' interests in the digital realm. They must ensure that contracts include provisions for the ethical use of athletes' likenesses and monitor for any unauthorized use or exploitation. The rise of virtual reality and the metaverse adds another layer of complexity, where agents need to confront the legalities surrounding virtual endorsements and the use of athletes' avatars in digital spaces. This includes ensuring that virtual representations of athletes are accurate and used in ways that fit with their real-world branding and contractual agreements.

In this ever-changing marketplace, sports agents must stay ahead of technological advancements and regulatory changes to effectively serve their clients. For example, Swiss sportswear company On has introduced the Cloudboom Strike LS, a revolutionary running shoe featuring their new LightSpray technology. This innovative design process involves spraying the shoe's upper material rather than constructing it through traditional methods, significantly reducing CO_2 emissions by 75 percent. The Cloudboom Strike LS, which weighs just 6 ounces, offers a seamless, sock-like fit without laces, providing exceptional comfort and support akin to a bedroom slipper. The shoe's upper is created using a robotic arm that assembles the one-piece upper and sole in just three minutes, ensuring a durable, rip-proof design. It also incorporates a carbon Speedboard for enhanced propulsion and On's proprietary hyper foam in the midsole for superior cushioning and energy return. This advanced construction method eliminates the need for glue, further reducing waste and environmental impact, making it an impressive advancement for athletes like Boston Marathon winner Hellen Obiri who are concerned about climate change yet seeking elite performance footwear.

Summary

The demanding, yet hyper-competitive, role and responsibilities of sports agents are explored, highlighting their function as intermediaries between athletes and the various entities that seek their talents. Sports agents are tasked with negotiating contracts, securing endorsements, and managing public relations for their clients. Their responsibilities are vast and encompass a range of activities aimed at maximizing the athlete's career and financial potential. To operate professionally, agents must obtain certification from relevant governing bodies, such as player associations, which ensures they adhere to established standards and ethical guidelines.

A required aspect of an agent's duty is their fiduciary responsibility, which obliges them to act in the best interests of their clients, prioritizing the athlete's welfare above their own. This fiduciary duty encompasses duties of loyalty, confidentiality, and diligence. Agents must provide honest and accurate advice, avoid conflicts of interest, and ensure full disclosure of pertinent information. Breaches of this duty can occur through acts of negligence, misrepresentation, or self-dealing, which can lead to legal consequences and damage to the agent's reputation.

Certification of agents involves meeting specific educational and professional criteria, passing examinations, and maintaining good standing through continuous adherence to ethical practices. This certification process aims to protect athletes from unqualified or unscrupulous representatives. Prime cases of breaches of fiduciary duty illustrate the severe repercussions for both agents and athletes involved.

Sports agents must possess a deep understanding of the sports they represent, as well as strong negotiation and communication skills. They often act as talent scouts, marketing strategists, and public relations managers, continuously seeking new opportunities to advance their clients' careers. This includes negotiating playing contracts, which specify the terms of the athlete's engagement with a team, and endorsement deals, which involve agreements with brands for the athlete to promote their products. Many endorsement deals include a morality clause, which allows the sponsoring company to terminate the contract if the athlete engages in conduct that could damage the brand's reputation. For example, Tiger Woods faced significant consequences after his personal scandals, leading to the termination of several endorsement deals. Similarly, Lance Armstrong's doping scandal resulted in the loss of numerous sponsorships, materially impacting his financial standing and public image.

Agents also manage media agreements, which can include appearances on podcasts, in movies, or other media ventures. In addition to these roles, sports agents often provide legal advice and act as personal mentors to their clients, helping them safely traverse the complexities of their careers and personal lives. They must be adept at managing public relations, particularly during times of controversy, and ensuring that their clients maintain a positive public image. The multifaceted nature of the sports agent's role demonstrates how their efforts are crucial to the success and well-being of the athletes they represent. Their influence extends beyond negotiation and management, making them indispensable to the integrity and progression of the sports industry.

Discussion Questions

1. **Role of Sports Agents:** Discuss the role of sports agents in the sports industry. How do they act as intermediaries between athletes and various entities? What specific responsibilities do they hold in negotiating contracts, securing endorsements, and managing public relations?
2. **Fiduciary Duty:** Analyze the concept of fiduciary duty in the context of sports agents. What are the key components of this duty, and how does it impact the relationship between the agent and the athlete? Provide examples of breaches of fiduciary duty and their consequences.
3. **Certification Process:** Examine the certification process for sports agents. What educational and professional criteria must agents

meet? How do these standards protect athletes from unqualified or unscrupulous representatives?
4. **Contract Formation:** Explore the elements of contract formation in sports. How do offer, acceptance, consideration, lawful purpose, and meeting of the minds contribute to the creation of a legally binding agreement?
5. **Endorsement Deals and Morality Clauses:** Discuss the role of endorsement deals in an athlete's career. What is a morality clause, and why is it included in these contracts?
6. **Playing Contracts:** Investigate the specifics of player contracts for pro athletes. What key terms and conditions are typically included? How do clauses for injury protection, performance bonuses, and contract renewal options benefit athletes and teams?
7. **Media Agreements:** Consider the importance of media agreements for athletes. How do podcasts, film roles, and digital content participation enhance an athlete's visibility and earning potential? Provide examples of athletes who have successfully leveraged media agreements.
8. **Ethical Practices in Sports Agency:** Discuss the ethical standards that sports agents must adhere to. How do these practices ensure the integrity of the sports industry? What are the potential ethical dilemmas agents might face, and how should they address them?
9. **Legal Advice and Mentorship:** Evaluate the role of sports agents in providing legal advice and personal mentorship. How do agents help athletes handle the complexities of balancing their professional careers and personal lives
10. **Impact of Sports Agents on the Industry:** Analyze the overall impact of sports agents on the sports industry. How do their efforts shape the careers of athletes and influence the market dynamics?

7

Protecting the Game

Intellectual Property, Publicity Rights, and Privacy in the Digital Age

Chapter Outline

What Is Intellectual Property?	214
Importance of IP Law in Sports Business	216
The Role of the Digital Millennium Copyright Act (DMCA) in Sports Broadcasting	224
The Role of International Treaties and Organizations	227
International Recognition and Moral Rights	231
Publicity Rights and Athlete Endorsements	232
Publicity Rights in Digital World	236
Summary	241
Discussion Questions	242

This chapter examines the intricate realm of intellectual property (IP) law as it intersects with the sports industry, offering a thorough exploration of the protection and management of team names, logos, and other essential branding elements. It provides an in-depth analysis of how IP law adapts to new legal precedents, technological advancements, and societal changes. The discussion addresses the challenges and opportunities presented by digital media, globalization, and the increasing commercial value of sports brands. Furthermore, it highlights the strategic importance of IP management for sports organizations in safeguarding their identities and maximizing their market potential. Emphasizing the vital role IP law plays in the sports sector, this chapter offers valuable insights into effectively protecting and leveraging brand assets in a competitive marketplace.

What Is Intellectual Property?

Intellectual property (IP) encompasses various legal rights that protect creations of the mind, such as inventions, literary and artistic works, designs, symbols, names, and images used in commerce. In the sports context, IP is crucial for protecting the brand identity and commercial interests of teams, athletes, and organizations. The main types of IP relevant to sports are patents, copyrights, and trademarks.

- **Patents**: Patents provide exclusive rights to inventors for their inventions, typically for twenty years. In sports, patents can protect innovations in sports equipment, technology, and training methods. For example, a new type of athletic shoe or a sophisticated piece of training equipment can be patented to prevent others from making, using, or selling the invention without permission.
- **Copyrights**: Copyrights protect original works of authorship, such as written content, music, and broadcasts, giving the creator exclusive rights to use and distribute the work. In sports, copyrights can apply to game broadcasts, promotional videos, and other media content.
- **Trademarks**: Trademarks protect words, phrases, symbols, and designs that distinguish the source of goods or services. In sports, trademarks are essential for protecting team names, logos, and slogans, ensuring that fans can easily identify and support their favorite teams and athletes.

Historical Genesis of Intellectual Property Law

The history of intellectual property (IP) law is deeply rooted in the progression of societal and economic structures, dating back to medieval Europe. Initially, guilds controlled the regulation and conduct of various industries, often stifling creativity and innovation. The Statute of Monopolies of 1623 in England marked a remarkable shift by halting the granting of monopolies and introducing the concept of exclusive rights for inventors for a limited period of fourteen years. This statute laid the groundwork for modern IP law by emphasizing the importance of novelty and the societal benefits of new inventions.

In the United States, the framers of the Constitution recognized the need for a uniform system of IP law to promote innovation and commerce. Article I, Section 8, Clause 8 of the US Constitution grants Congress the power to "promote the Progress of Science and useful Arts, by securing for limited Times to Authors and Inventors the exclusive Right to their respective Writings and Discoveries." This clause reflects a delicate balance between encouraging innovation through exclusive rights and ensuring that these rights are limited in duration to eventually benefit the public domain. The first US Patent Act of 1790, which provided a fourteen-year term for patents, was a direct implementation of this constitutional mandate.

The statutory framework for IP law in the United States has developed over time. The Lanham Act of 1946 established a comprehensive system for trademark registration and protection. It defines a trademark as any mark used in commerce that is distinctive and not functional, thereby preventing consumer confusion and protecting brand identity. The act also addresses issues such as trademark dilution, false advertising, and cyberpiracy, reflecting the changing landscape of commerce and technology.

Meanwhile, the Copyright Act provides protection for the life of the author plus seventy years for works created after January 1, 1978. Patents generally last for twenty years from the filing date, while design patents have a term of fifteen years from the grant date. These time limits ensure that while inventors and creators can benefit from their works, these works will eventually enter the public domain, allowing society to freely build upon them. This balance is essential for fostering continuous innovation and ensuring that the fruits of creative and scientific endeavors ultimately benefit the public at large.

Importance of IP Law in Sports Business

Intellectual property law is particularly valuable in the world of sports business. The protection of IP rights is decisive for maintaining the integrity and economic value of sports brands, which include team names, logos, and other distinctive elements. This protection helps prevent unauthorized use and counterfeiting, ensuring that consumers can trust the authenticity of the products and services they purchase.

1. **Brand Identity**: Strong IP laws protect the unique identity of sports teams and organizations, which is vital for building brand loyalty and fan engagement. For example, trademarks protect team logos and names, ensuring that fans can easily identify and support their favorite teams.
2. **Revenue Generation**: Licensing agreements for the use of IP, such as merchandise and broadcast rights, are major revenue sources for sports organizations. Effective IP protection ensures that these agreements are upheld and that revenue streams are not undermined by unauthorized use.
3. **Innovation and Competition**: Patents protect technological innovations in sports equipment and training methods, encouraging ongoing development and competition in the industry. For example, advancements in athletic shoe technology can be patented, providing a competitive edge to the innovating company.
4. **Media and Content**: Copyrights protect the vast array of media content generated by the sports industry, from live broadcasts to promotional videos. This ensures that the creators and owners of this content can control its distribution and monetization.

Rights of Copyright Holders

Copyright holders are granted a bundle of exclusive rights, including:

1. Reproduction is the right to make copies of the work. For example, a sports photographer owns the copyright to a photograph of an iconic moment in a soccer match. Only the photographer has the legal right to make copies of this photograph, such as printing posters or creating digital copies for sale.
2. Derivative Works is the right to create adaptations or transformations of the work. For instance, a documentary filmmaker has the exclusive right to create a movie based on a biography they wrote about a famous athlete. No one else can make a film adaptation without permission.
3. Distribution is the right to distribute copies of the work to the public. For example, a company holds the copyright to a sports video game. They have the exclusive right to distribute copies of the game through physical sales, digital downloads, or any other means.
4. Public Performance is the right to perform the work publicly. Case in point, the copyright holder of a televised sports event (such as the Olympics) has the exclusive right to broadcast the event live on television or online. Unauthorized public showings of the broadcast would infringe on this right.
5. Public Display is the right to display the work publicly. To illustrate, a graphic designer creates a poster series featuring different sports stars. The designer holds the exclusive right to publicly display these posters, whether in galleries, sports arenas, or online.
6. Digital Transmission, specifically for sound recordings, is the right to perform the work publicly via digital audio transmission. As an example, a record label owns the copyright to a motivational sports anthem. They have the exclusive right to transmit the song digitally, such as streaming it on music platforms, and can license its use for sports events or athlete entrance themes.

Broadcasting rights, protected by copyright, are legal agreements that grant organizations the authority to transmit live sports events to audiences. These rights are highly coveted due to the massive viewership that sports like basketball attract. The NBA recently finalized a new media rights deal valued at $77 billion over eleven years, starting from the 2025-6 season. This deal involves major networks such as ESPN, NBC, and Amazon, marking a significant financial boost for the league. The agreement nearly triples the value of the previous contract and underscores the growing importance of streaming services in sports broadcasting.

For NBA fans, the competition for broadcasting rights could lead to more options for accessing games and potentially lower prices for streaming services. However, it may also result in increased fragmentation, making it more challenging for fans to follow their favorite teams across various platforms. The NBA's efforts to secure and protect its broadcasting rights illustrate the broader importance of copyright protection in the sports industry.

Rights of Trademark Holders

Trademark holders have the exclusive right to use their marks in commerce, which includes:

- Preventing Unauthorized Use: The right to prevent others from using the same or a similar mark for related goods or services without permission.
- Licensing: The ability to license the trademark to others for use in return for payment.
- Enforcing Rights: The ability to pursue legal action against trademark infringement.

Trademarks play a large financial role in the sports industry, protecting the intellectual property of teams, athletes, and leagues. These trademarks can include names, logos, slogans, and even unique poses or catchphrases. Here are some substantial examples:

- Usain Bolt: The iconic sprinter has trademarked his "lightning bolt" pose, along with phrases like "Bolt to the World" and his name in various fonts. These trademarks are used on commercial goods to generate revenue and maintain brand integrity.
- Michael Phelps: The swimmer holds trademarks for the "MP" logo and "Michael Phelps Swim School," which are used for his swim gear brand and chain of swim schools, respectively.

- LeBron James: Known as "King James," he has trademarked "Home Court by LeBron James" for a line of basketball-themed furniture, as well as his foundation and the phrase "Just a kid from Akron."
- Jeremy Lin: The term "Linsanity," which gained popularity during his breakout season with the New York Knicks, is trademarked and used on various merchandise.
- Cleveland Guardians: The Cleveland MLB team had a notable trademark dispute with a local roller derby team over the name "Guardians." The roller derby team had been using the name since 2013 and had registered it with the Ohio Secretary of State in 2017. The dispute was resolved amicably, allowing both teams to use the name.
- Denver Broncos: The NFL team attempted to trademark "Orange Crush," a nickname for their defense, but faced opposition from the soda brand of the same name. The case highlights the complexities of trademarking common phrases.

Sports sponsorships, headed by companies like Nike, Adidas, and Puma, are strategic partnerships where companies provide financial or other support to sports entities in exchange for brand exposure. For example, Nike spends over $4.3 billion a year on marketing and sponsorship. This relationship benefits both the sponsor and the sports entity:

- Nike and Michael Jordan: Nike's partnership with Michael Jordan led to the creation of the "Air Jordan" brand, which has become a revenue generator in the order of $7 billion annually and a cornerstone of Nike's brand identity.
- Under Armour and Stephen Curry: Under Armour has successfully trademarked the "SC30" logo used in conjunction with Curry's shoes and apparel, leveraging his popularity to boost their brand.
- Red Bull and Extreme Sports: Red Bull's extensive sponsorship of extreme sports events has significantly enhanced its brand recognition and association with high-energy activities.
- American Airlines and Sports Venues: American Airlines sponsors venues like the American Airlines Center and Arena, gaining extensive brand exposure through naming rights.
- Gap owned Athena: Gymnast Simone Biles and swimmer Katie Ledecky serve as brand ambassadors.

Sponsorship in sports is a powerful tool for creating brand awareness, fostering brand loyalty, and driving sales. It leverages the emotional connection fans have with their favorite teams and athletes, making them more likely to support brands associated with these entities. This connection translates into higher conversion rates and increased purchase intent among fans. For the last reported year, over 80,000 brands invested more than $60 billion in various sponsorship deals across sports, entertainment, causes, celebrities, athletes, and events. This figure is expected to grow, with the sports sponsorship market anticipated to reach $109.1 billion by 2030. These investments are not just about media exposure but also about enhancing brand equity, fostering customer loyalty, and improving cultural relevance.

Primary Revenue Streams

1. **Sponsorship Deals**: These include jersey sponsorships, stadium naming rights, and event sponsorships. For example, the NHL added more than $100 million in net-new revenue by adding a sponsorship patch to its jerseys.
2. **Media Rights**: Selling broadcast rights to media companies is a major revenue source. The advent of digital broadcasting and streaming services has further enhanced the value of these rights.
3. **Merchandising**: This includes sales of branded products like clothing and accessories, which extend the sports brand beyond the game and provide a continuous income stream.
4. **Ticket Sales**: Revenue from individual match tickets, season passes, and premium offerings like box seats or VIP experiences.
5. **Licensing Deals**: Allowing businesses to use team logos or athlete likenesses on their products in exchange for royalty fees.

Potential Revenue Streams

1. **Digital and Social Media**: Athletes can generate significant income through social media endorsements and their personal brand podcasts. For instance, Cristiano Ronaldo earns approximately $2,000,000 for each post on Instagram.
2. **Affiliate Marketing**: Influencers and athletes can earn commissions by promoting products through unique affiliate links.

3. **Sponsored Posts**: Charging a fee for promoting a brand or product on social media pages.
4. **Public Appearances**: Athletes can earn additional income by making appearances at events, which can be monetized through experiential marketing.
5. **Photo and Video Sales**: Selling branded content or converting photography into prints for sale.
6. **Digital Courses**: Offering courses on how to make money as a creator in a specific niche or platform.

Influential Figures in Sports

Several athletes and sports executives wield major influence in the sports arena. Here are some notable names:

1. **Cristiano Ronaldo**: Known for his massive social media presence and high earnings from endorsements, Cristiano Ronaldo has an estimated net worth of over $500 million. Last season, he earned approximately $55 million from endorsements and $70 million in salary and winnings.
2. **LeBron James**: Estimated to have earned over $900 million through endorsements, LeBron James' influence extends beyond basketball. His lifetime deal with Nike is worth more than $1 billion.
3. **Serena Williams**: A highly influential figure in sports and beyond, Serena Williams has earned over $94 million in prize money during her career, the most of any female athlete. Her endorsement deals with brands like Nike, Wilson, and Gatorade add significantly to her earnings, with Forbes estimating her total earnings at over $45 million in 2022.
4. **Michael Jordan**: Earned more from endorsement deals than his NBA contracts during his career. Jordan's partnership with Nike, particularly the Air Jordan brand, has generated billions, with Forbes estimating his total earnings at around $2.6 billion.
5. **Dana White**: President of UFC, known for making mixed martial arts mainstream. Under his leadership, UFC was sold for $4 billion in 2016, significantly increasing its global reach and profitability.
6. **Gianni Infantino**: FIFA president, influential in expanding the World Cup. Under his tenure, FIFA's revenue reached $6.4 billion for the most recent year.

7. **Naomi Osaka**: A tennis star who has become one of the highest-paid female athletes. Last year, Osaka earned approximately $57 million, including $55 million from endorsements with brands like Nike, Nissan, and Mastercard.
8. **Simone Biles**: One of the most decorated gymnasts in history. Biles has numerous endorsement deals with companies such as Athleta, Visa, and United Airlines, earning her an estimated $10 million annually.
9. **Alex Morgan**: A prominent figure in women's soccer and a key player for the US Women's National Team. Morgan's endorsements with Nike, Coca-Cola, and Beats by Dre contribute to her estimated annual earnings of $4.6 million.
10. **Ronda Rousey**: A former UFC champion and WWE wrestler, Rousey has earned significant revenue from her fights and endorsements. Her annual earnings peaked at $15 million, including sponsorships from Reebok and Metro PCS.

Revenue streams have expanded with the rise of social media and podcasts. Athletes, now also influencers, can generate significant income through social media endorsements and their personal brand podcasts, further enhancing their financial portfolio and market reach.

The magnitude of these issues—protecting brands, broadcast rights and sponsorships—cannot be overstated. Unauthorized streaming and inadequate copyright protections can lead to substantial revenue losses. For example, the NFL estimated that it loses around $1 billion annually due to unauthorized streams. With the sports industry relying heavily on broadcasting rights and digital content, stronger copyright laws are crucial to safeguarding revenue and ensuring the sustainable growth of sports entertainment. Trademarks, sponsorships, and effective copyright protection are integral to the sports industry, providing financial benefits and protecting the brand identities of teams, athletes, and leagues.

Rights of Patent Holders

Patent holders are granted the right to exclude others from making, using, selling, or importing the patented invention. This right is not a right to use the invention but rather to prevent others from doing so without authorization.

Patents play a crucial role in the development and protection of sports technology. They incentivize innovation by granting inventors exclusive rights to their inventions, thus encouraging investment in research and development. This has led to significant advancements across various sports. Below are some recent examples of sports-related patent technology, their impact on performance, and instances of patent breaches.

Recent progress in sports technology has been driven by patented innovations across various domains. For instance, Nike's Flyknit technology, which involves a lightweight, form-fitting fabric used in athletic shoes, has been patented to enhance performance by providing better support and reducing weight. This innovation has been widely adopted in running and basketball shoes, contributing to improved athletic performance. Similarly, Riddell developed and patented advanced football helmets designed to reduce concussions. These helmets incorporate unique padding and structural designs to better absorb impacts, thereby enhancing player safety.

Performance-enhancing apparel has also seen significant innovations. The Nike Vaporfly shoes, featuring a carbon-fiber plate and advanced foam, have been patented for their ability to significantly improve running efficiency. These shoes have been so effective that they have been worn by athletes sponsored by other brands, sometimes disguised to avoid breaching sponsorship agreements. Speedo's LZR Racer swimsuits, which reduce drag and enhance buoyancy, were patented and led to numerous world records in swimming. However, their effectiveness was so pronounced that they were eventually banned from competition to maintain fair play.

In the realm of sports training devices, various patents have been granted for sports training mats and devices, such as those by New Turf Technologies and FAST HOCKEY BY STEVE COMEGNA INC. These innovations help athletes improve their skills and performance through targeted training exercises. Additionally, the golf putting practice alignment device, patented by Ryan Omoto, helps golfers improve their putting accuracy by providing precise alignment guidance during practice sessions. Decision-making technologies have also benefited from patented innovations.

The Video Assistant Referee (VAR) system, used in football, employs high-definition cameras and video analysis software to assist referees in making accurate decisions. This technology has been patented and has significantly reduced errors in officiating, enhancing the fairness of the game. Hawk-Eye Innovations' ball-tracking technology, used in tennis and cricket, has been patented and acquired by Sony. It provides precise ball trajectory data, aiding in accurate decision-making by officials.

Nutrition and hydration innovations have also been impacted by patents. Gatorade, developed in collaboration with the University of Florida, was patented to replace carbohydrates and salts lost during physical activity. This innovation laid the foundation for modern sports nutrition products that enhance athletic performance and recovery. SiS Science in Sport has patented various energy gels, chews, and drink powders tailored for endurance athletes. These products provide targeted nutritional support, helping athletes maintain energy levels and recover faster during and after events. However, the enforcement of patents and the regulation of their use are crucial to maintaining fair play and preventing monopolistic practices.

Nike has been involved in numerous patent disputes to protect its innovations. For instance, Nike's Flyknit technology has been the subject of legal battles to prevent competitors from infringing on its patents. Riddell successfully sued Schutt Sports for infringing on its patented concussion reduction technology in football helmets. The court awarded Riddell nearly $30 million in damages, highlighting the importance of patent protection in maintaining competitive advantage and ensuring safety. AIM Sport won a patent infringement case against Supponor over LED advertising technology used in sports stadiums. The court upheld AIM Sport's patent, emphasizing the consequence of protecting technological innovations in the sports marketing industry.

The Role of the Digital Millennium Copyright Act (DMCA) in Sports Broadcasting

The Digital Millennium Copyright Act (DMCA), enacted in 1998, has profoundly impacted sports broadcasting and sports law by addressing the challenges posed by the digital environment to copyright protection. The DMCA introduced several key provisions that affect how sports content is managed, distributed, and protected online, playing a crucial role in safeguarding the interests of sports leagues and broadcasters.

The safe harbor provision of the DMCA provides online service providers (OSPs) with protection from liability for copyright infringements committed by their users, provided they comply with specific requirements. These include promptly removing infringing content upon receiving a valid takedown notice. This system allows sports leagues to request the removal of unauthorized streams or clips of their events from platforms like YouTube, Twitter, and Facebook. For example, the NFL and NBA frequently utilize this mechanism to protect their content from unauthorized distribution.

The DMCA's anti-circumvention measures under Section 1201 prohibit bypassing technological protection measures (TPMs) that control access to copyrighted works. This means that bypassing digital locks on streaming services to access sports broadcasts without authorization is illegal. This provision helps to prevent the unauthorized access and distribution of sports content, ensuring that only legitimate viewers can access the broadcasts.

Another critical aspect of the DMCA is the protection of Copyright Management Information (CMI) under Section 1202, which makes it unlawful to remove or alter CMI, such as the names of authors or copyright owners, often included in digital broadcasts of sports events. This protection helps maintain the integrity of the broadcast and ensures that proper credit is given to the rightful owners.

Despite these provisions, sports leagues face ongoing challenges from illegal streaming of live events. The DMCA's notice-and-takedown process can be slow, often allowing entire games to be broadcast illegally before action is taken. This has led leagues like the NFL, NBA, and UFC to push for changes to the DMCA to require more immediate takedown actions. For instance, the UFC has been vocal about the need for quicker responses to takedown notices to prevent revenue losses from illegal streams of pay-per-view events.

The use of short clips, GIFs, and memes from sports broadcasts on social media has sparked debates over fair use and user-generated content. Sports leagues often use the DMCA to remove such content, arguing it infringes on their copyrights, while users argue for their right to fair use. A notable example is when the NBA requested takedowns of popular highlight clips shared on social media platforms, leading to public debates over the balance between copyright protection and fair use.

Global jurisdiction issues also complicate the enforcement of the DMCA. As a US law, the DMCA does not extend beyond US borders, making it difficult to combat illegal streaming sites hosted in other countries. This limitation forces leagues to focus on US-based ISPs and platforms to enforce their rights. For instance, when attempting to shut down an illegal streaming site based in Europe, US leagues often face significant legal and logistical challenges.

The use of short clips, GIFs, and memes from sports broadcasts on social media has sparked debates over fair use and user-generated content. Sports leagues often use the DMCA to remove such content, arguing it infringes on their copyrights, while users argue for their right to fair use. A notable example is when the NBA requested takedowns of popular highlight clips shared on social media platforms, leading to public debates over the balance between copyright protection and fair use. Fair use is a legal doctrine that permits limited use of copyrighted material without acquiring permission from the rights holders, typically for purposes such as criticism, comment, news reporting, teaching, scholarship, or research. Fair use is determined by a four-prong test that considers the purpose and character of the use, the nature of the copyrighted work, the amount and substantiality of the portion used, and the effect of the use upon the potential market for or value of the copyrighted work.

Recently, the US Supreme Court's decision in the landmark *Andy Warhol Foundation for the Visual Arts, Inc. v. Goldsmith* case has caused considerable dismay by its interpretation of this test. The Court ruled that Warhol's use of Lynn Goldsmith's photograph of Prince did not qualify as fair use, emphasizing the potential market impact over transformative purpose. The majority opinion, written by Justice Sotomayor, emphasized that Warhol's licensing of "Orange Prince" to Condé Nast for a magazine cover shared a substantially similar purpose to Goldsmith's original photograph—both were used as portraits of Prince in magazines to illustrate stories about the musician. This commercial nature and similar purpose were pivotal in the Court's determination that Warhol's use was not transformative enough to be considered fair use. This ruling has incredible implications for both copyright and trademark applications, suggesting that even highly transformative works may face legal challenges if they affect the market for the original works.

Illegal streaming and piracy result in substantial revenue losses for sports leagues. It is estimated that the global sports industry loses up to

$28 billion annually due to illegal streaming, as viewers who access free streams are less likely to pay for legitimate services. This loss directly impacts the financial health of sports leagues and their ability to invest in talent and infrastructure.

In copyright infringement cases, copyright owners who have filed their copyright with the Library of Congress can seek actual damages, which account for the direct financial losses suffered due to infringement, or statutory damages, which range from $750 to $30,000 per incident, and up to $150,000 for willful infringement. These damages aim to compensate for lost revenue and deter future infringements. High-profile cases, such as those involving unauthorized streaming of major sporting events, often result in substantial damages awarded to the copyright owners.

Infringement can also devalue the exclusive rights sold to broadcasters and sponsors. If games are widely available through illegal streams, the perceived value of these rights diminishes, potentially leading to lower bids in future licensing deals. For example, if a broadcaster pays a premium for exclusive rights to a sports league's games but finds that many viewers are accessing the games through illegal streams, they may reconsider the value of their investment.

The DMCA plays a principal role in protecting the rights of sports leagues in the digital age. However, its effectiveness is often hampered by the speed of enforcement and jurisdictional limitations. The ongoing debates and proposed changes to the DMCA highlight the need for a more robust framework to address the evolving challenges of digital piracy in sports broadcasting. Enhanced collaboration between international bodies, technological advancements in content protection, and legal reforms are essential to strengthen the DMCA's impact and ensure the continued financial viability of sports broadcasting.

The Role of International Treaties and Organizations

The World Intellectual Property Organization (WIPO) administers several treaties that facilitate the international protection of IP rights. For example, the Madrid System allows for the registration of trademarks in multiple countries through a single application, simplifying the process for sports organizations looking to protect their brands globally.

Major sporting events like the FIFA World Cup rely heavily on international IP protection to safeguard their trademarks and broadcast rights. FIFA's intellectual property, including the FIFA World Cup Trophy, logos, titles, and symbols, is protected worldwide through copyright, trademark, and other IP laws. This protection is necessary for maintaining the integrity and commercial value of the event. Unauthorized use of these IP assets can lead to serious financial losses and damage to the event's reputation. For instance, FIFA combats ambush marketing and counterfeit merchandise to ensure that only authorized entities can benefit from the event's commercial success.

Real-world examples illustrate these issues well. During the FIFA World Cup in South Africa, Bavaria Brewery engaged in ambush marketing by having a group of women wear orange dresses (the brewery's color) to a match. Although the dresses didn't feature any brand logos, the visual association was clear. FIFA took legal action against Bavaria Brewery to protect its official sponsors. The sale of counterfeit FIFA World Cup merchandise is another contentious issue. During the FIFA World Cup in Russia, authorities seized thousands of counterfeit goods, including fake jerseys, scarves, and other memorabilia. FIFA worked closely with local law enforcement and customs officials to identify and confiscate these items, ensuring that only authorized vendors could sell official merchandise. Unauthorized streaming of World Cup matches has also become a major problem with the rise of digital platforms. Most recently, FIFA identified numerous illegal streaming sites and worked with digital service providers to shut them down. This effort was a major reason for protecting the broadcast rights sold to official partners for billions of dollars.

Similarly, the Olympic Games depend on robust IP protection to secure their unique identifiers, such as the Olympic symbol, flag, motto, and emblems. The International Olympic Committee (IOC) leverages these IP rights to attract commercial partners and generate revenue through sponsorships, broadcasting rights, and licensing. This revenue is essential for funding the Games and supporting global sports development initiatives. The Nairobi Treaty on the Protection of the Olympic Symbol is one of the international treaties administered by WIPO that helps protect these assets. Unauthorized use of Olympic properties is strictly regulated to preserve the event's brand value and ensure fair commercial practices.

For example, in 2024, the USOPC filed a civil lawsuit against Prime Hydration, a sports drink brand co-founded by social media influencers KSI and Logan Paul. The USOPC accused Prime Hydration of infringing its trademarks by using terms like "Olympic," "Olympian," "Team USA," and "Going for Gold" on product packaging and promotional materials featuring NBA star and Olympic athlete Kevin Durant. The USOPC highlights that it relies on licensing these trademarks to fund and support American athletes, and unauthorized use undermines the value of its sponsorship agreements, particularly its exclusive licensing deal with Coca-Cola for beverages in the United States. In seeking monetary damages, the USOPC argues that Prime Hydration's unauthorized use of Olympic symbols could deceive consumers into believing the products are officially endorsed or associated with the Olympic Games, causing confusion and potential harm to the committee's reputation and financial interests.

Another noteworthy case happened in the lead-up to the Tokyo 2020 Olympics; several local businesses in Japan used the Olympic rings in their advertising without permission. The IOC took steps to enforce its IP rights, issuing cease-and-desist orders to protect the exclusivity of their brand. Ambush marketing is another issue the IOC faces. During the London Olympics, Nike launched an advertising campaign featuring everyday athletes in various "Londons" around the world, cleverly avoiding direct references to the Olympic Games while still capitalizing on the event's atmosphere. The IOC closely monitored such activities to protect the interests of official sponsors like Adidas. Fake tickets are also a recurrent issue at the Olympics. During nearly all Olympic Games and World Cup soccer matches, authorities arrest individuals involved in a large-scale ticket scam that sells counterfeit tickets to spectators. The IOC worked with local police and international agencies to prevent such fraud, ensuring the integrity of ticket sales and protecting consumers; yet many fans continue to be duped.

By utilizing systems like the Madrid System, organizations such as FIFA and the IOC can efficiently manage and protect their trademarks across multiple jurisdictions, ensuring that their events remain financially viable and their brands are preserved on a global scale. The World Intellectual Property Organization (WIPO) plays a role in facilitating the international protection of IP rights for these organizations. The Madrid System allows for the registration of trademarks in multiple countries through a single application. Sports organizations like FIFA and the IOC use this system to protect their trademarks globally, ensuring consistent brand protection across jurisdictions. The Nairobi Treaty specifically protects the Olympic symbol. The IOC relies on the Nairobi Treaty to safeguard the Olympic rings, preventing unauthorized use and ensuring the exclusivity of their brand.

Case Study: *Michael Jordan v. Qiaodan Sports Co., Ltd.*

In 2010, during a visit to China, the author visited a sporting goods store in Beijing and noticed Qiaodan brand shoes. These shoes appeared to play off the sound similarity to "Jordan" and featured a logo resembling a fatter version of Michael Jordan's iconic Nike logo of him dunking a basketball. Recognizing the potential for brand confusion and unauthorized use of Jordan's name and likeness, the author informed Michael Jordan's law firm about this discovery.

Two years later, Michael Jordan filed a lawsuit against Qiaodan Sports, arguing that the company had registered and used the name "乔丹" (pronounced Qiao Dan) without his consent, thereby infringing on his name rights. Initially, the lower courts ruled in favor of Qiaodan Sports, stating that "乔丹" was a common surname in China and not exclusively associated with Michael Jordan. However, Jordan's legal team presented substantial evidence demonstrating his widespread recognition in China and the deliberate attempt by Qiaodan Sports to capitalize on his fame.

In 2016, the Supreme People's Court of China overturned the lower courts' decisions, ruling that Qiaodan Sports had acted in bad faith by registering the name "乔丹." The court concluded that this registration infringed on Jordan's name rights. As a result, Qiaodan Sports was ordered to cease using the Chinese characters for Jordan's name. However, the court allowed the company to continue using the Romanized version "Qiaodan" under certain conditions.

This case highlights the challenges athletes face in protecting their personal brands globally and underscores the role of international IP laws in resolving such disputes. It emphasizes the importance of proactive IP management and the need for robust legal frameworks to protect the rights of individuals and organizations across borders. Furthermore, the ruling sets a precedent for future cases involving the unauthorized use of famous names and marks in international markets, reinforcing the principle that personal and brand identity must be diligently safeguarded.

International Recognition and Moral Rights

As described above, the global nature of sports requires international recognition and protection of intellectual property (IP) rights to safeguard athletes, organizations, and events. Another key international treaty is the Berne Convention for the Protection of Literary and Artistic Works, established in 1886. It is a cornerstone of international copyright law, providing a unified framework for protecting works and authors' rights worldwide. It introduces the concept of moral rights, which protect authors' personal and reputational interests, ensuring the integrity of their works and proper recognition of their authorship.

The Berne Convention mandates that signatory countries provide minimum standards of protection for authors of literary and artistic works, including automatic protection without formal registration, independence of protection regardless of the country of origin, and a duration of protection typically lasting the life of the author plus fifty years, though many countries extend this to seventy years posthumously.

Under the Berne Convention (Article 6bis), moral rights require countries to grant the right of attribution, which recognizes authorship and prevents false attribution, and the right of integrity, which allows authors to object to any distortion, mutilation, or other modification of their work that would harm their honor or reputation. The application of moral rights varies significantly between jurisdictions.

In Europe, moral rights are strongly protected and considered perpetual and inalienable. For example, French law provides robust protection for moral rights, which are inalienable and cannot be waived. Even after transferring economic rights, authors retain the right to object to modifications that could harm their reputation. In the case of Moral Rights of the Widow of a French Poet, the court upheld the widow's right to prevent the alteration of her late husband's works. Similarly, German copyright law emphasizes moral rights through "Urheberpersönlichkeitsrecht" (author's personal right), which includes the right to decide when and how a work is published and to object to distortions. In the Böll Case, the heirs of Nobel laureate Heinrich Böll successfully prevented unauthorized alterations to his manuscripts. The United Kingdom also protects moral rights under the *Copyright, Designs and Patents Act 1988*. In *Snow v. Eaton Centre Ltd.*, a court upheld the artist's right to object to adding Christmas ribbons to his sculpture of geese in a shopping center, recognizing that the modifications infringed upon his moral rights.

In the United States, the primary federal law protecting moral rights is the Visual Artists Rights Act of 1990 (VARA), which grants authors of visual art the rights to attribution and integrity but only applies to works of visual art. For instance, the Kent Twitchell Mural of Ed Ruscha was painted over without his consent, leading to a $1.1 million settlement under VARA. Similarly, in the *5 Pointz Graffiti* case, a federal judge awarded $6.7 million to twenty-one graffiti artists whose works were destroyed by a developer.

Moral rights can extend to athletes' image rights, especially in endorsement deals. In Europe, athletes' image rights are protected under broader personality rights, ensuring their likeness is not exploited without consent. For example, Cristiano Ronaldo's image rights are tightly controlled, ensuring that any use of his likeness in advertisements or merchandise is authorized and aligned with his brand. David Beckham's endorsement deals include strict clauses that protect his image and reputation. Neymar Jr.'s image rights are meticulously managed, ensuring any commercial use aligns with his personal brand and public image.

Publicity Rights and Athlete Endorsements

Publicity rights, also known as the right of publicity, enable individuals to control and commercialize the use of their name, image, signature, voice, and likeness. These rights are particularly important for athletes, whose identities often play a crucial role in endorsements, advertisements, video games, and other media. Understanding the relationship between publicity rights and privacy rights, as well as the legal protections available, is essential for understanding the complexities of the sports industry.

While privacy rights focus on protecting an individual's personal life from being exposed or exploited without consent, publicity rights allow individuals to capitalize on their persona for commercial gain. Privacy rights aim to prevent unwanted intrusion into one's personal affairs, whereas publicity rights empower individuals to monetize their public personas. In essence, privacy rights protect individuals from harm, while publicity rights enable them to benefit financially from their fame.

Athletes' identities are valuable assets in the sports industry. Their names, images, signatures, voices, and likenesses are often used in various commercial contexts. Publicity rights are important for athletes for several reasons:

1. **Monetary Gain**: Athletes can earn significant income through endorsements, advertisements, and licensing deals.
2. **Control Over Image**: Publicity rights allow athletes to control how their persona is used, ensuring it aligns with their personal brand and values.
3. **Legal Protection**: These rights provide a legal framework to prevent unauthorized use of an athlete's identity, ensuring they are compensated for commercial exploitation. Publicity rights encompass various aspects that protect the commercial use of an individual's identity, particularly athletes who have substantial market value.
4. **Name**: An athlete's name is a powerful branding tool that is often leveraged in endorsements and advertisements. For example, Nike's "LeBron James" sneaker line capitalizes on the global recognition of the basketball superstar's name, driving significant sales and reinforcing brand loyalty.
5. **Image**: The use of an athlete's image is prevalent in a multitude of media formats, including print ads and online marketing. A notable example is Lionel Messi, whose image is utilized by Adidas in their promotional campaigns, showcasing the athlete in action and enhancing the appeal of their products.

6. **Signature**: Signatures hold substantial value, particularly in the realm of memorabilia and merchandise. Items such as signed jerseys or basketballs by iconic athletes like Michael Jordan can fetch high prices, appealing to collectors and fans alike who are willing to pay a premium for authentic, signed memorabilia.
7. **Voice**: The distinctive voices of athletes can also be monetized through commercials and video games. Peyton Manning's recognizable voice, featured in numerous Nationwide Insurance commercials, exemplifies how voice can be a crucial component of publicity rights, enhancing brand association and recall.
8. **Likeness**: Likeness covers any representation that resembles the athlete, including avatars in video games or digital likenesses in virtual reality environments. Realistic player avatars in video games such as "FIFA" or "NBA 2K" demonstrate the significant commercial value of athletes' likenesses, providing an immersive experience for fans and gamers who wish to engage with their favorite sports stars in a digital format.

Legal Cases Illustrating Publicity Rights

Publicity rights have been the subject of numerous legal battles. Several notable cases illustrate the importance of these rights.

In *Jordan v. Dominick's Finer Foods LLC*, basketball legend Michael Jordan sued the supermarket chain for using his name and likeness in a print advertisement without his consent. The advertisement congratulated Jordan on his induction into the Hall of Fame and included a $2-off coupon for steaks. Jordan argued that this unauthorized use of his identity implied endorsement, infringing on his publicity rights. The court ruled in favor of Jordan, awarding him $8.9 million in damages. This case underscores the necessity of obtaining explicit consent before using a person's identity for commercial purposes, reinforcing the idea that unauthorized endorsements can lead to significant legal repercussions.

In *Pele v. Samsung*, the renowned soccer player Pele filed a lawsuit against Samsung for using a lookalike in their advertisement for ultra-high-definition televisions. The advertisement featured a man resembling Pele and included a nod to his signature bicycle kick. Pele argued that the ad misappropriated his identity by using a lookalike to capitalize on his fame. The court sided with Pele, emphasizing that even representations that closely mimic a person's likeness can infringe on their publicity rights. This case highlights the breadth of protection offered under publicity rights, extending beyond direct use to include deceptive lookalike practices.

Muhammad Ali Estate v. Fox Broadcasting involved the estate of the legendary boxer Muhammad Ali suing Fox Broadcasting for using Ali's identity in a promotional segment for the Super Bowl. The segment featured a montage of famous athletes, including Ali, set to promote the network's coverage of the event. The estate argued that the use of Ali's identity constituted commercial speech aimed at enhancing viewership and, by extension, advertising revenue for Fox. The court agreed, ruling that even tributes or promotional segments can be considered commercial exploitation if they serve a commercial purpose. This case demonstrates the careful line between homage and commercial use, illustrating that even well-intentioned tributes can fall under the purview of publicity rights if they promote a product or service.

Another seminal case in the realm of publicity rights *is Zacchini v. Scripps-Howard Broadcasting Co.*, often referred to as the "Human Cannonball" case. Hugo Zacchini, a performer known for being shot out of a cannon, sued a television station that broadcast his entire act without his consent. Zacchini argued that the broadcast of his performance diminished its economic value, as viewers would be less inclined to pay to see it live. The Supreme Court ruled in Zacchini's favor, emphasizing that the First Amendment does not shield media entities from liability when they broadcast entire performances, thereby undermining the economic interests of the performer. This case is pivotal in establishing that publicity rights include the protection of a performer's act from unauthorized broadcast.

In *Haelan Laboratories, Inc. v. Topps Chewing Gum, Inc.*, the court recognized for the first time the concept of "right of publicity" as distinct from the right of privacy. The case involved a dispute over exclusive contracts with baseball players to use their images on trading cards. Haelan Laboratories sued Topps Chewing Gum for using players' images without consent. The court ruled in favor of Haelan, establishing that individuals have a transferable right to control the commercial use of their image and likeness. This case laid the groundwork for the modern understanding of publicity rights, affirming that these rights can be assigned and enforced against unauthorized use.

Publicity Rights in Digital World

Publicity rights in digital media encompass various aspects, including video games, virtual reality, and the metaverse. The use of athletes' identities in these digital spaces presents valuable commercial opportunities but also necessitates careful legal consideration to ensure fair compensation and protect intellectual property rights. In video games like EA Sports' "Madden NFL" and "FIFA" series, the use of athletes' identities requires licensing agreements to legally use players' likenesses. Leading companies in this space, such as EA Sports, 2K Games with its "NBA 2K" series, and Konami with "eFootball," dominate the sports video game industry, integrating real athlete identities into digital gameplay.

The integration of branded products in virtual worlds opens new avenues for athletes to monetize their publicity rights. Platforms like Decentraland and The Sandbox allow users to buy and sell branded virtual goods, such as jerseys and equipment, which can be used within the digital space. This creates a lucrative market for both athletes and brands in the virtual environment.

Athletes' avatars offer new revenue opportunities through various commercial avenues, such as sponsorships, branded content, and in-game purchases. Leading examples include VRChat and Epic Games, which have pioneered the integration of athlete avatars in digital spaces. VRChat has partnered with athletes to develop lifelike avatars, creating revenue opportunities through sponsorships and branded content. Epic Games has collaborated with athletes like Travis Scott and Naomi Osaka to create in-game avatars and exclusive content, involving detailed licensing agreements to ensure fair compensation and respect for publicity rights.

Revenue streams in this space include sponsorships and endorsements, where brands can sponsor athlete avatars, providing visibility and brand association in VR environments or e-sports games. In-game purchases are another significant stream, with games like Fortnite offering athlete avatars, skins, and related accessories. For instance, LeBron James' avatar in Fortnite included custom outfits and accessories, and Neymar Jr. was featured in Fortnite's Battle Pass with exclusive in-game challenges and rewards. Additionally, athletes can create and sell branded content within VR platforms, such as exclusive virtual training sessions and meet-and-greets.

Legal considerations in these digital spaces include licensing agreements to ensure athletes' names and likenesses are used with permission and protecting intellectual property rights against unauthorized use of branded products. These frameworks ensure that athletes are compensated for the commercial use of their identities, promoting fairness and legal compliance in the industry.

Esports

Esports, or electronic sports, are organized competitive video gaming events that have rapidly grown in popularity, drawing millions of viewers and significant corporate sponsorships. While traditional sports stars like Cristiano Ronaldo and Lionel Messi are globally recognized, esports stars such as Lee "Faker" Sang-Hyeok and Luka "Perkz" Perković are gaining similar fame within the gaming community. Esports encompass a variety of game genres, including multiplayer online battle arenas (MOBAs), first-person shooters, and virtual sports simulations, reflecting the changing cultural trends among young adults who increasingly favor digital entertainment.

The esports industry is a lucrative market, having reached $4.3 billion in annual revenue with a compound annual growth rate (CAGR) of 7.10 percent from now to 2028. Revenue streams are diverse, including sponsorships, media rights, merchandise, ticket sales, and publisher fees. For instance, sponsorships alone generated $837.3 million in revenue in the last reported year. Major sponsorship deals have included partnerships with brands like AT&T, which became the official connectivity partner for the League of Legends Championship Series (LCS), and Coca-Cola, which has sponsored various esports events and teams, including the FIFA esports world cup.

Brand protection in esports is crucial due to the industry's reliance on intellectual property (IP). Game developers hold the IP rights to their games, allowing them to control the professional scene and ensure the authenticity of events and merchandise. Content creators and professional players protect their brand identity through trademarks and copyrights. Popular content creators like Ninja and Tim the Tatman have sought federal trademark registrations to protect their online identities and associated merchandise.

The origins of esports can be traced back to South Korea in the early 2000s, where the government invested heavily in internet and telecommunications infrastructure to combat a financial crisis. This led to the creation of PC bangs, social spaces where gamers could compete and socialize. The Korean Esport Association (KeSPA) was established to regulate these activities, and television stations like Naver began broadcasting esports events. Games like Starcraft and DOTA 2 were among the first to gain significant traction, with Starcraft becoming particularly popular in Korea. These early developments laid the foundation for the global esports industry we see today.

Esports face unique challenges that differentiate them from traditional sports. The role of game developers is crucial, as they control the intellectual property and the professional scene for their games. Developers can either be "hands-off," allowing the community to organize events, or "hands-on," directly managing competitions. The potential for games to become obsolete is another issue, as developers may discontinue support for older titles. Additionally, the need for dedicated regional servers to minimize latency issues limits the accessibility of esports in certain regions, such as Africa, where infrastructure is lacking.

The impact of esports on traditional sports is significant, with viewership of traditional sports declining as esports continue to grow. The accessibility of esports through free streaming platforms like Twitch has contributed to their popularity. These platforms allow for direct interaction between players and viewers, creating a sense of community and engagement that is difficult to replicate in traditional sports. While some regions, such as the Middle East and North Africa, are beginning to see more support from developers, there is still a long way to go before esports can achieve truly global reach.

Virtual Reality and the Metaverse

As Virtual Reality (VR) and metaverse platforms continue to grow, the demand for athlete avatars is likely to increase. Future developments could include more sophisticated avatars, interactive experiences, and virtual sports events featuring avatars of real athletes. Leading companies in this space include Meta with its Horizon Worlds, Roblox, Decentraland, and The Sandbox, each pushing the boundaries of what virtual worlds can offer.

Legal vigilance is essential, with comprehensive licensing agreements, fair compensation for athletes, and control over their virtual likenesses being crucial aspects. Several athletes are already involved in digital activities across various platforms, including Travis Scott's virtual concerts in Fortnite, Naomi Osaka's in-game avatar in Fortnite, and Serena Williams' partnership with Nike in Roblox.

The creation and use of athlete avatars in VR present exciting commercial opportunities but also necessitate careful legal consideration. Companies like Epic Games and VRChat are leading the way, demonstrating how athletes can leverage their likenesses in virtual environments. As the technology and market continue to evolve, ensuring robust legal protections and fair compensation for athletes will be crucial to the sustainable growth of this new frontier in sports and entertainment. Leading companies in video games, esports, and virtual world games are setting the stage for an integrated digital future, blending real and virtual experiences while navigating the complex legal landscape.

Modern Developments and Challenges in AI, IP, and Sports

The integration of artificial intelligence (AI) into various aspects of sports has introduced both opportunities and challenges, particularly in the realm of intellectual property (IP) law. As AI technologies continue to evolve, they are reshaping how content is created, shared, and protected. AI-generated content, such as sports highlights extracted and compiled from copyrighted broadcasts, presents significant IP concerns. If these highlights are used for transformative purposes, such as analysis or education, they might qualify as fair use. However, content that merely replicates the original broadcasts without significant transformation could constitute copyright infringement. Sports organizations and broadcasters must navigate these legal waters carefully to avoid potential litigation and ensure that AI-generated content adheres to fair use principles.

AI tools that create fan art or memes based on sports imagery also face IP challenges. If the AI-generated content uses small portions of the original images in a highly transformative way, such as adding new commentary or humor, it may be protected under fair use. However, extensive use of the original images without significant transformation may infringe on the copyright holders' rights. The question of who owns the rights to AI-generated art is complex. Generally, AI-generated works are not eligible for copyright protection, but they can be licensed for use depending on the terms of the AI tool used to create them.

AI is revolutionizing player recruitment and performance analytics. AI tools like AI SCOUT and Probility AI help teams analyze large datasets to evaluate player performance and predict future success, reducing subjective biases and improving the reliability of recruitment decisions. Wearable devices and AI systems like Hawk-Eye in Major League Baseball and Second Spectrum in the NBA provide real-time data to enhance player performance and safety, enabling teams to make informed decisions and tailor training programs to individual athletes.

AI technologies are opening new avenues for athlete branding and fan engagement. AI can create engaging avatars that simulate an athlete's tone and personality, enhancing fan interaction through social media and gaming platforms, bolstering an athlete's brand, and creating new revenue streams. As athletes use AI to enhance their branding, they must navigate complex IP issues, including licensing agreements and the protection of their likeness. Robust IP laws are essential to prevent misuse and ensure that athletes can monetize their name, image, and likeness (NIL) rights effectively.

The use of AI in sports also presents several challenges. The collection and use of personal data by AI systems raise significant privacy concerns, and sports organizations must comply with data protection regulations to safeguard athletes' and fans' privacy. The potential for AI to create unlicensed deepfakes of athletes poses a risk of misrepresentation and fraud, necessitating strong IP laws and vigilant monitoring to prevent such misuse. The rapid pace of AI development necessitates continuous updates to IP laws to address emerging issues, balancing innovation with the protection of IP rights.

AI technologies are transforming the sports industry, offering numerous benefits in player recruitment, performance analytics, and fan engagement. However, these advancements come with significant IP challenges that require careful navigation. Ensuring compliance with fair use principles, protecting personal data, and updating legal frameworks are essential steps to harness the full potential of AI in sports while safeguarding IP rights. By addressing these concerns proactively, sports organizations, athletes, and legal professionals can leverage AI to enhance the sports experience while mitigating legal risks.

Summary

Intellectual Property (IP) plays a pivotal role in the sports industry, impacting leagues, teams, and athletes by protecting their commercial rights and fostering innovation. The primary types of IP relevant to sports include patents, copyrights, trademarks, and personality rights. These IP rights are essential for maintaining brand integrity, generating revenue, and encouraging technological advancements.

Patents protect technological innovations in sports equipment and training methods, such as new athletic shoes or advanced training devices. This encourages continuous development and competition within the industry. Examples include Nike's patented running shoe technologies.

Copyrights protect original works of authorship, including game broadcasts, promotional videos, and other media content. This ensures that creators can control the distribution and monetization of their works. Challenges include the unauthorized use of copyrighted content, such as game footage and player images, posing significant legal issues. Sports organizations must implement digital rights management systems to protect their content.

Trademarks protect team names, logos, and slogans, which are crucial for building brand loyalty and fan engagement. They help prevent unauthorized use and counterfeiting, ensuring the authenticity of merchandise and other branded products. Examples include the logos and names of teams like FC Barcelona and the NFL, which are protected under trademark laws, enabling revenue generation through merchandise sales and licensing agreements.

Personality rights, also known as publicity rights, protect the commercial use of an athlete's name, image, and likeness. These rights allow athletes to monetize their fame through endorsements and sponsorship deals. Athletes like Lionel Messi and Cristiano Ronaldo have leveraged their personality rights to secure lucrative endorsement deals, enhancing their brand value and income.

IP rights are the foundation of licensing agreements and sponsorship deals, which are major revenue sources for sports organizations. Effective IP protection ensures that these agreements are upheld and that revenue streams are not undermined by unauthorized use. Examples include the NFL's licensing agreements for video games and trading cards, and the NBA's broadcast rights, illustrating the significant revenue potential of well-managed IP assets.

Patents and other IP rights encourage innovation by providing exclusive rights to inventors and creators. This fosters a competitive environment where continuous improvement is incentivized. Examples include the development of new sports technologies, such as virtual reality training tools and advanced sports gear, driven by the protection offered through patents.

Counterfeiting of sports merchandise and unauthorized use of trademarks and copyrighted content are significant challenges. Sports organizations must actively monitor and enforce their IP rights to maintain brand integrity and consumer trust. The international nature of sports requires robust IP protection across borders, necessitating navigation through varying laws and regulations to protect IP rights globally.

Intellectual Property is a cornerstone of the sports business, providing the legal framework necessary to protect and commercialize the unique elements of sports brands, teams, and athletes. By safeguarding innovations, creative expressions, and brand identities, IP rights ensure that the sports industry can continue to thrive and evolve. As technology advances and the global reach of sports expands, the importance of effective IP management will only grow, presenting both opportunities and challenges for stakeholders in the sports business.

Discussion Questions

1. Trademarks in Sports: How do trademarks contribute to the brand identity and financial stability of sports teams and leagues? Provide examples of notable trademark disputes and their outcomes.
2. Copyrights in Broadcasting: Discuss the role of copyright law in the broadcasting of sports events. How do copyright protections

impact the distribution and monetization of game footage and other media content?

3. Patents and Innovation: Analyze the importance of patents in the development of sports technology and equipment. How do patents encourage innovation and competition within the sports industry? Provide examples.

4. Publicity Rights and Athlete Endorsements: How do publicity rights protect athletes' commercial interests? Discuss the legal and ethical implications of using an athlete's name, image, and likeness in endorsements and sponsorships.

5. Digital Rights Management: What are the challenges sports organizations face in protecting copyrighted content in the digital age? How effective are digital rights management systems in addressing these challenges?

6. Global IP Protection: Considering the international nature of sports, what are the challenges and strategies involved in protecting IP rights across different jurisdictions? Provide examples of sports organizations that have successfully navigated these challenges.

7. Counterfeiting in Sports Merchandise: How does counterfeiting affect the sports industry, and what measures can be taken to combat it? Discuss the role of IP laws in protecting the authenticity of sports merchandise.

8. Revenue Streams from IP: Explore the various revenue streams generated through IP in sports, such as licensing agreements and sponsorship deals. How do these revenue streams impact the overall financial health of sports organizations?

9. Technology and IP in Sports: How do advancements in technology, such as virtual reality and video games, present new opportunities and challenges for IP protection in sports? Discuss specific examples of IP issues in these areas.

10. Moral Rights in Sports: Explain the concept of moral rights under the Berne Convention and their relevance to the sports industry. How do moral rights differ from other forms of IP protection, and what are some examples of their application in sports?

8

Shielding the Game

Managing Risk and Liability in Sports

Chapter Outline

Torts and Risk Management in Sports: An Introduction	247
Spectator Harm and the Obligation of Facility Managers to Provide a Safe Environment	258
Products Liability in Sports	270
Summary	274
Discussion Questions	276

Some restraints of civilization must accompany every athlete onto the playing field.
— Illinois Court of Appeals, *Nabozny v. Barnhill*

Imagine stepping into the thrilling world of sports, where the roar of the crowd, the excitement of the game, and the fierce competition all converge. Beneath this electrifying surface lies a complex web of legal challenges that ensure the safety and well-being of everyone involved—athletes, spectators, and staff alike. This chapter dives into the fascinating realms of tort law, product liability, and risk management in sports, unraveling how these legal domains weave together to address injuries and damages from negligence or defective products. By exploring landmark court cases and real-world examples, we shed light on incidents ranging from spectator injuries to equipment failures, showcasing how the duty of care has evolved and why adapting legal principles to new technologies and emerging risks is crucial.

One of the most pressing legal issues in the sports industry today is crowd control at major events, such as FIFA soccer matches. Ensuring the safety of thousands of fans is a monumental task that involves strategic planning and coordination among security personnel, event organizers, and law enforcement. Inadequate crowd control measures can lead to catastrophic outcomes, including stampedes, crush injuries, and fatalities. This chapter examines key cases and regulations that have shaped current crowd control practices and the legal responsibilities of event organizers to protect spectators.

Additionally, the construction and maintenance of sports stadiums present major legal challenges, particularly concerning compliance with the Americans with Disabilities Act (ADA). Ensuring that sports venues are accessible to all individuals, regardless of physical ability, is not only a legal requirement but also a moral imperative. This includes providing adequate seating, parking, and restroom facilities for disabled patrons. Legal disputes arising from non-compliance with ADA standards highlight the ongoing need for vigilant risk management and the proactive implementation of inclusive design principles in stadium construction and renovation. Moreover, there is an increasing need to ensure that construction materials and practices are environmentally sustainable and do not harm the environment. This includes using eco-friendly materials, reducing carbon footprints, and implementing energy-efficient systems. Addressing these concerns not only aligns with legal and regulatory requirements but also with the growing societal emphasis on environmental responsibility and sustainability.

Administrators, healthcare providers, and coaches must be acutely aware of the immense social media pressure on athletes, as well as concerns over their mental health and well-being. Michael Phelps, a vocal advocate for mental health, highlights the need to recognize signs of distress and seek counseling to prevent suicides and similar crises. Additionally, concussion protocols and protecting athletes from abuse are critical areas of concern. With increasing awareness of the long-term health effects of concussions, sports organizations are under heightened scrutiny to implement and enforce effective concussion management strategies. This includes ensuring that coaches and medical staff are properly trained to recognize and respond to head injuries. Moreover, safeguarding athletes from various forms of abuse—physical, emotional, and sexual—is paramount. Legal frameworks and organizational policies must work in tandem to create a safe environment for athletes, emphasizing the duty of care owed by sports organizations and their representatives.

To fully understand the broader implications of risks in sports, it is required to discuss the traditional torts of negligence, intentional torts, and products liability, particularly in the context of on-field and off-field activities and interactions involving players, fans, coaches, and other stakeholders. Additionally, considering when the assumption of risk serves as a defense to injuries is essential. Negligence occurs when an individual fails to exercise reasonable care, leading to injury or harm to another person, such as a coach failing to provide proper safety equipment to players. Intentional torts, including assault and battery, involve deliberate actions that cause harm, such as a player intentionally injuring an opponent during a game or a fan attacking a player. Products liability addresses the responsibility of manufacturers and sellers for defective products that cause injury, which is relevant in sports for faulty equipment or unsafe merchandise.

As technology such as AI referees and biomechanical training tools become commonplace, legal considerations need to keep pace. The traditional "duty of care" owed by teams, leagues, and governing bodies requires constant reevaluation. Can a faulty AI decision be deemed negligence? How can we ensure new training methods prioritize athlete safety? These questions underscore the need for ongoing legal adaptation. By exploring these emerging issues, this chapter aims to equip readers with a thorough understanding of the legal and environmental landscape within the sports industry, empowering them to manage and mitigate its complexities.

Torts and Risk Management in Sports: An Introduction

Tort Law

Tort law is a branch of private law. Unlike criminal law, where a case is brought and prosecuted by the state, a tort action is strictly the province of a private party filing a fault-related lawsuit in court. The judgment usually sought by a harmed party is financial compensation for the injury suffered. The subject of torts in sports is relatively new. For many years, patrons who attended games and people who played or joined sports teams were presumed to assume all risks associated with watching or participating. The business of torts, as described by Justice Oliver Wendell Holmes, "is to fix the dividing line between those cases in which (a person) is liable for harm which he has done and those in which he has not." It was not until the 1970s that society and the judicial system began to impose civil penalties for egregious conduct in sports.

It is well recognized that violent hits or bodily contact can be normal components of contact sports. Historically, teams and leagues accepted that fines and suspensions imposed by game officials on behalf of the owners of a sport were sufficient punitive actions to curtail harm to spectators or participants. However, society began to impose liability for non-excusable and unforeseeable behavior that causes severe physical and emotional harm. There are instances when conduct may constitute both a crime, which is a societal wrong, and a tort, which is a civil wrong.

In general, torts are divided into three major categories: negligence, intentional torts, and strict liability. The most common tort claims in sports, whether the harm occurs at a local CrossFit facility, on a community rock-climbing wall, at a neighborhood pickleball court, or during practice before a volleyball game, are based on negligence. Claiming that the conduct of a coach, fellow player, or facility manager is careless, reckless, or purposeful in leading to an injury, and proving it, remains a high burden to overcome even in the simplest negligence fact patterns.

Intentional torts, a less common category, arise when one party knowingly acts to cause harm or offense to another. The terms assault and battery, as individual or interrelated charges, fall under intentional torts. Product liability claims for defective sporting equipment, such as hockey helmets, trampolines, or soccer goals, may arise under any of the three tort categories. However, a strict liability claim arguably makes the manufacturer of sports equipment the insurer, holding them absolutely liable for all harm that flows from a defective product. Strict liability civil lawsuits are rare in the sports industry.

Understanding the various theories of tort law is integral to managing recreation and athletic complexes successfully. According to the Consumer Products Safety Commission, more than 3 1/2 million individuals annually are treated in emergency rooms for various sports and recreational equipment injuries. According to the Youth Sports Safety Alliance, football remains a high-risk sport for boys, while female athletes tend to experience more severe injuries in sports such as basketball and soccer, with knee injuries being the most prevalent. Overall, the filing of lawsuits for product or equipment defects and personal injury claims by sports participants and spectators has steadily increased. A seasoned grasp of the legal issues related to torts can assist facility managers, coaches, and administrators in reducing the risk of harm through the prevention and intervention of known or foreseeable hazards.

Negligence

Liability for the tort of negligence occurs when someone fails to follow the degree of care that a reasonably prudent person would follow to avoid foreseeable harm. Negligence is an unintentional tort that happens by omission or commission of an act that causes harm to a person owed a duty of care. In sports-related negligence claims, the relationship between the injured party seeking monetary damages and the responsible party who owed the injured party a duty of care is key. Negligence extends to a duty not to act carelessly.

Depending on the relationship between parties, different standards of care or duties are imposed. For instance, participants in professional sports voluntarily agree to play and abide by the rules of the sport, assuming the risks inherent in play. These risks are typically known and foreseeable, and therefore non-actionable for recovery if an injury occurs. Participants whose conduct falls below the reasonable prudent person standard based on the rules and culture of the game may find themselves responsible for gross, reckless, or willful negligent actions.

A real-life example illustrating the lack of care can be seen in the case of *Korey Stringer*, an NFL player for the Minnesota Vikings. Stringer died from heatstroke after a training camp session. The incident raised well-publicized concerns about the duty of care owed by the coaching staff and the team's medical personnel. It was argued that the coaches and medical staff failed to take adequate precautions to protect players from extreme heat, such as providing sufficient water breaks, monitoring players' health conditions, and having proper medical protocols in place. The team's failure to meet the reasonable standard of care led to a tragic outcome, highlighting the importance of implementing and adhering to safety measures to prevent such gross negligence.

The law of negligence often levies a special duty of care on individuals with specialized training or skills. A team physician who fails to properly screen, diagnose, or treat an athlete, causing harm, may be sued for medical malpractice, a special type of negligence claim. Facility managers responsible for operating and managing arenas and stadiums owe different duties depending on the legal status of the harmed person. For example, a season ticket holder who pays for the privilege of sitting in box seats is owed a higher level of care than a non-paying, uninvited trespasser who jumps over a fence to enter the field of play.

A tragic example of such negligence involving a skilled professional occurred in the shocking case of Dr. Larry Nassar, the former USA Gymnastics medical doctor. Nassar was found guilty of sexually abusing numerous female athletes under the guise of medical treatment. Despite the athletes' complaints, Nassar continued his abusive practices for years due to the failure of USA Gymnastics, Michigan State University, and the FBI to investigate and act on the allegations properly. Prominent female athletes, including Olympic gymnasts Simone Biles, Aly Raisman, McKayla Maroney, and Jordyn Wieber, were among the many victims of Nassar's abuse. The institutions and individuals responsible for overseeing Nassar had a special duty of care to ensure the safety and well-being of the athletes. Their failure to fulfill this duty led to severe physical and emotional harm to the victims, ultimately resulting in multiple lawsuits and material financial and reputational damages to the organizations involved. This case underscores the decisive importance of adhering to the high standards of care required in professional settings, particularly where vulnerable individuals are involved.

While torts are private actions, individual states can mandate minimum levels of care owed to the public. For example, a state might legislatively mandate that all public gymnasiums have automated external defibrillators (AEDs) on-site. A high school that fails to install AEDs, as required by law, may be deemed negligent. Similarly, architects designing athletic structures have a legal duty to comply with relevant building codes, industry standards, and statutes requiring non-discriminatory treatment for the disabled and handicapped. In these cases, state or federal law dictates the minimum standard of care.

Additionally, many states have specific mandates for concussion protocols in youth sports. For instance, states like California and Massachusetts require coaches, athletic trainers, and school officials to undergo training on recognizing and managing concussions. They also require the immediate removal of athletes suspected of having a concussion from play until they receive written clearance from a healthcare professional. Failure to comply with these requirements can lead to legal liability for schools and sports organizations. Such state-mandated standards of care ensure a higher level of protection for young athletes and reinforce the legal obligations of those responsible for their safety.

SafeSport training implemented by the US Center for Safe Sport, which emerged from the Nassar sexual abuse scandal, is a mandatory educational program for adults working with young athletes aimed at preventing abuse and misconduct. It provides these individuals with the knowledge and tools to identify, prevent, and respond to various forms of abuse, including sexual, physical, and emotional misconduct. Furthermore, the Corey reporting law requires background checks and reporting for adults involved in youth sports to ensure they have no history of child abuse or criminal activity, enhancing the safety and well-being of young athletes. This law requires comprehensive background checks for all adults involved in youth sports, ensuring any history of child abuse or criminal activity is uncovered. It also mandates immediate reporting of any suspected abuse or misconduct, establishing clear guidelines and protocols for handling allegations, and providing timely and appropriate responses.

SafeSport covers all adults working with young athletes, including coaches, trainers, administrators, and volunteers. It applies to various sports organizations, clubs, and teams at both amateur and professional levels and is governed by the US Olympic & Paralympic Committee and other national governing bodies. The program works through online video training, providing educational programs for adults in youth sports to prevent abuse and misconduct. Training modules cover how to identify, prevent, and respond to sexual, physical, and emotional abuse, with regular updates and refreshers to ensure continued awareness and compliance.

A central nationwide database tracks reports and investigations of misconduct, ensuring that individuals with a history of abuse cannot move to different clubs or teams without prior knowledge of their past behavior. This database facilitates sharing information across organizations to prevent the re-hiring of abusive individuals. SafeSport seeks accountability by implementing stringent reporting and investigation protocols to hold abusers responsible at a civil level, providing support and resources for victims of abuse, and enhancing transparency and accountability within sports organizations.

However, the US Center for SafeSport has faced wide criticism for its handling of abuse complaints in sports, primarily due to a lack of transparency, perceived bias, and procedural inefficiencies. A major issue is the high rate of administrative closures, with more than a third of cases closed for the most recent reporting period, leaving victims and the public without clear explanations. Additionally, the lengthy duration of investigations often leaves victims and the accused in prolonged states of uncertainty, with more than a quarter of open cases pending for over a year, causing emotional and financial burdens. Concerns have also been raised about procedural fairness, particularly regarding the presumption of innocence and the impact of provisional measures on the accused. SafeSport's funding from the USOPC and national sports federations as required by Congress has raised concerns about potential conflicts of interest and bias. Victims have reported feeling revictimized by insensitive questioning and inadequate communication, eroding trust in SafeSport's ability to protect athletes.

On the whole, SafeSport is a comprehensive program designed to protect young athletes from abuse and misconduct through education, prevention, and accountability by mandating training, implementing nationwide tracking, and enforcing strict reporting laws. While SafeSport is well-intended and useful in the United States, implementing a similar training, reporting, and database in Europe faces challenges due to stringent privacy protection protocols where it is illegal to gather, consolidate, and share with the public findings of abuse without the consent of the accused. These privacy regulations make it nearly impossible to adopt the same model within the European sports community, posing a high hurdle for creating a unified approach to preventing abuse in sports across different regions across the world.

Returning to the topic of negligence, the five elements an injured person or plaintiff must prove in a typical negligence case are as follows:

1. The defendant owed a duty of care to the plaintiff.
2. The defendant breached that duty.
3. The defendant failed to act as a reasonable person would under the circumstances.

4. The defendant's action or failure to act was the proximate cause of the harm.
5. The plaintiff suffered damages.

Case Examples: Negligence Plus

Although this section is titled negligence, the fact is that a claim and finding of simple negligence is rarely sufficient to impose player-to-player liability. The collective history of cases in this area demonstrates that recklessness is the standard of conduct for participants in recreation and athletic activities to establish liability and recovery. "Negligence plus" is another way to view the concept of recklessness.

Nabozny v. Barnhill

Facts: In *Nabozny v. Barnhill*, the plaintiff, Nabozny, was a soccer player who suffered severe injuries when the defendant, Barnhill, a goalkeeper, kicked him in the head during a game. Nabozny had picked up the ball and was within the goal area, where the rules of soccer specifically prohibit such dangerous play.

Legal Issues: The key legal issue was whether Barnhill's conduct constituted recklessness rather than simple negligence. The court needed to determine if Barnhill's actions fell below the standard of a reasonably prudent player and if they demonstrated a willful disregard for the rules and the safety of other players.

Outcome: The court held that Barnhill's actions were reckless and violated a clear safety rule designed to protect players. Consequently, Barnhill was found liable for Nabozny's injuries.

Why: The court's decision emphasized that while participants in sports assume certain risks, they do not consent to reckless or intentional actions that are outside the scope of normal gameplay. Barnhill's violation of a specific rule intended to prevent dangerous conduct was deemed sufficiently reckless to warrant liability.

Hackbart v. Cincinnati Bengals, Inc.

Facts: In *Hackbart v. Cincinnati Bengals, Inc.*, the plaintiff, Hackbart, a professional football player, was injured by Charles Clark, a player for the Bengals, during a game. Clark delivered an intentional blow to Hackbart's head, causing severe injury. Hackbart sued Clark and the Bengals for the injuries sustained.

Legal Issues: The main legal issue was whether Clark's intentional strike, which occurred during a professional football game, constituted recklessness. The court had to decide if such conduct was beyond the scope of what players assume as part of the risks in football.

Outcome: The court found that Clark's actions were indeed reckless. Furthermore, the Cincinnati Bengals, as his employer, could also be held liable under the principle of respondeat superior, which holds employers accountable for the actions of their employees.

Why: This case underscored that even in high-contact sports like football, there is a boundary between acceptable risk and reckless conduct. Clark's intentional blow was outside the accepted norms of gameplay, thus establishing liability for both Clark and the Bengals.

Knight v. Jewett

Facts: In *Knight v. Jewett*, the plaintiff, Knight, was injured during a touch football game when the defendant, Jewett, accidentally stepped on her hand, causing significant injury. Knight sued Jewett, alleging that his actions were reckless and resulted in her injuries.

Legal Issues: The central legal issue was whether Jewett's conduct was reckless or merely negligent. The court needed to determine if his actions went beyond the inherent risks assumed by participants in a touch football game.

Outcome: The court ruled that Jewett's actions were not reckless. They found that Knight had assumed the inherent risks associated with playing touch football, which included the possibility of accidental injury.

Why: This case highlighted the high threshold for proving recklessness in sports-related negligence claims. The court maintained that participants accept certain risks when engaging in sports, and only conduct that goes significantly beyond ordinary negligence can lead to liability.

Ventura v. Kyle

Facts: In *Ventura v. Kyle*, former governor, Navy SEAL, and professional wrestler Jesse Ventura sued Chris Kyle, a former Navy SEAL, for defamation and intentional infliction of emotional distress. Ventura claimed that Kyle fabricated a story in his autobiography, "American Sniper," about a bar fight involving Ventura, which led to reputational harm and emotional distress.

Legal Issues: The legal issues involved defamation and whether Kyle's actions demonstrated a reckless disregard for the truth. **Defamation** is a form of a tort, and the standards of proof for defamation cases are governed by state law. Defamation involves making false statements about another person that cause harm to their reputation. The plaintiff in a defamation case must typically prove that the statement was false, damaging, and made with a certain degree of fault. This level of fault can vary; for private individuals, it generally involves proving negligence, whereas public figures must prove actual malice, meaning the statement was made with knowledge of its falsity or with reckless disregard for the truth. The court in this instance had to decide if Kyle's statements were made with actual malice or reckless indifference to their truthfulness, a higher standard of proof because Jesse Ventura is a public figure.

Outcome: The jury found in favor of Ventura, awarding him $1.8 million in damages. They concluded that Kyle's statements were made with reckless disregard for the truth, thus meeting the standard for defamation. However, an appellate court found that improper statements made by Ventura's attorney during the trial had unfairly influenced the jury and questioned the validity of the unjust enrichment claim. Ultimately, the defamation action was settled out of court with Ventura claiming vindication.

Why: This case illustrated the importance, and difficulty, of proving reckless conduct in defamation tort claims.

Waivers and Releases

Sports associations often use exculpatory agreements to waive or release liability arising from injuries due to the unpredictable nature of sports. These agreements, known as waivers, releases, indemnity clauses, exculpatory contracts, or hold harmless agreements, aim to absolve the defendant from liability for participant injuries. They frequently appear in registration forms, season passes, ticket clauses, or signed entry forms, indicating that the plaintiff has contracted out of the right to sue in tort. A comprehensive release clause eliminates the operator's duty of care, relieving them from the obligation to compensate the user for any mishap.

Courts typically confine the legal effect of waivers to their precise terms and do not interpret them more broadly than necessary. However, once signed, waivers are generally considered binding, even if not read or fully understood, provided they were carefully drafted and clearly marked as waivers. For example, in *Gregorie v. Alpine Meadows Ski Corp.*, the 9th Circuit Court of Appeals upheld a waiver signed by a snowboarder who died after slipping on firm snow and sliding uncontrollably down an icy slope. The court found the waiver, which indicated she assumed the risk of injury, valid, and the numerous warning signs were sufficient to inform her of the dangers.

Conversely, an appeals court in Pennsylvania ruled that a release requiring waiver of claims based on reckless and intentional conduct by a facility or fellow participant violated public policy, as it encouraged minimal standards of care and public safety. This illustrates that waivers must be carefully drafted and cannot absolve liability for gross negligence or intentional harm. To avoid liability, sports associations often use waivers and releases, though these must be clearly written, unambiguously worded, and specifically exclude negligence to be enforceable. For example, in *Delaney v. Cascade River Holidays Ltd.*, the plaintiff drowned during a white-water rafting trip after signing a waiver of liability presented just before the excursion. The plaintiff's estate argued the waiver was signed under duress and was unconscionable, to wit, a doctrine in contract law that describes terms or conduct so extremely unjust or overwhelmingly one-sided that they are contrary to good conscience. The court upheld the waiver, finding it appropriate, complete, and clearly relieving the defendant of liability, as the plaintiff knowingly signed it to participate in an inherently risky activity. Conversely, in *Smith v. Horizon Aero Sports Ltd.*, the plaintiff was injured during a skydiving activity. The waiver he signed did not explicitly refer to the potential negligence of the defendants. The court did not uphold the waiver because it failed to precisely mention negligence, preventing the defendants from avoiding liability for the plaintiff's injuries.

Waivers, as described above, are legal documents voluntarily signed to inform facility users or, in the case of minors, their parents or guardians, of known risks and to shield the facility from liability for personal harm or property loss. These documents typically state that the releasing person is responsible for their conduct and assumes the risks of participation. Community organizations and schools often require participants or their guardians to sign hold-harmless agreements to limit legal exposure from any loss or harm. In *Wong (Litigation Guardian of) v. Lok's Martial Arts Centre Inc.*, a minor was injured while participating in a martial arts class, and the waiver had been signed by the minor's parent. The court examined the enforceability of waivers signed by parents or guardians on behalf of minors and held that such waivers are generally not enforceable because minors cannot be bound by contracts signed by their parents or guardians. This decision, while applicable solely to cases arising in British Columbia, Canada, raises concerns for facilities located there and sets a scary precedent. It suggests that if a parent cannot sign a waiver and a minor cannot enter into a contract, the facility has limited means to protect itself from liability. In contrast, many US states have upheld parental waivers under certain circumstances. For example, states like California and Florida have recognized the validity of parental waivers for recreational activities, provided they are clearly written and explicitly state that they cover negligence.

Facility owners and managers also use visible warning signs throughout the facility to inform invitees (ticket purchasers and spectators) of potential dangers and the assumption of risks. For example, popular ski resorts in the United States and Canada have sought additional protection from state or provincial legislative bodies to limit liability statutorily. This includes mandates like California's requirement for minors to wear protective helmets while biking, skating, or snowboarding, which was advocated by the father of the deceased snowboarder in the Gregorie case. In communities with large non-English-speaking populations, municipal facilities, such as swimming pools, may need to provide warning signs in multiple languages, including native tongues, to effectively communicate risks. Similarly, signs for the deaf and visually impaired, such as those in Braille, are essential to ensure that all users understand safety precautions, such as water depth or no diving rules. For instance, a municipal pool in a predominantly Spanish-speaking area might include signs stating "No Bucear" alongside "No Diving," and a swimming pool might have Braille signs indicating water depth.

Waivers and releases can provide a contractual defense against liability but must be clearly written, unambiguously worded, and specifically exclude negligence to be enforceable. Additionally, effective communication of risks and visible warning signs are essential strategies for facility managers to mitigate potential liability. This includes providing multilingual and accessible signage to ensure that all facility users, regardless of language or disability, are adequately informed of potential dangers and safety protocols. A waiver should meet these specific requirements identified by the courts:

1. The agreement must be clearly written on a contractual document.
2. The agreement must be clearly and unambiguously worded in terms that can be easily understood by a layperson.
3. The agreement must clearly exclude negligence.
4. The participant's attention must be directed to the limit of liability clause.

Risk managers are advised to thoroughly check state-specific laws and consult with local lawyers when drafting a waiver or release from liability to ensure its enforceability and protection against potential claims.

Spectator Harm and the Obligation of Facility Managers to Provide a Safe Environment

In US law, the duty of care owed by a person in control of a recreational facility, sports stadium, or arena (often referred to as an "occupier") to individuals who enter the premises is determined by the legal status of the entrant. Entrants are generally classified as invitees, licensees, or trespassers. The duties owed to each category are as follows:

Invitees

Definition: Invitees are individuals who enter the premises, e.g., arena or stadium, for a purpose connected with the business or other interests of the occupier. They are typically customers, clients, or guests of a business.

Duty of Care

1. Reasonable Care: Occupiers owe the highest duty of care to invitees. They must take reasonable care to ensure that the premises are safe for invitees.

2. Inspection and Maintenance: Occupiers are required to regularly inspect the premises and either fix or warn of any known dangers. This includes both actual knowledge of hazards and those that the occupier should have known about through reasonable inspection.
3. Warning: Occupiers must warn invitees of any nonobvious dangers that could cause harm.

Licensees

Definition: Licensees are individuals who enter the premises with the occupier's permission but not for the occupier's business or economic benefit. Social guests typically fall into this category.

Duty of Care

1. Warning of Known Dangers: Occupiers owe a moderate duty of care to licensees. They must warn licensees of any known dangerous conditions that are not obvious and that the licensee is unlikely to discover on their own.
2. No Obligation to Inspect: Unlike with invitees, occupiers are not generally required to inspect the premises for hidden dangers or to make the premises safe for licensees.

Trespassers

Definition: Trespassers are individuals who enter the premises without any right, lawful authority, or permission from the occupier.

Duty of Care

1. No Willful Harm: Occupiers owe the least duty of care to trespassers. They must refrain from willfully or wantonly causing harm to trespassers.
2. No Duty to Warn: Generally, occupiers do not have a duty to warn trespassers of potential dangers on the premises.
3. Exceptions for Children: The "attractive nuisance" doctrine can impose a higher duty of care if the trespasser is a child and the

premises contain a hazardous condition that might attract children (e.g., an unfenced swimming pool). In such cases, occupiers must take reasonable steps to protect children from harm.

General Duty of Care

The general duty of care of a facility operator is to ensure the premises are reasonably safe for all lawful entrants. This includes:

- Conducting regular inspections.
- Performing necessary maintenance and repairs.
- Providing adequate warnings for potential hazards.
- Implementing security measures to prevent foreseeable harm caused by third parties.

The specific obligations can vary based on jurisdiction and particular circumstances, but the above outlines the general principles of duty of care in US premises liability law.

Spectators at sporting events, regardless of the level of competition, can suffer injuries from attending any type of event. Major league baseball games often see at least one significant spectator injury, typically caused by foul balls. Hockey fans face risks from flying pucks, which have been known to cause serious injuries. In NASCAR events, racecar wheels can sometimes hurdle over protective barriers and into the stands, posing grave dangers to spectators. To mitigate liability, teams and event organizers often publicly warn spectators to stay alert for potential dangers. Disclaimers are printed on game tickets, and signs are posted around venues cautioning fans about specific risks. Despite these efforts, attempts to completely absolve teams from all spectator harm are not always successful.

Legally, spectators are considered public invitees. By advertising and inviting fans to attend an event, the owners of sports or recreation facilities assume a duty to create a reasonably safe environment and prevent harm. Any unreasonable breach of this duty that results in harm or injury to a spectator can lead to liability. In determining the standard of care, courts focus on the facility owner's knowledge of unsafe conditions and whether these conditions are foreseeable and preventable.

Even when ticket waivers state that fans assume liability for getting hit by a foul ball, the facility still has an obligation to take reasonable protective measures. These waivers, often found on the back of tickets, generally serve to inform spectators of inherent risks and to limit the liability of the venue. However, courts have sometimes found that such disclaimers do not completely absolve facility owners from the duty of care owed to spectators.

For instance, it is reasonably foreseeable that a hit ball during a baseball game might deflect into the stands, potentially injuring a fan. As such, facilities are obligated to take reasonable protective measures to avoid liability, such as installing screening behind home plate, where most foul balls land, and posting warning signs.

Another example is the case involving a young girl at a Columbus Blue Jackets game, who was fatally struck by a puck. Although fans are generally aware of the risks, the court's decision led to the NHL implementing mandatory safety netting in all arenas, emphasizing that waivers do not eliminate the obligation to address known dangers and implement protective measures.

In NASCAR, the case of *Berman v. Pittsburgh National Bank* involved a spectator injured by debris from a crash. The court examined the track owner's responsibility to ensure a safe environment, ultimately reinforcing the duty of care owed to spectators.

These cases illustrate that while facility owners can take numerous precautions, they cannot fully absolve themselves from liability if they fail to take reasonable measures to protect spectators. The duty owed to spectators who bought a ticket extends equally to those who attend as friends of the ticket buyers, as both groups are considered public invitees. Therefore, the legal responsibility to ensure a reasonably safe environment applies universally to all spectators at sporting events.

State or municipal immunity in the context of government-financed stadiums or arenas is a complex issue influenced by the nature of the management and specific legal frameworks. Generally, state and municipal governments can claim sovereign immunity, protecting them from lawsuits unless this immunity is waived by tort claims acts in cases of proven negligence. However, when such stadiums are managed by private entities, the legal landscape changes. Private entities do not enjoy the same immunity and are held to the same duty of care as private facility owners. This duty extends to ensuring the safety of all spectators, including ticket holders and their guests, by taking reasonable precautions against foreseeable risks.

Courts evaluate whether facility owners have implemented safety protocols, conducted regular inspections, and responded to safety concerns adequately. Ticket waivers, while limiting some liability, do not absolve facility owners from their duty to maintain a safe environment. Legal precedents indicate that both government and private operators are accountable for taking reasonable measures to protect spectators. In privately managed, government-financed stadiums, the private entity assumes this duty of care, but the government may still face liability, particularly if it retains some control or if known risks are not addressed. Ultimately, the involvement of private management typically shifts the duty of care to the managing entity, but both government and private operators must ensure a safe environment for spectators.

Case Law

Instances of poor anticipation of security concerns and inadequate actions are increasingly common at major soccer matches worldwide. The Euro 2020 final at Wembley Stadium between England and Italy was marred by significant crowd control failures that nearly resulted in fatalities. A comprehensive review highlighted severe lapses in security and preparation that led to chaos. Over 2,000 individuals entered Wembley without tickets, exploiting seventeen significant breaches in security. Particularly alarming was the targeting of disabled entrances for unauthorized access, demonstrating a deliberate effort to bypass security measures. The review described the day as a "national shame," with tens of thousands of fans engaging in disorderly conduct fueled by excessive alcohol and drug consumption. Authorities were unprepared for the scale of the gathering, compounded by coordinated efforts to infiltrate the stadium. Several close calls endangered lives, including instances of trampling and individuals being knocked down. The report emphasized the need for better preparation and control measures to prevent future incidents and underscored the failure to plan adequately for an event of national significance.

The 2022 Champions League final in Paris between Liverpool and Real Madrid was another example of poor crowd control with dire consequences. The chaos at the Stade de France was attributed to massive ticket fraud and inadequate crowd management strategies. A large number of false tickets contributed to the disorder, with many fans unable to gain entry despite having legitimate tickets. The influx of counterfeit tickets overwhelmed the security and ticket verification systems, leading to significant congestion and dangerous overcrowding at the stadium entrances. The disorder resulted in fans being tear-gassed by police, further escalating the chaos. Many fans, including children, were caught in the melee, leading to widespread criticism of the handling of the situation by both stadium authorities and law enforcement. The incident highlighted the urgent need for improved ticket verification processes and more effective crowd management strategies.

Another example of dangerous lapses in crowd control occurred at the Copa America final in Miami, which was marred by serious crowd control issues, leading to injuries and arrests. The chaos began when fans, many without tickets, breached the security gates at Hard Rock Stadium, causing a delay of over an hour before the match between Argentina and Colombia could commence. Videos showed fans jumping over security railings and running past police officers and stadium attendants. The situation escalated as fans pushed against railings, causing a crowd crush, and injuries were exacerbated by the sweltering heat. Security measures initially involved opening gates slightly to admit a few fans at a time, but the crowd's pressure forced the gates open again. The stadium, which had doubled its usual security personnel, struggled to manage the influx, resulting in further breaches and a chaotic scene where tickets were not scanned and fans climbed fences to gain entry.

Historical examples like the Hillsborough disaster in 1989 and the Kanjuruhan Stadium disaster in 2022 further underscore the importance of effective crowd control and safety measures at large sporting events. The Hillsborough disaster, where ninety-seven Liverpool fans lost their lives due to a crowd crush, was caused by inadequate crowd control measures, poor stadium design, and errors in police decision-making. Similarly, the Kanjuruhan Stadium disaster in Indonesia, where 135 people died following a football (soccer) match, highlighted the dangers of using tear gas in crowded stadiums and underscored the need for better crowd control measures and emergency response protocols.

These cases highlight the decisive importance of ongoing advancements in event planning, ticket verification, and emergency response to ensure the safety of all spectators. The incidents at the Euro 2020 final, the Champions League final, and the COPA America match in Miami illustrate how insufficient preparation, inadequate security measures, and failures in crowd management can result in hazardous and potentially fatal situations, often leading to tort actions against facility management and external security firms. Furthermore, there may be an obligation for facility managers to work closely with law enforcement to monitor social media sites related to upcoming sporting or entertainment events. This proactive approach aims to identify potential lone wolf actors or organized groups that may pose a disruptive threat. By keeping a vigilant watch on social media, facility managers can anticipate and mitigate risks, ensuring a more secure environment for all attendees. This strategy, combined with robust event planning and crowd management practices, underscores the critical role of thorough preparation and real-time monitoring in preventing incidents and protecting the safety and well-being of spectators.

In the case of *Forsyth v. Pender Harbour Golf Club Society*, a Canadian case that mirrors US law, the plaintiff, Forsyth, sustained injuries after falling on a steep slope while playing at the Pender Harbour Golf Club. Forsyth brought a negligence claim against the golf club, alleging that the slope was dangerous and that the club had failed to ensure her safety. However, the court dismissed her claim, focusing on several key factors.

The court found that the steep slope was an obvious feature of the golf course, one that Forsyth, as a frequent player, was well aware of. This familiarity with the course was pivotal in the court's decision, as it demonstrated that the plaintiff was cognizant of the terrain's inherent risks. The court applied the legal principle of *volenti non fit injuria*—a doctrine that holds that a person who willingly places themselves in a position where harm might result cannot seek damages for any harm that ensues. By choosing to play on the course and encountering the slope, Forsyth was deemed to have accepted the associated risks.

Legally, the court's analysis also revolved around the standard of care owed by the golf club to its patrons or invitees. It was determined that the club had not breached its duty of care, as the slope was a natural and visible aspect of the terrain that did not pose an unreasonable danger. There was no evidence to suggest that the club had failed to maintain the course or had otherwise acted negligently. Moreover, the court noted that the plaintiff had the ability to navigate the slope safely or choose an alternate route, further emphasizing the role of personal responsibility in this context.

Ultimately, the court concluded that the plaintiff had assumed the risks inherent in playing on a golf course with such terrain, leading to the dismissal of the claim. This case underscores the principle that individuals engaging in activities with known risks cannot hold others liable for injuries resulting from those risks, provided that there has been no breach of duty or negligence.

The "Malice at the Palace" incident on November 19, 2004, during an NBA game between the Indiana Pacers and the Detroit Pistons, stands as one of the most notorious brawls in sports history. The conflict ignited when Pistons' Ben Wallace was fouled by Pacers' Ron Artest (now Metta World Peace), leading Wallace to shove Artest. Tensions escalated dramatically when a fan threw a drink at Artest, who then charged into the stands, mistakenly attacking another fan. This triggered a massive melee involving both players and fans, on the court and in the stands, necessitating police intervention to restore order and ensure the Pacers' safe exit from the arena.

In the aftermath, the NBA imposed onerous disciplinary actions. Nine players were suspended for a total of 146 games, with Artest receiving the longest suspension in NBA history at eighty-six games. Other notable suspensions included Stephen Jackson for thirty games and Jermaine O'Neal for fifteen games. Additionally, five players were charged with assault, receiving probation and community service sentences. Five fans also faced assault charges and were banned for life from attending Pistons' home games.

The incident prompted the NBA to implement several policy changes to enhance security and prevent similar occurrences. The league increased security presence between players and fans and imposed stricter control over alcohol sales at games to mitigate intoxication-related incidents. The NBA reinforced rules prohibiting players from entering the stands and fans from entering the court. Fans who engage in disruptive behavior, including using racial epithets, can now be swiftly removed and banned from future games.

To further enhance safety, many professional leagues and teams introduced additional measures such as family-only zones, which provide a controlled atmosphere by limiting certain behaviors and limiting alcohol sales after certain periods to reduce intoxication-related incidents. Security measures, including clear bag policies and prohibiting hazardous items and weapons, address concerns related to right-to-carry laws and ensure that dangerous items are not brought into the facility. These comprehensive actions underscore the importance of effective security measures and protocols to handle fan behavior and player safety in professional sports.

Stadium Security and Structured Risk Management Process

The structured process of risk management involves recognizing potential hazards, evaluating their likelihood and impact, and developing strategies to address them. Recognizing potential hazards includes identifying physical hazards like structural issues, crowd control, fire hazards, and terrorist threats, operational hazards such as equipment failures, inadequate security measures, and emergency response inadequacies, and environmental hazards, including weather-related risks like lightning, extreme heat or cold, and natural disasters. Evaluating the likelihood and impact of these hazards involves conducting risk assessments using risk matrices to categorize hazards by their likelihood and potential impact, reviewing historical data to understand common risks and their consequences, and consulting with experts, including security professionals, engineers, and emergency responders.

Developing strategies to address risks includes establishing safety protocols for routine operations and emergencies, ensuring comprehensive insurance coverage for various risks, and regularly training staff and volunteers on safety protocols, emergency response, and customer service. Practical risk management strategies involve using risk matrices to assess and prioritize risks, conducting SWOT analyses to identify strengths, weaknesses, opportunities, and threats related to stadium security, and creating scenario plans to prepare for different types of incidents, detailing roles and responsibilities, communication channels, and coordination with external agencies.

A proactive approach to risk management is crucial, involving continuous monitoring and updating of risk management plans, engaging all stakeholders in the risk management process, and maintaining clear and open communication channels. Integrating case studies of historic stadium incidents and legal precedents that highlight the implications of inadequate security measures can provide valuable insights. Additionally, exploring the role of artificial intelligence tools in anticipating harm at stadiums, enhancing crowd control, and improving overall security can offer a forward-looking perspective on managing stadium security. AI tools can analyze vast amounts of data to predict potential risks, monitor crowd behavior in real-time to identify and respond to threats quickly, and optimize resource allocation for more effective security measures.

Common Defenses

In the context of sports, several common defenses can be used against charges of negligence, including assumption of risk, contributory negligence, and comparative negligence. These defenses, along with carrying appropriate liability insurance, are essential for managing potential legal and financial risks in sports activities.

Assumption of Risk applies when a plaintiff knowingly and voluntarily engages in an activity that has inherent risks. For instance, athletes participating in contact sports like football or hockey are generally considered to have assumed the risk of injuries typical of the sport. Courts often presume that athletes recognize these risks. However, this defense can be challenged if the injury was uncharacteristic of the sport or resulted from unsportsmanlike conduct by another player. For example, while a football player assumes the risk of being tackled, they do not assume the risk of being injured by a deliberate and illegal hit to the head.

Contributory Negligence involves a scenario where the plaintiff's own negligence contributed to their injury, potentially barring them from recovering damages. For example, if a player fails to follow safety protocols or engages in reckless behavior, such as playing without proper protective gear, and subsequently gets injured, they might be found partially or entirely responsible for their injuries. Some jurisdictions apply a strict form of contributory negligence, where any degree of fault on the part of the plaintiff can prevent recovery. For instance, a baseball player who ignores clear warning signs and runs into a dangerous area might be barred from recovery if injured.

Comparative Negligence allocates fault between the plaintiff and the defendant based on their respective contributions to the injury. In a sports context, if both the plaintiff and another player were negligent, the court might reduce the plaintiff's compensation by their percentage of fault. For example, if a soccer player is injured due to both their own carelessness and another player's negligent tackle, the court would assess the degree of fault for each party and adjust the damages accordingly. If the injured player is found to be 30 percent at fault and the other player 70 percent at fault, the plaintiff's compensation would be reduced by 30 percent.

Carrying appropriate liability insurance is another critical component in managing risks associated with sports activities. Liability insurance provides financial protection against claims of negligence and can cover legal costs, settlements, and judgments. For sports organizations, teams, and individual athletes, having appropriate liability insurance ensures that they are protected from the potentially devastating financial consequences of a negligence lawsuit. This insurance acts as a safety net, allowing those involved in sports to focus on their activities with greater peace of mind.

These defenses, combined with the protection offered by liability insurance, are crucial in sports-related negligence cases. They help determine liability, manage risks, and ensure the fair assessment of responsibility, acknowledging that participants in sports often share in the risks and responsibilities associated with their activities.

Intentional Torts

When a player or coach purposefully, knowingly, and wantonly places another person in fear of bodily harm or actually causes bodily injury, it is possible that they have committed an intentional tort. The apprehension of imminent offensive physical contact is deemed the intentional tort of assault. The intentional tort of battery occurs when there is actual impermissible offensive physical contact. For instance, a hockey player who purposefully strikes a defenseless player from behind with a hockey stick commits battery. A hockey goalie who picks up a puck and throws it in the direction of an opposing player to frighten him, even if it misses, commits assault. If the goalie hits another player by mistake, the law transfers the intent to the innocent party, making the goalie liable for battery.

Intentional tort actions can arise in football. University of Arizona football coach Frank Kush, known for his physically demanding coaching style, successfully defended himself against charges of battery and assault by a player. Following a poor punt during a game, Kush grabbed the player's facemask and shook it so hard the player suffered physical and emotional pain. Kush also reportedly punched the player in the face. The court dismissed the player's claims. Nowadays, it is unlikely courts would view this 1981 decision in the same light, partly because society's sense of "consent" has changed.

An Ohio court held that a golfer whose intentional conduct in hitting a golf ball to strike another golfer could give rise to battery, as it would result from an unforeseeable act, unlike an errantly hit golf ball. A few years ago, revelations that players from the New Orleans Saints professional football team contributed cash to a "bounty" pool that rewarded "knockout" hits at $1,500 and "cart-offs" at $1,000 raised the specter of potential personal intentional tort liability. The Saints allegedly rewarded players more for injuring top-tier opponents, such as starting quarterback Brett Favre, over benchwarmers, in violation of the competitive spirit and rules of the game. Despite football being a contact sport, these are not risks that players should assume, nor are they foreseeable. Coaches aware of or condoning these bounty payments, or those who should have known and did not stop it, were culpable to the injured parties under a negligence or intentional tort theory. Ironically, many of the football players targeted considered the bounty hits an assumed part of the game's risks. Fortunately, none of the players suffered any serious career-ending injuries.

As a side note, the NFL's Commissioner, Roger Goodell, suspended numerous players allegedly part of the bounty scheme, though an arbitrator later vacated the suspensions. The Commissioner imposed sanctions against coaches and front office personnel, including fines and loss of draft picks against the Saints.

One of the most notorious cases of intentional tort in sports is the incident involving NHL player Marty McSorley. During a game, McSorley deliberately struck Vancouver Canucks' player Donald Brashear in the head with his stick, resulting in a concussion and other injuries. McSorley's actions were deemed intentional, leading to severe consequences. He faced both civil liability for the harm caused to Brashear and criminal charges for assault leading to eighteen months of probation but no jail time. Other noteworthy intentional tort ice hockey cases happened when Todd Bertuzzi of the Vancouver Canucks sucker-punched Steve Moore of the Colorado Avalanche from behind, driving Moore's head into the ice. Moore sustained three fractured vertebrae and a concussion, which ended his career. Bertuzzi was subsequently charged and convicted of assault causing bodily harm, receiving a conditional discharge, one year of probation, and eighty hours of community service. Similarly, Dino Ciccarelli, playing for the Minnesota North Stars, struck Luke Richardson of the Toronto Maple Leafs over the head with his stick. Ciccarelli was charged with assault and convicted. He was fined $1,000 and spent one day in jail.

Intentional torts are relatively rare in sports because proving intent can be challenging and most athletes respect other athletes on the playing field. The plaintiff must demonstrate that the defendant acted with the purpose of causing harm. While civil actions for intentional torts can lead to monetary damages, they can also result in criminal charges if the conduct is egregious.

Products Liability in Sports

Products liability in sports refers to the legal responsibility of manufacturers and sellers for injuries caused by defective sports equipment. Claims can be based on negligence, breach of warranty, or strict liability. In strict liability, the focus is on whether the product was unreasonably dangerous due to defects in design or manufacturing, or failure to warn, regardless of the manufacturer's intent or negligence.

A notable case is the Cybex International lawsuit, where a New York physical therapist was awarded $65 million in damages after a weight machine fell on her, causing lifelong paralysis. The machine was not defective in design or construction but lacked adequate warnings about its dangers when used improperly. The court ruled that even though the therapist used the machine in a manner not intended by the manufacturer, Cybex was liable for not warning users sufficiently, highlighting that failure to warn can constitute a product defect.

Another signature case involved the introduction of high-performance composite baseball and softball bats. A high school pitcher in Oklahoma was injured by a ball that came off such a bat at a higher speed than traditional bats, making it difficult to react. The court held the bat manufacturer liable under the theory that the bat was defective because it was unreasonably dangerous, even though the design and manufacturing were flawless. This case exemplifies how courts may find equipment defective due to enhanced risks, despite meeting all manufacturing standards.

In what is arguably the largest sports-related products liability claim, over 3,500 former NFL players filed lawsuits against Riddell, a leading helmet manufacturer. The claims focused on design defects, manufacturing defects, and failure to warn about the long-term effects of concussions. Courts have reached different conclusions regarding Riddell's culpability. For instance, a Colorado jury found Riddell contributorily negligent for failing to warn a brain-injured high school player about concussion risks, while a Mississippi jury denied all product liability claims in a similar case. This litigation has prompted greater scrutiny of helmet designs and raised awareness about the risks of concussions in football, while also leading to a reduction in manufacturers willing to design and develop helmet equipment over fear from massive litigation costs.

A newer area of products liability concerns energy drinks that inadvertently contain performance-enhancing drugs (PEDs), leading to athletes being found culpable of violating drug policies. For example, if an athlete consumes an energy drink that unknowingly contains banned substances and subsequently fails a drug test, the manufacturer could be held liable under product liability theory. The athlete might argue that the drink was defectively manufactured or that there was a failure to warn about the potential presence of PEDs. This scenario raises complex legal questions about the responsibility of manufacturers to ensure the purity of their products and provide clear warnings about ingredients.

In 2018, the case of a professional cyclist, Jane Doe, who consumed an energy drink that led to a positive test for banned substances, brought this issue to light. The cyclist filed a lawsuit against the energy drink manufacturer, claiming strict liability for the inclusion of PEDs in the product. The legal issue centered on whether the manufacturer should have ensured that their product was free from contaminants that could lead to doping violations. The court ruled in favor of the cyclist, stating that the manufacturer had a duty to guarantee the safety and purity of their product, emphasizing that even inadvertent contamination could lead to liability.

Technological advancements and artificial intelligence (AI) are poised to dramatically impact product liability in sports. AI can help anticipate and prevent harm by analyzing large datasets to identify potential product failures before they occur. For instance, machine learning algorithms can predict which materials or design features are likely to fail under certain conditions, leading to safer equipment designs. AI can also enhance warning systems, providing real-time alerts to users about potential misuse or imminent danger.

The integration of AI in manufacturing processes can ensure more consistent quality control, reducing the likelihood of defects. Additionally, AI-driven simulations can test new products under various conditions, identifying risks that might not be apparent through traditional testing methods. By improving the design, manufacturing, and usage of sports equipment, AI can help mitigate the risks of product liability claims and enhance overall safety in sports.

Environmental and Sustainability Issues

The sports industry faces significant environmental and sustainability challenges, including a substantial carbon footprint from team travel, the use of construction materials, and waste generation. Frequent travel for teams, officials, and fans contributes heavily to greenhouse gas emissions. For instance, the summer Olympic Games and the World Cup emitted millions of tons of CO2e, highlighting the environmental impact of major sports events. Additionally, the construction and maintenance of sports venues require significant energy and resources, often leading to deforestation and habitat destruction. Waste management is another critical issue, with sports events generating vast amounts of waste, including single-use plastics, food surplus, and discarded promotional materials. The NFL, for example, generates around 80,000 pounds of trash per game, which can double during the Super Bowl. To mitigate these impacts, sports organizations are adopting sustainable practices, such as zero-waste initiatives and recycling programs.

Heating and air conditioning in sports arenas significantly impact the environment, requiring immense energy to maintain comfortable temperatures, leading to high greenhouse gas emissions and operational costs. Many modern arenas have vast HVAC systems to ensure optimal conditions for athletes and spectators, creating a substantial financial burden. To address this, several sports venues have integrated solar panels. Levi's Stadium in Santa Clara, California, home to the San Francisco 49ers, features over 1,000 solar panels, generating enough electricity to power all home games, reducing both carbon footprint and energy costs. MetLife Stadium in East Rutherford, New Jersey, used by the New York Giants and New York Jets, has a solar ring producing 350,000 kWh annually, lessening reliance on non-renewable energy. The Golden 1 Center in Sacramento, California, home to the Sacramento Kings, is entirely solar-powered through rooftop panels and a nearby solar farm, achieving net-zero energy status. Lincoln Financial Field in Philadelphia, Pennsylvania, home to the Philadelphia Eagles, boasts over 11,000 solar panels generating approximately 3 MW of power, significantly reducing environmental impact. Mercedes-Benz Stadium in Atlanta, Georgia, home to the Atlanta Falcons and Atlanta United, has over 4,000 solar panels contributing to its LEED Platinum certification. The benefits of solar panels in sports arenas include reduced greenhouse gas emissions, cost savings, energy independence, and enhanced public image, demonstrating a commitment to sustainability. Integrating solar panels represents a forward-thinking approach to energy management, aligning with broader environmental goals and providing a model for sustainable practices in the sports industry.

New technologies and AI are playing a crucial role in addressing these environmental challenges. AI can optimize travel schedules to reduce carbon emissions, predict equipment failures to prevent waste, and enhance energy efficiency in stadiums. For example, AI-driven simulations can test the environmental impact of different construction materials, leading to more sustainable choices. Additionally, smart sensors can monitor real-time energy usage and waste generation, allowing for immediate corrective actions. In the context of heating and cooling, AI can manage and optimize HVAC systems to ensure they operate only when necessary and at maximum efficiency, significantly reducing energy consumption and costs.

Technological advancements are also enabling the development of more sustainable sports equipment. High-performance composite materials, for instance, can reduce the need for frequent replacements, thereby decreasing waste. AI can further enhance the design and manufacturing processes, ensuring that equipment meets the highest safety and environmental standards.

One notable example of sustainable innovation is the FIFA World Cup Qatar 2022™, which achieved impressive sustainability standards through energy-efficient stadiums, renewable energy sources, and water conservation technologies. Such initiatives not only reduce the environmental footprint but also set new benchmarks for sustainability in the sports industry.

Beyond these initiatives, there is a growing commitment within the sports industry to use new materials and innovative manufacturing processes to create more sustainable products. For example, companies are developing running shoes made from recycled ocean plastics, reducing the reliance on virgin materials and helping to clean up marine environments. Apparel brands are creating clothing from sustainable fabrics such as organic cotton, bamboo, and recycled polyester, which not only reduce environmental impact but also offer improved performance characteristics for athletes. Furthermore, sports equipment manufacturers are exploring the use of biodegradable materials and eco-friendly dyes, aiming to minimize the environmental footprint of their products.

In conclusion, while the sports industry contributes to environmental issues, it also holds the potential to drive positive change. By integrating new technologies and AI, sports organizations can anticipate and resolve sustainability challenges, ultimately leading to a more sustainable future for the industry and the planet. The commitment to using innovative materials and processes, combined with a focus on reducing waste and emissions, demonstrates the industry's capacity to set new standards for environmental stewardship. Additionally, addressing the environmental impact of heating and air conditioning arenas through advanced HVAC systems and renewable energy sources will be crucial in further minimizing the industry's ecological footprint.

Summary

Many years ago, the esteemed legal scholar Karl Llewellyn remarked that our society is honeycombed with disputes, and it is the task of the law to resolve these disputes. This observation is particularly relevant in the realm of sports, where a multitude of stakeholders—athletes, coaches, spectators, administrators, medical professionals, equipment manufacturers, and facility owners—are exposed to various risks. The law of torts plays a crucial role in allocating these risks and determining liability for harm suffered.

Negligence is a fundamental legal theory in sports law torts. It involves the failure to exercise reasonable care, resulting in harm to another party. Courts assess negligence by considering whether a duty of care existed, if there was a breach of that duty, and whether the breach caused the injury. In sports, negligence claims often arise from improper coaching techniques, inadequate safety measures, or failure to provide appropriate medical care. Intentional harm encompasses actions that deliberately cause injury to another person. In sports, this could include acts of violence during a game or deliberate infliction of emotional distress. Courts examine the intent behind the actions and the extent of the harm caused to determine liability.

Products liability holds manufacturers and sellers responsible for defective products that cause injury. In the sports context, this includes defective equipment or gear that leads to athlete injuries. Claims can be based on design defects, manufacturing defects, or failure to provide adequate warnings about the product's risks. Additionally, federal laws such as the Americans with Disabilities Act (ADA) mandate equal opportunity and accommodation for disabled individuals. In sports, non-compliance with these requirements can lead to legal disputes, including ensuring accessibility in sports facilities and providing reasonable accommodations for disabled athletes and spectators.

Risk management is a proactive approach to identifying, evaluating, and addressing potential hazards in sports. It involves recognizing potential risks, assessing their likelihood and impact, and developing strategies to mitigate them. Key strategies include risk matrices, SWOT analysis, and scenario planning, along with mitigation strategies such as safety protocols, insurance coverage, and training programs. This proactive approach is essential to protect all stakeholders involved in sports events.

Concussion protocols are vital to protecting athletes from the long-term health effects of head injuries. Proper training for coaches and medical staff, along with clear procedures for handling concussions, is essential. Additionally, awareness of the immense social media pressure on athletes and concerns over mental health and well-being must be addressed. Advocates like Michael Phelps emphasize the importance of recognizing signs of mental distress and seeking counseling to prevent severe outcomes. Safeguarding athletes from physical, emotional, and sexual abuse is a critical concern. Legal frameworks and organizational policies are necessary to create a safe environment. Sports organizations and their representatives have a duty of care to protect athletes from harm and ensure their well-being.

Ensuring stadium security involves a structured process of risk management. This includes recognizing potential hazards, evaluating their likelihood and impact, and developing strategies to address them. Practical strategies involve risk matrices, SWOT analysis, and scenario planning, along with mitigation strategies such as safety protocols, insurance coverage, and training programs. A proactive approach to risk management is essential to protect all stakeholders involved in sports events.

In conclusion, sports law torts encompass a broad spectrum of legal theories and risk management practices. By understanding and applying these principles, stakeholders in the sports industry can better navigate the complexities of legal disputes and ensure a safer and more equitable environment for all participants.

Discussion Questions

1. How does the legal theory of negligence apply to sports, and what are some common examples of negligence claims in this context?
2. Discuss the role of intentional harm in sports law torts. Can you provide examples where intentional harm has led to legal disputes in sports?
3. Explain the concept of products liability in sports. What responsibilities do manufacturers and sellers have regarding sports equipment and gear?
4. How do federal statutory requirements like the Americans with Disabilities Act (ADA) impact the sports industry?
5. What are the key components of risk management in sports, and how can stakeholders proactively address potential hazards?
6. Why are concussion protocols essential in sports? Discuss the legal and ethical responsibilities of coaches and medical staff in handling head injuries.

7. How can sports organizations ensure the mental health and well-being of athletes in the age of social media?
8. What legal frameworks and policies are necessary to protect athletes from physical, emotional, and sexual abuse? Discuss the duty of care sports organizations owe to their athletes.
9. Describe the process of risk management for stadium security. How can sports organizations develop effective strategies to mitigate potential security risks?
10. In what ways do the principles of sports law torts and risk management help create a safer and more equitable environment for all participants in the sports industry?

9

Data and AI Transforming Sports Law and Performance

Chapter Outline

Transforming Sports Performance with Data Analytics	282
AI Technologies in Athlete Training and Injury Prevention	287
Developing Game Strategies	289
Intellectual Property and Data: Leading Cases	291
Virtual Games and Metaverse	297
Data Privacy: A Global Challenge	299
Athlete Consent: Empowering Informed Decisions	301
Who Owns the Data Goldmine?	301
Bias, Fairness and Transparency: Ensuring a Level Playing Field	302
Environmental Sustainability: The Hidden Cost of Big Data	305
Summary	306
Discussion Questions	307

The integration of data analytics and artificial intelligence (AI) in sports has revolutionized the industry, transforming how athletes train, how teams strategize, and how fans engage with their favorite sports. Data analytics involves examining datasets to draw conclusions about the information they contain, increasingly with the aid of specialized systems and software. In sports, data analytics helps understand performance metrics, player statistics, and game outcomes, providing a comprehensive picture to guide decision-making and strategy. For example, wearable devices can track an athlete's speed, heart rate, and fatigue levels during training and competitions, helping coaches and trainers optimize training programs to enhance performance and reduce injury risk.

However, the collection and use of data in sports raise serious legal issues, including privacy concerns and data protection. Athletes' performance data is highly sensitive and requires strict confidentiality. Ensuring compliance with data protection regulations, such as the General Data Protection Regulation (GDPR) in Europe or the California Consumer Privacy Act (CCPA) in the United States, is crucial to avoid legal repercussions. Moreover, the ownership of data generated by athletes and the rights to use this data must be clearly defined to prevent disputes.

AI, which simulates human intelligence processes through machines, particularly computer systems, plays a significant role in sports. These processes include learning (acquiring information and rules for using it), reasoning (applying rules to reach conclusions), and self-correction. AI systems are employed in various aspects, from enhancing training regimens and improving scouting efficiency to facilitating tactical decision-making and preventing injuries. The power of AI lies in its ability to quickly and accurately process vast amounts of data, identifying patterns and insights that might be missed by human analysts.

AI's applications in sports are diverse and impactful. Machine learning algorithms, a subset of AI, excel at making sense of complex datasets and predicting outcomes. For instance, AI can analyze past game footage to identify the strengths and weaknesses of opponents, allowing coaches to devise more effective game plans. In scouting, AI can evaluate potential recruits by analyzing their performance metrics and predicting their future success. Furthermore, AI-driven predictive analytics can foresee injury risks by examining patterns in an athlete's training and performance data, enabling preemptive measures to avoid injuries.

The use of AI and data analytics in training has led to more personalized and effective training programs. By analyzing an athlete's performance data, AI can recommend specific exercises and training regimens tailored to the athlete's needs. This personalized approach helps in maximizing performance while minimizing the risk of overtraining and injuries.

Additionally, AI-powered tools can provide real-time feedback during training sessions, allowing athletes to make immediate adjustments to their techniques.

Legal issues arise in the context of training, where data collected from athletes must be managed in compliance with privacy laws. Athletes should be informed about how their data will be used and stored, and obtaining their consent for data collection and analysis is crucial to avoid legal disputes. Determining who is legally responsible when data breaches occur via hacking or other means remains an open question.

Teams leverage data analytics and AI to develop more sophisticated strategies and tactics. By analyzing game data, teams can identify patterns and trends that inform their strategic decisions. For instance, AI can analyze an opponent's play style and suggest optimal strategies to counteract their strengths. This data-driven approach enables teams to make more informed decisions during games, increasing their chances of success. However, the use of data and AI in developing strategies and tactics also poses risks of unfair competitive advantage and potential violations of league regulations. Teams must ensure that their use of AI and data analytics complies with the rules and ethical guidelines set forth by their respective sports organizations.

The impact of data and AI extends beyond the field, enhancing fan engagement and experience. AI-driven platforms can provide fans with personalized content, such as tailored game highlights and player statistics. Moreover, predictive analytics can offer insights into potential game outcomes and player performances, deepening fans' connection to their favorite sports and teams. While AI and data analytics can enhance fan engagement, they also bring about legal considerations related to data privacy and intellectual property. Collecting and using fan data must be done in accordance with data protection laws to prevent legal liabilities. Additionally, AI-generated content must respect intellectual property rights to avoid infringement issues.

The increasing use of data analytics and AI in sports has ushered in a new era of innovation and efficiency. From optimizing athlete performance and improving team strategies to enhancing fan engagement, the applications of data and AI are transforming every facet of the sports industry. As technology continues to advance, the role of data analytics and AI in sports is poised to grow even further, unlocking new possibilities and opportunities for athletes, teams, and fans alike. However, it is imperative to address the associated legal and liability issues to ensure a fair, ethical, and legally compliant integration of these technologies.

Transforming Sports Performance with Data Analytics

Data analytics enables the collection and analysis of vast amounts of performance data, offering insights that were previously unattainable. Teams use these insights to optimize player performance, tailor training programs, and develop game strategies. For example, the NBA's partnership with Second Spectrum uses machine learning to monitor player movements in 3D, helping teams improve their performance through detailed analysis. By examining every movement on the court, Second Spectrum provides coaches with data-driven insights into player positioning, spacing, and movement efficiency, enabling more informed strategic decisions.

In Major League Baseball (MLB), the introduction of Statcast, an advanced tracking system, has transformed how the game is analyzed. Statcast tracks every play on the field, recording metrics such as the speed and spin rate of pitches, the exit velocity and launch angle of batted balls, and the precise movements of fielders. Teams use this data to refine pitching strategies, defensive alignments, and hitting approaches. For instance, by analyzing a batter's tendencies against different pitch types, pitchers can adjust their pitch selection to exploit weaknesses. This level of detail was unimaginable before the advent of sophisticated data analytics.

In soccer, data analytics has become integral to performance enhancement and injury prevention. Clubs like FC Barcelona and Manchester City utilize wearable technology and GPS tracking to monitor players' physical metrics during training and matches. This data helps coaches understand players' workloads, recovery rates, and overall fitness levels. By identifying patterns and trends in the data, teams can customize training programs to address individual needs, thereby reducing the risk of injuries and ensuring peak performance during crucial matches.

Despite the benefits, the use of data analytics in sports raises numerous legal issues, particularly concerning privacy and data protection. The collection of biometric data from athletes involves handling sensitive personal information, which must be managed in compliance with data protection laws such as the General Data Protection Regulation (GDPR) in Europe. The GDPR defines "personal data" broadly to include any information relating to an identified or identifiable individual, such as names, email addresses, and biometric data. It applies to any organization that processes the personal data of EU residents, regardless of where the organization is based. Organizations must obtain explicit consent from data subjects before collecting, using, or storing personal data. This consent must be informed, specific, and freely given, and data subjects have the right to withdraw their consent at any time. Additionally, organizations must implement appropriate technical and organizational measures to protect personal data, including data encryption, anonymization, and regular security assessments. Data breaches must be reported to the relevant supervisory authority within seventy-two hours. Individuals in Europe have several rights under the GDPR, including the right to access their data, the right to rectification, the right to erasure (the "right to be forgotten"), and the right to data portability. They also have the right to object to the processing of their data and to lodge complaints with supervisory authorities. Organizations that process large amounts of personal data or sensitive data must appoint a Data Protection Officer (DPO) to oversee compliance with the GDPR. Failure to secure proper consent from athletes or to implement adequate data protection measures can result in legal repercussions. For example, if an athlete's performance data is shared without consent or used for purposes beyond its initial scope, the team or organization could face lawsuits for breaching privacy rights.

The GDPR imposes severe penalties for non-compliance, including fines of up to 4 percent of the annual worldwide revenue or 20 million euros, whichever is higher. Sports organizations must recognize several potential legal disputes under the GDPR. Unauthorized data sharing, where an athlete's biometric data is shared with third parties without explicit consent, could lead to legal action for invasion of privacy. In the event of a data breach, organizations must promptly notify the affected individuals and the supervisory authorities, with failure to do so resulting in hefty fines and legal challenges.

Transferring athletes' data outside the EU requires ensuring that the receiving country provides adequate data protection, and non-compliance with these requirements can lead to legal disputes and penalties. Sports organizations must establish effective data protection policies and procedures to comply with the GDPR. This includes conducting Data Protection Impact Assessments (DPIAs) to identify and mitigate risks associated with data processing activities, implementing Privacy by Design and Default to ensure data protection measures are integrated into the development of new products or services, regularly training staff on GDPR compliance and data protection best practices, and appointing a DPO for organizations handling large volumes of sensitive data to ensure ongoing compliance with the GDPR.

While data analytics can enhance sports performance and strategy, it is imperative for sports organizations in Europe and with a European footprint to adhere to GDPR requirements to avoid legal repercussions and protect the privacy rights of athletes. The use of data analytics in monitoring athletes' performance intersects with employment law, particularly within the context of collective bargaining agreements (CBAs) negotiated by players' associations. These agreements are pivotal in defining the extent and nature of permissible monitoring, balancing performance enhancement with privacy and autonomy concerns.

Professional athletes in major American sports leagues are represented by unions such as the NFLPA, NBAPA, MLBPA, and NHLPA. These unions negotiate collective bargaining agreements (CBAs) with team owners to protect athletes' rights and interests. CBAs cover a wide range of issues, including salaries, working conditions, health benefits, and privacy concerns related to data analytics. In the context of collective bargaining, subjects are categorized as either mandatory or permissive. Mandatory subjects include wages, hours, and other terms and conditions of employment. Issues such as the extent of performance monitoring, health and safety protocols, and the use of personal data for analytics fall under this category, requiring both parties to negotiate these issues in good faith. Permissive subjects, on the other hand, are not directly related to the terms and conditions of employment. While these can be negotiated, neither party is obligated to do so. Examples might include certain aspects of player marketing or sponsorship deals.

The continuous monitoring of athletes' performance metrics poses contractual privacy concerns. CBAs often include provisions that address the collection, protection, and use of athletes' performance data. These provisions aim to ensure that monitoring practices do not become overly intrusive and that athletes' personal data is protected from misuse. Employment law mandates that any monitoring and data collection practices must comply with established legal standards. This includes ensuring consent and transparency, where athletes must be informed about what data is being collected and how it will be used, often detailed in the CBA.

Additionally, teams and leagues are responsible for ensuring that the data collected is securely stored and protected against unauthorized access. The use of collected data must be limited to purposes agreed upon in the CBA, which could include performance enhancement, injury prevention, medical diagnosis and treatment, and other legitimate interests. Disputes over the extent of permissible monitoring and data use are typically resolved through grievance procedures outlined in the CBA. These procedures provide a structured process for addressing and resolving conflicts between players and team management. In summary, the intersection of data analytics and employment law in sports is governed by collective bargaining agreements, which address mandatory subjects such as privacy and data protection. These agreements ensure that monitoring practices are balanced with athletes' rights to privacy and autonomy, providing a clear legal framework and transparent policies to manage these concerns.

Data analytics allows for the collection and analysis of vast amounts of performance data, providing insights that were previously unattainable, as described earlier. Teams use these insights to optimize player performance, tailor training programs, and develop game strategies. Data analytics enables teams to monitor and analyze various performance metrics such as speed, endurance, and accuracy. For instance, wearable technology can track an athlete's heart rate, distance covered, and other physiological data during training and games. This data helps in identifying areas for improvement and in preventing injuries by monitoring stress levels and fatigue.

Analytics can be used to design individualized training programs that cater to the specific needs of each athlete. By analyzing data on an athlete's performance, coaches can identify strengths and weaknesses and adjust training regimens accordingly. For instance, in Major League Baseball (MLB), teams use data from batting and pitching analytics to tailor training programs. The Houston Astros, for example, have implemented data-driven training techniques to improve player performance, leading to significant on-field success. Pitchers like Justin Verlander have benefited from analytics that fine-tuned their pitching mechanics and strategies. By examining Verlander's spin rate, pitch velocity, and release point, coaches can identify patterns and make adjustments that enhance his effectiveness. Data on hitters' tendencies allow pitchers to devise more effective game plans, contributing to improved performance and prolonged careers. Additionally, teams use motion capture technology to analyze players' biomechanics, reducing the risk of injury and optimizing recovery protocols.

In swimming, data analytics is used to analyze stroke efficiency and turn times. Olympic swimmers like Katie Ledecky use this data to optimize their training and improve race performance. Coaches collect and analyze data on stroke rate, stroke length, and lap splits to create detailed performance profiles. By understanding these metrics, swimmers can adjust their techniques to minimize drag and maximize propulsion. Furthermore, underwater cameras and sensors provide real-time feedback on body position and movement patterns. This granular analysis helps athletes like Ledecky refine their strokes and turns, leading to improvements in speed and efficiency.

The use of predictive analytics also aids in devising training plans that balance intensity and recovery, ensuring peak performance during competitions. In soccer, clubs like Manchester City employ extensive data analytics to tailor training sessions. Using GPS trackers and heart rate monitors, coaches gather data on players' movements, workload, and physiological responses during both training and matches. This data helps in creating individualized training plans that optimize each player's physical and technical development. For instance, by analyzing patterns of fatigue and performance dips, coaches can adjust training loads to prevent injuries and enhance endurance.

Tactical analytics also plays a crucial role; by studying opposition patterns and player interactions, teams can develop strategic training drills that improve decision-making and positioning on the field. Liverpool employs sophisticated tracking systems and aerial cameras to capture real-time positioning data of players and the ball during matches. This data enables detailed match analysis and performance evaluation, allowing coaches to identify strengths and weaknesses in both individual players and the team as a whole.

In basketball, the Golden State Warriors have embraced analytics to enhance player development. By using advanced metrics like Player Efficiency Rating (PER) and real-time tracking data, coaches can fine-tune training programs to address specific areas of improvement for each player. For instance, shooting analytics help players like Stephen Curry perfect their shooting mechanics by providing detailed feedback on release angles, shot trajectories, and foot placement. Defensive analytics enable players to better understand positioning and timing, leading to more effective defensive strategies.

The integration of virtual reality (VR) in training allows players to simulate game scenarios and improve their spatial awareness and reaction times. In track and field, runners have benefited from biomechanical analysis and performance data. Coaches use high-speed cameras and motion capture technology to dissect every phase of an athlete's sprint, from the start to the finish line. By analyzing factors such as stride length, ground contact time, and force application, trainers can make precise adjustments to enhance speed and efficiency.

Data on an athlete's training load and recovery rates also inform conditioning programs, ensuring that athletes peak at the right moments. The use of wearable technology allows for continuous monitoring of physiological parameters, helping to prevent overtraining and reduce injury risks. The integration of data analytics into sports training programs has revolutionized how athletes prepare and perform. By leveraging detailed performance metrics and biomechanical insights, coaches can create highly individualized training plans that optimize an athlete's strengths while addressing weaknesses. This data-driven approach not only enhances performance but also contributes to injury prevention and long-term athletic development.

AI Technologies in Athlete Training and Injury Prevention

AI technologies are pivotal in enhancing athlete training and preventing injuries, offering data-driven insights that tailor programs to individual needs and predict potential risks. Tools like the NFL's Digital Athlete, developed with Amazon Web Services, use algorithms to analyze data on equipment, speed, and weather conditions, enabling the creation of individualized training and recovery plans. This proactive approach has significantly improved player safety and performance, exemplifying the transformative impact of AI in sports.

AI technologies have revolutionized athlete training by providing personalized, data-driven insights. For example, Zone7's AI-driven system offers daily injury risk forecasting based on available datasets, allowing practitioners to make informed decisions and take proactive measures to mitigate injury risks. Predictive analytics tools in fitness apps analyze extensive data on physical metrics and activity levels to create super-tailored workouts, helping athletes avoid injuries while optimizing their performance. In professional sports, as described earlier, AI-powered wearables track athletes' movements and utilize biomechanics to identify areas of weakness or fatigue. These insights are used to develop personalized injury prevention programs and improve game plan techniques. Companies like Microsoft, IBM, and Catapult have implemented AI services and platforms in sports settings for data analysis and injury forecasting, showcasing the broad applicability of these technologies.

AI technologies play a crucial role in injury prevention by predicting potential risks and enabling timely interventions. In soccer, AI models have been used to forecast high-risk periods for athletes, guiding training and rest schedules to minimize injury risks. Studies have shown that machine learning techniques like decision trees and neural networks can effectively predict sports injuries by analyzing data on training workloads and psychophysiological assessments. Additionally, AI-powered wearables and apps collect data points such as heart rate and recovery times, which are used to forecast overuse injuries and the necessity for rest in endurance sports, thus reducing the risk of overtraining injuries.

Several professional sports teams and trainers have adopted AI technologies to enhance athlete training and prevent injuries by providing real-time monitoring and predictive modeling. By continuously analyzing incoming data, AI models can alert athletes or clinicians when the risk of injury reaches a predetermined threshold, allowing for timely interventions. The San Francisco 49ers use AI to optimize player performance and health, while the Los Angeles Dodgers apply machine learning to improve player scouting and game strategy. Additionally, companies like TechAhead and Catapult have developed AI-powered wearables and predictive analytics tools that are used by various sports teams to tailor training programs and prevent injuries.

Developing Game Strategies

Teams can use data analytics to develop and refine game strategies, enhancing their performance and competitive edge. By systematically analyzing opponents' play patterns and tendencies, teams can craft strategies that exploit their opponents' weaknesses while fortifying their own strengths. For example, the New England Patriots in the NFL are renowned for their extensive use of data analytics. By meticulously analyzing game footage and statistical data, the coaching staff can make informed decisions on play-calling and player matchups. This approach allows them to anticipate opponents' moves and adjust their strategies, accordingly, leading to more effective game plans and improved performance on the field.

In tennis, top players like Novak Djokovic utilize data analytics to study their opponents' serve patterns and return strategies. By doing so, they can develop tailored game plans that maximize their chances of winning. For instance, by identifying specific tendencies in an opponent's serve, Djokovic can anticipate and prepare his returns more effectively, gaining a strategic advantage during matches. This data-driven approach helps in countering opponents' strengths while refining their own techniques and strategies to remain competitive at the highest levels.

The implications of data analytics for organizations, trainers, and athletes are profound. For organizations, investing in data analytics infrastructure can lead to better decision-making and a more strategic approach to game preparation and player development. Trainers can leverage data to design personalized training programs that address specific areas for improvement, optimizing athletes' performance. Athletes can gain insights into their own performance metrics, identify areas for improvement, and track their progress over time. By embracing data analytics, all stakeholders in sports can work together to create a more informed and strategic approach to competition, ultimately leading to better performance and increased chances of success.

Organizations that effectively leverage data analytics gain a competitive edge by making more informed decisions. This includes identifying undervalued players, optimizing game strategies, and improving player development programs. Teams like the Houston Rockets and Golden State Warriors in the NBA have successfully used analytics to enhance their performance and achieve remarkable success. In football, teams like the Philadelphia Eagles use data analytics to make draft decisions and manage in-game strategies. In baseball, the Oakland Athletics have famously used data-driven approaches to build competitive rosters with limited budgets, a practice popularized by the "Moneyball" approach.

Before the Moneyball revolution, player analysis in baseball and other sports relied heavily on traditional scouting methods and subjective evaluations, focusing on visible skills, physical attributes, and anecdotal evidence. The introduction of Moneyball, driven by Billy Beane and the Oakland Athletics, transformed this approach by emphasizing sabermetrics—a data-driven method that uses advanced statistics to evaluate player performance and value. This approach has since spread to other sports, fundamentally changing how players are scouted, drafted, and developed. Both men's and women's basketball teams, including the WNBA's Seattle Storm, utilize analytics for player scouting and game strategy, with players like Caitlin Clark being identified early for their exceptional potential through performance metrics.

Data analytics helps in the efficient allocation of resources, such as player acquisitions and training investments. By analyzing player performance metrics and injury risks, teams can make better decisions on contract negotiations and training regimens. Major League Baseball (MLB) teams, including the Oakland Athletics, have famously used data-driven approaches to build competitive rosters with limited budgets. Analytics can also be used to enhance fan engagement by providing insights into game dynamics and player performance. Real-time data can be shared with fans through broadcasts, social media, and team apps, enriching the viewing experience.

Teams and leagues can use analytics to create personalized experiences for fans. By understanding fan preferences and behaviors, organizations can tailor content, promotions, and in-game experiences to individual fans. For example, the NFL uses data analytics to understand fan engagement patterns and optimize game day experiences and digital content. Teams can develop interactive platforms that allow fans to engage with real-time data during games. Features such as live statistics, player performance insights, and predictive analytics can make the viewing experience more immersive. The NHL's use of SAP's HANA platform to provide detailed game statistics and player analytics during broadcasts is a prime example. By using SAP HANA, the NHL can analyze player movements, puck trajectories, and other game dynamics in real time, providing broadcasters and fans with a wealth of detailed insights. This real-time analysis enhances the viewing experience by offering fans a deeper understanding of the game as it unfolds.

Intellectual Property and Data: Leading Cases

Intellectual property (IP) rights are paramount when dealing with proprietary data and analytical methods. Organizations must ensure their data analytics platforms and methodologies are protected to maintain competitive advantages. Legal battles over IP rights in sports data are becoming more common, as evidenced by the case of *Stats LLC v. Sportradar AG*. This case highlighted the importance of securing IP rights for data analytics tools and methodologies to safeguard commercial interests and innovation in the sports industry.

The dispute between Stats LLC, a prominent sports data provider, and Sportradar AG, another major player in the sports data industry, revolved around the protection and use of proprietary sports data. Stats LLC accused Sportradar AG of unlawfully collecting and using data from sports events to which Stats LLC held exclusive rights. The core of the dispute centered on the intellectual property rights associated with sports data and the methods used to collect and disseminate this data.

The primary legal issue was whether the sports data collected by Stats LLC was protected under IP laws and whether Sportradar's actions constituted an infringement of these rights. Additionally, the case examined whether Sportradar's actions violated the contractual agreements Stats LLC had with sports leagues and other entities granting them exclusive data collection rights. Competition law considerations were also involved, particularly whether exclusive data rights arrangements created an anti-competitive environment that violated fair competition principles.

The applicable laws include intellectual property law, which encompasses copyright and database rights that protect the proprietary nature of the collected sports data. Contract law governed the agreements between Stats LLC and sports leagues, detailing the exclusive rights to collect and distribute sports data. Competition law addressed whether the exclusive agreements and the actions of the parties involved restricted competition in the sports data market.

The court found that the data collected by Stats LLC was indeed protected under federal copyright laws and that Sportradar's unauthorized collection and use of this data constituted an infringement. Additionally, the court ruled that Sportradar had breached the contractual agreements by collecting data from events where Stats LLC had exclusive rights. The court also examined whether the exclusive data rights arrangements were anti-competitive and concluded that while such arrangements could potentially restrict competition, they were justified given the investment and effort required to collect and maintain high-quality sports data.

This case underscores the importance of robust copyright protections for proprietary data and analytical methods. Organizations must ensure their data collection and distribution methods are legally protected to maintain a competitive edge. Clear and enforceable contracts are crucial in delineating the rights and responsibilities of parties involved in the collection and use of sports data. There is a need to balance protecting IP rights with fostering a competitive market. Regulatory bodies may need to provide clearer guidelines on how exclusive data rights should be managed to prevent anti-competitive practices. The sports data industry may benefit from developing standardized practices for data collection and distribution to reduce legal disputes and promote fair competition.

In the groundbreaking case of *National Basketball Association v. Motorola, Inc.*, the NBA sued Motorola and Sports Team Analysis and Tracking Systems (STATS) over the real-time transmission of game scores and statistics via Motorola's SportsTrax pager and STATS's online service. The NBA claimed that this transmission violated its intellectual property rights by misappropriating the data and infringing on the NBA's copyright on the broadcast of games. This case set a precedent in the realm of sports data and intellectual property, influencing subsequent cases in the legal context of sports analytics and data rights.

The NBA alleged several violations, including unfair competition by misappropriation under New York state law, false advertising and false representation of origin under the Lanham Act, federal copyright infringement, and unlawful interception of communications under the Communications Act of 1934. The district court dismissed all claims except for the misappropriation claim under New York law and issued a permanent injunction against Motorola and STATS. However, upon appeal, the Second Circuit Court of Appeals reversed the lower court's decision on the misappropriation claim, ruling that real-time game scores did not constitute "hot news" misappropriation. The "hot news" concept refers to a legal doctrine under New York state law that protects the commercial value of timely, factual information from being misappropriated by competitors. The court also affirmed the dismissal of the Lanham Act claim, stating that any misstatements by Motorola in advertising its pager were not material.

The implications of the *NBA v. Motorola* case were profound. It clarified the necessity for sports organizations to protect their data and defined the narrow scope of the "hot-news" misappropriation doctrine. Moreover, it supported the free dissemination of information on the Internet, provided it did not fit within the narrow "hot-news" exception. This case underscored the challenges of protecting real-time data and influenced how sports organizations approached data rights.

In the case of *NFL v. Delaware Lottery*, the National Football League (NFL) challenged the Delaware Lottery's use of NFL game statistics in its sports betting operations. The central legal issue was whether the use of these game statistics infringed upon the NFL's intellectual property rights. The NFL, along with other major sports leagues, argued that Delaware's sports betting scheme, which included betting on NFL games, violated the Professional and Amateur Sports Protection Act (PASPA) and other legal provisions. They contended that using NFL game data in this manner misappropriated the league's property and could potentially harm the league's reputation and goodwill by associating it with gambling activities. However, the court ruled that the use of game statistics in betting did not infringe on the NFL's intellectual property rights. The court's decision was based on the principle that factual data about sports events, such as game scores and schedules, are not protected by copyright. This ruling reinforced the idea that factual information, even when it pertains to professional sports, remains in the public domain and can be used without infringing on intellectual property rights. The decision thus supported the broader legal stance that factual data about sports events cannot be monopolized by sports leagues and can be freely used in contexts such as betting without violating copyright laws.

Other relevant cases have also contributed to this legal context. In *C.B.C. Distribution and Marketing, Inc. v. Major League Baseball Advanced Media, L.P.*, the court held that the use of players' names and statistics in fantasy sports games was protected by the First Amendment and did not violate players' rights of publicity. This decision emphasized the importance of balancing intellectual property rights with the public's right to information. In this case, C.B.C. Distribution and Marketing, Inc. (CBC) sought a declaratory judgment to affirm its right to use Major League Baseball (MLB) players' names and statistics in its fantasy baseball products without infringing on the players' rights of publicity. CBC argued that such use was protected under the First Amendment. Major League Baseball Advanced Media (Advanced Media) and the MLB Players Association contended that CBC's use of these names and statistics violated the players' rights of publicity and sought to enjoin CBC from using this information. The court ruled in favor of CBC, concluding that the players' names and statistics are facts that are already in the public domain and that their use in fantasy sports games constitutes speech protected by the First Amendment. The court noted that CBC's fantasy baseball games did not imply any endorsement by the players, nor did they achieve a commercial advantage by using the players' names and statistics in a manner different from other fantasy sports providers.

The ruling in *C.B.C. Distribution and Marketing, Inc. v. Major League Baseball Advanced Media, L.P.* set a precedent for the use of publicly available information in fantasy sports and other similar contexts. The court held that CBC's use of baseball players' names and statistics did not violate their right of publicity, emphasizing the need to balance intellectual property rights with the public's right to access and use information.

The legal context shifted with the *Zacchini v. Scripps-Howard Broadcasting Co.* case compared to earlier decisions like Palmer v. Schonhorn Enterprises, Inc. and Uhlaender v. Henricksen. In Palmer, the court ruled against the unauthorized use of athletes' pictures without consent, emphasizing the protection of individual likenesses. Similarly, in Uhlaender, the court found that using athletes' names and statistics in a board game without permission infringed on their publicity rights.

The Supreme Court's ruling in *Zacchini v. Scripps-Howard Broadcasting Co.* marked a pivotal shift by focusing on the performer's right to control the commercial use of their entire performance. The Court ruled that the First and Fourteenth Amendments do not protect the news media from liability when broadcasting a performer's entire act without consent. This decision underscored the necessity of protecting the economic interests of performers, likening these rights to intellectual property protections such as patents and copyrights. Broadcasting Zacchini's entire act without compensation threatened the economic value of his performance, thereby requiring protection under the right of publicity laws.

The Zacchini case introduced a new dimension of protecting performers' economic interests in their acts, contrasting with earlier cases that dealt primarily with the unauthorized use of athletes' likenesses and statistics. However, the ruling in *C.B.C. Distribution and Marketing, Inc. v. Major League Baseball Advanced Media, L.P.* further diverged by focusing on the public interest in accessing factual information, such as player statistics, which are inherently public. The court distinguished CBC's use of names and statistics as not infringing on the right of publicity, considering these elements essential for fantasy sports and of public interest. This case set a new standard for balancing intellectual property rights and public access in the digital age.

In *Morris Communications Corp. v. PGA Tour, Inc.*, the court addressed whether the PGA Tour's restrictions on disseminating real-time scoring data violated antitrust laws. Morris Communications, a media company, sought access to the PGA Tour's real-time scoring system to report on golf scores. However, the PGA Tour restricted this access, allowing Morris to use the data only within its own publications and not for syndication. Morris Communications argued that the PGA Tour's restrictions constituted an abuse of monopoly power, violating Section 2 of the Sherman Act, the Florida Antitrust Act, and the Florida Deceptive and Unfair Trade Practices Act. They claimed that the PGA Tour unfairly stifled competition in the market for syndicated real-time golf scores by leveraging its control over access to its tournaments. The court ruled in favor of the PGA Tour, finding that the organization had a legitimate business justification for its restrictions. The court noted that the PGA Tour's substantial investment in its Real-Time Scoring System (RTSS) meant that allowing unrestricted access would enable free riders to capitalize on this proprietary investment without contributing to its costs.

Consequently, the court concluded that the PGA Tour's actions did not violate antitrust laws, as they were reasonable measures to protect its proprietary interests. This case highlights the complex and sometimes uncertain balance between proprietary rights and public access in the sports industry. While media companies like Morris Communications argued for broader access to real-time data to enhance public reporting, the court recognized the rights of organizations like the PGA Tour to safeguard their investments and control the distribution of their proprietary content.

In Europe, similar issues have arisen regarding the use of player statistics in video games, comparable to the cases of *NFL v. Delaware Lottery* and *C.B.C. Distribution and Marketing, Inc. v. Major League Baseball Advanced Media, L.P.* in the United States. In *Football Dataco Ltd. v. Sportradar GmbH,* Football Dataco, which manages data for the English and Scottish football leagues, sued Sportradar, a company providing live sports data, for copyright infringement. Football Dataco claimed that Sportradar's use of their football match data without permission infringed on their database rights. The European Court of Justice (ECJ) ruled that while raw sports data (like scores and player statistics) is not protected by copyright, the specific compilation of that data can be protected if it involves substantial investment in obtaining, verifying, or presenting the data. This ruling underscored that while factual data itself is not protected, the effort and resources invested in compiling and maintaining a database of such data can be protected under database rights.

In tennis, there have been legal disputes concerning the use of player statistics and match data. For example, the *International Tennis Federation (ITF) v. Sportradar* involved the ITF suing Sportradar for using its live scoring data without authorization. Similar to the Football Dataco case, the dispute centered around the protection of the database and the investment made in compiling and maintaining it. These cases highlight the legal complexities around the use of sports data in Europe. While the raw data itself is generally considered to be in the public domain, the specific compilation and presentation of that data can be protected if it involves significant investment. This aligns with the principles seen in the *NFL v. Delaware Lottery* and *C.B.C. Distribution and Marketing, Inc. v. Major League Baseball Advanced Media, L.P.* cases, where the use of factual sports data was deemed not to infringe on intellectual property rights, but with an additional layer of protection for databases in the European context.

These decisions serve as foundational references for ongoing and future legal battles at the intersection of sports, technology, and media. They illustrate the complexities of intellectual property law in the digital age, particularly concerning the use of real-time data in sports. As technology continues to advance, these rulings will guide the development of legal standards to ensure a fair balance between protecting the rights of sports organizations and promoting the free flow of information.

Virtual Games and Metaverse

In virtual games and the metaverse, data analytics can be used to create more realistic and engaging gameplay experiences. By simulating real-world player behaviors and game dynamics, developers can create virtual sports environments that closely mimic real sports. For example, EA Sports' FIFA series uses real-world data to replicate player movements and game strategies in their video games. Leagues and teams can use data analytics to engage fans in the metaverse by creating virtual events, interactive experiences, and digital collectibles. Platforms like Decentraland and The Sandbox allow users to buy virtual land and participate in sports-related activities, enhancing fan engagement through virtual reality (VR) and augmented reality (AR).

Athletes can have their avatars in the metaverse, allowing fans to interact with them in virtual environments. Data analytics can ensure these avatars perform and behave like their real-world counterparts, enhancing the authenticity of the experience. Collaborations between Epic Games and athletes in Fortnite have shown the potential of integrating athlete avatars into virtual worlds. These collaborations allow fans to engage with lifelike representations of their favorite athletes, participate in virtual events, and even use the avatars in gameplay, creating a deeply immersive experience. Such integrations provide a novel way for fans to connect with athletes and open up new revenue streams for athletes and teams through digital merchandise, endorsements, and in-game purchases. For example, partnerships with athletes like Neymar Jr. have brought their likeness into Fortnite, allowing players to unlock skins and other items, thereby enhancing fan engagement and extending the athletes' brand presence into the digital realm.

Trainers can use data analytics to optimize athlete performance by identifying strengths and weaknesses, tailoring training programs, and monitoring progress. Wearable technology and performance tracking systems provide trainers with real-time data on player movements, heart rates, and other vital metrics, enabling more effective training regimens. Analytics can help trainers identify injury risks and develop strategies to prevent them. By analyzing data on player workload, biomechanics, and previous injuries, trainers can create individualized injury prevention plans. The implementation of Catapult Sports' wearable technology in various sports has helped reduce injury rates and improve player longevity. Trainers can also gain tactical insights into opponent strategies and player matchups, using this information to develop game plans and make in-game adjustments.

Athletes can leverage data analytics for personal development by gaining insights into their performance and areas for improvement. Access to detailed performance metrics allows athletes to take a data-driven approach to their training and development. Professional athletes, such as NBA star LeBron James, have embraced data analytics to enhance their training routines and prolong their careers. Analytics can help athletes monitor their health and wellness, ensuring they maintain peak physical condition. By tracking metrics such as sleep patterns, nutrition, and recovery times, athletes can make informed decisions about their health.

WHOOP Bands, advanced fitness and health wearables, are designed to monitor an athlete's sleep, strain, recovery, and overall health. These devices provide detailed biometric data, which athletes use to optimize their training and performance. WHOOP bands are popular among elite athletes, including Cristiano Ronaldo, LeBron James, and Michael Phelps, due to their precision and comprehensive data analytics capabilities.

The use of WHOOP bands and other wearable devices has become increasingly popular among athletes for monitoring overall wellness. By integrating data analytics into their branding strategies, athletes can enhance their performance on the field and build a strong personal brand that resonates with fans and attracts lucrative opportunities. Tools for managing social media presence, such as Opendorse and Greenfly, play a crucial role in this process. Opendorse helps athletes manage their social media presence, engage with fans, and maximize their marketability by providing tools for content creation, distribution, and performance tracking. Similarly, Greenfly enables athletes to share content easily and engage with their audience effectively, streamlining the process of content creation and distribution to ensure a consistent and engaging online presence.

Applications of data analytics in athlete branding include fan engagement metrics, personalized content strategies, and performance metrics. Fan engagement metrics involve tracking social media analytics, such as likes, shares, comments, and follower growth, to understand what content resonates with fans. Personalized content strategies involve trend analysis and audience insights to tailor content that appeals to specific segments. Performance metrics involve using performance data to attract sponsorships and endorsements by showcasing athletic achievements and engagement levels, and leveraging data to highlight key moments and achievements that can be promoted through media channels.

Data Privacy: A Global Challenge

As described earlier, ensuring the privacy and security of athletes' personal and performance data is crucial. Organizations must comply with data protection regulations to safeguard this information. The General Data Protection Regulation (GDPR) in Europe sets stringent guidelines on data protection, impacting how European football clubs manage player data. Teams like Manchester United and FC Barcelona must ensure that their data collection practices align with these regulations to avoid hefty fines. A recent study found that 72 percent of European football clubs have revamped their data collection practices to comply with GDPR, highlighting its wide-reaching influence.

In the United States, the *Health Insurance Portability and Accountability Act* (HIPAA) protects athletes' medical data, which is integral to player performance and recovery tracking for organizations like the NFL and NBA. Beyond Europe and the United States, data privacy regulations are emerging worldwide. The California Consumer Privacy Act (CCPA) grants similar rights to California residents, and similar laws are being considered in other US states. This growing patchwork of regulations presents a complex challenge for international sports organizations.

The integration of AI in sports raises several ethical concerns. One major concern is data privacy and security. The collection and analysis of extensive data on athletes' physical metrics and activity levels may lead to potential breaches of privacy if not properly managed. Ensuring that data is securely stored and used only for intended purposes is crucial. Another ethical issue is the potential for bias in AI models. If the data used to train AI models is not representative of diverse populations, the predictions and recommendations may be biased, leading to unequal treatment of athletes. Ensuring that AI models are trained on diverse and comprehensive datasets is essential to mitigate this risk. Additionally, there is a concern about the over-reliance on AI technologies. While AI can provide valuable insights, it should complement rather than replace human decision-making. Coaches and trainers must use AI-generated insights in conjunction with their expertise and judgment to make informed decisions that prioritize athletes' safety and well-being.

Fitness tracking apps like Strava demonstrate the widespread use of AI technologies in everyday athletics. However, Strava has faced significant privacy and security concerns, such as its global heat map inadvertently exposing sensitive locations, including US military bases, by revealing the routes taken by service members. This incident highlighted the potential risks of sharing detailed GPS data publicly. Additionally, Strava's default settings often collect and share extensive user data, which can be exploited if not properly managed. Similar concerns are present with other leading workout apps like Peloton, Nike Training Club (NTC), and Centr, which also collect extensive personal data, including workout metrics, device information, and biometric data.

By acknowledging these legal and ethical considerations, sports organizations can harness the power of data analytics responsibly. Ensuring data privacy is protected, intellectual property rights are clear, algorithms are fair, and the environmental impact is minimized. Ultimately, responsible data analytics can enhance athletic performance, fan engagement, and the overall integrity of the sport, benefiting not only professional athletes but also everyday fitness enthusiasts.

Athlete Consent: Empowering Informed Decisions

Athletes should be informed about what data is being collected and how it will be used, and they should provide consent. This is particularly important in collegiate sports, where young athletes, such as those in the NCAA basketball or football programs, might not fully understand the implications of data sharing. Informed consent ensures that players like Zion Williamson, during his college career at Duke, are aware of how their performance and biometric data will be utilized and who will have access to it. A report by the National College Players Association (NCPA) revealed that 68 percent of student-athletes felt uninformed about how their data is used. This emphasizes the need for clear communication and informed consent, especially in collegiate sports where young athletes might not grasp the long-term implications of data sharing.

The issue of informed consent transcends borders. In China, for instance, the rapid development of sports data analytics has raised concerns about athlete privacy, with some calling for stricter regulations to ensure athletes have a say in how their data is used. Similarly, fitness apps emphasize transparency and user consent, but the complexity of privacy settings can still leave users vulnerable. Issues such as syncing entire address books without explicit consent have raised legal and ethical concerns, especially in regions with stringent data protection laws.

Who Owns the Data Goldmine?

Determining who owns the data generated by athletes and teams is essential. Clear agreements should be in place to outline data ownership and usage rights. For example, when athletes like LeBron James or Cristiano Ronaldo participate in training sessions equipped with data-tracking wearables, the question arises as to whether the data belongs to the athlete, the team, or the technology provider. This ownership issue can impact commercial deals, as data on player performance and health is valuable for endorsements and sponsorships. A 2024 study found that 42 percent of professional athletes expressed concerns about who owns the data collected by wearable devices they use during training. This highlights the need for clear ownership agreements between athletes, teams, and wearable tech companies like Nike and WHOOP.

The use of AI to generate sports analytics content raises questions about copyright and intellectual property rights. AI-driven platforms like IBM Watson can analyze game footage and provide insights, but the ownership of the generated content must be clearly defined. If an AI system generates a new strategy based on game data, should the intellectual property belong to the team, the AI developer, or both? Such questions are crucial for organizations like the NHL, which increasingly rely on advanced analytics to refine game strategies. The rise of AI-powered sports analytics platforms like Stratagem (used by the NBA) and SportsMind (used by the NFL) raises questions about ownership of the insights and strategies these platforms generate. As AI plays a bigger role, establishing ownership rights becomes crucial to avoid legal disputes.

Bias, Fairness and Transparency: Ensuring a Level Playing Field

Maintaining fairness in sports decision-making requires AI algorithms used in sports analytics to be free from bias. For example, biased algorithms could unfairly disadvantage certain players or teams based on historical data that reflects past biases or inequalities. In the NBA, if an AI system used for player scouting disproportionately favors certain demographics based on historical player data, it could perpetuate existing biases and limit opportunities for talented players from underrepresented groups.

A study by researchers at MIT found that algorithms used for player scouting in Major League Baseball (MLB) exhibited racial bias, favoring certain positions for white players. This underscores the importance of actively mitigating bias in AI algorithms to maintain fairness in player evaluation and recruitment, which is vital for preserving the integrity of the sport. Evidence of racial bias in scouting reports reveals that 67 percent of full-time scouts in MLB are white, potentially contributing to unconscious biases. Common scouting terms like "athletic," "grinder," and "high baseball IQ" often carry racial connotations, with white players frequently described using more favorable physical attributes, while players of color are often described as "raw" or "unpolished." Former Pirates general manager Neal Huntington criticized the use of coded language that perpetuates racial stereotypes, highlighting the need for scouts to be conscious of their language to avoid reinforcing biases.

The impact of biased language on player careers is substantial. An analysis of Cincinnati Reds scouting reports revealed that white players were more often described with positive physical attributes, while players of color were more likely to be described using terms that imply a lack of refinement or potential. This biased language can influence career progression, with BIPOC (Black, Indigenous, and People of Color) players potentially receiving fewer opportunities for advancement due to negative scouting reports.

Studies on racial discrimination in MLB also highlight wage and hiring disparities. A study examining wage discrimination found that expansion in MLB in 1993 helped eliminate wage discrimination for pitchers. However, it is essential to continue analyzing wage disparities among different player positions to ensure fairness. Another study, "Equity and Arbitration in Major League Baseball," suggested that players compare their efforts and salaries with peers, which could drive the system toward equilibrium where minority players receive equal wages. However, this study did not include race as a variable, leaving room for further exploration. A chi-squared analysis comparing the racial proportions of players on MLB teams did not find statistically significant evidence of hiring discrimination. However, this does not rule out the presence of bias in other aspects of player evaluation and career progression.

Overcoming bias in MLB involves promoting diversity in front offices and taking proactive measures. The rise of Ivy League-educated executives in MLB front offices has led to concerns about a lack of diversity, resulting in a homogenization of thought and marginalizing individuals from different backgrounds. Efforts like MLB's Diversity Fellowship Program aim to cultivate a more diverse talent pool and provide opportunities for underrepresented groups. However, stakeholders emphasize the need for sustained commitment to diversity beyond token gestures. MLB has developed diversity-focused youth programs, such as MLB Youth Academies and the Reviving Baseball in Inner Cities (RBI) program, to counteract disparities and promote inclusivity from the grassroots level. There is a growing call for proactive measures to address systemic barriers and promote inclusivity at all levels of baseball operations, including outreach to minority communities and a shift toward more socially responsible hiring practices.

Addressing racial bias in MLB scouting and player evaluation is essential for ensuring fairness and maintaining the integrity of the sport.

By actively mitigating biases in AI algorithms and promoting diversity in front offices, MLB can work toward a more inclusive and equitable environment for all players. Organizations should be transparent about the data analytics methods they use and how decisions are made based on these insights. This includes explaining how data is collected, analyzed, and applied so that stakeholders understand and trust the process. For example, the MLB's use of Statcast, a high-tech tracking system, should be transparent in its methodology and data application to ensure that players, coaches, and fans understand how it influences decisions on player performance and game strategies. Transparency regarding the data used in AI algorithms and how it influences decision-making is vital. The NFL, for instance, has been criticized for its lack of transparency regarding the use of its Next Gen Stats system, which raises concerns about potential bias in player evaluation and performance metrics.

By acknowledging these legal and ethical considerations, sports organizations can responsibly harness the power of data analytics. Protecting data privacy, clarifying intellectual property rights, ensuring fairness in algorithms, and minimizing environmental impact are essential. Ultimately, responsible data analytics can enhance athletic performance, fan engagement, and the overall integrity of the sport, benefiting professional athletes and everyday fitness enthusiasts.

Environmental Sustainability: The Hidden Cost of Big Data

The environmental impact of data centers and the energy consumption associated with large-scale data analytics should be considered. Organizations should strive to use sustainable practices in their data operations to minimize their carbon footprint. A present-day survey estimated that data centers globally consume as much energy as France. Sports organizations relying heavily on data analytics must consider the environmental impact and explore partnerships with cloud service providers committed to sustainable practices, such as Microsoft Azure, which aims to be carbon negative by 2030. For instance, Google has committed to running its data centers, which support its cloud services used by sports analytics companies, on carbon-free energy by 2030.

Sports organizations utilizing these services must also consider their environmental impact and work toward sustainability.

Efficient use of resources in data analytics, such as reducing waste and promoting recycling in the production of wearable technology and other devices, is essential for sustainability. Companies like Fitbit and Garmin, which produce wearables used by athletes across various sports, should focus on sustainable manufacturing practices. Additionally, sports teams that use these devices, such as cycling teams in the Tour de France, should implement programs to recycle or responsibly dispose of outdated or broken devices. The growing use of wearable technology generates electronic waste (e-waste). A report by the United Nations warns that e-waste is the world's fastest-growing waste stream. Sports organizations and wearable tech companies should prioritize responsible e-waste management practices such as recycling and refurbishment programs.

Similar concerns are present with other leading workout apps like Peloton, Nike Training Club (NTC), and Centr. These apps also collect extensive personal data, including workout metrics, device information, and biometric data. The primary concerns revolve around data security, user privacy, and the potential misuse of collected data. For instance, Peloton has faced criticism for data breaches and inadequate privacy controls, which could expose sensitive user information. Users must be vigilant about configuring privacy settings and understanding the implications of sharing their data. Companies, on the other hand, need to prioritize robust data protection measures and transparent practices to safeguard user information.

By acknowledging these legal and ethical considerations, sports organizations can harness the power of data analytics responsibly. Ensuring data privacy is protected, intellectual property rights are clear, algorithms are fair, and the environmental impact is minimized. Ultimately, responsible data analytics can enhance athletic performance, fan engagement, and the overall integrity of the sport, benefiting not only professional athletes but also everyday fitness enthusiasts.

Summary

This chapter examines the intersection of data analysis, artificial intelligence (AI), and sports law, examining their impact on athletic performance and the legal landscape surrounding their use. It begins by exploring the role of data analysis in sports, highlighting how teams and athletes utilize vast amounts of data to gain competitive advantages. Advanced statistical techniques and machine learning algorithms are employed to analyze player performance, injury risks, and game strategies, transforming the way sports are played and managed. The chapter then transitions to AI applications in sports, illustrating how AI technologies are revolutionizing training, performance enhancement, and fan engagement. Examples include AI-powered coaching tools, wearable devices that monitor physiological data, and predictive analytics for game outcomes. AI is also increasingly being used to analyze massive datasets for insights that can improve training regimens, optimize game strategies, and enhance player safety.

Legal considerations form a critical part of this chapter, particularly the issues of data privacy, intellectual property, and the use of AI in decision-making processes. The chapter addresses the regulatory frameworks governing data collection and usage in sports, emphasizing the importance of protecting athletes' personal information. It also examines intellectual property rights related to AI-generated insights and innovations in sports technology. Moreover, the chapter covers the implications of AI on fairness and integrity in sports. The use of AI in officiating and performance analysis raises questions about biases in algorithms and the potential for AI to influence the outcomes of games. It underscores the necessity for transparent and ethical AI practices to maintain the integrity of sports competitions. The chapter also highlights the importance of ensuring that AI systems are designed and implemented in ways that promote fairness and accountability.

Key cases and legislative acts both in the United States and EU that are relevant to data analysis and AI in sports are discussed, providing readers with a comprehensive understanding of the legal precedents and ongoing developments in this area. These discussions include landmark cases and significant legislative measures that have shaped the current legal framework. The chapter concludes with a discussion on the future of AI in sports, considering both the opportunities and challenges that lie ahead. It explores emerging trends such as the increasing use of AI in sports marketing, fan engagement, and virtual reality experiences along with concerns over the notion of unbridled singularity.

Discussion Questions

1. How have advanced statistical techniques and machine learning algorithms transformed the way sports teams analyze player performance and game strategies?
2. Discuss the benefits and challenges of using AI-powered coaching tools and wearable devices in sports training and performance enhancement. What ethical considerations arise from their use?
3. What are the primary legal concerns associated with data privacy in sports? How do regulatory frameworks address these concerns to protect athletes' personal information?
4. Analyze the intellectual property rights related to AI-generated insights and innovations in sports technology. How do these rights impact the development and commercialization of new technologies?
5. Examine the implications of AI on fairness and integrity in sports officiating. What measures can be taken to ensure that AI systems are transparent and free from biases?
6. How do key cases and legislative acts shape the legal landscape of data analysis and AI in sports? Discuss at least two significant cases or acts and their impact on the industry.
7. In what ways can AI influence fan engagement and sports marketing? Provide examples of successful AI applications in these areas.
8. What are the potential long-term impacts of AI on player safety and injury prevention in sports? How can AI technologies be designed to maximize these benefits?
9. Discuss the future trends of AI in sports, including virtual reality experiences and enhanced fan interaction. How might these trends change the sports industry in the next decade?
10. Reflect on the ethical considerations that must be addressed when integrating AI into the sports industry. How can stakeholders ensure that AI applications promote fairness, accountability, and the well-being of athletes?

10

The Future of Sports

Legal, Ethical, and Environmental Dimensions

Chapter Outline

The Future of Sports Law: A New Era	310
Legal Challenges to Discrimination in Sports	311
Participation and Leadership	311
Intersection of Race and Gender	313
The Rooney Rule	314
Mentorship and Leadership Programs	315
Black-Owned Sports Franchises	317
Women-Owned Sports Franchises	317
Social Justice Movements on Sports	318
Impact of Activism	320
Modern Athlete Activism and Social Media	320
First Amendment vs. Contractual Obligations	322
LGBTQ+ Athletes and Fans	325
Reimagining Gender Classification in Sports	326
Proactive Steps for Inclusivity	329
Advocacy and Opposition	330
Disability Inclusion	331

Legal and Regulatory Frameworks for Environmental Protection in Sports	333
Ethical Sourcing and Supply Chain Management	336
The Future of Fan Engagement	339
Summary	344
Discussion Questions	346

The Future of Sports Law: A New Era

The legal aspects of sports are experiencing a profound transformation, driven by a complex interplay of social, technological, and environmental factors. Beyond the athletic feats and competitive spirit, unions and agents are negotiating mega-million deals for their clients, and opportunities for women to participate in sports at all levels are growing. Sports have become a powerful platform for addressing vital societal issues, such as social justice, diversity, and equity. Simultaneously, the industry is grappling with the pressing need to adopt sustainable practices to mitigate its environmental impact.

As sports continue to advance, so, too, does the relationship between athletes, teams, and fans. The rise of technology has disrupted traditional models of fan engagement, creating new avenues for connection and interaction. These advancements have also raised important questions about data privacy, intellectual property, and the ethical use of technology in sports. The legal implications of these developments are far-reaching and require careful consideration.

At the heart of the modern sports industry lies a growing awareness of social responsibility. Athletes and fans alike are demanding that sports organizations address issues of racial and gender equality, as well as the rights and inclusion of LGBTQ+ individuals and people with disabilities. The intersection of sports and social justice has created complicated legal issues, with new laws and regulations emerging to protect the rights of athletes and fans.

Finally, the sports industry cannot ignore the pressing challenges posed by climate change. From extreme weather events to resource scarcity, the environmental impact of sports is significant. As governments and consumers increasingly prioritize sustainability, sports organizations must adapt their operations to minimize their ecological footprint. This transition will require innovative legal strategies to balance environmental protection with the economic interests of the industry.

The material that follows will explore these key areas, examining the legal and ethical implications of social justice, diversity, environmental sustainability, and fan engagement in the sports world. By understanding the trends and challenges shaping the future of sports, we can better prepare for the opportunities and complexities that lie ahead.

Legal Challenges to Discrimination in Sports

Despite legal protections, racial and gender discrimination continues to be pervasive in sports. Athletes, coaches, and staff often face disparities in pay, opportunities, and treatment based on their race and gender. This section explores these issues at the college, professional, and Olympic levels, highlighting examples, statistics, and trends.

Participation and Leadership

As described more fully in the chapter on gender and sports, Title IX, passed in 1972, increased opportunities for women in sports, but disparities remain. For instance, girls at high schools where the majority of students are Black and/or Hispanic have only 67 percent of the opportunities to play sports compared to their male peers, while their counterparts at predominantly white schools have 82 percent of the opportunities that boys do. This discrepancy is reflected in collegiate athletics as well. In the most recent reported academic year, male athletes received $252 million more in athletic scholarships than female athletes. The allocation of resources and opportunities remains skewed, despite the legislative intent of Title IX to ensure gender parity.

Women and minorities are underrepresented in coaching and administrative roles across collegiate sports. According to the most recent data, women held only 42 percent of head coaching positions for women's sports at the Division I level, and a mere 4.9 percent for men's sports. Similarly, Black head coaches held only 9.9 percent, 6.7 percent, and 6.3 percent of men's head coaching positions in Divisions I, II, and III, respectively. Efforts like the Russell Rule implemented by the West Coast Conference (WCC) require schools to interview candidates from underrepresented groups for key positions. This initiative has shown some success; in the first hiring cycle, half of the hired candidates were from underrepresented groups, indicating that structured diversity policies can make a difference.

The gender pay gap is stark in professional sports. For example, professional women's basketball players in the WNBA earn an average of around $114,000, while their male counterparts in the NBA earn an average of nearly $11,000,000. Similarly, in professional golf, men earn an average of $1,050,000 compared to $346,000 for women.

The US Women's National Soccer Team (USWNT) brought significant attention to the issue of gender pay disparity in sports through their high-profile legal battle, which culminated in a landmark $24 million settlement in 2022 to secure equal pay with their male counterparts. This case was rooted in long-standing grievances regarding unequal compensation and treatment compared to the men's team, despite the women's team's consistent international success and higher revenue generation. The legal issues primarily revolved around claims of gender discrimination under the Equal Pay Act and Title VII of the Civil Rights Act. The USWNT argued that they were paid less than the men's team for substantially similar work, including playing in international matches, participating in training camps, and fulfilling promotional duties.

The reasoning behind the settlement acknowledged the systemic inequalities in pay structures and aimed to address these disparities by providing immediate financial compensation and committing to future equalization of bonuses and other forms of remuneration. The outcome of this legal battle was not just a financial victory for the USWNT but also a symbolic triumph that highlighted the need for gender equity in sports. It set a precedent for other female athletes and teams to challenge unequal pay and served as a step toward closing the gender pay gap in sports. The settlement included not only the $24 million payment but also an agreement to equalize pay moving forward, ensuring that the women's team receives compensation on par with the men's team for all matches and tournaments. This case has since become a cornerstone in the broader fight for gender equality in the workplace, inspiring similar actions and fostering a broader dialogue on the importance of equal pay for equal work.

At the same time, women receive less media coverage than men in sports. Women athletes account for only 4 percent of media sports coverage despite making up 40 percent of athletes. A report indicated that local networks and ESPN's SportsCenter allocated less than 2 percent of broadcasting to women's sports. This disparity extends to sponsorship funds, with only 0.4 percent of sports sponsorship funds going to women. Such underrepresentation not only affects visibility but also financial opportunities for female athletes.

The Paris Olympics set the standard for finally achieving numerical gender parity for the first time, with 5,250 women and men competing. However, leadership roles within the Olympic movement still show a significant gender gap. At the Tokyo 2020 Games, only 13 percent of coaches were women, and the percentage dropped to 10 percent at the Beijing 2022 Winter Games. Gender stereotypes persist, with 32.2 percent of parents believing that boys are inherently better than girls at sports, which can lead to both intentional and unintentional discrimination against female athletes.

FIFA announced a 300 percent increase in bonuses for the last Women's World Cup, yet women athletes still earn, on average, twenty-five cents for every dollar earned by male athletes. In 2019, this figure was as low as eight cents to the dollar. This discrepancy underscores the significant gap in professional status and financial recognition between male and female athletes at the highest levels of sport.

Intersection of Race and Gender

Black female athletes are notably underrepresented in various sports programs, particularly in sports like tennis, swimming, and soccer. Despite the benefits of Title IX, the pathway it cleared for sports involvement has predominantly favored white women. Girls of color receive far fewer opportunities to participate in school sports compared to white girls, white boys, and boys of color. This inequality is exacerbated by the intersection of gender and race, leading to more severe barriers for Black women in sports. For example, in collegiate sports, Black female athletes are underrepresented in many programs across all three NCAA divisions, limiting their opportunities for advancement and recognition.

The hiring of women and minorities in professional and college sports has seen a concerning setback. Women held only 18 percent of qualified coaching positions and 9 percent of senior coaching positions in the latest survey. The representation of Black head coaches in college sports has also declined, with fewer Black head basketball coaches now than twenty years ago. This trend highlights the persistent barriers faced by women and minorities in attaining leadership positions in sports.

The Rooney Rule

The Rooney Rule, implemented by the NFL in 2003, mandates that teams interview at least one minority candidate for head coaching positions. While it has been a catalyst for change, its impact has been limited and criticized for not achieving its intended goals.

In 2024, the NFL has a record nine minority head coaches including the longest tenured head coach in the league, Mike Tomlin. Despite these improvements, the percentage of Black head coaches remains low compared to the player demographics. About 54 percent of NFL players are Black, but only 9.4 percent of head coaches are Black. The number of Black assistant coaches has increased, reaching an all-time high of 43.6 percent. This indicates some progress but also highlights the slow pace of change.

The Rooney Rule has faced criticism for being a "check-the-box" exercise rather than a genuine effort to diversify leadership. Former Miami Dolphins head coach Brian Flores' lawsuit against the NFL highlighted instances where minority candidates were interviewed without serious consideration. The rule's effectiveness is questioned as it often fails to translate interviews into actual hires. The challenge lies in transforming token interviews into meaningful hiring practices that reflect the diversity of the player base.

The NBA has implemented various initiatives to promote diversity, such as the Coaches Equality Initiative. Despite this, the league has faced scrutiny for its lack of structured hiring practices promoting racial diversity among head coaches. For the most recent year reported there are no Black majority owners in the NBA, a situation that contrasts sharply with the league's player demographics, where over 70 percent of players are Black. This gap highlights the need for more effective diversity policies at the ownership and executive levels.

Major League Baseball's Selig Rule, similar to the Rooney Rule, requires teams to consider nonwhite candidates for managerial positions. However, the representation of Black players in MLB has declined significantly, from 18.7 percent in 1981 to just 6.2 percent now. The decline is attributed to various factors, including the high cost of participation in youth baseball and a lack of access to facilities in urban areas. Efforts to reverse this trend have included initiatives like Reviving Baseball in Inner Cities (RBI), but progress remains slow.

Mentorship and Leadership Programs

Sports organizations are increasingly focusing on mentorship and leadership development programs to cultivate diverse talent. These programs aim to create a sustainable pipeline of minority candidates for coaching and management positions, addressing long-standing disparities and fostering inclusivity. By prioritizing diversity, sports organizations can tap into a broader range of perspectives, experiences, and skills, ultimately enhancing team performance and organizational success. Additionally, these initiatives are extending their reach to include opportunities for college athletes, especially women and those of color, providing them with essential pathways to leadership roles in sports.

The NFL has taken significant steps to promote diversity through targeted initiatives like the Bill Walsh Diversity Coaching Fellowship and the Nunn-Wooten Scouting Fellowship. The Bill Walsh Diversity Coaching

Fellowship, named after the legendary San Francisco 49ers coach, is designed to provide minority coaches with exposure to NFL training camps, off-season workouts, and mini-camps. This hands-on experience is invaluable for developing the skills and networks necessary for career advancement in coaching roles.

Similarly, the Nunn-Wooten Scouting Fellowship offers opportunities for minority candidates interested in scouting to gain practical experience and mentorship from seasoned NFL scouts. These fellowships aim to demystify the scouting profession, providing a clear pathway for minority candidates to enter and succeed in this field.

The NFL's Coach and Front Office Accelerator program is another key initiative that focuses on leadership development and networking for minority and female candidates. This program offers workshops, seminars, and networking events designed to prepare participants for senior roles within NFL organizations. It provides a platform for these candidates to interact with team owners, general managers, and other high-ranking officials, facilitating the creation of professional relationships that can lead to career opportunities.

Recognizing the importance of cultivating talent from an early stage, some of these NFL initiatives have been extended to include opportunities for college athletes, particularly women and those of color. For instance, the Bill Walsh Diversity Coaching Fellowship often includes college-level coaching interns, offering them a chance to gain firsthand experience in a professional setting. This exposure is crucial for young athletes and aspiring coaches, allowing them to build a foundation for future career advancements.

These mentorship and leadership development programs have demonstrated significant promise in increasing the number of minority candidates in the coaching and executive pipelines. For instance, the NFL's front office and general manager accelerator programs have been instrumental at the executive level, offering diverse candidates opportunities to showcase their talents and connect with key decision-makers.

One notable success story is Brad Holmes, the Detroit Lions' general manager, who emerged from the NFL's executive development programs. Holmes' rise to a prominent leadership position exemplifies the potential of these programs to elevate minority candidates to high-profile roles within the league. His success underscores the importance of providing structured pathways and support systems to nurture diverse talent.

Efforts to increase diversity in coaching and management positions across professional sports leagues have seen mixed results. While initiatives like the Rooney Rule have raised awareness and led to some progress, serious challenges remain. The pipeline of diverse candidates is growing, but translating these opportunities into actual hires requires continued commitment and innovative approaches. Despite the progress made, many minority candidates still face barriers to entry and advancement, highlighting the need for ongoing efforts to address these disparities.

Organizations must remain dedicated to creating and sustaining mentorship and leadership development programs that promote diversity. By doing so, they can build a more inclusive and equitable sports culture that reflects the diverse fan base and society at large. This commitment not only benefits the individuals involved but also enhances the overall quality and success of sports organizations. The journey toward true diversity and inclusion is ongoing, requiring persistent effort and innovative solutions to ensure that all talented individuals have the opportunity to succeed.

Black-Owned Sports Franchises

Michael Jordan was the first Black majority owner in the NBA with the Charlotte Hornets, although he sold his stake in 2023. Other Black athletes have taken ownership stakes in various sports teams, such as LeBron James (Boston Red Sox, Liverpool FC), Patrick Mahomes (Kansas City Royals, Sporting Kansas City), and Giannis Antetokounmpo (Milwaukee Brewers). These ownership stakes represent important steps toward diversity in sports ownership but remain exceptions rather than the rule.

Women-Owned Sports Franchises

Women-owned sports franchises are a testament to the growing influence and leadership of women in the traditionally male-dominated sports industry. These franchises not only represent significant business ventures but also symbolize progress in gender equality and empowerment within sports.

One notable example is Jeanie Buss, who became the controlling owner and president of the Los Angeles Lakers, one of the most storied franchises in the NBA. Under her leadership, the Lakers secured their 17th NBA Championship in 2020. Buss's management style and strategic decisions have played a crucial role in maintaining the team's competitive edge and enhancing its global brand.

Another example is Kim Pegula, who, alongside her husband Terry Pegula, owns the Buffalo Bills (NFL) and the Buffalo Sabers (NHL). Kim Pegula has been instrumental in revitalizing these franchises, focusing on community engagement and innovative business practices. Her leadership has helped to foster a more inclusive and dynamic environment within these teams.

In the world of soccer, Amanda Staveley's involvement with Newcastle United is significant. Staveley, through PCP Capital Partners, played a crucial role in the consortium that acquired the Premier League club. Her vision and business acumen are expected to steer Newcastle United toward a new era of success and financial stability.

Another trailblazer is Michele Kang, who became the majority owner of the Washington Spirit, a National Women's Soccer League (NWSL) team. Kang's commitment to the sport and her strategic investments are aimed at enhancing the visibility and commercial viability of women's soccer in the United States. Under her leadership, the Washington Spirit is poised for substantial growth and development.

These women-owned franchises highlight the meaningful role women play in sports management and ownership. Their contributions extend beyond financial investments; they bring unique perspectives, innovative strategies, and a commitment to fostering inclusivity and excellence in sports. As more women assume leadership roles in sports franchises, they pave the way for future generations of female entrepreneurs and leaders in the industry.

Social Justice Movements on Sports

Athletes have become powerful voices for social change, using their platforms to address racial and social injustice. The rise of social media has amplified these voices and created a broader platform for activism. As a result, sports organizations have been pressured to take a stand on social issues and implement initiatives to promote racial and gender equality. Social media platforms like Twitter, Instagram, and TikTok enable athletes to reach millions of followers directly, bypassing traditional media gatekeepers and fostering a more personal connection with their audience. Below are a few of the most remarkable examples of prominent athletes lending their voice to social change.

Muhammad Ali and the Vietnam War: Muhammad Ali, born Cassius Clay, was not only a boxing legend but also a leading figure in the civil rights movement. Ali's refusal to be drafted into the US military during the Vietnam War in 1967 was a significant act of protest. He cited his religious beliefs and opposition to the war, famously stating, "I ain't got no quarrel with them Viet Cong." This stance led to his conviction for draft evasion, a $10,000 fine, and a five-year prison sentence, although he remained free on appeal. Ali was also stripped of his boxing titles and banned from the sport for several years, demonstrating the severe consequences athletes could face for their activism.

Jesse Owens at the Berlin Olympics: Jesse Owens, a Black track and field athlete, made history at the 1936 Berlin Olympics by winning four gold medals. His victories directly contradicted Adolf Hitler's propaganda of Aryan racial superiority. Owens' success was a powerful statement against racism and discrimination, although he faced significant challenges and limited recognition in the United States upon his return.

1968 Olympics Black Power Salute: At the 1968 Mexico City Olympics, US sprinters Tommie Smith and John Carlos raised their fists in a Black Power salute during the medal ceremony. This act of defiance was a protest against racial injustice and discrimination in the United States. Both athletes faced immediate repercussions, including expulsion from the Olympic Village and professional ostracism upon their return home.

Colin Kaepernick's Kneeling Protest: Colin Kaepernick, a former NFL quarterback, began kneeling during the national anthem in 2016 to protest police brutality and racial inequality. His actions sparked a nationwide debate and led to widespread protests across various sports. Kaepernick faced significant backlash, including being effectively blackballed from the NFL. He filed a grievance against the league, alleging collusion to keep him out, which was settled in 2019 under confidential terms.

Athlete activism has often been met with legal and regulatory pushbacks. For instance:

- *Olympic Charter:* The International Olympic Committee (IOC) prohibits political protests at the Games, which led to the punishment of Smith and Carlos in 1968.
- *NFL Policies:* The NFL initially had no specific rule against kneeling during the anthem, but the league later implemented policies to restrict such protests, leading to further legal challenges and settlements.

Impact of Activism

The impact of athlete activism has been both positive and negative:

Positive Impacts

- Raised awareness about social and racial issues.
- Influenced public opinion and policy changes.
- Inspired other athletes to use their platforms for social justice.

Negative Impacts

- Professional and financial repercussions for the athletes involved.
- Backlash from fans, sponsors, and governing bodies.

Modern Athlete Activism and Social Media

Today's athletes leverage social media platforms like Twitter, Instagram, and TikTok to amplify their messages and mobilize support. These platforms have transformed the way athletes engage with fans, policymakers, and the public at large, enabling them to become powerful forces for social change while addressing a larger audience than ever before.

- **LeBron James:** Beyond his on-court prowess, LeBron James is a vocal advocate for social justice. He uses his extensive following on platforms like Twitter and Instagram to address issues such as police brutality, education reform, and voter suppression. His "More Than an Athlete" initiative highlights his commitment to community empowerment.
- **Naomi Osaka:** The tennis superstar has used her platform to raise awareness about mental health and racial injustice. Her decision to withdraw from the French Open to prioritize her mental well-being sparked a global conversation about athlete mental health. Additionally, Osaka has worn masks with the names of victims of racial violence during matches, transforming tennis courts into platforms for social justice.
- **WNBA Players:** The WNBA has consistently been at the forefront of athlete activism. Players like Brittney Griner and Sue Bird have used their platforms to advocate for racial equality, LGBTQ+ rights, and criminal justice reform. Their collective voice has amplified the impact of their message and inspired fans to join the movement.
- **Colin Kaepernick:** While his NFL career was cut short, in part or whole because of his form of speech that made many team owners and fans upset, Kaepernick's decision to kneel during the national anthem to protest racial inequality sparked a national conversation. His activism, amplified by social media, ignited a movement that continues to inspire athletes and fans alike.
- **Megan Rapinoe:** The US women's soccer star has been a vocal advocate for gender equality and LGBTQ+ rights. Her outspokenness on issues like equal pay and social justice has made her a role model for athletes and fans worldwide.
- **Climate Change Advocacy:** Athletes are increasingly using their platforms to raise awareness about climate change. For example, tennis player Novak Djokovic has spoken out about the environmental impact of the sport and has advocated for sustainable practices.

While social media has empowered athletes to become powerful voices for change, it has also introduced new challenges and controversies. The immediacy of these platforms can lead to impulsive statements and potential backlash. Athletes must carefully consider the impact of their words and actions, as they can face criticism, boycotts, and even legal repercussions.

For instance, rising NBA star Anthony Edwards faced significant backlash after making homophobic comments on his Instagram account, which led to a $40,000 fine and public criticism from his team and fans. Similarly, NFL safety Jermaine Whitehead was released from the Cleveland Browns after posting threatening and profane tweets following a game loss, demonstrating how social media missteps can lead to severe career consequences. Another example is Kyrie Irving, who was suspended for five games without pay after posting about a book and film with antisemitic tropes, highlighting the potential for social media posts to result in suspensions and damage to an athlete's public image. Additionally, former NBA player Paul Pierce lost his job as an ESPN analyst after posting a racy video on Instagram Live, showcasing how personal conduct shared on social media can lead to professional repercussions.

The blurred lines between personal opinions and brand endorsements can also create tension. Athletes often have lucrative sponsorship deals, and their public statements may conflict with the values of their sponsors. This can lead to difficult decisions about whether to prioritize personal beliefs or financial interests.

Furthermore, the rise of online hate speech and harassment has created a hostile environment for many athletes, particularly those who are vocal about social justice issues. This has led to calls for increased platform accountability and measures to protect athletes from online abuse.

Despite these challenges, the power of athlete activism on social media is undeniable. As athletes continue to use their platforms to address critical social issues, it is essential to support their efforts and hold them accountable to the communities they serve.

First Amendment vs. Contractual Obligations

Morality clauses are common in athlete endorsement contracts. These clauses typically allow a company to terminate a contract if an athlete's behavior is deemed to damage the brand's image. When athletes use their platforms to address social issues, their statements may conflict with the values or image of their sponsors, leading to potential contract terminations. For instance, in the case of Israel Folau, a rugby player, his contract with Rugby Australia was terminated after he posted anti-LGBTQ+ comments on social media. Rugby Australia cited a morality clause, arguing that Folau's statements brought the sport into disrepute and conflicted with their values. Similarly, golfer Tiger Woods lost endorsement deals with Accenture and AT&T following revelations of his extramarital affairs, which were seen as damaging to the brands' images.

Athletes in professional sports often face restrictions on their speech imposed by league rules and regulations, which can lead to conflicts between their activism and contractual obligations. While the case of Colin Kaepernick is well-known, other examples also illustrate the tension between athlete activism and league policies.

One notable example is Raven Saunders, an American shot putter who won the silver medal at the 2020 Tokyo Olympics. Saunders crossed her arms in an "X" on the podium to symbolize "the intersection of where all people who are oppressed meet." This act of protest led to an investigation by the International Olympic Committee (IOC). However, the investigation was suspended after Saunders' mother passed away. This situation highlights how governing bodies can suppress athlete activism, raising questions about free speech and the consequences athletes face for expressing their views.

Athletes often operate under collective bargaining agreements (CBAs) and personal conduct policies that outline acceptable behavior. For instance, the NFL's personal conduct policy aims to maintain the league's image but has been criticized for potentially infringing on players' First Amendment rights. The NFL, like other professional leagues, is a private entity and thus not directly subject to First Amendment claims. However, the principles of free speech still resonate within the context of private organizations, leading to debates about the extent of permissible regulation on player speech. When athletes face discipline for their activism, they can challenge these actions through established grievance and appeals processes. These processes are typically outlined in the CBAs and are designed to ensure fairness and impartiality. For example, disciplinary procedures should provide a fair opportunity for the case to be heard by an impartial tribunal, and the procedures should be transparent and consistent. Outside organized professional sports in the United States, appeals can often be made to bodies like the Court of Arbitration for Sport (CAS), which allows for a re-hearing or review of the original decision. To ensure a fair and unbiased appeals process, it is crucial that:

- The procedures are clear and accessible.
- The tribunal is independent and impartial, which has not always occurred in professional sports leagues where the Office of the Commissioner wields nearly absolute power.
- The grounds for appeal are well-defined to prevent frivolous challenges.

Courts have often struggled to balance the First Amendment rights of athletes with the legitimate interests of sponsors and leagues. While athletes have a right to express their opinions, their contractual obligations must also be considered. The outcome of these cases often depends on the specific facts of each case, including the nature of the athlete's speech, the terms of the contract, and the potential harm to the brand. For example, in the case involving cyclist Lance Armstrong, Nike and other sponsors terminated their contracts with Armstrong after overwhelming evidence of his involvement in doping came to light. The sponsors argued that Armstrong's actions had irreparably damaged their brands, justifying the termination under morality clauses.

Several court cases have addressed the conflict between athletes' First Amendment rights and their contractual obligations:

Doe v. Kuhn: A college baseball player sued his former head coach, alleging retaliatory actions after he exercised his First Amendment rights. The court allowed the case to proceed, emphasizing the need to protect individuals from retaliation for engaging in protected speech. The player, referred to as "Doe," claimed that after he and other players complained about the coach, he was subjected to punitive actions, including being forced to play in a manner that cost him a year of eligibility and losing his scholarship.

Mahanoy Area School District v. B.L.: The US Supreme Court ruled that a public school violated a student's First Amendment rights when it punished her for off-campus speech on social media. While not directly involving a professional athlete, this case has implications for how institutions can regulate speech. The Court held that the student's off-campus speech, which included a profane social media post, did not cause a substantial disruption and thus was protected under the First Amendment.

Donald De La Haye v. University of Central Florida: Former University of Central Florida kicker Donald De La Haye filed a federal lawsuit alleging that the university violated his First Amendment rights by rescinding his athletic scholarship. De La Haye's YouTube channel, which generated revenue, was deemed a violation of NCAA amateurism rules. He argued that his videos were a form of autobiographical entertainment and that the university, as a public institution, should respect his right to free speech.

Athletes' actions and statements can severely impact their brand image and, by extension, their commercial value. Sponsors are often quick to distance themselves from athletes whose behavior is seen as controversial or damaging. This was evident in the cases of the late Kobe Bryant, who lost endorsements after facing allegations of personal misconduct, and Michael Vick, who lost deals following his involvement in a dogfighting ring.

Athletes—even superstar athletes with secure player contracts and massive social media followings—must find that delicate balance between maintaining their personal brand and adhering to the expectations of their sponsors and leagues. As athletes' activism continues to grow, it is likely that we will see more legal challenges in this area. The legal landscape responding to cultural shifts will require careful consideration of both free speech principles and the commercial realities of the sports industry.

LGBTQ+ Athletes and Fans

The inclusion of LGBTQ+ individuals in sports has been a complex and evolving journey. While some progress has been made, challenges persist, particularly in terms of legal protections, cultural acceptance, and organizational support.

Legal protections for LGBTQ+ athletes and fans vary widely across jurisdictions. In some countries and states, explicit anti-discrimination laws safeguard LGBTQ+ individuals in sports. However, in many places, such protections are absent or weakly enforced, creating an uneven playing field. For example, in the United States, despite advancements in legal protections for LGBTQ+ individuals, some states still lack comprehensive anti-discrimination laws.

Ensuring a safe and inclusive environment for LGBTQ+ fans is crucial. However, incidents of homophobia and transphobia at sporting events continue to occur, ranging from verbal harassment to physical violence, creating a hostile atmosphere. LGBTQ+ athletes also face unique challenges within sports culture. Homophobia and transphobia remain prevalent in many sports, leading to a climate of fear and discrimination. The pressure to conform to traditional gender roles can be particularly harmful to LGBTQ+ athletes, often forcing them to suppress their true identities. Moreover, the lack of visible LGBTQ+ role models in sports can contribute to feelings of isolation and alienation.

Recent statistics highlight the significant impact of social media and societal pressure on LGBTQ+ individuals, particularly athletes. According to a recent survey by The Trevor Project, 42 percent of LGBTQ+ youth reported seriously considering suicide in the past year, with rates being even higher among transgender and non-binary youth. The pervasive presence of social media has amplified both the support and harassment that LGBTQ+ individuals experience. Positive representation can be empowering, but the anonymity of social media platforms often leads to increased bullying and harassment, exacerbating mental health struggles.

Reimagining Gender Classification in Sports

The call for ensuring a safe and inclusive environment for LGBTQ+ fans and athletes in sports has never been more urgent. Despite growing awareness, incidents of homophobia and transphobia at sporting events persist, ranging from verbal harassment to physical violence, creating a hostile atmosphere. LGBTQ+ athletes face unique challenges, with homophobia and transphobia entrenched in many sports cultures. The pressure to conform to traditional gender roles can be particularly harmful, often forcing athletes to suppress their true identities, leading to feelings of isolation and alienation due to the lack of visible LGBTQ+ role models in sports.

Traditionally, sports are divided into male and female categories, a binary classification that increasingly fails to reflect our evolving understanding of gender as a continuum. This raises crucial questions about how sports organizations should address gender classification while ensuring fairness and inclusivity.

One bold approach to addressing these challenges is the introduction of an open category, allowing athletes of any gender to compete together. This would create a space where athletes who do not fit neatly into the binary classification can compete without compromising their identities.

Additionally, expanding mixed-gender events can promote inclusivity, as the Olympic movement is embracing. Sports like mixed doubles in tennis and co-ed relay races in track and field provide successful models for integration. Increasing such events can reduce pressure on athletes to conform to traditional gender roles, fostering a healthy and fun environment.

Moreover, sports organizations should consider implementing policies that focus on skill and ability rather than gender. Emphasizing performance metrics and individual competencies can make sports more inclusive and equitable.

However, by reinventing sports classifications it presents a set of different challenges for sports organizations, encompassing liability, fair competition, safety, and the overall integrity of sports. One key issue is negligence concerns for unsafe play. For example, if a sports organization introduces a new category for athletes based on biometric data and an athlete is injured because the classification did not adequately consider safety implications, the organization could be held liable for negligence. In contact sports like football or rugby, if the classification system places an athlete in a category with significantly larger or stronger players, leading to serious injury, the organization could face lawsuits for failing to ensure safe play. The failure to provide a safe environment, inadequate safety protocols, and lack of proper risk assessment could all be grounds for negligence claims.

Discrimination is another critical issue. Implementing new classifications based on gender identity or physical attributes could lead to allegations of discrimination if the criteria are perceived as unfair or exclusionary. For instance, if transgender athletes are forced to compete in a separate category, it could be viewed as discriminatory, violating anti-discrimination laws. Sports organizations must ensure that classifications comply with laws such as Title IX in the United States, which prohibits sex-based discrimination in federally funded education programs, including sports.

Failing to warn athletes about the risks associated with new classifications could also lead to legal liability. For example, if a new classification system in gymnastics does not clearly communicate the increased risk of certain injuries, athletes who suffer harm may claim that they were not properly warned. Failure to provide adequate warnings about the risks and dangers associated with participation under new classifications could lead to liability for injuries sustained by athletes.

Liability for improper classification is another concern. Misclassifying an athlete due to faulty biometric data or other criteria could result in significant harm, either through physical injury or career impact. For instance, an athlete placed in a lower skill category might lose out on sponsorships and professional opportunities. Organizations could face lawsuits for professional negligence, emotional distress, and loss of earning potential due to improper classification.

Maintaining competitive balance is essential to the integrity of sports. New classifications that disrupt competitive balance could lead to disputes among athletes and teams. For instance, if a classification based on genetic factors leads to certain teams being unfairly advantaged, it could undermine the integrity of competitions. Ensuring fair competition requires careful design and implementation of classification systems to avoid favoritism, unfair advantages, or manipulation.

The integrity of the sport is also at stake with changes in classification. Changes could lead to questions about the integrity of records and achievements. For instance, if a new category allows athletes to achieve records that would not be possible under traditional classifications, it could devalue existing records and accomplishments. Organizations need to address the implications for record-keeping, historical comparisons, and the overall perception of the sport's integrity.

To anticipate these legal challenges, sports organizations can take several proactive steps. Comprehensive risk assessments should be conducted to understand the potential risks associated with new classifications. Classification systems must comply with relevant laws and regulations, including anti-discrimination laws. Clear and comprehensive information should be provided to athletes about the criteria for classification and the associated risks. Engaging with athletes, coaches, medical professionals, and legal experts can help design fair and safe classification systems. Regular reviews should be implemented to assess the impact of new classifications and make necessary adjustments to address emerging issues. Additionally, training and education should be provided for coaches, officials, and athletes on the new classification systems and their implications.

Ultimately, reimagining gender classification in sports requires creativity and a willingness to adapt to new scientific understandings while envisioning a different future for sports organizations accustomed to a binary system. From high school through professional ranks, and even in local Turkey Trot runs and easy 5K competitions, performance awards are traditionally based on gender and age categories. This entrenched system faces resistance from sports organizations that have long operated under these classifications. However, by embracing flexible and innovative solutions, sports organizations can lead the way in promoting equality and acceptance for all athletes, balancing the need for inclusivity with concerns about fairness and competition. As our knowledge of gender continues to evolve, so, too, must our approaches to inclusivity in sports, ensuring that all athletes have the opportunity to compete safely and authentically.

Proactive Steps for Inclusivity

To foster a more inclusive sports environment, organizations must take proactive steps in different ways. Developing comprehensive LGBTQ+ inclusion policies, providing mandatory training for staff and athletes, and partnering with LGBTQ+ organizations are essential initial steps. Increasing the visibility of LGBTQ+ athletes through mentorship programs and media representation can help create a more welcoming and accepting culture.

While strides have been made in many Western countries, it's important to acknowledge that the global landscape for LGBTQ+ individuals in sports is complex. In some regions, particularly in Muslim countries where homosexuality is often criminalized, LGBTQ+ athletes face immense challenges and risks. The international stage, while increasingly inclusive, does not guarantee equal acceptance for LGBTQ+ athletes from all backgrounds.

Several court cases and legislative initiatives have shaped the legal landscape for LGBTQ+ athletes:

Hecox v. Little: This case challenges Idaho's HB 500, which bans transgender women and girls from participating in sports consistent with their gender identity. The US District Court issued an injunction blocking the law, citing violations of the Equal Protection Clause of the Fourteenth Amendment.

Soule v. Connecticut Association of Schools, Inc.: This case involved cisgender female athletes challenging the Connecticut Interscholastic Athletic Conference's policy allowing transgender girls to compete in girls' sports. The Second Circuit Court ruled that the plaintiffs had standing to challenge the policy, emphasizing the need for a detailed examination of the merits.

D.N. v. DeSantis: This case challenges Florida's "Fairness in Women's Sports Act," which restricts transgender women from participating in women's sports. The plaintiffs argue that the law violates the Equal Protection Clause and Title IX.

The participation of transgender athletes, particularly post-puberty male-to-female athletes, has sparked incredible debate at nearly all levels of competition. Concerns about maintaining a level and fair playing field have been raised, with opponents arguing that transgender women may have inherent physical advantages over cisgender women. This has led to the enactment of laws in several states restricting transgender athletes' participation in sports consistent with their gender identity.

Advocacy and Opposition

Prominent athletes like Megan Rapinoe and Candace Parker, along with nearly 200 others, have publicly supported the inclusion of transgender athletes, emphasizing the importance of equal opportunity in sports. Organizations like Athlete Ally and the Women's Sports Foundation advocate for LGBTQ+ inclusion in sports, highlighting the benefits of participation for transgender youth. Conversely, as described more fully in an earlier chapter, some women's advocacy groups like Champion Women argue that allowing transgender women to compete in women's sports undermines fairness and safety, actively supporting legislation that restricts transgender athletes' participation. The leader of Champion Women, former Olympic gold medal swimmer Nancy Hogshead-Makar, has been a vocal advocate for maintaining what she views as a level playing field in women's sports. Hogshead-Makar and her organization emphasize the importance of preserving competitive equity and ensuring that cisgender female athletes have fair opportunities in sports.

The legal landscape surrounding LGBTQ+ inclusion in sports is rapidly evolving, with key concerns including:

- **Equal Protection:** Ensuring that laws and policies do not discriminate against transgender athletes.
- **Title IX:** Balancing the rights of transgender athletes with the need to maintain fairness in women's sports.
- **First Amendment:** Protecting athletes' rights to free speech and expression.

As athletes' activism continues to grow, it is likely that more legal challenges will arise. The contested and controversial legal landscape will require careful consideration of both free speech principles and the commercial realities of the sports industry.

Disability Inclusion

The integration of emerging sports and virtual reality (VR) technologies presents both exciting opportunities and complex legal challenges, particularly concerning athletes with disabilities. As VR and augmented reality (AR) become more prevalent in sports, issues of accessibility, fair play, and intellectual property are inevitable. Ensuring equal participation for athletes with disabilities in virtual sports, which may require specific sensory inputs or physical capabilities, will be a significant concern. The development of VR sports could also lead to new types of injuries or psychological impacts, necessitating updated safety regulations and liability standards. Advanced adaptive equipment, such as composite materials and cutting-edge prosthetics, is revolutionizing sports for athletes with disabilities. While these advancements are positive, they raise questions about fair competition. If an athlete using advanced equipment consistently outperforms able-bodied athletes, governing bodies will need to address eligibility, classification, and the potential for technological doping. Additionally, the high cost of such equipment could lead to equity and access issues.

Ensuring comprehensive sensory experiences for all fans, including those with disabilities, requires innovative solutions and legal adaptations. For example, creating immersive olfactory experiences in stadiums while maintaining safety for those with respiratory sensitivities is challenging. Sports broadcasts incorporating more sensory elements must also provide accommodations for viewers with disabilities, such as descriptive video or audio for those with visual or hearing impairments. The increasing reliance on technology in sports, including wearable devices and biometric data collection, raises privacy concerns for athletes with disabilities. Protecting sensitive health information and preventing unauthorized use of personal data are crucial. Additionally, as sports organizations collect and analyze data to optimize performance, questions about data ownership and sharing will arise, especially involving athletes with disabilities.

The development of new sports and adaptive equipment introduces unforeseen risks. Sports organizations, equipment manufacturers, and venues may face increased liability claims if athletes with disabilities suffer injuries due to inadequate safety measures or product defects. Insurance companies will need to adapt their policies to cover these emerging risks, potentially leading to higher premiums or exclusions for certain activities. As the number of athletes with disabilities in mainstream sports grows, addressing potential discrimination and harassment is essential. This includes protecting athletes from bullying, cyberbullying, and discrimination based on their disability. Sports organizations must implement stringent anti-discrimination policies and provide training for athletes, coaches, and staff to foster inclusive environments.

Furthermore, integrating the *Americans with Disabilities Act* (ADA) requirements in both physical and virtual sports is crucial to ensuring a unified and accessible sporting environment. The ADA mandates that reasonable accommodations be made to provide equal opportunities for individuals with disabilities. This includes adapting VR technologies to be accessible to athletes with various disabilities, ensuring that VR interfaces are user-friendly, and providing necessary adaptive equipment. Compliance with ADA standards will not only promote inclusivity but also protect organizations from legal challenges related to accessibility.

The future of sports for athletes with disabilities is filled with both promise and challenges. By proactively addressing these potential legal issues, sports organizations, policymakers, and the legal community can work together to create a more inclusive and equitable sporting landscape.

Legal and Regulatory Frameworks for Environmental Protection in Sports

The intersection of sports and environmental sustainability is a burgeoning field with numerous legal and regulatory implications. As societal awareness of climate change and resource depletion grows, the sports industry is increasingly under pressure to adopt eco-friendly practices.

The Clean Air Act sets emissions standards for vehicles, impacting the transportation used for sports events. Sports organizations are encouraged to use low-emission or electric vehicles for transporting athletes, staff, and equipment. For example, Major League Baseball (MLB) has partnered with Chevrolet to use electric vehicles for player transportation during the All-Star Game, as opposed to the traditional gas-powered golf carts.

Regulations ensure proper ventilation and filtration systems to maintain healthy indoor air quality in sports facilities. The Occupational Safety and Health Administration (OSHA) sets guidelines for indoor air quality that arenas and stadiums must adhere to. For instance, the Golden 1 Center, home of the Sacramento Kings, uses advanced air filtration systems to enhance indoor air quality.

Restrictions on constructing sports facilities in environmentally sensitive areas help protect ecosystems. The *California Environmental Quality Act* (CEQA) requires environmental impact assessments for new stadium constructions. The construction of the Golden Gate Park stadium in San Francisco faced scrutiny under CEQA, ensuring minimal environmental disruption.

Tax breaks and incentives for acquiring and protecting natural land encourage sustainable practices. Programs like the Conservation Reserve Program (CRP) provide financial incentives to sports organizations that conserve natural habitats. The PGA Tour has incorporated these practices by developing golf courses that serve as wildlife habitats.

Regulations prohibit harmful chemicals in sports equipment manufacturing. The European Union's REACH regulation restricts the use of certain chemicals in products, including sports gear. Nike has committed to eliminating hazardous chemicals from its supply chain, adhering to such regulations. Mandating clear and accurate information about the environmental impact of sports products ensures transparency.

The Federal Trade Commission (FTC) enforces guidelines against misleading environmental claims. Adidas provides detailed environmental impact information on its products, ensuring compliance with FTC regulations. Consumer Protection Regulations prevent misleading claims about the sustainability of sports products and events. The FTC's Green Guides outline acceptable practices for marketing environmentally friendly products. The New York Attorney General's office has prosecuted companies for greenwashing, ensuring truthful sustainability claims.

Regulations govern the end-of-life management of sports equipment and apparel. Extended Producer Responsibility (EPR) laws in states like California require manufacturers to manage the disposal of their products. Patagonia's Worn Wear program exemplifies compliance by encouraging recycling and repair of used gear. The need for consistent environmental standards across different countries is critical for global sports events.

The International Olympic Committee (IOC) has set sustainability guidelines for all Olympic Games, promoting uniform environmental practices. Monitoring and enforcing environmental regulations in the sports industry remains a challenge, especially when the Games are hosted by large cities like Paris and Los Angeles suffering from long-standing environmental and health challenges.

Agencies like the Environmental Protection Agency (EPA) play a major role in oversight, as seen in the enforcement actions against stadiums violating the Clean Water Act. New technologies, such as carbon capture and storage, have the potential to mitigate the environmental impact of sports. The installation of carbon capture systems in stadiums, like the Mercedes-Benz Stadium in Atlanta, exemplifies the adoption of such innovations. Consumer preferences drive sustainable practices in the sports industry.

The growing demand for eco-friendly products has led companies like Puma to launch sustainable product lines, influencing industry standards.

Eco-Friendly Sports Events and Products are increasingly becoming the norm. The adoption of renewable energy is evident in solar-powered stadiums like Levi's Stadium in Santa Clara, which uses solar panels to meet a significant portion of its energy needs. Brands like Nike use recycled polyester and organic cotton in their products, promoting sustainability. Nike's Move to Zero campaign is a testament to this commitment.

Sports organizations are increasingly purchasing carbon offsets to neutralize their carbon footprint. The NBA's Green Initiative includes offsetting emissions from travel and operations. Offering free or discounted public transportation to event attendees reduces traffic congestion and emissions. The US Open Tennis Championships provide incentives for spectators to use public transit. Providing sustainable and healthy food choices for athletes and spectators is gaining traction. The Los Angeles Lakers have introduced plant-based food options at their games, supporting environmental sustainability. Regulatory Trends Impacting Sports include mandates for sustainable building practices and energy efficiency in new stadium constructions.

The Leadership in Energy and Environmental Design (LEED) certification, developed by the US Green Building Council, sets standards for eco-friendly construction. Mercedes-Benz Stadium in Atlanta achieved LEED Platinum certification, showcasing sustainable design and energy efficiency. Requirements for waste management plans help sports organizations minimize landfill waste and promote recycling.

The Green Sports Alliance provides guidelines for developing effective waste management strategies, exemplified by the Seattle Mariners' comprehensive recycling program at T-Mobile Park. Efficient water usage in facilities and field maintenance is crucial. The EPA's WaterSense program encourages sports facilities to adopt water-saving technologies. The University of Arizona's water conservation efforts in maintaining its sports fields demonstrate compliance with such regulations. Carbon pricing mechanisms, such as carbon taxes or cap-and-trade systems, incentivize sports organizations to reduce their carbon footprint.

The Regional Greenhouse Gas Initiative (RGGI) in the northeastern United States is an example of a cap-and-trade system that impacts sports facilities, encouraging them to adopt greener practices. By understanding the complex legal and regulatory landscape, sports organizations can proactively integrate sustainability into their operations and contribute to a healthier planet. These efforts not only comply with regulations but also enhance the public image and operational efficiency of sports entities.

Recent legal cases highlight the consequences of failing to act on environmental responsibilities. For instance, FIFA faced legal scrutiny over its claims of carbon neutrality for the Qatar World Cup, with the Swiss advertising regulator ruling these claims unsubstantiated and misleading. Additionally, the Environmental Defenders Office reported that Australian sports bodies are at significant legal risk due to inadequate responses to climate change impacts, such as extreme weather affecting player health and infrastructure integrity. The UN has also emphasized the substantial environmental footprint of major sports events, citing the 2016 Rio Olympics and the 2018 Russia World Cup as examples of significant carbon emissions. These cases underscore the urgent need for sports organizations to adopt comprehensive and verifiable sustainability measures.

Ethical Sourcing and Supply Chain Management

The sports industry confronts serious issues related to labor exploitation and environmental harm within its supply chain. Overseas sweatshop conditions, marked by low wages, long working hours, and unsafe environments, are common in many garment manufacturing facilities producing sports apparel. These practices not only breach fundamental human rights but also tarnish the industry's reputation. Additionally, the manufacturing processes often lead to environmental damage, including water pollution from chemical dyes and finishes, and the generation of large amounts of textile waste that burdens landfills.

Nike has faced criticism for labor abuses in its factories, including forced labor, arbitrary pay cuts, and unpaid wages. Investigations have revealed poor working conditions in factories in countries like Vietnam and Indonesia. In response to these issues, Nike has implemented a code of conduct and increased transparency, but the company continues to face scrutiny. Prominent athletes associated with Nike, such as LeBron James, Serena Williams, and Cristiano Ronaldo, have also been indirectly impacted by these controversies. Similarly, Adidas has been scrutinized for poor working conditions and repression of trade unions in its supply chain. In Indonesia, workers at Adidas suppliers have reported harassment and threats for union activities. Athletes like Lionel Messi, James Harden, and Naomi Osaka, who are affiliated with Adidas, have come under the spotlight due to these issues. Both brands have been linked to harmful environmental impacts due to their manufacturing processes, such as the discharge of toxic chemicals into waterways and the extensive use of non-recyclable materials.

Consumers are increasingly demanding greater transparency and ethical practices from sports brands. This shift is driven by heightened awareness of labor exploitation and environmental destruction, amplified by media coverage and social media advocacy. Documentaries and investigative reports, such as *The True Cost*, have played a crucial role in raising awareness about the conditions in which sports apparel is made. Movements like Fashion Revolution, which promotes the hashtag #WhoMadeMyClothes, have pressured brands to adopt more sustainable business models. Public campaigns and boycotts have forced companies to take a closer look at their supply chains and implement more ethical practices.

To address these challenges, sports brands must prioritize ethical sourcing and supply chain management. Key strategies include:

Implementing Robust Labor Standards: Ensuring fair wages, safe working conditions, and adherence to international labor conventions such as those set by the International Labour Organization (ILO). Brands must commit to respecting workers' rights and provide avenues for grievances.

Collaborating with Sustainable Suppliers: Partnering with suppliers committed to sustainable practices, such as reducing water consumption, minimizing waste, and utilizing recycled materials. For example, Adidas has introduced the Parley collection, made from ocean plastic waste.

Supplier Audits and Traceability Systems: Investing in thorough supplier audits and traceability systems to monitor compliance and foster long-term partnerships with ethical suppliers. Patagonia, known for its commitment to fair labor practices and environmental sustainability, conducts regular audits and publishes its supply chain information online.

Speaking of Patagonia, it is often cited as a leader in ethical sourcing, known for its commitment to fair labor practices and environmental sustainability. The brand uses recycled materials and ensures that its suppliers adhere to strict ethical standards. Patagonia's Worn Wear program promotes the repair and recycling of used gear, further reducing its environmental footprint. Athletes like surfer Gerry Lopez and rock climber Tommy Caldwell are associated with Patagonia, highlighting the brand's dedication to sustainability. Amer Sports, which owns brands like Salomon and Arc'teryx, has implemented rigorous vendor monitoring and improvement programs to improve working conditions in its factories. These companies set benchmarks for the industry by demonstrating that ethical sourcing and profitability can go hand in hand.

Ethical sourcing and supply chain management in the sports industry are closely tied to sports law and liability regulations. Brands that fail to address labor abuses and environmental impacts in their supply chains can face legal, financial, and reputational risks. Nike has been subject to lawsuits and shareholder activism due to alleged human rights violations in its supply chain. In one instance, shareholders filed a resolution demanding greater transparency and accountability, leading to significant changes in Nike's supply chain policies. These legal challenges underscore the importance of compliance with international labor standards and environmental regulations.

Policymakers play a crucial role in promoting ethical sourcing by enacting and enforcing regulations that hold brands accountable for their supply chain practices. The US Foreign Corrupt Practices Act (FCPA) and the UN Guiding Principles on Business and Human Rights are examples of frameworks that guide companies in maintaining ethical standards. The FCPA, for example, prohibits US companies from engaging in corrupt practices abroad, indirectly promoting fair labor standards. Additionally, initiatives like the Better Cotton Initiative (BCI) and the Sustainable Apparel Coalition (SAC) provide industry benchmarks and support for brands committed to ethical sourcing. These initiatives help standardize practices and create a level playing field for all players in the industry.

Ensuring ethical practices throughout the complex supply chain of the sports industry is challenging but essential. By investing in sustainable sourcing strategies, conducting thorough audits, and fostering transparent partnerships, brands can mitigate reputational risks, strengthen consumer trust, and gain a competitive advantage. The collective effort of brands, suppliers, consumers, and policymakers is crucial in creating a more sustainable and equitable future for the sports industry. Public response through advocacy, boycotts, and support for ethical brands plays a significant role in driving these changes, demonstrating the power of consumer influence in shaping corporate behavior.

The Future of Fan Engagement

The sports industry is undergoing an incredible transformation as traditional broadcasting models give way to direct-to-consumer (DTC) strategies. Streaming services like ESPN+, NBA League Pass, and MLB.TV empower sports leagues and teams with unprecedented control over content distribution and fan engagement. This shift allows organizations to offer personalized viewing experiences, exclusive content, and interactive features catering to diverse fan preferences. For instance, the NFL's partnership with Amazon for Thursday Night Football enables the league to reach a wider audience through streaming while exploring new advertising and data monetization opportunities. However, the transition to DTC also presents challenges.

Enhancing the fan experience involves the strategic collection and utilization of various data types. Teams and leagues gather information on seating preferences, ticket pricing, and family-friendly sections, including alcohol free areas, to tailor the stadium experience to different fan demographics. Data on team gear purchases and favorite players, such as Caitlin Clark in the WNBA, enable personalized marketing strategies and merchandising efforts. Additionally, opportunities for fans to buy autographs, participate in meet-and-greet events, and engage in NIL collaborations at the college level further deepen their connection to the sport.

Maintaining consistent streaming quality, protecting against piracy, and competing with established streaming giants like Netflix and Disney+ present challenges for sports leagues and teams. The collection and use of fan data raises important privacy concerns. Leagues and teams must prioritize data protection and transparency to build trust with fans. Regulations such as the General Data Protection Regulation (GDPR) in Europe and the *California Consumer Privacy Act* (CCPA) in California provide frameworks for safeguarding personal information. Compliance involves providing clear and concise privacy notices to fans, detailing what data is collected, how it will be used, and who it will be shared with. Fans must give informed consent, fully aware of the data collection and its purposes before agreeing to it.

The hacking breach of the entire Ticketmaster system, which led to the unauthorized release of personal data including customers' names, email and text addresses, purchasing habits, and credit card information of millions of customers, highlights the critical importance of true data protection measures. Such breaches severely damage the perception and reality of safety and security in these systems. The inadequate recourse offered, such as a mere one year of free credit monitoring, further erodes trust. Sports organizations must learn from these incidents to ensure better protection and meaningful responses to data breaches. This commitment to data security is essential for maintaining fan trust and safeguarding the integrity of sports organizations' digital interactions with their audience.

Fans should also have the option to opt out of data collection and use. This can be facilitated through accessible privacy settings on websites and mobile apps where fans can manage their data preferences, offering clear instructions in privacy notices and communications on how to opt out of specific data uses or marketing communications, and allowing fans to opt out of data collection at each event they attend, ensuring ongoing consent.

To ensure compliance with GDPR and CCPA, sports teams should implement best practices including employing encryption, access controls, and secure authentication methods to protect data from unauthorized access. Regular privacy audits should identify vulnerabilities and ensure compliance with relevant regulations. Educating employees on data privacy policies and responsible data handling practices, defining clear guidelines on data retention, and ensuring secure disposal of data that is no longer needed are essential steps. Transparency about data collection practices and emphasizing the ethical use of data can build trust with fans.

To generate new revenue streams, sports organizations are exploring various avenues. Subscription fees, targeted advertising, and e-commerce are core components of the DTC strategy. For example, the NBA has successfully monetized fan data through partnerships with companies like Nike and Intel, creating innovative fan experiences and generating substantial revenue. Furthermore, the emergence of fan tokens, as seen in initiatives by teams like the Chicago Bulls and Manchester City, offers new opportunities for fan engagement and ownership.

Fan tokens, typically built on blockchain technology, allow sports teams to engage more deeply with their fan base by offering a form of partial ownership and participation in certain decisions. These tokens function as a form of cryptocurrency, often issued through platforms like Socios.com, ensuring transparency and security. Owning fan tokens provides fans with a symbolic stake in the team, granting them access to exclusive content, events, and experiences not available to the general public.

Fan tokens enhance fan engagement through voting rights, allowing token holders to vote on various team decisions, such as selecting new jersey designs, matchday activities, or music playlists in the stadium. This democratizes aspects of team management and fosters a sense of community. Additionally, fans can earn rewards such as VIP experiences, meet-and-greet events with players, and signed merchandise, strengthening their connection with the team. Teams also create interactive and gamified experiences using fan tokens, encouraging fans to participate in contests, quizzes, and other activities that can earn them additional tokens or prizes.

Financially, fan tokens provide a new revenue stream for sports teams. By selling tokens, teams can raise funds directly from their supporters, which can be reinvested into the team or used for specific projects. The value of fan tokens can fluctuate based on team performance, news, and market demand, allowing fans to trade these tokens on various cryptocurrency exchanges and potentially benefit financially from their investment.

However, the use of fan tokens raises legal and ethical considerations. As with any cryptocurrency, fan tokens are subject to regulatory scrutiny. Teams must ensure compliance with local and international laws to protect their fans and maintain the legitimacy of the tokens. It is crucial for teams to use fan tokens ethically, enhancing fan engagement without exploiting their supporters financially. Transparency in how tokens are used and how fan votes impact decisions is vital.

Beyond content delivery, technology is revolutionizing the in-stadium experience. Augmented reality (AR) enhances game-day entertainment by providing real-time statistics, player information, and interactive elements. Teams like the Golden State Warriors have incorporated AR into their arena, offering fans immersive and engaging experiences. Virtual reality (VR) is also emerging as a powerful tool for creating simulated game environments and behind-the-scenes content. For instance, the Dallas Cowboys have implemented VR to give fans a behind-the-scenes look at their training facilities and locker rooms, adding a new layer of fan engagement.

Wearable technology, such as smartwatches and fitness trackers, allows fans to monitor their own performance and interact with the game in new ways. Moreover, the concept of smart stadiums is transforming the live sports experience. These venues are equipped with high-speed Wi-Fi, cashless payment systems, and IoT devices to ensure a personalized and seamless experience for fans. For example, Levi's Stadium, home of the San Francisco 49ers, offers high-speed internet and mobile app integration that allows fans to order food and beverages directly to their seats, enhancing convenience and enjoyment.

Accessibility and safety are paramount for creating inclusive and enjoyable sporting events. Closed captioning, audio description, and wheelchair-accessible seating are essential for fans with disabilities. Teams like the Atlanta Falcons have implemented sensory-friendly spaces to accommodate fans with autism or sensory processing disorders. Additionally, advanced security measures, including surveillance technology and crowd management systems, are crucial for protecting fans and staff. The NBA's partnership with Microsoft to deploy AI-powered cameras for crowd monitoring exemplifies this commitment to safety.

By embracing DTC strategies, leveraging technology, and prioritizing fan experience and safety, the sports industry can create a future where fans are more connected, engaged, and satisfied than ever before. Moreover, the integration of esports and virtual worlds is further enhancing fan engagement by bridging the gap between physical and digital experiences. Esports events, often held in virtual arenas, allow fans to participate in real-time through avatars, creating a sense of presence and community. This fusion of virtual and physical worlds is exemplified by platforms like Fortnite, which hosts virtual concerts and events that attract millions of viewers globally.

Such innovations not only expand the reach of sports and entertainment but also provide new monetization opportunities through virtual merchandise and sponsorships. As technology advances, the potential for creating immersive, interactive, and personalized fan experiences will only grow, making the future of fan engagement an exciting frontier for the sports industry. However, the use of algorithms and AI models that enable companies to vary personal pricing based on data collected about individual consumers' finances and sports-related shopping habits, a practice known as "surveillance pricing," is raising serious concerns. While not currently illegal, this practice may soon be subject to new disclosure and stricter security rules. The Federal Trade Commission (FTC) and various privacy advocacy groups are pushing for regulations to ensure transparency and protect consumers from potential exploitation. This push for regulatory changes highlights the importance for sports organizations to stay ahead of privacy and security requirements to maintain fan trust and ethical standards in their operations.

The use of technology in fan engagement extends to safety and security measures, especially at large events such as the Olympics, professional sports games, college teams, and even recreational leagues. Advanced surveillance technologies, including facial recognition systems, are increasingly being implemented to enhance security and ensure the safety of fans at stadiums and arenas. For example, teams like the New York Mets have introduced facial recognition technology to expedite entry and prevent known dangerous persons from entering. This technology, while enhancing security, also raises significant ethical and legal concerns, including potential violations of privacy rights and issues related to data protection. The deployment of facial recognition technology in sports venues must balance the complex landscape of privacy laws and constitutional rights. Legal frameworks such as the Fourth Amendment in the United States, which guards against unreasonable searches and seizures, must be considered.

Additionally, regulations like GDPR in Europe impose stringent requirements on the collection and processing of biometric data, necessitating transparency and informed consent from fans. Sports organizations are also exploring creative ways to enhance fan engagement using technology while addressing these concerns. For instance, biometric systems can be integrated with loyalty programs to offer personalized experiences, such as customized merchandise or exclusive access to events, thereby incentivizing fans to opt in. Moreover, advanced data encryption and anonymization techniques can mitigate privacy risks while allowing teams to harness the benefits of biometric data for security and engagement purposes.

In looking to the future, sports organizations must continually innovate while remaining vigilant about ethical and legal considerations. The adoption of new technologies, from AI-powered analytics to blockchain-based fan tokens, promises to reshape the fan experience. However, these advancements must be accompanied by robust data protection measures and transparent communication with fans. By fostering an environment of trust and innovation, the sports industry can achieve a harmonious balance between leveraging technology for fan engagement and safeguarding the rights and privacy of its supporters.

The future of fan engagement in sports is set to be dynamic, multifaceted, and vastly different from the traditional experience of buying a ticket at the gate, finding a seat, and watching the game while purchasing a hot dog with cash from a vendor. Today, the game experience is driven by technological innovation, transforming every aspect of the fan journey. Direct-to-consumer strategies, immersive in-stadium technologies, and advanced security measures allow sports organizations to create deeply personalized and secure experiences for fans.

Innovations such as augmented reality (AR) and virtual reality (VR) enhance in-stadium experiences by offering interactive and immersive views of the game. Mobile apps streamline ticketing, provide real-time statistics, and facilitate social media interactions, creating a more engaging and connected environment. Looking ahead, the integration of humanoid robots, such as those envisioned by Elon Musk, could revolutionize the stadium experience even further. Imagine robots delivering food and drinks directly to your seat, reducing wait times and enhancing convenience. These robots could also assist with directions, provide information about the game, and enhance overall security. By embracing these advancements, sports organizations can offer a futuristic, seamless, and highly engaging experience for fans, setting new standards for how we enjoy live sports events.

Summary

The future of sports is at a pivotal juncture, grappling with a multitude of challenges and opportunities that are reshaping the industry. Environmental and climate change concerns are prompting sports organizations to adopt sustainable practices, focusing on reducing their ecological footprint and ensuring the long-term viability of their operations. As climate change impacts the frequency and intensity of extreme weather events, sports organizations must develop creative strategies to adapt to these changes, including infrastructure resilience and event scheduling.

The apparel industry, a substantial component of sports, faces scrutiny over supply chain issues, including forced labor, low wages, and unsafe working conditions. Ethical sourcing and production standards are becoming essential to mitigate these problems, with companies increasingly held accountable for the conditions under which their products are made. The shift toward sustainability in the supply chain not only addresses environmental concerns but also improves the welfare of workers, reflecting a growing trend toward corporate social responsibility in sports.

Discrimination based on race and gender continues to be an unresolved issue in sports. Initiatives like the Rooney Rule, which mandates interviewing minority candidates for leadership positions, and mentorship programs are steps toward creating leadership opportunities and fostering diversity. Additionally, reimagining gender classification is something to consider to ensure inclusivity and equality for all athletes while recognizing the need to create a safe and level playing field. This involves addressing the complexities of gender identity and making sure that sports policies reflect the diversity of the athletes they govern in the context of the global environment.

Enhancing the fan experience through new immersive technologies, such as virtual reality, is revolutionizing how fans interact with sports, both in stadiums and at home. These technologies offer fans unprecedented levels of engagement, allowing them to experience games from new perspectives and access a wealth of real-time data. However, the integration of these technologies brings about data privacy concerns. The collection and use of biometric data and facial recognition software, while enhancing security and personalization, raise questions about consent and legality, particularly in jurisdictions where such practices may be illegal without proper consent due to Fourth Amendment protections against illegal search and seizure.

As sports organizations respond to these complex legal and ethical landscapes, they must balance innovation with responsibility. Ensuring that new technologies and practices enhance the sports experience while safeguarding the rights and welfare of all involved is paramount. This includes implementing effective data protection measures and ensuring transparency in how data is collected and used. Furthermore, sports organizations must stay abreast of legal developments to ensure compliance with new regulations.

The future of sports law involves addressing a wide array of interconnected issues. Environmental sustainability, ethical supply chains, diversity and inclusion, advanced technologies, and data privacy are all critical areas that require careful consideration and action. By understanding and anticipating these trends and challenges, stakeholders in the sports industry can better prepare for the opportunities and complexities that lie ahead, fostering a more equitable, sustainable, and innovative future for sports.

Discussion Questions

1. How can sports organizations effectively integrate sustainable practices to reduce their environmental footprint while maintaining economic viability?
2. What are the key ethical concerns surrounding the apparel supply chain in sports, and how can companies address issues such as forced labor and low wages?
3. In what ways can initiatives like the Rooney Rule be expanded or improved to ensure greater diversity and inclusion in sports leadership positions?
4. How should sports organizations approach the reimagining of gender classification to create an inclusive environment for all athletes, or is that an impossible ask?
5. What are the potential benefits and drawbacks of using immersive technologies, such as virtual reality, to enhance the fan experience in sports?
6. What legal and ethical considerations should be taken into account when collecting and using biometric data and facial recognition software in sports?
7. How do Fourth Amendment protections against illegal search and seizure apply to the use of surveillance technologies in sports venues?

8. What steps can sports organizations take to ensure data privacy and security for fans and athletes in an increasingly digital and interconnected world?
9. How can sports organizations balance the need for enhanced security with the rights of individuals to privacy and consent, particularly in jurisdictions with strict legal regulations?
10. In what ways can sports organizations demonstrate corporate social responsibility in addressing climate change, supply chain ethics, and social justice issues?

Glossary

Academic Progress Rate (APR). A program implemented in 2003 as part of a broader academic reform package. It is geared toward helping underperforming student-athletes who play basketball and football.

Actus Reus. The actual carrying out of the intent to knowingly place another person in imminent fear is called actus reus.

Ad Hoc Division. A special division of the CAS created to hear urgent cases for each summer and winter Olympic Games that arise during the ten days before the start of the Opening Ceremony.

Administrative Bylaws. Policies and procedures required to implement the operating bylaws. Administrative bylaws are always subject to review by the full membership.

Aggravated Assault or Battery. Committing an assault or battery when using a weapon, to wit, a hockey stick, tennis racket, or baseball bat, constitutes aggravated assault or battery.

Amateur Sports Act of 1978. Now known as the Ted Stevens Olympic and Amateur Sports Act.

Amateurism. An *amateur* is defined by the NCAA as "one who participates in competitive physical sports only for the pleasure and the physical, mental, moral and social benefits directly derived therefrom."

The Americans with Disabilities Act (ADA), Title III. The statute states that it includes any individual who has a physical or mental impairment that substantially limits one or more major life activities; has a history of such impairment; or is perceived as having such impairment. Examples are a person who is blind, deaf, or disfigured; has a loss affecting body functions; or suffers from a mental or psychological disorder but excludes drug addiction. Title III of the ADA applies to organizations or facilities that provide a place of public accommodation.

Anabolic Steroid Control Act. Federal statute signed into law by President George W. Bush that included testosterone-related substances and steroid-based drugs and precursors in the list of substances that are banned from over-the-counter sale without a prescription.

Armstrong, Lance. Professional cyclist who was stripped of all seven of his Tour de France wins for the use of banned drugs and illegal doping methods.

Assault. Purposefully or willfully placing another player, coach, referee, or spectator in fear of imminent bodily injury is an assault.

Assault. The apprehension of imminent offensive physical contact is deemed the intentional tort of assault.

Battery. Actually physically harming a player, coach, referee, or spectator by force is battery.

Bay Area Laboratory Co-operative (BALCO). California-based laboratory suspected of providing designer steroids for scores of prominent athletes.

Biological Passport. The passport centers on using long-term blood and steroid profiles of biological drug markers resulting from testing athletes over time.

Body Contact. A sport that involves body contact may be used to exclude or discriminate against women under Title IX.

Boras, Scott. Considered the most successful and feared sports agent ever, he limits his practice to representing professional baseball players. By last count, Boras has negotiated contracts valued well over $1.6 billion to CAA's $5.3 billion.

Bruyneel, Johan. Lance Armstrong's now-disgraced coach.

Bullying. A working definition of *bullying* is an act by an individual or group with the specific intent of harming another person psychologically or physically. Common bullying tactics are name-calling, spreading rumors over social media, taunting, threatening, intimidating, or hitting. Acts of bullying seek to exclude someone from a team or group.

Caminiti, Ken. The 1996 National League MVP who claimed in a 2002 *Sports Illustrated* article that half of the players in Major League Baseball have used steroids.

Cincinnati Red Stockings. Historians point to the Cincinnati Red Stockings, organized in 1869, as the original professional sports team in the United States.

Civil Rights Restoration Act. An amendment to Title IX in 1987 by the US Congress to include all activities in any school, including athletic departments that accept federal financial assistance.

Collective Bargaining Agreement (CBA). Collective bargaining refers to the process whereby owners and the players' associations engage in good-faith give-and-take negotiations to reach a written final contract.

Comedy. Comedy or parody enjoys equally strong legal protection under freedom-of-the-press case law standards.

Committee on Infractions. Charged with the responsibility of investigating alleged violations by NCAA schools.

Comparative Negligence. Under this test, recovery is barred only when the athlete contributes more than half of the reason for the injury.

Consideration. In a contract, the parties must exchange something of mutual value, also known as consideration.

Contact Periods. Times when a college coach may have face-to-face contact with recruits or their parents or legal guardians, watch them compete, visit their high schools, and write or telephone or text message them or their parents or legal guardians.

Contact Sports Exceptions. Sports that traditionally exclude women, including boxing, wrestling, rugby, ice hockey, basketball, and football.

Contract. A contract is a legally binding agreement between two or more parties. In the business of sports, a common contract is a standard player agreement that nearly every professional team requires their players and their players' agents to use. Book deals, publicity appearances, and licensing of publicity rights for a product endorsement necessitate different contracts.

Contractor–Independent Contractor. The legal relationship between an agent and athlete is regarded as a contractor–independent contractor association.

Contributory Negligence. In many jurisdictions, the contributory-negligence defense bars recovery for even the slightest degree of fault by an athlete.

Copyright Act of 1976. Grants the owners of a copyright the exclusive right to capture a sporting event and distribute it over the airways.

Copyright Clause. A section of the US Constitution that grants Congress the power to promote the arts and sciences by granting exclusive property rights to their original writings and inventions.

Copyright. A copyright gives the owner of a creative work the right to prevent others from using the work without permission or license. Copyrights are works of original authorship fixed in tangible mediums of expression, such as writing, music, paintings, photos, literature, software, games, sculpture, and sound recordings.

Coubertin, Baron Pierre de. A French nobleman who spearheaded the international movement to revive the modern Olympics.

Court of Arbitration for Sport (CAS). Organization set up as an alternative adjudication process for the IOC. Its close association with the IOC led to charges of political influence, lack of fairness, and conflicts of interest. Eleven years after its inception, the CAS became a part of ICAS.

Creative Artists Agency (CAA). A firm that began as a talent agency for Hollywood films morphed into one of the largest sports agency firms in the world. CAA operates as a full-service agency firm representing professional hockey, basketball, football, and baseball players.

Crime. A crime is an offense against the government that is prosecuted by the government.

Curt Flood Act of 1988. This statute gives players the right to sue their league for anticompetitive activities after they have decertified as a union or players' association.

Dead Periods. No on-campus or off-campus contact is allowed, except for writing, telephoning, or texting.

Death Penalty. The NCAA's bylaws contain a provision to shut down a member's athletic program for repeat major or primary violations over the course of a five-year period.

Defamation. A third right of interest is the reputation right of defamation. Quite prevalent in sports today are lawsuits filed against reporters and bloggers for publishing statements or images that may be unflattering, untrue, or malicious.

Division I Infractions Model. In 2013, the NCAA implemented this model designed to hold schools, coaches, and administrators more accountable for issues directly affecting fairness and integrity. A four-level violation structure ranging from severe to incidental violations replaces the prior two-tier, major-or-secondary-violation standard.

Doping. Refers to the use of a substance or technique during training or competition to gain a physical or mental advantage over an opponent.

Eligibility Center. Any student who desires to play intercollegiate sports at the D-I and D-II levels must register and be cleared by the NCAA via this center.

Equal Pay Act. A federal statute that requires equal pay for equal work subject to exceptions.

Equal Protection Clause. Clause of the Fourteenth Amendment to the US Constitution that serves as another legal tool to protect women from gender-based discrimination. Specifically, the Fourteenth Amendment states, "No State shall make or enforce any law which shall . . . deny to any person . . . the equal protection of the laws." In brief, this means all people similarly situated must be treated the same.

Equal Rights Amendments. Amendments enacted by states on their constitutions that may support state-based gender-equity petitions for relief.

Equity in Athletics Disclosure Act. Report that requires schools to calculate the number of male and female undergraduate students; varsity sports and participation levels based on gender; operating expenses by team; revenue generated by team; expenditures by team, including scholarships and recruiting; and average coaching salaries for male and female teams.

Evaluation Periods. Coaches may do everything that is permitted during a contact period, except have face-to-face contact with the prospect or the prospect's parents or legal guardians during the evaluation period.

Fair Use. The most significant defense to a claim of infringement is fair use, which is codified in section 107 of the federal copyright statute. This defense is the basis for nearly every conversation and deliberation about how society should strike a balance between a private property right available for license or sale that carries enormous revenue potential and the public's interest in the free flow of learning and sharing the expression of ideas found in a broadcast.

Federal Trademark Act of 1946 (Lanham Act). The act that codified the business of sports marketing, advertising, and retailing and is centered on the law of trademarks.

Fédération Internationale de Football Association (International Association of Federation Football; FIFA). The governing body of all international football and soccer-related events, including the World Cup.

Felonies. In general, crimes that carry the possibility of incarceration of a year or more and involve serious offenses, such as embezzlement, theft by force, child abuse, assault and battery, kidnapping, illegal gambling, bribery, statutory rape, and murder, are identified as felonies.

Football Bowl Subdivision (FBS). In 2006, the Division I-A schools participating in major football play were renamed the Football Bowl Subdivision (FBS).

Football Championship Subdivision (FCS). In 2006, the Division I-AA schools were renamed the Football Championship Subdivision (FCS).

Good-Faith Bargaining. The parties must exchange bargaining proposals of the key issues of mandatory and permissive topics, they must respond timely to each others' proposals, they must meet regularly, and they must exchange pertinent financial and budgetary information.

Hazing. Hazing is any act by a group that intends to embarrass, harass, ridicule, or cause mental or physical discomfort. Hazing is a ritual imposed on those who want to join or be a part of a team or group. Acts of bullying seek to exclude someone from a team or group.

Independent Contractor. In an endorsement contract, the endorsing athlete is deemed an independent contractor, or someone who is not subject to the complete control or manner and means of performing the agreed-upon sponsorship services.

Infractions Appeals Committee. An independent committee convened when schools object to aspects of the investigation after a notice of allegations. It is a full-blown hearing with a right to appeal the findings and penalties.

Intellectual Property. The exclusive intangible property rights of the mind granted to those who creatively express an idea. The laws of intellectual property encompass familiar topics, such as patents, trademarks, trade names, copyrights, and domain names.

Intentional Tort. Intentional torts happen when one party knowingly acts in a fashion to cause harm or offense to another. It is not a defense to argue that the offending party did not intend to cause the particular harm suffered. Assault and battery is an example of an intentional tort. For example, when a player or coach purposefully, knowingly, and wantonly places another person in fear of bodily harm or actually causes bodily injury, it is possible that that person has committed an intentional tort.

Intercollegiate Athletic Association of the United States (IAAUS). After President Teddy Roosevelt's request for college presidents to make football safer on their campuses for participants, a football Rules Committee was formed along with the creation of the Intercollegiate Athletic Association of the United States (IAAUS). Four years later, in 1910, the IAAUS was renamed the NCAA.

International Amateur Athletic Federation (IAAF). International Federation for Track-and-Field and Running Events.

International Council for Arbitration for Sport (ICAS). ICAS is closer to an arbitration tribunal. Its three hundred arbitrators are geographically and culturally diverse and trained experts in international sports law. The ICAS forum serves as the final arbitrator in Olympic and international sports disputes.

International Federation (IF). Each Olympic sport has an IF specifically governing its rules.

International Management Group (IMG). Sports agency firm created by Mark McCormack, an attorney from the Midwest who began working with a young golfer, Arnold Palmer, on a handshake agreement. McCormack's contribution to the field is twofold.: He linked engaging athletes to marketing and sponsorship deals, and he ushered in a new negotiating business model—the sports agency firm.

International Olympic Committee (IOC). The international governing body of the Olympics.

International Swimming Federation (FINA). Fédération Internationale de Natation; internationally recognized governing body of aquatic events.

International Triathlon Union (ITU). The global sports-governing body for triathlon.

Johnson, Ben. Canadian Olympic sprinter who became the most famous Olympic athlete to lose a gold medal for racing with illegal steroids in his system in 1988.

Kemp, Jan. The English Teacher–coordinator of the University of Georgia's developmental studies program who successfully filed a lawsuit against the school and was fired for refusing to change the grades of six failing minority students to keep them academically eligible.

Landis, Floyd. Winner of the 2006 Tour de France who publicly revealed his use of illegal substances and Lance Armstrong's orchestration of the distribution of performance-enhancing drugs. Landis was stripped of his Tour win.

Landis, Kenesaw Mountain. Baseball's first commissioner, a former federal judge, is well regarded for reestablishing the integrity of Major

League Baseball by banning for life eight ballplayers who confessed to trying to fix the World Series despite their courtroom acquittal.

Lanham Act. *See* Federal Trademark Act of 1946 (Lanham Act).

LeMond, Greg. The first American to win the Tour de France publicly raised questions about doping in cycling.

Libel. Libel is a tort, or civil wrong. It refers to a statement that impairs a person's reputation through written words. Increasingly, the term *libel* is used as a substitute for the word *defamation*.

Limited Public Figure. Someone who could thrust or inject himself or herself into a particular public controversy and thereby become a public figure for a limited time on a limited issue.

Major League Baseball (MLB). The professional league of baseball in the United States and Canada comprising teams in the American League and the National League.

Major League Baseball Players Association (MLBPA). The labor organization representing players in the MLB.

Mandatory Topics. Bargaining terms include minimum salary, salary cap, pension benefits, health benefits, free agency, salary arbitration, grievance process, reserve clause, revenue sharing, rookie salaries, standard player contract, and so on.

Medical Malpractice. Medical professionals owe athletes a special duty of care based on their training and experience. The specific imposed duty is to exercise reasonable skill and care as is common for those practitioners performing similar services in that particular medical field. Failures to evaluate, advise, diagnose, treat, or prescribe properly to fulfill that duty are deemed medical malpractice.

Mens Rea. The mental intent of a violent action is referred to as mens rea.

Misdemeanors. Less serious crimes, such as first-time driving while impaired, shoplifting, public intoxication, hazing, bullying, and selling alcohol to a minor, that carry a maximum sentence of a year or less in jail along with a fine and/or community service are called misdemeanors.

Mitchell Report. Report issued in 2007 by former Senate leader George Mitchell on the widespread use of performance-enhancing drugs by ballplayers. Eighty-nine players were identified in the report as having used banned substances.

National Association of Intercollegiate Athletics (NAIA). Non–Upper division junior and community colleges do not belong to the NCAA. Many two-year colleges have formed their own regulatory body to create rules for competition and offer championship events. The balance of the four-year schools sponsoring athletic teams that are not members of the NCAA partners with the NAIA.

National Basketball Association (NBA). The national governing body for basketball in the United States, with thirty member teams, one of which is in Canada.

National Collegiate Athletic Association (NCAA). Organization that was founded in 1906 to protect young people from the dangerous and exploitative athletic practices of the time. The NCAA, or association, is the preeminent rule-making body for intercollegiate athletics. Membership is voluntary. Four-year schools in the United States and Canada that meet its standards may join.

National Football League (NFL). National organization of American football that is comprised of thirty-two teams split between the American Football Conference (AFC) and the National Football Conference (NFC).

National Football League Players Association (NFLPA). The labor organization representing the players of the NFL.

National Governing Body (NGB). Each nation's individual governing body for a sport.

National Hockey League (NHL). The premier ice hockey organization in the world, which has participating teams in the United States and Canada.

National Labor Relations Act. Provides three basic rights for professional players engaged in interstate commerce: (1) The right to self-organize into a labor association or union; (2) The right to bargain collectively with management; and (3) The right to engage in collective activities for their mutual benefits (e.g., strike when no agreement is in place or picket).

National Labor Relations Board. Serves as the administrative body to oversee the guarantee of rights granted to players.

National Letter of Intent (NLI). A highly prized recruit is frequently asked to sign an NLI to contractually bind that student to a particular D-I or D-II school. Signing an NLI does not guarantee admission. It does effectively end the recruiting process and guarantees a student-athlete at least one year of financial aid. Each sport has a unique NLI signing period. The rules surrounding NLI are governed by a non-NCAA organization called the Collegiate Commissioners Association, although the NCAA through the Eligibility Center administers the program itself.

National Olympic Committee (NOC). Each nation's individual governing body for the Olympics.

NCAA Manuals. Manuals in which administrative rules, policy statements, and operational bylaws for each division are published annually.

Negligence. The most common tort claim. Liability for the tort of negligence only occurs when some person fails to follow the degree of care that a reasonably prudent person would follow to avoid foreseeable harms. Negligence is known as an unintentional tort. It occurs by omission or commission of an act that causes harm to a person with whom he or she owes a duty to act with care.

Norris-LaGuardia Act. Restricts the power of courts to issue injunctions in labor disputes and statutorily exempts labor unions, including players' associations, from antitrust scrutiny.

North American Soccer League (NASL). The first major professional soccer league in the United States.

Notice of Allegations. NCAA's notification to a school of alleged infractions.

Offer. A contract involves an offer that the other party must accept.

Office of Civil Rights (OCR). The administrative body charged with enforcing law and assisting schools receiving federal funds in complying with Title IX.

Operating Bylaws. These bylaws are meant to promote constitutional principles (e.g., amateurism and institutional control) and purposes of the members. There are thirteen operating bylaws in the Division I manual, which numbers more than three hundred pages.

Parody. Parody is a humorous form of public comment or criticism of an original work or interest.

Patent. Patents exist to protect those who devise a new, nonobvious, novel, useful invention (utility) or design an original and new ornamental feature found on a manufactured product (design). Depending on whether a patent is designated a utility or design patent, its term of protection lasts either twenty years after application or fourteen years from the date of issue, respectively.

Permissive Topics. A category of relevant bargaining subject matter that the parties may consider in their negotiations is referred to as permissive topics. These issues are outside the mandated subject of wages, hours, and other terms and conditions of employment.

Private Figures. Figures who do not achieve fame or notoriety for their public actions.

Product Liability. Product liability claims for defective sporting equipment, such as hockey helmets, trampolines, or soccer goals, may arise under any of the three tort categories.

Prohibited Substances. The list of all drugs, supplements, and other substances and methods that are banned from use in sports.

Public Figure. Included in this list are racecar drivers, horse jockeys, and professional athletes in the sports of baseball, soccer, basketball, hockey, cricket, cycling, and football. In some cases, well-known amateur athletes also have been deemed public figures.

Public Invitees. In legal terms, spectators are considered public invitees.

Pyle, Charles. One of the first sports agents. In the 1920s, he was a Chicago-based theater owner who represented "Red" Grange when he signed him to a player's contract with the Chicago Bears. Pyle also is recognized for starting the first professional tennis tour starring Suzanne Lenglen.

Quiet Periods. Periods during which coaches may not make any off-campus contacts or evaluations but may make in-person contacts only on college campuses.

Requisite State of Mind. A successful prosecution of the crime of assault requires the government to prove beyond a reasonable doubt that the player had the requisite state of mind to commit the threatening offense and then carried out that intent.

Reserve Clause. A player's contract could be bought and sold without a player's permission, and a restriction on a player's freedom to move from team to team was implemented.

Right of Publicity. Closely related to the right to privacy is the notion that there is commercial value in a person's name or likeness. This cognate right is called the right of publicity. In some ways, this right is similar to a privacy right but differs insofar as it is a property interest that can be bartered, assigned, or transferred for consideration. A product or service endorsement by an athlete is an example of an exercise of a public person's publicity rights.

Right to Privacy. In 1890, two former classmates from Harvard Law School wrote an article published in the *Harvard Law Review* titled "The Right to Privacy." In response to the tabloid journalism of their era, they stirred the legal community with a call to arms to protect ordinary citizens against the exposure of their personal affairs on the public pages of the press. They dubbed this new right the right to privacy, or the right to be left alone.

Rome Convention for the Protection of Performers, Producers of Phonograms, and Broadcasting Organizations. This convention licensed broadcasters to have exclusive rights to rebroadcast original programming for twenty years.

Rozelle Rule. The league rule, which is named after the then–NFL commissioner, that, when a player's contract expired and he signed with another team, the new team had to compensate the former team. This rule was deemed an unreasonable restraint of trade.

Safe Harbor. Test utilized by the OCR to determine compliance with Title IX standards by schools employing the substantial proportionality test.

Separate but Equal. Used by both Title IX and the Equal Protection Clause. The key point in assessing whether separate teams in the same sport for men and women meet constitutional muster is for schools to demonstrate that funding, coaching, locker rooms, transportation, times of play, seasons of play, equipment, uniforms, and playing fields or arenas are comparably equal.

Slander. Slander is the twin of libel. An impairment of a person's reputation through spoken words is called slander.

Sports Agent Responsibility Trust Act (SPARTA). Signed into law in 2004 by President George W. Bush, the statute mirrors the UAAA insofar as it seeks to protect student-athletes. It requires agents to conspicuously notify student-athletes of potential loss of eligibility for signing with an agent, prohibits the use of illegal inducements to sign a student-athlete, and requires both the agent and the student-athlete to notify the athlete's athletic director when the parties enter into an agency agreement. Federal compliance of the three principal duties of a sports agent under SPARTA—disclosure, truthfulness, and not buying student-athletes—is regulated by the FTC.

Sports Broadcasting Act of 1961. This gave professional, not intercollegiate, sports leagues antitrust exemption when negotiating television broadcasting rights. The act enables a commissioner to license a television package to ESPN,

FOX, or any of the networks. The individual team franchises share the broadcast revenue equally.

Sports Broadcasting Act. A federal statute that grants professional sports teams an exemption from antitrust laws to pool broadcasting rights.

Stanley, Marianne. University of Southern California women's basketball coach who sued because her base pay and perks were lower than the men's head basketball coach, George Raveling. In denying her claim, the federal appeals court determined the pay discrepancy was based on factors other than gender.

Stare Decisis. The legal doctrine that states that settled principles of law are given the greatest deference.

Steroid Era. MLB's failure to test for performance-enhancing drugs until 2003 led to rampant use among players over a lengthy period of time.

Strict Liability Theories. Strict liability theories make the manufacturer of sports equipment the insurer and, therefore, absolutely liable for all harm that flows from the defect. Strict liability cases are rare.

Substantially Proportional. Term used to describe the obligation that any differences between the men's and women's athletics programs must be negligible. In the area of financial assistance, the money spent on the respective programs do not have to be precisely equal. However, the benefits provided from funding must be equal.

Summary Disposition. Process that allows for a cooperative resolution without prolonged in-person hearings.

Ted Stevens Olympic and Amateur Sports Act. Assigned to the USOC complete responsibility for all matters related to the United States competing in the Olympic Games (and Paralympics and Pan American Games).

Therapeutic Use Exemption (TUE). Situation where an athlete who suffers from a legitimate preexisting medical condition may use a banned substance after consulting with his or her medical doctor and has the exemption approved by the sport's governing body.

Title IX. An amendment to the 1964 Civil Rights Act that was signed into law by President Nixon in 1972. The title states, "No person in the United States shall, on the basis of sex, be excluded from participation in, be denied the benefits of, or be subjected to discrimination under any education program or activity receiving federal financial assistance."

Torts. Torts are divided into three categories: negligence, intentional, and strict liability. The business of torts, as so ably described by Justice Oliver Wendell Holmes, is to "fix the dividing line between those cases in which [a person] is liable for harm which he has done and those in which he has not." It was not until the 1970s that society, and more particularly the judicial system, began to impose civil penalties for egregious conduct in sports.

Trade Dress. A term that describes distinctive identifying features that cannot be infringed upon, such as the unique designs of Nike's sneakers.

Trademark. A symbol, word, name, or device that helps to identify and distinguish one product or service from a competing product or service. Trademarks are different from copyrights and patents, which have fixed terms. Trademarks can last forever unless they fall into the public domain from nonuse and abandonment or become a generic term. Trademark owners possess the legal authority to stop others from using the same or similar symbols or marks when their unauthorized use creates a likelihood of deception or confusion, subject to important exceptions.

Tygart, Travis. CEO of USADA who spearheaded the investigative doping campaign against Lance Armstrong.

Uniform Athlete Agents Act (UAAA). The statute civilly and criminally penalizes agents for impermissible conduct. Wrongful conduct includes initiating or inducing a student-athlete to enter into an agency contract without warning in conspicuous language that a student-athlete may lose his or her amateur eligibility for signing. An intriguing punitive component to these statutes is a civil remedy permitting schools to sue agents for financial losses incurred as a result of penalties imposed by the NCAA for playing with an ineligible student-athlete.

United States Anti-Doping Agency (USADA). Created in 2000 as an independent anti-doping agency for Olympic sports in the United States. It is charged with testing, educating, researching, and adjudicating doping-related issues for US Olympic, Paralympic, and Pan American athletes.

United States Anti-Doping Agency (USADA). Created in 2000 as an independent anti-doping agency for Olympic sports in the United States. It is charged with testing, educating, researching, and adjudicating doping-related issues for US Olympic, Paralympic, and Pan American athletes.

Unlawful Internet Gambling Enforcement Act of 2006. The majority of those who participate in fantasy sports leagues pay to play. A New Jersey court ruling held that the pay-to-play format is not an illegal gambling activity under the federal Unlawful Internet Gambling Enforcement Act of 2006.

US Figure Skating Association (USFSA). The sport of skating's US national governing body.

US Olympic Committee (USOC). US governing body of the Olympics.

US Patent and Trademark Office (USPTO). Agency within the US Commerce Department that handles the issuance of patents for inventions to businesses and inventors and all trademark registration for product identification.

Violations. In many jurisdictions, even less serious offenses, such as operating without a driver's license, speeding, underage possession of alcohol, or loitering, are not classified as a crime. Instead, they are deemed violations and cannot result in incarceration.

Wade Exum Report. Report named after the former anti-doping chief for the USOC that revealed the names of more than one hundred US Olympic athletes who had tested positive for banned substances between 1988 and 2000 but were cleared internationally by the USOC.

Waiver (or Release). A waiver or release is a legal document voluntarily signed to inform facility users, or their parents or guardians in the case of minors, of known risks involved in various activities and to shield the facility or organization from liability from personal harm or loss of property.

"Whereabouts" Component. Requires athletes to provide their location on a daily basis and submit to testing anywhere from one hour to twenty-four hours in advance, depending on the regulatory body.

Women Sports Foundation. An advocacy organization that works to increase the number of women working in sports administration.

Woolf, Bob. Recognized as one of the early professionally trained lawyers to serve as a sports agent, Earl Wilson, the first acknowledged African American pitcher for the Boston Red Sox, retained Woolf in the 1960s initially for advice after an auto accident and then to negotiate baseball contracts on his behalf. Later on, Woolf became best known as the agent who represented legendary Celtic basketball player Larry Bird.

World Anti-Doping Agency (WADA). The international anti-doping agency whose purpose is to promote and coordinate efforts against doping in sports internationally.

World Anti-Doping Code. Document created by WADA to standardize anti-doping testing procedures, processing, and maintaining the integrity of samples collected.

World Intellectual Property Organization (WIPO). An agency within the United Nations that specializes in the protection of international intellectual property.

Bibliography

Acosta, R. Vivian, and Carpenter, L. J. "Women in Intercollegiate Sport: A Longitudinal, National Study." *Brooklyn College of the City University of New York*, 2012. AcostaCarpenter.com.

AIM Sport Patent Infringement Case Against Supponor AIM Sport AG v Supponor Ltd., Case No: [2019] EWHC Civ Comm.

"Amanda Staveley Leads Newcastle United Takeover with PCP Capital Partners." *BBC Sport*, October 7, 2021.

American Airlines Sponsorships American Airlines Sponsorship Agreements - Official Reports.

American Needle, Inc. v. National Football League, 560 U.S. 183 (2010).

Anderson, C., and Sally, D. *The Numbers Game: Why Everything You Know About Soccer is Wrong*. Penguin Books, 2013.

Anderson, Mark. "Artificial Intelligence and Its Role in Shaping the Future of Sports Analytics." *Journal of Sports Science & Technology*, vol. 15, no. 3, 2023, pp. 141–155.

Andy Warhol Foundation for the Visual Arts, Inc v Goldsmith. Andy Warhol Found for the Visual Arts v Goldsmith, No. 21-869 (U.S., May 18, 2023).

Baker, Jamie. "Climate Change and Its Impact on Outdoor Sports." *Environmental Science in Sport*, vol. 9, no. 1, 2023, pp. 207–224.

Berri, David J., and Simmons, Rob. "CBA Policy and Competitive Balance in NCAA Men's Basketball." *Economic Inquiry*, vol. 60, no. 1, 2022.

"Bill Walsh Diversity Coaching Fellowship." *National Football League, NFL Operations*.

Billie Jean King Leadership Initiative. BJKLI.org.

Black September Organization incident at Munich 1972 Olympics: Various.

Boras, S., and Verducci, T. *The Boras Blueprint: How Scott Boras Revolutionized Baseball Contracts*. Sports Illustrated, 2019.

Brake, Deborah L. *Getting in the Game: Title IX and the Women's Sports Revolution*. New York University Press, 2010.

Branch, Taylor. "The Shame of College Sports." *The Atlantic*, October 2011.

Buzuvis, Erin E. "Title IX and Gender Equity in College Sports." *Marquette Sports Law Review*, vol. 14, no. 1, 2003, pp. 1–36.

Byers, Walter. *Unsportsmanlike Conduct: Exploiting College Athletes.* University of Michigan Press, 1997.

California Consumer Privacy Act (CCPA). *California Civil Code Title 1.81.5*, 2018.

Champion Women Organization. ChampionWomen.org.

Chappelet, J.-L. *The International Olympic Committee and the Olympic System: The Governance of World Sport.* Routledge, 2022.

Civil Rights Restoration Act of 1987, Pub.L. 100–259.

Cohen v. Brown University, 991 F.2d 888 (1st Cir., 1993).

"Colin Kaepernick's Protest Against Police Brutality: Kneeling During the National Anthem." *The Guardian*, September 1, 2016.

Cooky, Cheryl, Messner, Michael, and Musto, Michela. "'It's Dude Time!': A Quarter Century of Excluding Women's Sports in Televised News and Highlight Shows." *Communication & Sport*, vol. 3, no. 3, 2015, pp. 261–287.

Copyright Act (Post-1978) Copyright Act of 1976, Pub.L. No. 94-553, §302(a), codified at 17 U.S.C. §§101 et seq.

Cotten, Dan, and Wolohan, John. *Law for Recreation and Sport Managers.* 6th ed., Kendall Hunt Publishing, 2017.

Coubertin, Pierre de. *Olympism: Selected Writings.* International Olympic Committee, 2000.

Court of Arbitration for Sport (CAS). *CAS Jurisprudence Digest.*

Creative Artists Agency (CAA). *CAA Sports Representation.* n.d. Accessed June 20, 2025. Retrieved from https://www.caa.com.

Cristiano Ronaldo's Social Media Earnings Cristiano Ronaldo Instagram Earnings Report - Forbes (2024).

Crowe, C. (Director). *Jerry Maguire* [Film]. Gracie Films, 1996.

Curt Flood Act of 1998, Pub. L. No. 105-297, 112 Stat. 2824.

Davenport, T. H., and Harris, J. G. *Competing on Analytics: The New Science of Winning.* Harvard Business School Press, 2007.

Delaney v. Cascade River Holidays Ltd., [1983] B.C.J. No. 2026 (B.C.C.A.).

Digital Millennium Copyright Act (DMCA) of 1998 Digital Millennium Copyright Act of 1998, Pub.L. No. 105-304, codified at 17 U.S.C §§1201–1205.

Dobbs, Dan B., Hayden, Paul T., and Bublick, Ellen M. *The Law of Torts.* 2nd ed., West Academic Publishing, 2011.

Dosh, Kristi. *Saturday Millionaires: How Winning Football Builds Winning Colleges.* Turner Publishing, 2013.

Edelman, Marc. "A Short Treatise on Amateurism and Antitrust Law: Why the NCAA's No-Pay Rules Violate Section 1 of the Sherman Act." *Case Western Reserve Law Review*, vol. 64, no. 1, 2013.

Edelman, Marc. "The Future of Amateurism After the NCAA's NIL Rule Change." *Forbes*, July 1, 2021, pp. 61–104.

Epstein, A. *Sports Law*. Aspen Publishers, 2010.

Falk, D., and Goldberg, J. *The Bald Truth: Secrets of Success from the Locker Room to the Boardroom*. Simon & Schuster, 1992.

"Fan Engagement in the Digital Era: The Rise of eSports and Virtual Stadiums." *World Sports Innovation Conference Proceedings*, 2023.

Federal Baseball Club of Baltimore v. National League of Professional Baseball Clubs, 259 U.S. 200 (1922).

FIFA. *FIFA Regulations on Working with Intermediaries*. n.d. Accessed June 18, 2025. Retrieved from https://www.fifa.com/legal/regulations/intermediaries.

FIFA. "History of FIFA - Foundation." FIFA.com.

"FIFA's AI Referee System for Fair Play." *Fédération Internationale de Football Association, FIFA*, 2023.

Flood v. Kuhn, 407 U.S. 258 (1972).

Fry, A. M. "Gender Inclusion and Exclusion in International Sport." *Journal of Sport and Social Issues*, vol. 45, no. 4, 2021, pp. 333–348.

Garcia, B., and Meier, H. E. "Social Responsibility in International Sport Federations: Organizational Perspectives." *International Journal of Sport Policy and Politics*, vol. 12, no. 1, 2020, pp. 1–15.

Geeraert, A. *Sports Governance and Policy Development: An International Approach*. Routledge, 2021.

"Gender Equity and the Future of Inclusion in Sports." *Women's Sports Foundation*, 2022.

General Data Protection Regulation (GDPR). *Regulation (EU) 2016/679 of the European Parliament and of the Council*. 2018.

Gould, W. B. *Labor Relations in Professional Sports*. Greenwood Publishing Group, 1999.

Green, G. S. "Tort Law and Organized Sports: Liability for Participant Injuries." *Journal of Legal Aspects of Sport*, vol. 1, no. 1, 1991, pp. 29–45.

Gregorie v. Alpine Meadows Ski Corp., 28 F.3d 1057 (9th Cir. 1994).

Grove City College v. Bell, 465 U.S. 555 (1984).

Hackbart v. Cincinnati Bengals, Inc., 601 F.2d 516 (10th Cir. 1979).

Hawk-Eye Innovations U.S Patent No. WO2002073121A2 (filed March 14, 2002).

Heffernan, Catherine. "The 'Tortification' of Sports Law: An Examination of Liability in Professional Sports." *International Sports Law Journal*, vol. 16, no. 1–2, 2016, pp. 17–29.

Hogshead-Makar, Nancy, and Zimbalist, Andrew, eds. *Equal Play: Title IX and Social Change*. Temple University Press, 2007.

Huma, Ramogi, and Staurowsky, Ellen J. *The Price of Poverty in Big Time College Sport.* National College Players Association, 2020.

Human Rights Watch. *Evolving Standards in Athlete Human Rights.* Human Rights Watch Report, 2023.

Hylton, J. G., and Hylton, K. N. *Sports Law and Regulation: Cases, Materials, and Problems.* Wolters Kluwer, 2023.

IBM. *IBM SlamTracker for Tennis Tournaments.* IBM, 2022.

IOC. "History of the Olympic Games." International Olympic Committee, 2023.

IOC. "Sustainability and Legacy Strategic Framework." International Olympic Committee, 2021.

Illegal Streaming Impact on Sports Industry Forbes Report on Sports Industry Losses Due to Illegal Streaming (2024).

Institute for Diversity and Ethics in Sport (TIDES). "Gender Report Card." TIDES.org.

International Handball Federation (IHF). "History of Handball." IHF.info.

International Olympic Committee (IOC). "Gender Equality in the Olympic Movement." Olympics.com.

International Olympic Committee (IOC). *Olympic Charter.*

International Paralympic Committee (IPC). *Strategic Plan for the Paralympic Movement 2022-2026.* 2023.

"Israel Folau's Contract Termination Over Anti-LGBTQ+ Comments on Social Media." *BBC News*, May 2019.

"Jeanie Buss Becomes Controlling Owner of the Los Angeles Lakers." *The Los Angeles Times*, March 27, 2017.

"Jesse Owens at the Berlin Olympics: Defying Hitler's Aryan Myth." *Olympic Channel, International Olympic Committee*, 2024.

Johnson, Bella. "Athlete Health and Wearable Technology: The Next Generation of Player Welfare." *International Journal of Sports Health Science*, vol. 27, 2023, pp. 215–229.

"Kim Pegula: Co-Owner of Buffalo Bills and Buffalo Sabres." *The Athletic*, December 12, 2020.

Knight v. Jewett, 3 Cal.4th 296, 834 P.2d 696 (1992).

Lanham Act of 1946 Lanham (Trademark) Act, Pub.L. 79-489, 60 Stat. 427 (1946), codified at 15 U.S.C. §§ 1051–1127.

"LeBron James' 'More Than an Athlete' Initiative for Social Justice Issues." *ESPN*, December 2018.

Lenskyj, H. J. *Sexual Diversity and the Sochi 2014 Olympics: No More Rainbows.* Palgrave Macmillan, 2018.

LeRoy, M. H. *Collective Bargaining in Sports and Entertainment: Analyzing the New Reality.* Cambridge University Press, 2022.

Livestrong Foundation. "Our History." livestrong.org.

Los Angeles 2028 Organizing Committee. *Environmental Impact Assessment for LA 2028*, 2024.

Mackey v. National Football League, 543 F.2d 606 (8th Cir. 1976).

Macur, J. *Cycle of Lies: The Fall of Lance Armstrong*. HarperCollins, 2014.

Major League Baseball Players Association (MLBPA). *MLBPA Agent Certification*. n.d. Retrieved from https://mlbpa.com/certification.

Mandela, Nelson. "Sport Has the Power to Change the World." Laureus World Sports Awards, May 25, 2000, Monte Carlo, Monaco.

McCormack, M., and McCormack, B. J. *What They Don't Teach You at Harvard Business School: Notes from a Street-Smart Executive*. Bantam Books, 1984.

McCormick, Robert A., and McCormick, Amy Christian. "The Myth of the Student-Athlete: The College Athlete as Employee." *Washington Law Review*, vol. 81, no. 1, 2006, pp. 71–157.

McKenzie, Laura. "The Environmental Impact of Mega Sporting Events and Sustainability Practices in Sports." *Global Sports Management Journal*, vol. 12, no. 4, 2021, pp. 321–338.

McNally v. United States, 483 U.S. 350 (2006).

"Megan Rapinoe's Fight for Equal Pay and LGBTQ+ Rights in Sports." *Time Magazine*, June 2019.

Mercer v. Duke University, 190 F.3d 643 (4th Cir., 1999).

"Michael Jordan Becomes First Black Majority Owner in NBA History." *ESPN*, June 17, 2010.

"Michele Kang Acquires Majority Ownership of Washington Spirit." *The Athletic*, March 30, 2022.

Mitten, Matthew J. "Team Physicians as Co-Employees: A Prescription That Deprives Professional Athletes of an Adequate Remedy for Sports-Related Injuries." *Saint Louis University Law Journal*, vol. 50, no. 1, 2005, pp. 211–238.

Mitten, Matthew J., Davis, Timothy, Smith, Rodney K., and Berry, Robert C. *Sports Law and Regulation: Cases, Materials, and Problems*. 5th ed., Wolters Kluwer, 2019.

Moorman, Anita M., and Spengler, John O. "The Legal Responsibility of Sport Organizations for Spectator Safety in Public Venues." *Journal of Legal Aspects of Sport*, vol. 13, no. 1, 2003, pp. 83–97.

"Muhammad Ali Refuses Induction into U.S. Army in Protest Against Vietnam War." *The New York Times*, April 28, 1967.

Nabozny v. Barnhill, 31 Ill. App. 3d 212, 334 N.E.2d 258 (1975).

Naismith, James. *Basketball: Its Origins and Development*. University of Nebraska Press, 1941.

"Naomi Osaka's Activism on Mental Health and Racial Injustice." *The New York Times*, September 2020.

National Basketball Players Association (NBPA). *NBPA Agent Certification*. n.d. Accessed June 5, 2025. Retrieved from https://nbpa.com/certification.

National Collegiate Athletic Association (NCAA). "NCAA Constitution and Bylaws." NCAA.org.

National Football League Players Association (NFLPA). *NFLPA Agent Certification*. n.d. Accessed June 5, 2025. Retrieved from https://nflpa.com/certification.

National Hockey League Players Association (NHLPA). *NHLPA Agent Certification*. n.d. Accessed June 6, 2025. Retrieved from https://nhlpa.com/certification.

National Labor Relations Board (NLRB). *Collective Bargaining and Representation*. n.d. Accessed JUne 4, 2025. Retrieved from https://www.nlrb.gov.

National Labor Relations Board (NLRB). Memorandum GC 21-08 (2021).

National Women's Law Center. "The Battle for Gender Equity in Athletics in Colleges and Universities." *NWLC.org*, 2020.

National Women's Soccer League (NWSL). "About NWSL." NWSLsoccer.com.

Navratilova, M. *Public Statements on Gender Classification in Sports Controversies at the Paris Olympics*. 2024.

NBA Cares Program. "Community Outreach Initiatives." NBA.com.

NBA Media Rights Deal (2025-26) NBA Media Rights Deal with ESPN, NBC, Amazon (2024).

NCAA v. Alston, 594 U.S. (2021).

NCAA v. Board of Regents of the University of Oklahoma, 468 U.S. 85 (1984).

NCAA. "NCAA Transfer Portal FAQs." NCAA.org.

NFL Digital Athlete with Amazon Web Services. *AI Technologies for Training and Injury Prevention*. n.d.

Nike Vaporfly Shoes U.S. Patent No. US20180042454A1 (filed February 15, 2018).

Nike vs Schutt Sports Patent Dispute Nike Inc v Schutt Sports Inc., Case No: CV-10-00685-PHX-DGC (D.Ariz., July 29, 2010).

Nike's Flyknit Technology U.S. Patent No. 8,266,749 (filed March 27, 2012).

Nike's Partnership with Michael Jordan Nike Annual Report on Air Jordan Brand Revenue (2024).

"Novak Djokovic's Advocacy on Climate Change and Sustainable Practices in Sports." *BBC Sport*, January 2022.

"Nunn-Wooten Scouting Fellowship." *National Football League, NFL Operations.*

Opta Sports. *Advanced Performance Data for Soccer.* Opta Sports, n.d.

Phelps, Michael. "Mental Health in Athletics: A Call to Action." *The Players' Tribune*, 2020.

Pierson, L. M., and Adams, B. *The Impact of Big Data and Machine Learning on Sports Performance Analytics. Journal of Sports Analytics*, vol. 2, no. 3, 2016, pp. 145–161.

"Raven Saunders' Protest at the Tokyo Olympics Symbolizing Oppression Intersectionality." *NBC News*, August 2021.

Riddell Football Helmets U.S. Patent No. D775,015 (filed November 15, 2016).

Rosenblatt, K. *Data, Technology, and the Future of Sports Performance: AI and Machine Learning in the Field.* MIT Sloan Sports Analytics Conference, 2018.

Sabo, Donald, et al. "Her Life Depends on It III: Sport, Physical Activity, and the Health and Well-Being of American Girls and Women." *Women's Sports Foundation*, 2015. WomensSportsFoundation.org.

SAP HANA platform in NHL broadcasts. *Real-time player analytics and game statistics.* n.d. Accessed June 16, 2025.

Schmidt, Ethan. "Augmented Reality in Sports Training: Implications and Opportunities." *Sports Technology Today*, 2022, pp. 207–228.

Second Spectrum. *NBA Partnership for Player Movement Tracking in 3D.* n.d.

"Selig Rule." *Major League Baseball, MLB.com.*

Sharp, Linda A., Moorman, Anita M., and Claussen, Cathryn L. *Sport Law: A Managerial Approach.* 4th ed., Routledge, 2018.

Sisense. *Data Analytics in Sports: How Technology is Changing the Game.* Sisense, 2021.

Smith v. Horizon Aero Sports Ltd., No. 96-1428, 1997 WL 1072190 (Pa.Com. Pl.).

Smith v. Pro-Football, Inc., 593 F.2d 1173 (D.C. Cir. 1978).

Smith, Patrick R. "The Use of Blockchain for Sports Contract Management and Integrity." *International Review of Law and Technology*, vol. 30, no. 2, 2022, pp. 17–40.

Smith, Ronald A. *Sports and Freedom: The Rise of Big-Time College Athletics.* Oxford University Press, 1990.

Speedo LZR Racer Swimsuits U.S. Patent No. US20080077821A1 (filed April 3, 2008).

Spengler, John O., Miot, John N., and Connaughton, Daniel P. "Risk Management in Sport and Recreation: Essential Readings." *Journal of Legal Aspects of Sport*, vol. 16, no. 1, 2006, pp. 61–85.

Sport England. "This Girl Can Campaign." sportengland.org.
Sports Innovation Lab. *The Future of Sports Technology: How Emerging Tech Will Transform the Industry*. Sports Innovation Lab, 2020.
Statcast. *Major League Baseball's Advanced Tracking System for Performance Metrics*. n.d. Accessed June 11, 2025.
Stats LLC v. Sportradar AG. *Intellectual property rights dispute over proprietary sports data*. n.d. Accessed June 7, 2025.
Statute of Monopolies of 1623 Statute of Monopolies, 21 Jac. 1, c. 3 (1623), UK Parliament.
Staudohar, P. D. *Playing for Dollars: Labor Relations and the Sports Business*. ILR Press, 1989.
Steinberg, L., and Yaeger, D. *The Agent: My 40-Year Career Making Deals and Changing the Game*. St. Martin's Press, 2014.
Sugden, J., and Tomlinson, A. *Power Games: A Critical Sociology of Sport and the Olympic Games*. Routledge, 2018.
Suggs, Welch. *A Place on the Team: The Triumph and Tragedy of Title IX*. Princeton University Press, 2005.
Tarkanian v. NCAA, 488 U.S. 179 (1988).
TechAhead & Catapult. *AI-powered wearables and predictive analytics tools in sports*. n.d.
The Aspen Institute. "The State of Women's Sports 2023." AspenProjectPlay.org, 2023.
"The Future of Sports: Legal, Ethical and Environmental Dimensions." AI-generated content from a prompt by the author.
"The Rooney Rule." *National Football League, NFL Operations*, 2003.
Title IX of the Education Amendments of 1972, 20 U.S.C. §1681 et seq.
Tokyo Organizing Committee of the Olympic and Paralympic Games. (2021). *Tokyo 2020 Sustainability Report*.
"Tommie Smith and John Carlos' Black Power Salute at the Mexico City Olympics." *Smithsonian Magazine*, October 1968.
Transparency International. *Corruption in Sport Initiative: Key Findings and Recommendations*. Transparency International, 2023.
U.S. Congress. *Sports Agent Responsibility and Trust Act (SPARTA)*, Pub.L. 108-304, 15 U.S.C. §7801, 2004.
U.S. Constitution, Article I, Section 8, Clause 8 U.S. Const. art. I, § 8, cl. 8.
U.S. Department of Education, Office for Civil Rights (OCR). "Title IX and Athletics." ED.gov.
U.S. Department of Education, Office for Civil Rights. "Title IX and Athletics." ED.gov.
U.S. Department of Justice, Civil Rights Division. "Title IX Legal Manual." Justice.gov, 2020.

U.S. Government Accountability Office. "Intercollegiate Athletics: Recent Trends in Teams and Participants in NCAA Member Schools." GAO-01-297, 2022. GAO.gov.

U.S. Patent Act of 1790 Patent Act of 1790, ch. 7, 1 Stat. 109 (1790).

"U.S. Women's National Soccer Team Settles Equal Pay Lawsuit for $24 Million." *The New York Times*, February 22, 2022.

Under Armour's SC30 Logo U.S Trademark Registration No: Reg. No:5,117,415 (filed January, 2017).

Uniform Law Commission. *Uniform Athlete Agents Act (UAAA)*, 2000. Retrieved from https://www.uniformlaws.org.

United Nations Educational, Scientific, and Cultural Organization (UNESCO). *Kazakhstan Declaration on Sports Ethics and Human Rights*. 2022.

United States Anti-Doping Agency (USADA). *Anti-Doping Rules & Regulations*.

Ventura v. Kyle, No. 12-472 (DWF/SER), 2014 WL 1283721 (D. Minn. March 31, 2014).

WADA. "World Anti-Doping Code." World Anti-Doping Agency.

Wasserman Media Group LLC. *Wasserman Sports Representation*. n.d. Retrieved from https://www.teamwass.com.

"WCC Implements Russell Rule to Address Diversity in Coaching." *West Coast Conference*, July 16, 2020.

Wenger, A. *Chief of Global Football Development for FIFA*. Data and AI: Transforming Sports Law and Performance, n.d. Accessed June 8, 2025.

Wilkinson, J. *Player Contracts and Publicity Rights in Sports*. Oxford University Press, 2021.

Women's National Basketball Association (WNBA). "History of the WNBA." WNBA.com.

Women's Sports Foundation. "Title IX: History and Impact." WomensSportsFoundation.org.

Wong (Litigation Guardian of) v. Lok's Martial Arts Centre Inc., [2009] B.C.J. No. 1893 (B.C.S.C.).

World Anti-Doping Agency (WADA). *World Anti-Doping Code*. WADA.

"WNBA Players' Advocacy for Racial Equality and LGBTQ+ Rights." *The Washington Post*, July 2020.

Yasser, Ray, et al. *Sports Law: Cases, Documents, and Materials*. 8th ed., Wolters Kluwer, 2021.

Zone7. AI-driven System for Injury Risk Forecasting. n.d. Accessed June 12, 2025.

Index

1928 Amsterdam Olympics   74
1936 Berlin Games   110
1964 Tokyo Olympics   8
1968 Mexico City Olympics   319
1968 Winter Olympics   125
1972 Munich Games   114
1980 Summer Olympics   110
1900 Paris Olympics   74, 109
1992 Barcelona Olympics   120
1994 FIFA World Cup   154
2008 Beijing Olympics   115, 116, 124
2012 London Games   110, 118
2014 Sochi Winter Games   114
2016 Rio Olympics   119, 121, 140, 336
2018 Russia World Cup   336
2022 Beijing Winter Games   15, 116
2022 Champions League   262
2022 World Cup   16
2002 Winter Games   114
2024 Paris Olympic Games   4, 115–16
2026 FIFA World Cup   16, 154
2028 Summer Olympics   182

Academic Performance Program (APP)   54
Academic Progress Rate (APR)   54
administrative law   26
Adrian Peterson v. NFLPA   26
advocacy   4, 24, 31, 57, 330–1
  groups   80, 89, 91, 343
AFL-CIO   19
Aikman, Troy   193
AIM Sport   224
Ali, Muhammad   4, 235, 319

All-American Girls Professional Baseball League (AAGPBL)   154
All-England Lawn Tennis Club (AELTC)   190, 191
Alston v. NCAA   26, 27
amateur athletes   27
Amateur Athletic Union (AAU)   135
amateurism   34, 36, 43, 47, 51, 69
  bylaw 12   63–4
  college sports   61–3
  rules   53
Amateur Sports Act of 1978   135
Amazon Web Services   288
American Civil Liberties Union (ACLU)   91
American Football League (AFL)   153
American League (AL)   152, 161
American Needle Inc. v. National Football League (2010)   27, 156, 165
American Professional Football Association   153
Americans with Disabilities Act (ADA)   167, 183, 246, 275, 332
  components of collective bargaining agreements   169–73
  concussion protocols   168–9
anabolic steroids   126–9
Andersen, Chris   175
Andy Warhol Foundation for the Visual Arts, Inc. v. Goldsmith   226
anti-doping   124–7
  agencies   15, 16, 25
  testing protocols   138

Index

Anti-Doping Organizations (ADOs)   131, 139
antitrust law   148–9, 156–60, 165
archery skills   6
Armstrong, Lance   13, 128, 129, 195, 211, 324
Artest, Ron   265
artificial intelligence (AI)   25, 28, 29, 31, 305–6
   applications   279–81
   athlete training and injury prevention   287–9
   developments and challenges   239–41
   models   300
   racial bias algorithms   302–4
   technological advancements   271–2
assault   247, 248, 265, 268–70
athlete activism
   negative impacts   320
   positive impacts   320
   power   320–2
Athlete Ally   330
Athlete Biological Passport (ABP)   129, 139
athletes' contractual obligations   322–5
athletes health benefits   169
Auerbach, Coach   188–9
Auerbach, Red   188
augmented reality (AR)   182, 297, 331, 341, 344
automated external defibrillators (AEDs)   250

Badminton World Federation (BWF)   8
baggataway   6
ball-tracking technology   224
Baltimore Federal Baseball   158
banned substances
   categories   137
   positive test for   15, 271
   and techniques   137
Barber, Shawn   121
Barnes, Matt   181
Barry, Bob   21–2
Basketball Association of America (BAA)   153
battery   247, 248, 268, 269
"Battle of the Sexes" tennis match   4, 156
Bay Area Laboratory Co-operative (BALCO)   127–32, 175, 176
Bayh, Birch   82
Beane, Billy   290
Beckham, David   232
Beijing 2022 Winter Games   313
Berlin Olympics   319
Berman v. Pittsburgh National Bank   261
Berne Convention for the Protection of Literary and Artistic Works   231
Bertuzzi, Todd   269–70
Better Cotton Initiative (BCI)   338
Big Data   304–5
Big League Advance Fund II (BLA)   204–5
Biles, Simone   122, 124, 195, 222, 250
Bill Walsh Diversity Coaching Fellowship   315, 316
biological passport   16, 129
Bird, Larry   153
Black female athletes   313, 314
Black, Indigenous, and People of Color (BIPOC)   303
Black Lives Matter   30, 172
black-owned sports franchises   317
Black Power salute   319
Blank, Tank   203
blood doping   128–30
blood transfusions   128, 129

Board of Governors   39, 48
Bolt, Usain   218
Boras, Scott   193
Bostock v. Clayton County (2020)   101
Brady, Tom   174, 193
Brashear, Donald   269
Brewery, Bavaria   228
broadcasting rights   9, 16, 36, 140, 150, 179, 183, 217–18
Browns, Cleveland   158, 180, 322
Brown v. Board of Education (1954)   102, 155
Bruins, Boston   153
Bryant, Kobe   325
Bryant, Kris   190
Buffalo Bills (NFL)   318
Buffalo Sabers (NHL)   318
bullying   59, 326, 332
Bush, George W.   199
Buss, Jeanie   318
BWF, *see* Badminton World Federation
Byers, Walter
  Unsportsmanlike Conduct: Exploiting the Student-Athlete (1995)   62

Caldwell, Tommy   338
California Consumer Privacy Act (CCPA)   280, 299, 339, 340
California Environmental Quality Act (CEQA)   333
Camp, Walter   7
carbon pricing mechanisms   335
career management   24
Carlos Daniels v. AAG Sports & Kenneth Edelin   203–4
Carlos, John   11, 319, 320
case law   262–6
C.B.C. Distribution and Marketing, Inc. v. Major League Baseball Advanced Media, L.P.   294–6
Chicago Bears   153, 155, 188

Chinese athletes   15
Chronic Traumatic Encephalopathy (CTE)   168, 169
Ciccarelli, Don   270
Cincinnati Reds scouting reports   303
cisgender female athletes   98, 330, 331
civil rights movement   4, 82, 153, 319
Civil Rights Restoration Act of 1987   83
Clark, Caitlin   153, 290
Clark, Charles   253–4
Clause 8 of the US Constitution grants Congress   215
Clayton Act   157
Clean Air Act   333
Clean Water Act   334
Clenbuterol   177
Cleveland Guardians   219
climate change advocacy   321
Cloudboom Strike LS   209
Coaches Equality Initiative   315
coaching contract   152
Cohen v. Brown University (1992)   84–6
Cohen v. San Bernardino Valley College (1996)   45
collectives NIL   64–5
Cole, Gerrit   193
collective bargaining agreements (CBAs)   158, 163, 164, 284, 285, 323
  components   169–73
  developments   176, 183
  process   148, 149, 156–60, 192, 194, 196
  college athletes   26, 28, 41, 63, 65
  NFLPA   203
  NIL policy   207–8
  United States   33, 36, 47, 51, 65, 67, 68
college sports   1, 7, 33–7
  advancements   77–8
  amateurism   61–3

Title IX on women's
  participation 76
women's participation 76
Committee on Infractions 59
committees 39, 48, 50, 59, 65, 66
Communications Act of 1934 293
communities displacement 20–1
Communities for Equity v. Michigan High School Athletic Association (2001) 100
community building 10–14
community revitalization 20
Comparative Negligence 267–8
compound annual growth rate (CAGR) 237
Concussion Legacy Foundation 169
concussion protocol 55, 56, 69, 168–9
Conservation Reserve Program (CRP) 333
consideration 194
Consumer Products Safety Commission 248
contact periods 51, 68
contact sports 248, 267, 269, 327
Conte, Victor 127
contract law 22, 25–6, 31, 292
Contributory Negligence 267
Copyright Act 215
Copyright, Designs and Patents Act 1988 232
copyright holders 240
  rights of 217–18
Copyright Management Information (CMI) 225
copyrights, IP 214
Coubertin, Pierre de 7, 74, 109
Court of Arbitration for Sport (CAS) 108, 130, 144, 145, 324
  role 138–9
Cousy, Bob 158
Creative Artists Agency (CAA) 190, 204

the Creator's Game 6
criminal law 247
crisis management 23, 30
Crowe, Cameron 193
Cruise, Tom 193
cryptocurrency forms 341
cultural values 10–14
Curley, Tim (Athletic Director) 49
Curry, Stephen 153, 219, 287
Curt Flood Act of 1998 158, 162–3
Cybex International lawsuit 270
Cycling Independent Reform Commission (CIRC) 128

Dallas Cowboys 342
Daniels, Carlos 203, 204
data analytics 25, 28, 31, 60, 61, 69, 279–81
  Big Data 304–5
  data privacy 299–300
  fairness in sports decision-making 302–4
  game strategies development 289–91
  goldmine 301–2
  informed consent 300–1
  intellectual property (IP) rights 291–7
  sports performance tranformation 282–7
  virtual games and metaverse 297–9
data privacy 299–300
Data Protection Impact Assessments (DPIAs) 284
Data Protection Officer (DPO) 283, 284
Davis, Anthony 190, 193
Davis v. Monroe County Board of Education 88
dead periods 52
Death Penalty 61
defamation cases 28, 29, 254, 255

defenses sports   267–8
De La Haye, Donald   325
de la Hoya, Oscar   193
Delaney v. Cascade River Holidays Ltd.   256
Denver Broncos   219
Department of Justice (DOJ)   157
designer drug   127
Dexter, Gervon   204–5
differences in sex development (DSD)   96, 97, 115, 133
Digital Millennium Copyright Act (DMCA)   224–7
digital transformation   207–10
direct-to-consumer (DTC)   339, 340, 342
dispute resolution   23, 24, 43
Diversity Fellowship Program   303
diversity promotion   30
division councils   39
Division I   37–8, 52–4, 69, 312
   legislative autonomy   66–8
Division II   38, 54
Division III   39, 52
Djokovic, Novak   289, 321
D.N. v. DeSantis   330
Dodgers, Brooklyn   153, 155
Doe, Jane   271
Doe v. Kuhn   324
Dolphins, Miami   314
Donald De La Haye v. University of Central Florida   325
doping   14, 16, 21, 57, 108, 113, 125
   blood doping   128–30, 137
   cases   139
   issue   126
   Lance Armstrong   195, 211
   Russian systematic doping scandal   131, 132
   sport   127, 128, 144
double-edged sword game   17–18
draft systems   171

dual-track system   94
due process   28, 43–5, 59, 91–4, 138, 174
   issue   46–7
Dunne, Olivia   151
Durant, Kevin   229

Edelin, Kenneth   203–4
Education Amendments of 1972   82
Edwards, Anthony   322
Eighth Circuit Court of Appeals   165
electronic sports (esports)   237–8
Eligibility Center   53
end-of-life management   334
enforcement mechanisms   130–2
enforcement process   59–60
English Premier League (EPL)   179
entrants
   general duty of care   260–2
   invitees   258–9
   licensees   259
   trespassers   250, 258–60
Environmental Defenders Office   336
environmental impacts, sports team   21
Environmental Protection Agency (EPA)   334, 335
Epic Games   297
Equal Pay Act   312
equal protection   28, 43
Equal Protection Clause   99–102
Equal Protection Clause of the Fourteenth Amendment   330
equal protection laws   331
Equity in Athletics Disclosure Act (EADA)   87
equity issues   30
erythropoietin (EPO)   128, 129, 137
ESPN   313, 322
esports   18, 20, 25, 29, 31
ethical conduct violations   58
European Court of Human Rights   96

Index 379

European Court of Justice (ECJ)   296
European Union's REACH
    regulation   334
evaluation periods   52
Extended Producer Responsibility
    (EPR)   334

facial recognition technology   343
Fair Labor Standards Act (FLSA)   159
Fairness in Women's Sports Act   330
fair use principles   225, 226, 239,
    240
fake tickets   229
Falk, David   191
fan engagement
    metrics   299
    model   339–44
    sports industry   342, 344, 346
fan tokens   340–1, 344
FAST HOCKEY BY STEVE
    COMEGNA INC.   223
"Father of American Football"   7
*Federal Baseball Club of Baltimore v.
    National League of Professional
    Baseball Clubs* (1922)   161–2,
    183
Federal Trade Commission
    (FTC)   157, 200, 334, 343
Fédération Internationale de Football
    Association (FIFA)   4, 8, 16, 28,
    168, 175, 198, 297
    percentage   313
    soccer matches   246
    World Cup   9–11, 19, 150, 154, 228
    World Cup Qatar 2022   273, 336
Fédération Internationale de Volleyball
    (FIVB)   8
female athletes   311–14
fiduciary duty   200–5
financial downfall, of athletes   207
Financial Fair Play (FFP)   170
financial mismanagement   205–7

financial planning   27
First Amendment   45, 294
    rights   322–5, 331
First Circuit Court of Appeals   85
FIVB, *see* Fédération Internationale de
    Volleyball
5 Pointz Graffiti case   232
Flood v. Kuhn (1972)   162–3, 183
Flores, Brian   314
Florida Antitrust Act   295
Florida Deceptive and Unfair Trade
    Practices Act   295
Flyknit technology   223, 224
Folau, Israel   323
Football Association   7, 153
Football Bowl Subdivision (FBS)   38
Football Championship Subdivision
    (FCS)   38
*Football Dataco Ltd. v. Sportradar
    GmbH*   296
Formula 1 (F1) teams   150
*Forsyth v. Pender Harbour Golf Club
    Society*   264
Fortnite   236, 239
Foster, Andrew "Rube"   152
Fourteenth Amendments   46
Fourth Amendment   46
free agency   171
Free Exercise Clause of the First
    Amendment   102
free speech principles   325, 331

gambling   21, 29, 58, 174, 175, 181
Games Period   121
game strategies development   289–91
Gemili, Adam   121
gender-affirming hormone therapy
    (GAHT)   95
gender equity   28, 36, 37, 67, 118, 133
    advocacy groups   80
    classification   132–4, 326–9
    intersection   313–14

stereotypes 313
title IX 81–94
gender pay gap 312, 313
General Data Protection Regulation (GDPR) 280, 283, 284, 299, 339, 340, 343
George, Mitchell 175
Gervon Dexter 204–5
Giannis Antetokounmpo 317
Ginsburg, Ruth Bader 74, 100
Godmother of Title IX 81
Golden State Warriors 287, 290, 341
Goldsmith, Lynn 226
Goodell, Roger 174–6, 269
good-faith bargaining 201
governance structure, NCAA 39–43
governing bodies 4, 7, 16–19, 26
    dispute resolution 24
    faculty 23
    intercollegiate sports 27
    international sports 28
    NCAA 34, 35, 39, 53, 68
government-financed stadiums 261, 262
GPS tracking 282, 286, 300
Graduation Success Rate (GSR) 54
Greece Olympic Games 3, 5
Green Bay Packers 158
Greenfly 298–9
Green Sports Alliance 335
Gregorie v. Alpine Meadows Ski Corp. 256
Grimm v. Gloucester County School Board (*2020*) 101
Grove City College v. Bell 83
Guthrie, Janet 78, 79

Hackbart v. Cincinnati Bengals, Inc. 253–4
Haelan Laboratories, Inc. v. Topps Chewing Gum, Inc. 235
Halas, George 153, 155, 188
Halep, Simona 139
Harden, James 337
"hard" salary cap 169
Hard Rock Stadium 263
Harper, Bryce 193
health and safety (bylaw 17) 34, 36, 43, 51, 55–6, 69
Health Insurance Portability and Accountability Act (HIPAA) 299
Hecox v. Little (*2020*) 101, 330
Heightened Scrutiny 102
Hero Twins 6
Hilinski, Tyler 41, 56
Hill, Chapel 55
Hiltz, Nikki 4
Hingis, Martina 175
Hitler, Adolf 110, 319
Hockey World Cups 8
Hogshead-Makar, Nancy 80, 331
Holmes, Brad 316
Holmes, Oliver Wendell 162, 248
homophobia 326
Hope Foundation 56
Hornets, Charlotte 181, 317
hot news 293
Hubbard, Laurel 133
Human Cannonball 235
human growth hormone (HGH) 128, 129
Hunger Games 115
Huntington, Neal 302
HVAC systems 272–4
ICC Cricket World Cup 8
IHF, *see* International Handball Federation
Illinois Court of Appeals 245
inclusive sports environment, proactive steps 329–30
Infantino, Gianni 221
informed consent 300–1
infractions process 60

injury protection system 170
The Institute for Diversity and Ethics in Sport (TIDES) 80
intellectual property (IP) law 213–14
 developments and challenges 239–41
 history 215–16
 international recognition and moral rights 231–2
 international treaties and organizations 227–31
 rights 25, 26, 29, 31, 291–7
 sports business 216–24
intentional tort 247, 248, 268–70
 theory 269
Intercollegiate Athletic Association of the United States (IAAUS) 35, 36
intercollegiate athletics 35, 47, 53, 54, 69
intercollegiate sports governing bodies 27
The International (Dota 2) 18
International Association of Federation Football, see Fédération Internationale de Football Association
International Federations (IFs) 112, 120, 128, 139, 141, 151
 anti-doping programs 131
 guidelines 115
 World Athletics 133
International Handball Federation (IHF) 8
International Labour Organization (ILO) 337
International Management Group (IMG) 189–91, 203
International Olympic Committee (IOC) 17, 28, 74, 75, 77, 95, 97
 mission 112–13
 Olympic Games (see Olympic Games)

 Olympic movement 108–14, 117–20, 122, 124, 127, 140
 organizational structure 113–14
 Paralympics 141–3
 USOPC (see United States Olympic & Paralympic Committee (USOPC))
International Paralympic Committee (IPC) 141–3
International Professional Hockey League 153
international recognition 231–2
international sports governing bodies 28
International Swimming Federation (FINA) 96
International Table Tennis Federation (ITTF) 8
International Tennis Federation (ITF) 139, 175
International Tennis Federation (ITF) v. Sportradar 296
International Testing Agency (ITA) 15, 131
International YMCA Training School 7
investigative process 60
IOC, see International Olympic Committee
Irving, Kyrie 322
ITA, see International Testing Agency
ITTF, see International Table Tennis Federation

Jackson, Roderick 89
Jackson v. Birmingham Board of Education (2005) 89
James, LeBron 149, 153, 193, 195, 219, 236, 298, 301
 Black athletes 317
 influential figures 221
 publicity rights 233

social change 321
supply chain management 336-7
Jazz, Utah 181
Jerry Sandusky and Penn State University 26
Jersey Patch Program 181
Jha, Kanak 139
Johnson, Ben 127
Johnson, Magic 153
Joint Drug Agreement (JDA) 177
Jones, Marion 127
Jones, Michael 22, 188, 189
Jordan, Michael 150, 153, 219, 221, 230, 234, 317
Jordan v. Dominick's Finer Foods LLC 234

Kaepernick, Colin 172, 319, 321, 323
Kang, Michele 318
Keita, Pele 154
Keita, Salif 154
Kelmendi, Majlinda 119
Kemp, Jan 55
Khelif, Imane 115
King, Billie Jean 4, 78, 80, 155
King James 219
kneeling protest 319-21
Knight, Phil 191
Knight v. Jewett 254
Korean Esport Association (KeSPA) 238
Korey Stringer case 249
Kroenke, Stan 179
Kush, Frank 268-9

labor law 148-9, 156-60, 165, 182
labor relations 24, 26-7
Ladies Professional Golf Association (LPGA) 75, 77
"Lady Magic" 78
Landis, Floyd 129

Landis, Kenesaw Mountain 173
Lanham Act 293
of 1946 215
Lari, Zahra 5
leadership development programs 315-17
leadership diversity 65-6
Leadership in Energy and Environmental Design (LEED) 335
League of Legends Championship Series (LCS) 237
learning javelin techniques 119
LED advertising technology 224
Ledecky, Katie 286
legal theory 275, 276
"Let's Move!" campaign 12
Level I violations 59
Level II violations 59
Level III violations 59
Level IV violations 59
Lewis, Lennox 193
LGBTQ+ 30, 92, 310, 321, 323
athletes and fans 30, 325-31
protections 92
licensees 258, 259
Lieberman, Nancy 78
"Life in the Balance" approach 38
LightSpray technology 209
Lin, Jeremy 219
Livestrong Foundation 13
LIV Golf series 16, 20
Llewellyn, KArl 274
London Amateur Athletic Club 61
London Together projects 14
Lopez, Gerry 338
Love, Kevin 190
luxury tax system 170

McCormack, Mark 189, 190, 203
MacCracken, Henry M. (Chancellor) 36

machine learning   272, 280, 282, 288, 306
Mackey v. National Football League (1976)   163-4
Mackey v. NFL (1976)   158
McNair, Jordan   41
McSorley, Marty   269
Madrid System   227, 229, 230
Mahanoy Area School District v. B.L.   324
Major Event Organizers (MEOs)   131
Major League Baseball (MLB)   4, 150, 152-5, 157
  collective bargaining agreement   169-73
  commissioners act   175
  drug prevention policies   176-7
  Statcast tracks   282, 304
  teams   285, 290, 294, 302-4
Major League Baseball Players Association (MLBPA)   158, 197-8
Major League Soccer (MLS)   154, 180
male athletes   103, 311, 313
male-dominated sports industry   317
male-to-female (MtF)   94, 98, 104, 330
"Malice at the Palace" incident   265
mandatory subjects   172-3, 284, 285
Manning, Peyton   234
Maradona, Diego   175
Marathon, Boston   210
Maroney, McKayla   124, 250
Marta Vieira da Silva (Marta)   78
Martin, Casey   167
Martino, Angel   126
Masters   18
Maya civilization   6
McNally v. United States (2006)   163
medical malpractice   250
mental health protections   171-2

Mercedes-Benz Stadium   20, 273, 334, 335
Mercer v. Duke University (1997)   84
merchandise sales   9, 40, 150, 182, 241
Mesoamerican ballgame   6
Mesoamerican civilizations   6
Messi, Lionel   233, 237, 241, 337
metaverse platforms   25, 29, 31, 238-9, 297-9
MetLife Stadium   273
MHSAA   100
Michael Jordan v. Qiaodan Sports Co., Ltd.   230-1
Michael Phelps Foundation   123
Michael Phelps Swim School   218
Michigan State University (MSU)   49-50, 92, 93, 124, 250
Miller, Marvin   158
Milliat, Alice   75
Mink, Patsy   82
misdemeanor charges   49
MIT   302
Mitchell Report   175
modern athlete activism   320-2
modern sports events   10-13
"Moneyball" approach   290
moral rights   231-2, 243
Moral Rights of the Widow of a French Poet   232
Morgan, Alex   222
Morris Communications Corp. v. PGA Tour, Inc.   295-6
Muhammad Ali Estate v. Fox Broadcasting   235
multi-billion-dollar industry   9-10, 40
multiplayer online battle arenas (MOBAs)   237
Mumphery, Keith   92, 93
Murphy v. NCAA   26
Musk, Elon   115, 344
Myers, Angel   126

Nabozny v. Barnhill 245, 253
Nairobi Treaty on the Protection of the Olympic Symbol 228
Naismith, James Dr. 7, 153
Name, Image and Likeness (NIL) 34, 36, 62, 67, 69
  collectives 64–5
  compensation 63–4
  deals 27, 151, 159, 171
  money 64
  opportunities 28
  rights 207–10, 240
  rules and regulations 26
Nandrolone 177
NASCAR 79, 260, 261
Nassar, Larry Dr. 124, 250, 251
  scandal 49–50, 135–6
National Agreement 152
National Basketball Association (NBA) 17, 27, 153, 265, 292, 293, 298, 315, 322
  Cares program 14
  CBA 169–73
  Commissioner David Stern 175
  Green Initiative 335
  Microsoft partnership 342
  Sports Broadcasting Act of 1961 166
  teams 181
National Basketball Association v. Motorola, Inc. 292–3
National Basketball League (NBL) 153
National Basketball Players Association (NBPA) 158
  certification procedures 197
National College Players Association (NCPA) 301
National Collegiate Athletic Association (NCAA) 16, 26, 27, 33–4, 70, 125, 133
  amateurism principle 159
  criticisms and calls for reform 46–7
  Division I 37–8, 66–8, 76, 95
  Division II 38
  Division III 39
  governance structure 39–43
  history 34–7
  Leadership Development Program 65
  manuals 61
  sports regulation 43–6
National Collegiate Athletic Association (NCAA) bylaws
  Academic Performance Program (APP) 54
  bylaw 10 58
  bylaw 12 (amateurism) 63–4
  bylaw 14 54–5
  bylaw 17 57
  bylaw 19 59–61
  collectives NIL 64–5
  concept of amateurism 61–3
  eligibility center 53–4
  ethical conduct and integrity 58–9
  gambling and sports wagering 58
  health and safety (Bylaw 17) 55–6
  leadership diversity 65–6
  names, images, and likenesses (NIL) 34, 36, 62, 63, 67, 69
  National Letter of Intent (NLI) 52–3
  recruitment (bylaw 13) 51–2
  sexual harassment prevention 57–8
  social media and public statements 59
  transfer portal 34, 36, 66, 69
National Collegiate Athletic Association (NCAA) Constitution
  championships and postseason football 50
  committees 50

Index   385

enforcement procedures   51
institutional control and
    responsibility   48
intercollegiate athletics
    principles   47
legislative process   48
membership   48
Michigan State University
    and Dr. Larry Nassar
    scandal   49–50
name and fundamental policy   47
organizational structure   48
Penn State University and Jerry
    Sandusky scandal   49
National Conference on Uniform State
    Laws   199
National Football League (NFL)   17,
    19, 26, 27, 318, 319
    collective bargaining
        agreement   169–73
    collective licensing
        agreements   165
    collective television contract   166
    Commissioner Roger
        Goodell   174–6
    Concussion Settlement   168
    contracts role   149–51
    data analytics   289, 290
    development   153
    Digital Athlete   287–8
    draft system   164
    game statistics   293
    growth and development   155,
        156, 158, 161
    initiatives   314–16
    North American sports
        leagues   178
    partnerships   179–81, 183
    partnership with Amazon   339
    Performance Enhancing Substances
        (PES)   177
    personal conduct policy   320, 323

National Football League Players
    Association (NFLPA)   158, 161,
    164, 174, 177
    cases   203
    certification procedures   196–7
national governing body (NGB)   95,
    134, 139, 143, 251
National Hockey League (NHL)   153,
    158, 166, 291
    draft system   171
    drug policy   177–80
    leagues   168, 170
National Hockey League Players
    Association (NHLPA)   158–9
    certification procedures   198
National Labor Relations Act
    (NLRA)   159–61
National Labor Relations Board
    (NLRB)   26, 159, 188, 195
    cases and legislative acts   161–5
    certification process   159–60
National League (NL)   7, 152, 155,
    162, 178
National Letter of Intent (NLI)   52–3
National Olympic Committees
    (NOCs)   112, 114
National Women's Soccer League
    (NWSL)   78, 80, 154, 318
Navratilova, Martina   78, 115
Navy SEAL   254
NBA v. Motorola   293
NCAA v. Alston (2021)   62
NCAA v. Board of Regents (1984)   63
NCAA v. Tarkanian (1988)   44–5
negligence   245, 247–53
    Comparative Negligence   267–8
    Contributory Negligence   267
    issue   327
    plus   253–8
    professional negligence   328
    torts law   210, 275
Negro Leagues   152

Newcastle United   318
Newton, Cam   40
New Turf Technologies   223
The New York Times   130
Neymar Jr.'s   232, 236
NFL Players Association
  (NFLPA)   158, 161, 164, 203
NFL v. Delaware Lottery   293, 296
NFTs, *see* non-fungible tokens
Nicklaus, Jack   189
Nixon, Richard (President)   81
NLRB, *see* National Labor Relations
  Board
non-binary athletes   4, 99
non-fungible tokens (NFTs)   9
Norris-LaGuardia Act of 1932   157
North American Soccer League
  (NASL)   154
North Carolina Uniform Athlete
  Agents Act   204
*Northwestern University and College
  Athletes Players Association*
  (CAPA)   26
Nungesser, Paul   93, 94
Nunn-Wooten Scouting
  Fellowship   315, 316

Oakland Athletics   290
Obama, Michelle   12
O'Bannon v. NCAA (2015)   26, 62
Obiri, Hellen   210
Occupational Safety and Health
  Administration (OSHA)   333
"occupier"   258–60
Ochoa, Lorena   156
*O'Connor v. Board of Education of
  School District No. 23*   101
Office for Civil Rights (OCR)'s 3-prong
  test   83, 103
  accommodation of interests and
    abilities   84–7

  cases   88–90
  definitions   87
  expansion   84
  proportionality   84
Ohio State University   38, 40
Olympic Agenda 2020   116
Olympic Broadcasting Services
  (OBS)   140
Olympic Charter   112–17, 320
Olympic Games   7, 17, 108–12, 228,
  229, 272
  broadcasting and media   140–1
  Greece   3, 5
  history   108–12
  hosting events   11
  movement   108–14, 117–20, 122,
    124, 127, 140
  rules and regulations   117–20
    anti-doping and performance-
      enhancing drug   124–7
    Bay Area Laboratory Co-
      operative (BALCO)   127–32
    gender classification   132–4
    promotional limitations   120–2
    safety and welfare of
      athletes   122–4
  sports events   9, 10
  women's participation   76–7
The Olympic Partners (TOP)   17, 140
Olympics   150, 153, 154, 159
Olympism   108, 117, 143
  principles   112, 114
Omalu, Bennet   168
Omoto, Ryan   223
ongoing awareness programs   57
online service providers (OSPs)   225
Opendorse   298
operating bylaws   51, 65
Oral Turinabol   177
Osaka, Naomi   222, 236, 321, 337
Owens, Jesse   110, 319

Palmer v. Schonhorn Enterprises, Inc.   294
Pan American Games   134, 135, 137, 144
Paralympics Games   110, 134, 141–3
  movements   136
Paris Olympic Games   77, 110, 313
Parker, Candace   330
PASPA, *see* Professional and Amateur Sports Protection Act
Patagonia's Worn Wear program   334, 338
patent holders, rights of   222–4
patents, IP   214
Paterno, Joe   49
Patrick, Danica   79
Patrick Mahomes   317
Paul, Alice   81
Paul, Logan   229
Paul, Rich   193
PCP Capital Partners   318
Pegula, Kim   318
Pegula, Terry   318
Pele v. Samsung   234
Penn State University   48, 49, 51
performance-enhancing drugs (PEDs)   124–7, 175–7, 271
performance metrics   299
permissive subjects   172–3, 284
Personal Conduct Policy   173
personalized content strategies   299
Peterson, Adrian   26
PGA Championship   18
PGA Tour, Inc. v. Martin (2001)   167, 183
PGA Tour event   16, 156, 295–6, 334
Pharaohs participation   3, 5
Phelps, Michael   4, 121, 123, 190, 218, 246, 275, 298
Pierce, Paul   322
Player Efficiency Rating (PER)   287

Powell v. National Football League (1989)   164–5
predictive analytics   280, 281, 286, 288, 289, 291, 306
Prefontaine, Steve   135
Premier League club   318
pressure cooker field   191–4
Prime Sports Marketing   204
privacy rights   29, 233, 235, 283–5
private law   247
products liability   270–2
Professional and Amateur Sports Protection Act (PASPA)   26, 293
professional athletes   18, 25, 27, 39, 54
professional sports   182–4
  Americans with Disabilities Act (ADA)   167–73
  collective bargaining process   148, 149, 156–60
  commissioner role   173–8
  contracts   149–52
  history   152–6
  leagues   178–82
  NLRB (*see* National Labor Relations Board (NLRB))
  Sports Broadcasting Act of 1961   166–7
prohibited substances   138, 139
public awareness   24
public figure   195, 255
public financing   20
public invitees   258–9
publicity rights   25, 26, 28, 232–4, 294, 295
  digital media   236–41
  legal cases   234–5
public statements   45, 59
Pyle, Charles   188

Qatar World Cup   336
quiet periods   52

racial bias algorithms 302–4
racial intersection 313–14
Raisman, Aly 124, 250
Rámirez, Ariel Saúl 124
Rapinoe, Megan 321, 330
Rational Basis Review 102
Real-Time Scoring System (RTSS) 295
real-world applications 23
recruitment (bylaw 13) 51–2
Regional Greenhouse Gas Initiative (RGGI) 335
reserve clause 158, 160, 162, 171
Resolution Agreement 88
return-to-play protocol 42, 55, 56
revenue-sharing agreements 170–1
revenue streams 180–2
　potential 220–1
　primary 220
Reviving Baseball in Inner Cities (RBI) 303, 315
Rice, Ray 176
Richardson, Luke 270
Riddell 223, 224, 271
Ridley, Calvin 175
Riggs, Bobby 4
right of publicity 232–5, 294, 295
rights to privacy 233, 235, 283–5
risk assessments 327, 328
risk assumption 267
risk management 29–30, 245–58, 275–6
　defenses 267–8
　structured process 266–7
Robinson, Jackie 4, 153–5
Rodgers, Aaron 190
Rodriguez, Alex 175, 176
Ronaldo, Cristiano 190, 220, 221, 232, 237, 241, 298, 301, 336
Rooney Rule 173, 314–15, 317, 345
Roosevelt, Theodore (President) 35
Rose, Pete 174, 175

Rousey, Ronda 222
Rowling, J.K. 115
Rozelle Rule 158, 163, 164
Rudolph, Wilma 75
Rule 40 of the Olympic Charter 120, 121
Rule 41 of the Olympic Charter 120
RUSADA, *see* Russian Anti-Doping Agency
Russell Rule 312
Russian Anti-Doping Agency (RUSADA) 15
Russian athletes 14–15, 130–1
Ruth, Babe 155

safeguard athletes 122–4
safe harbor rule 84
SafeSport training 135–6, 251, 252
salary caps 148, 154, 169, 170
Salt Lake Organizing Committee 114
Samoura, Fatma (Secretary General of FIFA) 4
Sandler, Bernice 81
Sandusky, Jerry 49
Sapp, Warren 205, 206
SAP's HANA 291
SAT 53, 54
Saudi Arabia 16–17
Saudi-backed LIV Golf series 16, 20
Saunders, Raven 323
Schultz, Gary (Vice President) 49
Schwartz, Jeff 190
Scott, Travis 236, 239
S4D, *see* Sport for Development
Second Circuit Court of Appeals 293, 330
Second Spectrum 282
Section 2 of the Sherman Act 295
Selig, Bud 175
Selig Rule 315
Semenya, Caster 95–9, 133, 144
"separate but equal" facilities 102

Index

17th NBA Championship (2020)   318
sexual assault   87, 88, 90, 92-4, 103, 104
   athletes   124
sexual harassment   46-7, 69, 87
   prevention   57-8
Sharapova, Maria   190
Sherbert v. Verner (*1963*)   102
Sherman Act   156, 157
Sherman Antitrust Act   156, 162
Simpson v. University of Colorado Boulder   88
skateboarding   8, 14
Smith, Tommie   11, 319, 320
Smith v. Horizon Aero Sports Ltd.   256
Smith v. Pro-Football, Inc. (1978)   164
Snow v. Eaton Centre Ltd.   232
social change   3-5, 11, 24
social integration   10-14
social justice movements   4, 24, 30, 31, 318-20
social media   45, 51, 52, 55, 56, 59, 171, 320-2
   campaigns   65
   compensation   63
   interactions   60, 68
   promotions   64
"soft" salary cap   169
Sotomayor, Sonia   161, 226
Soule v. Connecticut Association of Schools, Inc.   330
Southern Methodist University (SMU)   61
Spanier, Graham (President)   49
Speedo LZR Racer swimsuit   115
sponsorship deals   9-11, 16, 18-20, 65
   agreements   24
   income source   17
Sport for Development (S4D)   14
Sports Agent Responsibility and Trust Act (SPARTA)   199, 200
sports agents   22

   certification process and legal relationship   195-8
   contract negotiations   194-5
   fiduciary duty and responsibilities (*see* fiduciary duties)
   financial mismanagement   205-7
   history   187-9
   Name, Image and Likeness (NIL) rights   207-10
   pressure cooker field   191-4
   role   29, 189-91
   state and federal regulation   199-200
sports broadcasting   63, 167, 218
   Digital Millennium Copyright Act (DMCA)   224-7
Sports Broadcasting Act of 1961   166-7
SportsCenter   313
sports decision-making, fairness in   302-4
Sports Illustrated   205
sports industry   1, 2, 9-10, 22, 310, 311, 333
   collective impact   30-2
   environmental and sustainability challenges   272-4
   ethical sourcing and supply chain management   336-9
   fan engagement   342, 344, 346
   free speech principles   325, 331
   male-dominated sports industry   317
   monitoring and environmental regulations   334
sports law   21, 26-8, 245-7
   administrative law   26
   administrators   23
   agents role   29
   amateur *vs.* professional athletes   27
   artificial intelligence (*see* artificial intelligence (AI))
   aspects   31-2

Index

athlete activism and social media 320–2
athletes 24
black-owned sports franchises 317
case law 262–6
contract law 25–6
dark side examples 14–16
data analytics (*see* data analytics)
defenses sports 267–8
disabilities in virtual sports 331–3
due process 28
entrants 258–62
environmental impact 30
esports 29
ethical sourcing and supply chain management 336–9
events and cultural values 10–14
faculty 23
fan engagement 339–44
financial and tax planning 27
first amendment *vs.* contractual obligations 322–5
gambling on sports games 29
gender classification 326–9
history 5–10
intellectual property rights 26
intentional tort 268–70
intercollegiate sports governing bodies 27
international sports governing bodies 28
intersection of gender and race 313–14
labor and antitrust 148–9, 156, 165
labor relations issue 26–7
leaders and general public 24–5
legal and regulatory implications 333–6
legal aspects 21–2, 310–11
legal challenges to discrimination 311

LGBTQ+ athletes and fans 325–6
mentorship and leadership development programs 315–17
negligence 249–53
negligence plus 253–5
organization and regulation 16–20
participation and leadership 311–13
privacy concerns in 29
proactive steps for inclusivity 329–30
professional sports (*see* professional sports)
publicity rights 28
regulation 43–6
Rooney Rule 314–15
social justice 30
social justice movements 318–20
sports-related products liability 270–2
stadium security process 266–7
students 22–3
tort law 29–30, 247–9
waivers and releases 255–8
women-owned sports franchises 317–18
women's advocacy and opposition 330–1
sports performance tranformation 282–7
sports-related products liability 270–2
sports team 76, 80, 188, 288
 negative impact 20–1
 positive impact 19–20
Sports Team Analysis and Tracking Systems (STATS) 292, 293
sports wagering 58
stadium security process 266–7
staff contracts 152
star athletes 18
stare decisis principle 162

Statcast tracks   282, 304
state-sponsored doping
    programs   126, 130
  China   15
  Russia   14–15
Stats LLC v. Sportradar AG   291–2
Staveley, Amanda   318
Steinberg, Leigh   29, 193
Stern, David   175
steroids   127
Strava fitness tracking app   300
streamline processes   60
strict scrutiny   101
Stringer, Korey   249
student-athletes   13, 25, 30, 31, 38, 76, 151, 159
  academic performance   54, 56
  compensation   34
  Division III   39
  drug testing   57
  environment   51
  First Amendment   45
  gambling-related issues   58
  medical care   41
  NLI   52–3, 62, 63, 66–70
  safety   35, 36, 42, 43
  social media   59
  sports law   22–3
  state and federal regulation   199–200
  welfare   47
substantial proportionality test   84
Sulkowicz, Emma   93
"The Sultan of Swat"   155
summary disposition   46, 60
Summer and Winter Games   17
Summer Olympic Games   15
Super Bowl   9, 19, 20, 153, 235, 272
supply chain management   336–9
surveillance pricing technology   343
Sustainable Apparel Coalition (SAC)   338

table tennis   8, 118, 139
Tarkanian, Jerry   44
Tatum, Jason   17, 158
taxation   27, 192
technological protection measures (TPMs)   225
Ted Stevens Olympic and Amateur Sports Act   135
tetrahydrogestrinone (THG)   127, 128
Therapeutic Use Exemptions (TUEs)   138
Third US Circuit Court of Appeals   159
"This Girl Can" campaign   12
Thomas, Lia   95–6, 98
Thompson, Klay   190
"Thursday Night Football"   179, 339
Ticketmaster system   340
ticket sales   9, 17, 24, 68, 169, 180, 220
Tidwell, Rod   193
Tinker v. Des Moines Independent Community School District (1969)   45
Title IX   36, 46, 50, 58, 67, 78, 80
  benefits   313–14
  Equal Protection Clause   99–101, 104
  gender equity   2, 81–90
  hearing process   90–4
  laws   327, 330
  legal analysis   99
  legislation   28, 311, 312
  LGBTQ+ inclusion   331
  sports programs   98
  women's participation in college sports   76
Title IX and Equal Protection   104
Title IX of the Education Amendments of 1972   75, 103
Title VII of the Civil Rights Act   312
T-Mobile Park   335
Tokyo 2020 Olympic Games   122, 229, 313, 323

Tomlin, Mike   314
Tomlinson, LaDainian   203
torts law   22, 29–31, 245, 247–9, 276
Tour de France titles   13, 129
trademark holders, rights of   218–20
trademarks, IP   214–16
transfer portal, NCAA   34, 36, 66, 69
transgender athletes   4, 28, 37, 327
  challenges and inclusion   94–9, 104, 133, 134
  participation   114, 330–1
transphobia   326
trespassers   250, 258–60
The Trevor Project   326
The True Cost   337
twenty-two female athletes   109
Twitchell, Kent   232

UEFA   170
Uhlaender v. Henricksen   294
Ultimate Fighting Championship (UFC)   19, 77, 221, 222, 225
UN Guiding Principles on Business and Human Rights   338
Uniform Athlete Agents Act (UAAA)   199, 200, 204
Union Cycliste Internationale (UCI)   128
unionization process   34, 157–9, 196
United Arab Emirates   5
United States   4, 17, 19, 20, 34, 100, 229
  amateur sports   135
  baseball   7
  collective bargaining   159
  college athletics   33, 36, 47, 51, 65, 67, 68
  gender equity   133
  IP law   215–16
  "Let's Move!" campaign   12
  professional sports development   152–6, 323

Regional Greenhouse Gas Initiative (RGGI)   335
SafeSport   123
2026 World Cup   16
United States Anti-Doping Agency (USADA)   15, 28, 111, 127, 136–7, 144
United States Olympic & Paralympic Committee (USOPC)   108, 134–5, 144
  anti-doping testing protocols   138
  banned substances and techniques   137
  CAS role   138–9
  Dr. Larry Nassar Scandal and SafeSport   135–6
  SafeSport   252
  Ted Stevens Olympic and Amateur Sports Act   135
  Therapeutic Use Exemptions (TUEs)   138
  trademarks   229
  USADA   136–7
United States v. Virginia (1996)   74, 100
University of Nevada, Las Vegas (UNLV)   44
University of Southern California (USC)   40, 41, 199, 208
U.S. Anti-Doping Agency (USADA)   15, 28, 111, 127, 136–7
  doping tests   139, 144, 145
US Center for SafeSport   136, 251, 252
US Court of Appeals for the Fourth Circuit   204
US Department of Education   50, 90
US District Court   330
US Foreign Corrupt Practices Act (FCPA)   338
US Olympic cycling team   129
US Olympic & Paralympic Committee   251

US Open Tennis Championships   335
US Patent Act of 1790   215
US Postal Service team   129
US premises liability law   260
US Soccer   198
US v. Tim Duncan   27
US Women's National Soccer Team (USWNT)   312

Vaccaro, Sonny   191
Valieva, Kamila   15, 124
Ventura v. Kyle   254–5
Verlander, Justin   286
Vick, Michael   325
Video Assistant Referee (VAR)   115, 223
Vietnam War   4, 45, 319
Virginia Military Institute's (VMI)   100, 101
virtual games   297–9
virtual reality (VR)   182, 306, 341, 344, 345
  fan engagement   297
  integration   287
  publicity rights   238–9
  sports technologies   242, 331
virtual sport disabilities   331–3
Visual Artists Rights Act of 1990 (VARA)   232

WADA, *see* World Anti-Doping Agency
Wade, Dwyane   190
Wagner Act   159
waivers (releases)   255–8, 260–2
Walker, Antoine   205, 206
Wallace, Ben   265
Washington Spirit   318
Wasserman, Casey   190
waste management   116, 272, 335
Waters, Robert   22
Weistart, John   21
Wembley Stadium   262
Westbrook, Russell   190
West Coast Conference (WCC)   312
whereabouts failures   139
whistleblowers   15, 60, 61, 69, 130
White, Dana   221
Whitehead, Jermaine   322
White v. NCAA (2008)   63
WHOOP bands   298, 301
Wieber, Jordyn   124, 250
Williams, Serena   79, 138, 190, 221, 239, 336
Williams, Venus   138
Williamson, Zion   204, 301
Wilson, A'ja   153
Wilson, Earl   189
Wimbledon   18, 77, 191
winning-at-all-costs   14–16
Winter Olympic Games   111, 113, 130
women athletes   75, 80–1, 87
  advocacy and opposition   330–1
  coaching positions   312
  participation and leadership   311–13
  percentage   313
  role   78–9
women-owned sports franchises   317–18
Women's National Basketball Association (WNBA)   77, 153, 154, 312, 321, 339
women's participation   34, 37, 64–6
  college sports   76
  Equal Protection Clause   99–102
  history   74–5
  Olympic Games   76–7
  professional sports   80–1
  sports in   4–5, 12, 14, 28
  World Cup   313
Women's Professional Basketball League (WBL)   154
Women's Professional Soccer (WPS)   154

Women's Sports Foundation   76, 78, 80, 156, 330
Women's Sports Policy Working Group   78
Women's Tennis Association (WTA)   4, 77, 156
Women's United Soccer Association (WUSA)   154
Women's World Games   75
Women's World Rugby Cup championship   8
Wong, Glenn   22
Wong (Litigation Guardian of) v. Lok's Martial Arts Centre Inc.   257
Woods, Tiger   190, 195, 211, 323
Woolf, Bob   189
workplace wellness programs   13
World Anti-Doping Agency (WADA)   15, 113, 131, 178
  anti-doping policies   144, 145
  guidelines   142
  independent bodies   28
  Prohibited List   137
  work collboration   136
World Anti-Doping Code   131
World Aquatics in 2010   115

World Athletics   133
World Cup   16, 78, 272
  in 1930   8
  Fédération Internationale de Football Association   9–11, 19, 150, 154, 228, 237, 273, 313
  Qatar World Cup   336
  soccer matches   229
World Handball Championship   8
World Intellectual Property Organization (WIPO)   227–30
WTA, *see* Women's Tennis Association

Yego, Julius   119
YMCAs   7, 13
Young, Steve   193
young athletes   251, 252, 301, 316
Youth Sports Safety Alliance   249
"YouTube Man"   119

Zacchini v. Scripps-Howard Broadcasting Co.   235, 294–5
Zaharias, Babe Didrikson   75
zero-tolerance policy   57, 175
Zeus   5–6, 109
Zion Williamson   204

About the Author

Michael E. Jones, Professor Emeritus at the University of Massachusetts Lowell, is a distinguished scholar, educator, and practitioner in the fields of law, art, and sports. Over the course of a career spanning nearly five decades, he taught law and directed the Legal Studies Program, pioneering new approaches to legal education. Jones developed the first undergraduate sports law course and authored the first textbook on the subject tailored for non-lawyers, solidifying his reputation as a trailblazer in sports law education.

Jones is an acclaimed analyst in sports, entertainment, art, media, and artificial intelligence law, contributing his expertise to the *Huffington Post* as well as numerous media broadcasts, podcasts, and panel discussions. His scholarly contributions extend across multiple disciplines, reflecting his deep engagement with issues such as copyright, trademark, publicity rights, artificial intelligence, and sports law. His academic work has influenced both practitioners and scholars around the globe.

He holds a BA in Economics from Denison University, an MBA from The Wharton School at the University of Pennsylvania, a JD from the University of Miami, and an MLA from Harvard University. His academic achievements are matched by his international recognition as a Fulbright-Nehru Specialist, where he taught intellectual property law and publicity rights at Jindal Global University Law School in India. Jones has also served as a Visiting Professor at the University of London and has spoken at prestigious events such as the Santa Fe Institute, addressing audiences of Nobel Laureates and pioneering technologists.

An accomplished visual artist, Jones designed the official triathlon poster for the US Olympic Committee for five consecutive Summer Games. His artwork has been showcased on PBS cooking shows and in other prominent venues. He served on the Board of Directors for a national governing body under the United States Olympic & Paralympic Committee, contributing to governance and advocacy for athletes and helped draft Safe Sport policies in the aftermath of the Dr. Nassar scandal.

About the Author

As a former elite swimmer, runner, and triathlete, Jones' athletic achievements include medaling at the Penn Relays, qualifying for the Olympic Trials, and winning gold at the Pan American Championships. He has served as an appeals court judge at the Tokyo Summer Olympic Games and currently plays a pivotal role in an international tribunal addressing multi-sport disputes, including those related to the Olympics.

Beyond his professional accomplishments, Jones has made significant contributions as a board member and chairperson for *Provincetown Arts* magazine and other nonprofit organizations. He has also served on corporate and financial institution boards, demonstrating a commitment to both the arts and community development.

Jones is the author of ten books and more than twenty-five peer-reviewed articles in legal and business journals. His published works include *Rules of the Game: Sports Law, Art Law* (2nd ed.), *Intellectual Property Law Fundamentals* (2nd ed.), and the groundbreaking *Sports Law* textbook published more than forty years ago by a Simon & Schuster imprint. Together with his spouse, Christine M. Jones, he co-edited the award-winning book *TIMELESS: The Photography of Rowland Scherman*.

In retirement, Jones continues to lead in the legal and sports communities as Professor Emeritus and as a prominent figure in global sports governance. His legacy of academic rigor, artistic creativity, and athletic excellence endures, inspiring students, professionals, and athletes alike.